JACKY ICKX

Viel mehr als Mister Le Mans
Mister Le Mans, and much more

Inhalt Contents

Vorwort von Mario Andretti / Foreword by Mario Andretti	4
Danksagung / Acknowledgements	6
Jacky Ickx – Einer, der seinen eigenen Weg geht / Jacky Ickx, doing it his own way	8
1963 – 1966 Die ersten Jahre im Motorsport / His early racing activities	12
1967 Erfolge in der Formel 2 und im Sportwagen / Worldwide success both in Formula Two and sportscars	28
1968 Der erste Formel-1-Sieg und ein Beinbruch / A Formula One victory but also a major injury	50
1969 Ickx schreibt Geschichte in Le Mans / Making history at Le Mans	74
1970 Die Rückkehr zu Ferrari / Back with Ferrari	94
1971 – 1972 Höhen und Tiefen mit Ferrari / Mixed success with Ferrari	114
1973 Das letzte Jahr bei Ferrari / The final year with Ferrari	132
1974 Ein Neustart als Nummer zwei bei Lotus / A new start as second driver at Lotus	144
1975 – 1976 Talfahrt in der F1, Triumphe im Sportwagen / Fewer races in F1, more success at endurance	154
1977 – 1978 Fokus auf Sportwagenrennen / Concentrating on sportscars	174
1979 – 1981 Abenteuer in Amerika und Afrika / Adventures in America and Africa	192
1982 – 1985 Zum Abschluss im Rothmans-Porsche / The Rothmans Porsches	202
1986 – 2000 Wüstenabenteuer und ein Sieg als Teamchef / Desert adventures and a win as a team boss	224
Das Leben abseits der Rennstrecke / Personal life away from racing	232
Statistik / Statistics	236
John Horsman	48
Jackie Oliver	88
Hans Herrmann	92
Jackie Stewart	112
Brian Redman	142
Derek Bell	222
Jochen Mass	230

Impressum Imprint

Editor: Reinhard Klein, Author: Ed Heuvink, Revision English text: John Davenport, German translation: Sebastian Klein, German proof-reading: Mona-Lisa Kinting, Design and layout: Ellen Böhle-Hanigk, Coordination: Sarah Vessely

Editorial staff: Alexander Galitzki, Daniel Klein, Reinhard Klein, Sebastian Klein, Colin McMaster, Sarah Vessely

Photography from the McKlein archive with the work of: Antonio Biasioli, Foster & Skeffington, Hans Georg Isenberg, Reinhard Klein, Walter Kotauschek, Robert Kroeschel, Peter Kumpa, Lars O. Magnil, Heide & Peter Nicot, Dieter Noellner, Kalle Riggare, Alois Rottensteiner, Colin Taylor Productions, Gerhard D. Wagner. Other images: LAT (p.32, 46, 50, 53, 66, 78, 81, 85, 90, 97, 163, 173, 193, 232), Ed Heuvink (p.6, 14, 19, 41, 53), Rob Wiedenhoff (p.12, 16, 17, 27), DPPI (p.198)

Special thanks to: Mario Andretti, Derek Bell MBE, Bernard Cahier (†), John Davenport, Marc Duez, David Hobbs, Ursula Kleinmanns, Jochen Mass, Luis Podenco, Brian Redman, Sir Jackie Stewart OBE

Bibliography: Automobile Year (Edita sa), MotorSport, Autosport, L'Automobile, Racing in the Rain (John Horsman)

Reproductions: McKlein Publishing/Verlag Reinhard Klein GbR, Printing: Himmer AG, Augsburg, Germany, Distribution: RallyWebShop (www.rallywebshop.com)

Copyright and publisher:
McKlein Publishing/Verlag Reinhard Klein GbR
Hauptstr. 172
51143 Köln
Germany
Tel.: +49-(0)2203-359239
Fax: +49-(0)2203-359238
publishing@mcklein.de
www.mckleinstore.com
www.mcklein.de

1st edition – 2014
ISBN: 978-3-927458-74-1

All right reserved. No part of this book may be reproduced, stored or transmitted by any means, mechanical, electronic, or otherwise without written permission of the publisher. Sämtliche Rechte der Verbreitung – in jeglicher Form und Technik – sind vorbehalten.

Note from the publisher: This book was written without the personal contribution of Jacky Ickx. Hinweis in eigener Sache: Dieses Buch ist ohne einen persönlichen Beitrag von Jacky Ickx entstanden.

Vorwort von Mario Andretti

Foreword by Mario Andretti

Jacky Ickx hat früher gesagt, dass Freundschaften zwischen Fahrern selten sind. Man kann Respekt haben, aber keine Freundschaft. Er hat das mit solcher Überzeugung gesagt, als hätte es die Gewissheit einer mathematischen Gleichung. Die Tatsache, dass wir trotzdem Freunde wurden, und das in so kurzer Zeit, ist also außergewöhnlich.

Bei Ferrari war ich für elf Grands Prix sein Teamkollege, sechs 1971 und fünf 1972. In derselben Zeit fuhren wir zusammen neun Langstreckenrennen, dabei holten wir sechs Pole Positions, vier Siege und einen zweiten Platz. So viel Erfolg hatten wir in unserer kurzen gemeinsamen Zeit.

Als ich ins F1-Team von Ferrari kam, war Jacky schon etabliert. Ich war der Neue. Anfangs dachte ich, ich müsste jeden Schritt überdenken, um nicht auf eine versteckte Falltür zu treten. Aber es gab keine. Er behandelte mich ab dem ersten Tag mit Respekt. Ich fühlte mich gleichberechtigt und akzeptiert. Bei Jacky gab es kein: „Ich zuerst." Wenn du ein Teamkollege von Jacky bist, teilst du dir das Rampenlicht. Das bedeutete mir viel und das habe ich bis heute nicht vergessen. Ich habe daraus etwas mitgenommen. Er hat großen Einsatz gezeigt: Er hat mir Respekt entgegengebracht, bevor ich ihn mir verdient habe.

Jacky Ickx has said that friendship between drivers is rare. You can have respect, but not friendship. He says this with such conviction as if it has the certainty of a mathematical equation. So the fact that we became friends, especially over a short period of time, is out of the ordinary.

I was his team-mate in eleven GP races for Ferrari, six in 1971 and five in 1972. In the same timeframe, we drove nine long distance races, were on pole six times and gained four wins and a second place. That's how much success we had in our brief time together.

When I joined the Ferrari F1 team, Jacky was already well established. I was the new guy. I came in and I was thinking I might need to watch my step around the open manholes ... but there weren't any. He treated me with respect from day one. He made me feel equal and accepted. There was no me-first system with Jacky. When you're a team-mate of Jacky's, the spotlight is shared. That meant a lot to me and I never forgot it to this day. And there was a lesson in it for me. Think about it for a minute. The effort he made was huge. He handed me respect before I even earned it.

Neben dem herzlichen Empfang strahlte Jacky Ruhe und Selbstvertrauen aus. Dieses Verhalten half mir, auch selbstbewusst zu sein. Jedes Mal, wenn ich Jacky begegnete, fühlte ich mich selbstbewusster.

Jacky und ich waren als Team so perfekt, wie es nur irgendwie geht. Zum einen passten wir physisch zusammen, wir hatten fast dieselbe Größe und Sitzposition. Beim Sitz haben wir einen perfekten Kompromiss gefunden, jeder hat ein Stück nachgegeben. Zum anderen hat sich das Kräfteverhältnis zwischen uns nahtlos hin und her bewegt. Er war berechnender, ich aggressiver. Er wusste, dass ich gern das Qualifying fuhr, also ließ er mich. Da war etwas Besonderes zwischen uns, ein Verständnis. Er wusste, was ich wollte. Und ich wusste, was er wollte. Wir waren beide stark, aber nicht so, dass es für Konflikte gesorgt hätte. Wir hatten einen starken Glauben in den anderen, wie eine eigene Religion.

Abseits der Strecke redete Jacky nicht viel über die Rennen. Er war ein kluger Kopf, hatte etwas von einem Philosophen. Für einen jungen Kerl hatte er so viel Weisheit, Reife und gesunden Menschenverstand. Ich habe mich manchmal gefragt, wie ich auch so werden kann. Vielleicht hat etwas davon auf mich abgefärbt. Er war kultiviert, zurückhaltend und bescheiden und hatte gute Manieren. Wenn er einen Raum betrat, hatte er immer ein Lächeln auf den Lippen. Auf diesen Qualitäten beruhte seine Anziehungskraft.

Einmal habe ich in seinem Haus in Belgien übernachtet. Nach den 9 Stunden von Kyalami bin ich über Brüssel in die USA zurückgeflogen. Er lud mich zu sich nach Hause ein, was ich sehr aufmerksam fand. „Komm mit, komm mit", sagte er und zeigte damit seine warme, gastfreundliche Seite.

Freundschaft ist eine Wahl. Manche Beziehungen – zu Vätern, Söhnen oder Brüdern – kann man sich nicht aussuchen. Bei Freundschaften kann man sich dafür oder dagegen entscheiden. Dass sich Jacky trotz seiner Auffassung zu Freundschaften zwischen Fahrern dafür entschied, war eine Bereicherung für mich. Er sagte, Freundschaften sind selten. Für mich war er aber ein großartiger Freund. Ich weiß, dass das Nehmen nur die halbe Miete ist. Ich hoffe, dass ich ihm das, was er mir gegeben hat, auf irgendeine Weise zurückgeben konnte.

Wenn ich auf diesen Teil meines Lebens zurückblicke, muss ich unweigerlich an Jacky denken. Er hat dazu beigetragen, dass die Erfahrung bei Ferrari für mich eine sehr gute war. Er war ein traumhafter Teamkollege. Wenn ich jetzt und hier jemanden wählen müsste, den ich mir am meisten für mein Team wünschen würde, mit der einzigen Einschränkung, dass ich nicht meinen Sohn Michael nehmen dürfte, dann würde ich Jacky nehmen.

Dieses Vorwort hätte ich so nicht schreiben können, als wir Teamkollegen waren. Es brauchte Zeit, um die Gefühle sacken zu lassen. Und ich brauchte die Distanz, um die Dinge geistig zu verarbeiten. Wenn ich heute zurückblicke, dann sehe ich diese wunderbare, erfolgreiche Zeit, die ich mit dem faszinierendsten Teamkollegen, den ein Mann sich wünschen kann, verbracht habe.

Nazareth, USA, April 2012
Mario Andretti

On top of his warm welcome when I arrived, Jacky instilled calm and confidence and I found his demeanour was helping me to be confident. Every time I encountered Jacky, I began to feel more confident.

He and I were as close to a perfect team as you can get. First, we were a good match physically with almost the same size and driving position. We could make a perfect compromise with the seat position – he gave up a little, I gave up a little. Second, the balance of power could shift between us seamlessly. We got along very well and didn't have any trouble finding our middle ground. He was more calculated. I was more aggressive. He knew I liked to qualify and he'd always let me. There was something between us, an understanding. He knew what I wanted. I knew what he wanted. We were both strong, but not in a way that produced conflict. We had sort of a faith in each other, our own kind of religion.

Away from the track, he didn't talk much about racing, but he had a great mind and superior intellect. He was somewhat of a philosopher. He had so much wisdom, maturity and just plain common sense for a young guy. I wondered how I could get to be like that. Maybe some of it would rub off on me. He was polished, well mannered, sophisticated – always floating into a room with a smile – and always humble and modest. It was these qualities that made people gravitate to him.

I stayed at his house once in Belgium. We were coming from South Africa after the 9 Hours of Kyalami and I connected through Brussels on my way back to the USA. He invited me to stay at his home, which was extremely considerate. "Come in, come in" he said, revealing his warm, hospitable side.

I know that friendship is a choice. Some relationships you don't get to choose, like fathers, sons and brothers. But friendship you can opt into and out of. It was my gain that Jacky opted in, especially given his theory on friendship between drivers. While he said friendship is not common, he was sure being a great friend to me. And I know that receiving is only half of the friendship equation. I hope I gave it back to him in one form or another.

When I look back at that part of my life, I can't do it without remembering Jacky. He helped make that experience a very good one for me. He was a dream team-mate. In fact, if I had to pick a guy I'd most like on my team, right here, right now, with the only stipulation being that I can't pick my own son Michael, I would pick Jacky.

This is not a foreword I could have written while we were team-mates. It has needed time. I needed to wait for lifelong, career-long feelings to settle and sort themselves out. I needed to distance myself – then look back and see things again – and turn them over in my mind and reflect. And when I do that today, I see this wonderfully successful time that I shared with the most amazing team-mate a guy could wish to have.

Nazareth, USA, April 2012
Mario Andretti

Danksagung
Acknowledgements

Meine erste Begegnung mit Jacky Ickx war unmittelbar nach seinem Sieg am Nürburgring 1969. An jenem Tag war er ein F1-Auto von Brabham gefahren und hatte eines dieser fantastischen Rennen abgeliefert. Ein paar Monate später haben wir uns in Spa wieder getroffen – vor dem 1000-Kilometer-Rennen auf dieser wunderbaren Rennstrecke. Und wieder war er in Topform: Er hat zwar nicht gewonnen, aber alles aus seinem Ferrari 512S herausgeholt, den er sich mit John Surtees geteilt hat. Ich erinnere mich auch noch an den GP der Niederlande 1971. Im strömenden Regen haben Ickx und Pedro Rodriguez das ganze Feld überrundet. Das sind nur drei von ganz, ganz vielen Rennen, bei denen ich ihn live erlebt habe. Wenn Jacky im richtigen Auto saß, war er einer der weltbesten Fahrer seiner Zeit.

Die Arbeit an diesem wunderschönen Bildband über die Motorsport-Karriere von Jacky Ickx hat mir extrem viel Spaß gemacht, weil ich einige der Fahrer der damaligen Zeit wieder treffen konnte: Derek Bell, Jackie Stewart, Hurley Haywood, Jochen Mass, Vic Elford, David Hobbs, Nino Vaccarella und besonders Brian Redman, mit dem Jacky so viele Siege errungen hat. All diese Fahrer haben diese gefährliche Ära des Motorsports überlebt, in der tödliche Unfälle fast alltäglich waren. Sie alle haben ihre ganz persönlichen Erinnerungen und erzählten gerne über ihre Erlebnisse als Teamkollegen, Rivalen oder Freunde von Jacky.

Dieses Buch ist eine Hommage von einem passionierten Motorsportler im Allgemeinen und Jacky-Ickx-Fan im Speziellen. In meinen Augen ist er einer der größten Allrounder in der Geschichte des Motorsports. Er hat sein Talent auf der Rundstrecke in Formel-Autos, Sport- und Tourenwagen gezeigt und seine Vielseitigkeit durch seine Rallyeabenteuer in den Wüsten dieser Welt noch mehr unterstrichen. Alles in diesem Buch ist ein persönliches Zeugnis meiner Bewunderung für ihn und sein Können.
Chapeau, Jacky!

Ed Heuvink
De Bilt, Holland, Oktober 2014

The first time I encountered Jacky Ickx was straight after his win at the Nürburgring in 1969. He had just had one of those fantastic races in a Brabham F1 that drivers dream about. Some months later we met again at Spa prior to the 1,000-kilometre race at that wonderful Belgian track. And once more, that day he was on top form. He did not win, but he extracted everything he could from the Ferrari 512S that he shared with John Surtees. I also remember the Dutch GP of 1971. In the pouring rain, he and Pedro Rodriguez lapped the whole field in a demonstration of how to drive fast in soaking wet conditions. These are just three of the many races where I saw him drive and there were many, many more. When he was sitting in the right car, Ickx was on top and one of the best drivers in the world of his particular era.

Working on this book about Ickx's motor sports career with all its wonderful photographs gave me the great pleasure to once again meet several of the drivers from that time including Derek Bell, Jackie Stewart, Hurley Haywood, Jochen Mass, Vic Elford, David Hobbs and Nino Vaccarella and especially Brian Redman with whom Jacky shared so many wins. These are all drivers who survived that dangerous period in which fatal accidents were an almost everyday part of motor racing. They all have their own memories and talked with pleasure about their experiences with Jacky as a team-mate, a driver, a rival and a friend.

I have written this book as a tribute from someone who is both a passionate fan of motor sport in general and of Jacky Ickx in particular. To my mind, he is one of the greatest all-round drivers in the history of motor sport and has demonstrated that on race tracks with single seaters, sports cars and touring cars and then added to that versatility with his exploits across the deserts of the world on rallye-raids. Everything in this book is a personal manifestation of my admiration for him and his ability.
Jacky, chapeau!

Ed Heuvink
De Bilt, Holland, October 2014

Jacky Ickx – Einer, der seinen eigenen Weg geht
Jacky Ickx, doing it his own way

Jacky Ickx war schon immer einzigartig, ein Außenseiter. Bereits in seiner Kindheit, die er auf dem Anwesen seiner Eltern – dem ehemaligen Kloster „Prieuré de l'Ermite" vor den Toren von Brüssel – verbrachte, zeigte sich, dass Jacky gern seinen eigenen Weg geht. Durch seinen Vater, den Automobiljournalisten und Hobby-Motorsportler Jacques Ickx, und seinen älteren Bruder Pascal, der sich ebenfalls im Motorsport engagierte, hatte Jacky schon als Kind viel mit Autos zu tun. Die Schule lag dem kleinen Jacky dagegen nicht so sehr, er konnte sich einfach nicht konzentrieren. „Ich war kein schlechter Schüler, aber ich konnte nicht den ganzen Tag im Klassenraum sitzen", erklärte er dem niederländischen Journalisten Rob Wiedenhoff zu Beginn seiner Karriere. Zum 16. Geburtstag bekam Jacky von seinem Vater ein Motorrad geschenkt. Ickx senior hoffte, dass Jacky einen Teil seiner großen Energie auf diese Maschine verwenden würde. Es war diese frühe Motorrad-Erfahrung, durch die Jacky ein so gutes Balancegefühl entwickelte, von dem er in seiner Motorsportlaufbahn sehr profitierte.

Jacky Ickx was always a unique person, an outsider. He grew up at the beautiful 'Prieuré de l'Ermite', a beautiful country style mansion just outside Brussels and from an early age, it was clear that Jacky would be going his own way. Born into a well-known automotive family, he was raised with all that material benefits could provide as well as many opportunities to get to know all about cars. His father, Jacques Ickx, was a famous automotive journalist and competitor while his elder brother, Pascal, also had a motor sport involvement and a career involving cars. However at school, young Jacky did not feel comfortable and could not concentrate. "I was not a bad pupil, but I could not sit in a classroom all day long", he told Rob Wiedenhoff, a Dutch journalist who visited him at the beginning of his racing career. On his sixteenth birthday, Jacky was given a motorcycle by his father who hoped that his son could dissipate some of his enormous energy by using the machine. It was this early acquaintance with motorcycles that gave Jacky a good feeling of balance from which he was to benefit later in his motor sport career.

Als Wiedenhoff den jungen Ickx am Saisonende 1967 besuchte, lebte der 22-Jährige noch bei seinen Eltern. „Als ich bei ihm ankam, hörte ich aus einem der Nebenräume Orgelmusik", erinnert sich Wiedenhoff. „Ich glaube, es war Bach. Ich dachte: Das ist aber merkwürdig für einen Rennfahrer, besonders für einen so jungen. Nach dem Treffen wusste ich aber, dass es perfekt zu Ickx' Charakter passte, der für seine 22 Jahre sehr mysteriös und nachdenklich war." Diese mysteriöse Aura versprüht Ickx übrigens auch heute noch.

Nach dem Aufstieg zum Vollzeit-Rennfahrer sorgte Ickx für eine strikte Trennung von Privat- und Berufsleben. Er konzentrierte sich zwar voll auf den Rennsport, lebte abseits der Strecke, aber sein eigenes Leben. Er ging seinen eigenen Weg ohne dem Klischee des Rennfahrers zu entsprechen. Er war ein Individuum, ganz anders als seine Kollegen. Er war ein Egozentriker. Er machte die Dinge, die ihm gefielen, nur zur eigenen Freude und nicht für andere.

Die Risiken des Rennsports betrachtete Ickx als selbstverständlich. Sie hielten ihn nicht davon ab, seinen Job ohne wenn und aber zu erledigen. Als Jackie Stewart seinen Feldzug für mehr Sicherheit begann, unterstützte Ickx ihn nicht. Daher war er bei den anderen Fahrern nicht besonders beliebt. „Ich bin meinen eigenen Weg gegangen, den ich für richtig hielt. Das machte mich zu einer Art Außenseiter", sagte Ickx zu Wiedenhoff. „Mein Vater sagte immer: ‚La Liberté de risquer sa vie, c'est une liberté.' Das bedeutet übersetzt: ‚Die Freiheit zu haben, sein eigenes Leben zu riskieren, ist eine Freiheit.'" Wiedenhoff empfand diese Überzeugung als angeboren: „Ich glaube nicht, dass ihm diese Herangehensweise beigebracht wurde. Sie war eher in seinen Genen verwurzelt. Bei der Karriere seines Bruders Pascal gab es viele Ähnlichkeiten."

„Anders als Jackie Stewart, der der perfekte PR-Mann ist, habe ich nie viel Wert auf PR gelegt", sagte Ickx bei einem zweiten Interview mit Wiedenhoff nach seinem Rücktritt. Am selben Tag gab Ickx ein langes Zitat des früheren US-Präsidenten Abraham Lincoln wieder. „‚Du kannst keinen Wohlstand erzeugen, indem Du Sparsamkeit verhinderst. Du kannst die Schwachen nicht stärken, indem Du die Starken schwächst. Du kannst dem Lohnempfänger nicht helfen, indem Du den Lohnzahler unterdrückst.' Ich finde es wunderbar, dass ein Mann so etwas vor mehr als 150 Jahren gesagt haben soll", sagte Ickx und fuhr fort: „‚Du kannst nicht des Menschen Charakter und geistige Stärke aufbauen, indem Du seine Initiative und Unabhängigkeit zerstörst.'" Wiedenhoff war von diesen Worten sehr überrascht. „Ich war total perplex. Ickx hat mich mit diesem Text direkt zu Beginn unseres Interviews konfrontiert. Das bringt seinen Charakter sehr gut auf den Punkt: Er geht seinen eigenen Weg. Und ich bin sicher, dass ihm seine späteren Erfahrungen, als er bei der Paris–Dakar durch die leeren Wüsten Afrikas gefahren ist, einen noch breiteren Horizont verschafft haben. Das und sein unabhängiger Charakter haben ihn zu dem Menschen gemacht, der er heute ist."

Rob Wiedenhoff ist ein geschätzter Motorsportjournalist aus den Niederlanden. Er hat den Sport seit den frühen 60er-Jahren begleitet und hatte in dieser Zeit engen Kontakt zu Jacky Ickx. 30 Jahre lang hat er die Karriere des Belgiers rund um den Globus verfolgt.

When Wiedenhoff visited Ickx at the end of the 1967 season, the twenty-two year old driver was still living at home with his parents. "When I arrived at his place, I heard organ music – I think it was Bach – coming out of one of the adjoining buildings. I thought this was a bit odd for a racing car driver, especially one so young," remembers Wiedenhoff. "But after our meeting, I found it fitted in perfectly with the character of Ickx who was very mysterious and pensive for a twenty-two year old." After all these years, that mysterious aura is still with him today

Once Jacky Ickx became a full-time racing driver, he kept his private life and his professional life strictly separated. Although he was fully committed to racing, away from the circuits he liked to live his own life in his own way without having to conform to any racing driver stereotype. He was very much an individual, different from the others. He was if anything, egocentric, doing things he liked to do purely for his own fun and not for anyone else's benefit.

He took the dangers inherent in racing for granted and did his job without fuss. When Jackie Stewart started his safety crusade, Ickx did not join him. As a result, he was not terribly popular with the other drivers. "But I acted in my own way, for what I thought was right. This made me a kind of outsider." Ickx said to Wiedenhoff. "My father had a personal saying 'La Liberté de risquer sa vie, c'est une liberté', or 'to have the freedom to risk one's own life, is a freedom'." Wiedenhoff commented: "I don't think he got that approach through being taught it. More likely it was in his genetic make-up. For instance, there were similarities in the career of his brother, Pascal."

"I never paid much importance to doing PR, unlike Jackie Stewart who is the perfect PR guy", Ickx said to Wiedenhoff when they met again after he had retired from circuit racing. That same day, when they met in Brussels, Ickx gave the journalist a long quotation from Abraham Lincoln, the former American president. 'You cannot bring about prosperity by discouraging thrift. You cannot strengthen the weak by weakening the strong. You cannot help the wage earner by pulling down the wage payer'. "I think that it's wonderful that a man should have said this more than one hundred and fifty years ago", Ickx said. "'You cannot build character and courage by taking away man's initiative and independence'," the quotation continued. "I was totally surprised when he came up with a text like this," Wiedenhoff said. "He hit me with it right at the start of our interview. But it sums up his character pretty well: going his own way. And I am sure, that his later experiences when driving through the empty deserts of Africa on Paris-Dakar and other such events, have given him a yet broader view of life. This and his independent character have made him the man he is today."

Rob Wiedenhoff is a well-regarded Dutch motor sport journalist who has covered the sport since the early sixties. In this period, he was very close to Jacky Ickx, attending the races in which Ickx competed for thirty years all over the world.

RAC British Grand Prix 1972, Brands Hatch, Ferrari 312B2

1963 – 1966

Die ersten Jahre im Motorsport
His early racing activities

Jacques Bernard „Jacky" Ickx ist der zweite Sohn des belgischen Motorjournalisten Jacques Ickx, der als Redakteur für die offizielle Zeitschrift des Royal Automobile Club of Belgium namens Royal Auto arbeitete. Daher kam Jacky früh mit Autos in Berührung. Manchmal sogar mit Rennwagen, denn sein Vater nahm nebenbei an Rennen und Rallyes teil. Als Jacky am 1. Januar 1945 geboren wurde, war sein Vater 34 und sein Bruder Pascal acht Jahre alt. In seiner Jugend zeigte Jacky ein zunehmendes Interesse an Autos und allem, was mit Geschwindigkeit zu tun hatte. Seine Eltern unterstützten diese Begeisterung: Da Jackys schulische Leistungen nicht herausragend waren, wollten sie ihm etwas geben, worauf er sich konzentrieren konnte. Als Jacky 16 Jahre alt war, kauften sie ihm sein erstes Motorrad – eine Puch. Die 50-Kubik-Maschine wurde aber schnell durch ein Trial-Motorrad mit 125 Kubik ersetzt, und damit nahm der junge Jacky schon bald an Rennen teil. Ein Jahr später wurde Ickx Trial-Europameister in seiner Klasse. Im Alter von 17 Jahren probierte er sogar eine richtige Suzuki-Rennmaschine aus, die er jedoch nie im Wettbewerb einsetzte, weil er noch zu jung war. Durch die Trials entwickelte Jacky einen hervorragenden Gleichgewichtssinn, der ihm später bei Autorennen enorm zugute kam.

Jacques Bernard "Jacky" Ickx was the second son of motoring journalist Jacques Ickx, the editor of Royal Auto, which is the official publication of the Royal Automobile Club of Belgium. Thus, right from his early childhood, Jacky was surrounded by cars. Sometimes even racing cars as his father was a part-time racer and drove in rallies. Jacky was born on January 1st, 1945, when his father was thirty-four years old and brother Pascal, eight. As he grew up, Jacky got more and more interested in automobiles and anything related to speed. His parents did not oppose this trend. Indeed, Ickx got his first motorcycle from them – a 50 cc Puch – at the age of sixteen. This was partly because he was not distinguishing himself in his academic studies at school and they felt he needed something that he could focus on. The 50 cc bike was soon replaced by a bigger 125 cc machine, a proper trials bike, and the young Jacky was soon competing with it. A year later, he became European champion in his trial class. At the age of seventeen, he even had a go on a proper Suzuki racing bike, but, since he was too young, he could not actually use it in a race. By doing trials, Jacky developed an excellent feeling of balance, which later helped him when driving cars.

Großer Preis der Tourenwagen 1966, Nürburgring

Nach den ersten Erfahrungen bei Trials 1961 und 1962 wechselte Ickx schon bald auf vier Räder, 1963 nahm er die ersten Wettbewerb in einem BMW 700 in Angriff. Um das richtige Feeling fürs Rennfahren und die wichtigsten Tricks zu lernen, ging Jacky nach Zandvoort zu Paul Frère, dem berühmten belgischen Journalist und Rennfahrer. Im April nahm Ickx mit dem BMW, der ihm vom belgischen BMW- und Zündapp-Importeur Albert Moorkens zur Verfügung gestellt wurde, an einem Bergrennen in den belgischen Ardennen teil. Leider endete die Automobil-Premiere in einem Baum, an dem der kleine BMW stark demoliert wurde. Nach erfolgreicher Reparatur nahm Ickx sein zweites Bergrennen in Angriff. In Gives war Ickx entspannter, blieb auf der Straße und gewann seine Klasse. Außerdem ging Ickx in jenem Sommer das erste Mal auf einer Rennstrecke an den Start. In Zolder wurde er Dritter in der Klasse. Der brandneue Kurs, der offiziell den Namen „Omloop van Terlaemen" trug, war erst im Juni 1963 eingeweiht worden und sollte hinter Spa-Francorchamps die zweitwichtigste Rennstrecke Belgiens werden.

Ende September nahm Ickx mit dem BMW 700 an der Tour de France Automobile teil. Die einwöchige Veranstaltung bestand aus 16 Prüfungen, darunter Rallye-WPs, Bergrennen und Rennen auf verschiedenen Rundstrecken wie Spa-Francorchamps, Reims und Le Mans. Ickx und sein erfahrener Beifahrer Georges Harris zeigten in dem kleinen Auto eine gute Leistung. Beim Rennen in Le Mans endete jedoch die Vorstellung der Belgier wegen einer defekten Lichtmaschine. Der Gesamtsieg bei der 12. Tour de France Automobile ging an die Franzosen Jean Guichet und José Behra im Ferrari 250 GTO.

Beim Bergrennen von Namur Ende September fuhr Ickx sowohl den BMW als auch einen Ford Lotus Cortina Mk1. Das brandneue Fahrzeug, das erst im September die Gruppe-1-Homologation erhalten hatte, bekam er von Ford Belgien zur Verfügung gestellt. Der Lotus Cortina sollte sein Rennwagen für die nächsten zwei Jahre sein und in dieser Limousine sollte im Frühjahr 1964 auch die internationale Karriere von Ickx beginnen. Im März war Ickx bei zwei Bergrennen und bei kleineren Rennen in Zolder erfolgreich. Darüber hinaus bewies Ickx bei einer Rallye im belgischen Huy seine Vielseitigkeit mit dem zweiten Gesamtrang. Bei der 12-Stunden-Rallye fuhr Ickx einen Hillman Imp – ein Kleinwagen mit Heckmotor, der von der Veranlagung her große Ähnlichkeit mit dem BMW 700 hatte.

Im Mai war Ickx erneut in Zolder und nahm an zwei Rennen zum „Bekers van Terlaemen" (Pokal von Terlaemen) teil. Dabei fuhr er sowohl den BMW als auch den Cortina, schied aber beide Male aus. Das gleiche Schicksal ereilte ihn eine Woche später bei den „Coupes de Spa". Im berühmt-berüchtigten Masta-Knick musste Ickx einem sich drehenden Alfa Romeo ausweichen und verlor dabei die Kontrolle über seinen Wagen. Der Cortina erwischte einen kleinen Jungen, der in einer Sperrzone stand und bei dem Unfall ums Leben kam. In den Tagen nach dieser Tragödie gab es viele negative Schlagzeilen um Jacky, obwohl dieser an dem Unfall wenig Schuld hatte.

Drei Klassensiege bei Bergrennen in Belgien und ein dritter Platz bei einem Rennen in Zolder brachten dagegen positive Ablenkung. Eine große Herausforderung erwartete Ickx aber im Juli. Zusammen mit Teddy Pilette sollte Ickx den Lotus Cortina, mit dem er vorher in Spa verunfallt war, bei den 24 Stunden von Spa-Francorchamps pilotieren. Das Langstreckenrennen feierte 1964 nach zwölfjähriger Pause ein Comeback, anders als zuvor waren jetzt aber nur noch Tourenwagen zugelassen.
Zahlreiche internationale Werksteams gingen an den Start, darunter Mercedes-Benz, BMW, Ford und Lancia. Die jungen Belgier schlugen

After his experiences with trials bikes in 1961 and 1962, Ickx started driving cars in a BMW 700 in 1963. To get the feeling of racing and to learn the basic tricks, the young driver went to Zandvoort in the Netherlands to be taught by Paul Frère, the famous Belgian journalist and racing car driver. With this small BMW lent to him by the Belgian BMW (and Zündapp) importer, Albert Moorkens, Ickx entered his first event in April at a hill climb in the Belgian Ardennes. Unfortunately, his first outing ended in a collision with a tree in which Ickx almost demolished his little car. With it repaired, at the second hill climb in Gives he was more relaxed, stayed on the road and won his class. Later that summer, Ickx got his first circuit experience, when he raced at the new track of Zolder and finished third in the smallest class. The 'Omloop van Terlaemen', as the track was officially known, had opened in June 1963 and was to be the second most important racetrack in Belgium after Spa-Francorchamps.

In late September of that year, Ickx drove the BMW 700 in the Tour de France Automobile, a weeklong racing and regularity event in France and surrounding countries. For this event, he was partnered by fellow Belgian, the experienced Georges Harris. The event included sixteen special stages and hill climbs as well as races at several circuits such as Spa-Francorchamps, Reims and Le Mans. Although they showed some good performances in the little car, they were unable to finish thanks to a broken alternator during the race at Le Mans. Overall winners of this 12th edition of the Tour de France Automobile was the much more powerful Ferrari 250 GTO of Frenchmen Jean Guichet and José Behra.

For the hill climbs at Namur at the end of September, Ickx drove both the BMW and a new Ford Lotus Cortina Mk1. This brand new car – which was homologated by Ford as a Group 1 touring car during September – was loaned to him by Ford Belgium. It was to be his racing car for the next two years. With the Ford Lotus Cortina, Ickx would kick off his international career at the beginning of 1964. During March, he was successful at two hill climbs as well as at some minor races at Zolder. But before the professional racing season got under way, Ickx demonstrated his adaptability by finishing second in a 12-hour rally in Huy, Belgium. On this event, Ickx drove a Hillman Imp, a small rear-engined family car not so very different from the BMW 700 with which his career in cars had started.

In May, Ickx drove two races at Zolder using both the trusty BMW 700 and the new Lotus Cortina. Unfortunately, in neither of the races did he finish. When he entered the 'Coupes de Spa' a week later, again he failed to finish. At the ultra-fast Spa-Francorchamps circuit, Ickx lost control of his Cortina at the infamous Masta kink while trying to avoid a spinning Alfa Romeo. He crashed, killing a young boy who was standing in an unauthorised area. During the days that followed this unfortunate incident, Jacky received a lot of negative publicity for the result of an accident that was not of his making.

He went on to win his class at three hill climbs in Belgium and came third at a race at Zolder. But the real challenge for Ickx came in July, when he was asked to drive the 24 Hours of Spa-Francorchamps in the Lotus Cortina – the car he had crashed earlier at Spa – and he would share the driving with Teddy Pilette. After a twelve-year break, this famous event was now back on the international calendar and was open to touring cars. It received a large international entry with several works teams including Mercedes-Benz, BMW, Ford and Lancia. The two young Belgians in the Lotus Cortina had a good race until a wheel broke on Sunday morning. After limping back to the pits on three wheels and then

Coupes de Spa 1964, Spa-Francorchamps, Ford Lotus Cortina n°30

sich in diesem starken Feld gut, bis sonntagmorgens eine Felge brach. Der Cortina humpelte auf drei Rädern an die Box zurück und wurde dort 40 Minuten lang repariert. Ickx/Pilette schafften es trotzdem auf Gesamtrang 14 und Platz vier in der Klasse ins Ziel. Die Gesamtsieger – Robert Crevits und Gustave Gosselin im Mercedes 300SE – legten innerhalb der 24 Stunden fast 4.000 Kilometer zurück.

Die gute Leistung in Spa zahlte sich für Ickx aus: Für den Lauf zur Tourenwagen-Europameisterschaft in Zandvoort bot ihm Alan Mann Racing einen seiner Lotus Cortina an. Im Qualifying platzierte Ickx das Auto in der ersten Startreihe neben dem BMW von Hubert Hahne und dem Cortina seines Teamkollegen Sir John Whitmore. Der Engländer führte das Rennen an, bis er durch Motorprobleme eingebremst wurde. Da Whitmore so viele Meisterschaftspunkte wie möglich mitnehmen sollte, musste Ickx hinter seinem Teamkollegen bleiben und wurde Vierter, während Hahne zum Sieg fuhr. Der nächste EM-Lauf war das Bergrennen am Timmelsjoch in Österreich. Ickx durfte erneut im Lotus Cortina von Alan Mann Racing ran und wurde diesmal Zweiter, direkt hinter seinem Teampartner Whitmore.

enduring a 40-minute pit stop to correct the damage, they continued and finally crossed the line in fourteenth place overall and fourth in class. The overall winners of that race – the Belgians, Robert Crevits and Gustave Gosselin – covered nearly 4,000 kilometres in their powerful Mercedes-Benz 300SE.

For the Zandvoort round of the European Touring Car Championship later that summer, Jacky Ickx was offered a Lotus Cortina prepared and run by Alan Mann Racing as a reward for his good effort at Spa. He managed to qualify the car on the front row alongside the BMW of Hubert Hahne and Ickx's team-mate, Sir John Whitmore. The Englishman took the lead and led until he encountered engine problems and had to back off. Since it was important for Whitmore to score as many points as possible for the ETC, Ickx stayed behind his team-mate. Hahne won the race with Ickx classified fourth. The next round of the ETC was a hill climb at Timmelsjoch in Austria. Once more, Ickx drove an Alan Mann Lotus Cortina and this time finished second, again right behind Sir John Whitmore.

Der vorletzte Lauf zur Tourenwagen-EM war ein Rennen in den Straßen von Budapest, wo Ickx erneut in einem Alan-Mann-Cortina saß. In Ungarn schied Ickx zwar vorzeitig aus und überquerte nicht die Ziellinie, dennoch wurde er als Dritter in der Klasse gewertet. Zum Abschluss der Saison stand wie schon 1963 das Bergrennen von Namur auf dem Programm, wo Ickx erneut im Ford und im BMW 700 antrat. Es war ein erfreulicher Ausklang, denn Ickx gewann beide Klassen.

Im Laufe des Jahres 1964 hatte Jacky Ickx auf internationaler Bühne einige gute Resultate erzielt und Erfahrungen in einem der besten Tourenwagen-Teams Europas gesammelt. Das Beste aber war, dass Alan Mann ihn 1965 erneut in seinem Team haben wollte. Die Autos des schüchternen Engländers hatten 1964 bei der Rallye Monte Carlo, der Tour de France Automobile (mit dem Gesamtsieg) und in der Tourenwagen-EM für Schlagzeilen gesorgt. 1965 sollte Ickx also Teil des starken Teams von Ford of Europe sein.

So kam es, dass Jacky Ickx im Alter von 20 Jahren plötzlich ein professioneller Rennfahrer war. Zu Beginn der neuen Saison sollte er in einem Lotus Cortina sitzen, der damals ohne Zweifel stärkste Tourenwagen in der 1.600er-Klasse. Und dank der Unterstützung von Ford Belgien konnte Ickx auch abseits der EM die Autos von Alan Mann fahren. Seine Saison begann im März mit einigen Bergrennen, die er wenig überraschend alle gewann. Die ersten Rennen fanden am 21. März in Zolder statt. Im Rahmen der „Coupes de Belgique" nahm er im Lotus Cortina in der 1.600er-Klasse teil und im starken Ford Mustang am Rennen der Tourenwagen ohne Hubraumlimit. Ein ähnliches Auto hatte 1964 die Tour de France Automobile gewonnen. In beiden Rennen sah Ickx als Erster die Ziellinie! Und kurz darauf ließ er diesem Doppelsieg zwei Triumphe bei Bergrennen in den Ardennen folgen.

Um seine Vielseitigkeit zu demonstrieren, durfte Ickx zusammen mit Gilbert Staepelaere die Tulpenrallye bestreiten – den niederländischen Lauf zur Rallye-Europameisterschaft. Obwohl es bei der Veranstaltung reichlich Eis, Schnee und Nebel gab, schlug sich Ickx gut. Nach Anwendung des Klassenaufwertungssystems wurde Ickx auf Platz elf gewertet, der Sieg ging an Rosemary Smith im Hillman Imp.

Am Morgen vor dem 500-Kilometer-Rennen der Sportwagen in Spa-Francorchamps nahm Ickx am Tourenwagenrennen im Rahmen der „Coupes de Spa" teil. In einem von Alan Mann aufgebauten Ford Mustang fuhr Ickx auf die Pole und führte ein starkes internationales Feld an. Wegen Motorproblemen konnte er das von Alan Hutcheson im Ford Galaxie vorgegebene Tempo aber nicht halten. Am Ende wurde Ickx sogar überrundet und musste sich mit Platz 14 begnügen. Einen Monat später hatte Ickx am Nürburgring ähnlich viel Pech. Beim deutschen Lauf zur Tourenwagen-EM schied der Mustang, den er sich mit Sir Gwaine Baillie teilte, schon in der ersten Runde aus. Zwei Wochen später war dann aber der lang ersehnte erste EM-Sieg im Ford Mustang fällig: Bei seinem Heimspiel zur Tourenwagen-EM siegte er vor seinem Landsmann Lucien Bianchi in einem weiteren Alan-Mann-Mustang. Erstaunlicherweise reichte dieses eine Ergebnis aus, um am Jahresende den Titel in der Division 3 zu gewinnen. Beim separaten Rennen der Zweiliter-Tourenwagen setzte Ickx den Lotus Cortina von Ford Belgien ein, konnte damit aber nicht das Tempo der Alan-Mann-Autos von John Whitmore und Peter Procter mitgehen. Ickx beendete das Rennen auf Rang vier hinter dem Alan-Mann-Duo und dem BMW 1800 TISA von Hubert Hahne, mit dem sich Ickx das ganze Rennen einen spektakulären Zweikampf geliefert hatte.

Um den Lotus Cortina in den USA zu promoten, beauftragte Ford das Team von Alan Mann Racing, ein Auto beim Trans-Am-Rennen in Maryland einzusetzen.

The penultimate round of the ETC was a race held on the streets of Budapest and Ickx was given another opportunity by Alan Mann Racing. This time however, he failed to finish but was eventually classified, though not crossing the finish line, as third in class. To finish off the season, Ickx – just as he had done in 1963 – competed in the Namur Hill Climb with both the Ford and the BMW 700. It was a satisfactory conclusion to the year since he won both classes that he entered.

During that 1964 season, Jacky Ickx got some good international results and gained experience with one of the best saloon car teams in Europe. What was best of all was that they wanted him back so that, for the 1965 season, he would be part of the strong Ford of Europe team run by Alan Mann. This quiet Englishman had made headlines in 1964 by preparing Ford cars for the Monte Carlo Rally, the Tour de France Automobile (which they won outright) and the European Touring Car Championship.

So it was that at twenty years of age, Jacky Ickx became a fully professional racing driver. For the 1965 season, he would start by driving a Lotus Cortina, which at that time was demonstrably the most competitive touring car in the 1,600 cc class. With the help of Ford Belgium, Ickx was also able to drive Alan Mann cars in other events outside the ETC and in March, he began the new season by tackling a number of hill climbs all of which he – as expected – won. His first racing that year was at the circuit of Zolder where on March 21st, he drove in two races in two different classes; the 1,600 cc class with a Lotus Cortina and also in the unlimited touring car class with a powerful Ford Mustang similar to the one that had won the Tour de France Automobile in 1964. In both of these 'Coupe de Belgique' races, he crossed the finish line as the winner. These victories were followed by two more hill climb wins in the Belgian Ardennes.

To underline his diversity, it was arranged that Ickx would partner Gilbert Staepelaere for the Tulip Rallye, the Dutch round of the European Rally Championship. Despite there being lots of snow, ice and fog, Ickx coped pretty well and they finished a respectable eleventh overall. The results were calculated on a class improvement basis and thus Rosemary Smith in her little Hillman Imp came out as the winner.

Held on the morning before the 500-kilometre sportscar race at Spa-Francorchamps, there was the traditional 'Coupes de Spa' touring car race. Behind the wheel of an Alan Mann-prepared Ford Mustang, Ickx qualified on pole and led from the start ahead of a strong international field. However, because of engine problems, Ickx could not keep up the pace set by the Ford Galaxie of Englishman, Alan Hutcheson. Towards the end of the race, Ickx was even lapped and finally finished a rather disappointing fourteenth. A month later at the Nürburgring, Ickx was again out of luck. He retired on the first lap of the German round of the European Touring Car Championship in a Mustang that he was sharing with Sir Gwaine Baillie. At the Belgian round of the ETC, two weeks later at Zolder, Ickx was finally able to pull off the ETC victory that had been eluding him with the Ford Mustang. Second behind him was his compatriot, Lucien Bianchi, in a similar Alan Mann Mustang. Amazingly, this single result was enough at the end of the season to give Ickx the Division 3 title. In the separate race for the two-litre class, Ickx was entered in the Belgian Lotus Cortina and found himself unable to fight with the faster Alan Mann cars of John Whitmore and Peter Procter. He consequently ended up fourth behind them as well as behind one of the more powerful BMW 1800 TISAs driven by Hubert Hahne with whom he had a monumental race-long struggle.

Coupes de Spa 1965, Spa-Francorchamps, Ford Mustang

Coupe Terlaemen 1965, Zolder, Ford Lotus Cortina

Coupes de Spa 1966, Spa-Francorchamps, Ford Mustang n°1

Für Ickx war es der erste Besuch in Amerika und er war erfolgreich: Ickx und sein Teampartner Trevor Taylor brachten den rot-goldenen Cortina auf Platz neun ins Ziel.

Nach der Rückkehr aus Amerika war Ickx auch in Zandvoort erfolgreich: Er gewann beide „Coupes du Benelux"-Rennen. In der 1.600er-Klasse fuhr er einen Lotus Cortina, in der Klasse ohne Hubraumlimit einen Mustang. Das US-Muscle-Car setzte Ickx im August auch beim Marathon de la Route ein. Die von der Lütticher Royal Motor Union organisierte Veranstaltung wurde 1965 wegen des zunehmenden Verkehrsaufkommens erstmals nicht als Rallye von Lüttich nach Sofia und zurück ausgetragen, sondern als Langstreckenrennen: 82 Stunden nonstop auf dem Nürburgring! Bei dieser Ausdauerschlacht teilte sich Ickx das Cockpit erneut mit Gilbert Staepelaere. In knapp drei Tagen und Nächten legte das Duo von Ford Belgien 310 Runden zurück – genauso viele wie Henri Greder und Johnny Rives in einem weiteren Ford Mustang. Die Franzosen hatten am Ende aber knapp die Nase vorn, und Ickx musste sich mit Platz zwei begnügen.

Bei den 24 Stunden von Spa-Francorchamps ging Ford nicht werksseitig an den Start, also folgte Jacky Ickx einer Einladung von BMW. Für die Bayern fuhr er zusammen mit Dieter Glemser einen von vier BMW 1800 TISA. Zu Jackys Teamkollegen zählte übrigens auch sein älterer Bruder Pascal. In der Qualifikation erzielte Jacky die zweitbeste Zeit und startete daher aus der ersten Reihe. Sein Rennen endete jedoch vorzeitig mit defekter Zylinderkopfdichtung. Immerhin sahnte ein anderer Ickx die Lorbeeren ein: Pascal Ickx gewann das Langstreckenrennen zusammen mit dem belgischen Sportwagenfahrer Gérard Langlois van Ophem.

Ab September nahm Ickx nur noch an kleineren Rundstrecken- und Bergrennen teil, die er größtenteils gewann. Ickx erlebte ein sehr gutes erstes Jahr als Profi-Rennfahrer. Viele Teamchefs waren auf ihn aufmerksam geworden und wollten ihn für 1966 unter Vertrag nehmen. Dazu zählte auch Ken Tyrrell. Der Brite hatte bereits Jackie Stewart für die Formel 2 verpflichtet und fragte jetzt bei Ickx an, ob dieser ausgewählte Formel-2- und Formel-3-Rennen für ihn fahren wollte. Das Tyrrell-Team hatte in der Motorsport-Szene einen exzellenten Ruf in Bezug auf die Vorbereitung, Präsentation und vor allem die Ergebnisse ihrer Rennwagen. Diese Chance hätte für Ickx den großen Durchbruch bedeutet – und das sollte sie auch.

1965 hatte Ickx die Belgische Tourenwagen-Meisterschaft gewonnen – und das im zarten Alter von 20 Jahren! Und das Jahr 1966 begann gleich mit einer neuen Herausforderung: Leon Dernier fragte bei Ickx an, ob dieser seinen Ferrari 250 LM bei den 24 Stunden von Daytona fahren wollte. Es sollte nicht nur Jackys Debüt auf dem Florida-Speedway, sondern auch seine Premiere in einem Ferrari sein. Die 24 Stunden von Daytona bildeten den Auftakt zur Internationalen Markenmeisterschaft 1966 und lockten daher Werksteams von Ford, Ferrari und Porsche an. In diesem starken Feld teilte sich Ickx den zwei Jahre alten Ferrari mit Dernier und Jean Blaton, alias Beurlys. Eingesetzt wurde das Auto von der Ecurie Francorchamps, der Rennschmiede des belgischen Ferrari-Importeurs Jacques Swaters. Nach einer problemlosen Qualifikation startete das Trio von der 20. Position ins Rennen, doch nach 80 Runden war schon wieder alles vorbei. Der 250 LM strandete mit defekter Kraftübertragung.

Die Europa-Saison begann für Ickx mit einigen Bergrennen im Lotus Cortina und einem Rennen in Zolder im Ford Mustang, welches er gewann. Es war sein erster Triumph im neuen Jahr. 1965 hatte Ickx seine größten Erfolge auf Ford gefeiert, und auch dieses Jahr setzte der junge Belgier fast immer auf Ford-Power. Die von Tyrrell eingesetzten Matra wurden bei den meisten Rennen von

To promote the Lotus Cortina in the USA, Alan Mann was asked by Ford to run a car at the Marlboro Trans Am event in Maryland. The team entered Ickx together with Trevor Taylor in one of the red and gold Cortinas and, on Ickx's first visit to North America, he and Taylor finished ninth overall.

Back in Europe, Ickx won both the races he entered at Zandvoort at the 'Coupes du Benelux' race meeting. In the 1,600 cc class he drove a Lotus Cortina while in the unlimited class he was at the wheel of a Mustang. That same Mustang was then used in August to compete in the Marathon de la Route. This had been a famous rally also known as the Liège-Sofia-Liège but increasing traffic on European roads – even in Yugoslavia – had forced the Royal Motor Union of Liège to convert their long-distance road rally into a gruelling, 82-hour event at the Nürburgring. For this marathon, Ickx was again partnered by his fellow Ford Belgium driver, Gilbert Staepelaere. In the three full days and nights of racing, they covered three hundred and ten laps. That was the same number of laps covered by the French Mustang team of Henri Greder and Johnny Rives but it was the French pair who finished ahead and the Belgians had to be content with second place.

For the 24 Hours of Spa-Francorchamps, with no official entries from Ford, Jacky Ickx was invited by BMW to drive one of their factory cars alongside Dieter Glemser. This would be one of four BMW 1800 TISAs entered by the Bavarian manufacturer. Driving in one of the other BMWs was Jacky's elder brother Pascal. After practice, Jacky Ickx was second fastest and thus at the front of the grid, but he failed to finish the race when the BMW's head gasket failed. But it was another Ickx in a BMW who tasted victory since Pascal Ickx won the event partnered by Belgian sportscar driver Gérard Langlois van Ophem.

From September on, Ickx only competed in some minor races and hill climbs but he did have the satisfaction of winning most of them. For Ickx, this first full year as a professional driver was satisfying and he received a lot of interest from team owners who were interested in having him drive for them in 1966. One of these was Ken Tyrrell, who had already contracted Jackie Stewart to drive his Formula Two car and he now asked Ickx to join him to drive Formula Three and some Formula Two races in the coming year. The Tyrrell Organisation was well-known in the motor racing world for its car preparation, excellent presentation and, of course, its good results. This opportunity could, and would, be a big breakthrough for Jacky Ickx.

One of the things that he had collected during 1965 was the Belgian Touring Car crown and that already at the age of just twenty. And now the year of 1966 started with an exciting new experience for Jacky Ickx since he was asked by Leon Dernier to drive his Ferrari 250 LM at the 24 Hours of Daytona. Not only would it be Jacky's first race at the Florida speedway but also his first time in a Ferrari. The 24 Hours of Daytona was a relatively new event and was also the opening round of the 1966 International Championship of Makes with works entries from Ford, Ferrari and Porsche. The two-year old car to be driven by Ickx was entered by Ecurie Francorchamps, the racing arm of the Belgian Ferrari importer Jacques Swaters. Joining Jacky in the Ferrari LM were Dernier and Jean Blaton, also known as 'Beurlys'. After a trouble-free practice, the team started from twentieth position on the grid but unfortunately transmission problems forced them to retire after only eighty laps with six hundred laps still remaining.

Back in Belgium, Ickx did some hill climbs in a Lotus Cortina and a race at Zolder in the Ford Mustang, which he won. That win would

24 Heures de Spa-Francorchamps 1965, BMW 1800 TISA n°5

24 Hours of Daytona 1966, Daytona Beach, Ferrari 250LM

Copyright: From the collections of The Henry Ford.

Ford-Aggregaten mit einem Liter Hubraum angetrieben. Im F2-Auto arbeitete ein reinrassiger Rennmotor, im F3-Boliden ein seriennahes Triebwerk. Jacky sollte beide Monoposti fahren und seine Saison sollte zu Ostern in Oulton Park beginnen. Das Meeting musste jedoch wegen Schneefalls abgesagt werden. Also wurde Ickx' Monoposto-Debüt auf den 11. April vertagt. Auf der schnellen Strecke von Goodwood im Süden Englands fuhr Ickx vorsichtig und wurde Sechster. Im Rennen musste er sich das Auto jedoch mit Teamkollege Jackie Stewart teilen. Beim Schotten riss der Gaszug und so übernahm er das Ickx-Auto. Eine Woche später zeigte sich im französischen Pau das gleiche Spiel: Diesmal teilten sich Stewart und Ickx den Matra, nachdem Stewarts Auto wegen eines Problems mit der Kraftstoffversorgung gestrandet war. Ein Woche später gewann Ickx ein Tourenwagenrennen in Zolder am Steuer seines Mustangs. Am 8. Mai hatten die belgischen Fans dann erstmals die Möglichkeit, den kommenden Star in einem Monoposto zu sehen. Das aber nicht sehr lange, da Ickx nach 18 Runden des ersten von zwei Heats mit Motorschaden aufgeben musste. Am selben Tag holte er bei einem Tourenwagenrennen, welches im Beiprogramm stattfand, im Lotus Cortina den zweiten Platz.

■ *Jackie Stewart: „Ickx war sehr talentiert. 1966 war er bei Tyrrell mein Teamkollege. Da hatte ich die Chance, ihn fahren zu sehen. Ken [Tyrrell] traf eine gute Wahl, ihn zu verpflichten. Es ist verwunderlich, dass Jacky in seiner Karriere nicht mehr Formel-1-Rennen gewonnen hat. Aber es gibt keinen Zweifel, dass er im Sportwagen einer der besten war."*

Beim Formel-3-Auftritt in Monaco gelang es Ickx nicht, sich zu qualifizieren, da er durch einen Trainingsunfall keine gezeitete Runde zustande gebracht hatte. Im Ford Mustang blieb er mit einem Sieg bei den „Coupes de Spa" jedoch in der Erfolgsspur. Dann reiste er in die USA, genauer gesagt zum Trans-Am-Rennen auf der Strecke von

thus turn out to be his first of the New Year. After all the successes with Ford in 1965, Ickx was still Ford-powered as Ken Tyrrell's Matras were most of the time powered by one-litre Ford engines, the F2 car having a fully developed race engine and the F3 car a production-based unit. Jacky was scheduled to drive both and his season was due to start at Easter in Oulton Park but the meeting was cancelled thanks to a fall of snow. Thus his race debut was on April 11th at Goodwood where Ickx finished a somewhat cautious sixth at the fast circuit in southern England. During the race, he had to share his car with Jackie Stewart after a broken accelerator cable forced the Scot to retire and take over Ickx's car. A week later in France at Pau, the two drivers again shared a Matra but this time it was a fuel supply problem that forced Stewart to retire early in the race. The following week, Ickx won a touring car race at Zolder, driving his Mustang. On May 8th, Ickx's Belgian fans had their first opportunity to see him racing a Matra when he drove one at Zolder. But it was only for a very short time since Ickx had to retire with engine problems in the first of two heats after only completing eighteen laps. The same day, he came second in a Lotus Cortina in a touring car race that was supporting the main event.

■ *Jackie Stewart: "Ickx was highly talented. He was my partner at Tyrrell in 1966 where I had a chance to see him drive. Ken [Tyrrell] made a good choice when he hired him. Actually, it is quite surprising that Jacky did not win more Formula One races in his career, but there can be no doubt that he was one of the best in sportscars."*

Down in Monaco in May, Ickx was unable to qualify for the Formula Three race as he crashed in practice and was thus unable to set a time. But there was more success with his Ford Mustang at home. He won the 'Coupes de Spa' before going to America to drive in another Trans Am event, this time sharing an Alan Mann Lotus

Mid-America in Ohio. Zusammen mit Hubert Hahne wurde er im Lotus Cortina gegen starke Konkurrenz aus Amerika Dritter. Von Ohio flog Ickx direkt nach Le Mans, um erstmals an dem 24-Stunden-Klassiker teilzunehmen. Ford setzte an jenem Wochenende nicht weniger als 14 Autos ein und daher stieß die „Ford-Familie" bei der Suche nach Top-Fahrern auf den jungen Belgier. An der Sarthe teilte er sich einen Ford GT40 Mk1 mit Jochen Neerpasch. Das Monster mit 4,7-Liter-Motor lief zwar unter der Flagge der amerikanischen Firma Essex Wire – einer der großen Zulieferer der Ford Motor Company –, wurde aber vom Engländer David Yorke eingesetzt. Ickx/Neerpasch platzierten den GT40 im Training auf Platz 14 und arbeiteten sich im Rennen auf die siebte Position nach vorn, ehe sie nach 154 Runden durch Motorschaden ausfielen. Das andere Auto von Essex Wire – ein GT40 Mk2 mit 7,0-Liter-Triebwerk – brachte dem Sponsor dagegen mehr Erfolg. Die Amerikaner Ronnie Bucknum und Dick Hutcheson fuhren den Ford auf Rang drei ins Ziel.

Der Juli brachte für Ickx viel Abwechslung mit sieben Rennen in ganz unterschiedlichen Autos: Er fuhr einen Formel-2-Boliden in Reims und Rouen, ein Formel-3-Auto in Silverstone, den Alan-Mann-Cortina am Nürburgring, einen BMW in Spa und einen Gruppe-7-Sportwagen in Brands Hatch. Während er bei den F2-Rennen ausfiel, schaffte Ickx in Silverstone den Sprung aufs Treppchen. Der Matra-Pilot nahm das Rennen von ganz hinten in Angriff, kämpfte sich bei strömendem Regen durch das Feld und wurde beeindruckender Dritter. Das 6-Stunden-Rennen auf dem Nürburgring endete wiederum vorzeitig: Der Cortina von Ickx und Paul Hawkins strandete mit einem Lagerschaden. Bei den 24 Stunden von Spa startete Ickx erneut für BMW, wo sich der Belgier einen BMW 2000 TI mit Hubert Hahne teilte. Das Duo holte die Pole Position, ging sofort in Führung und fuhr überlegen zum Sieg. In 24 Stunden legten sie 4.048 Kilometer zurück, das entspricht einem Schnitt von mehr als 168 km/h!

Cortina at the Mid-America track in Ohio with Hubert Hahne. They finished third overall in a strong field of American cars and drivers. Immediately after this American race, Ickx flew to Le Mans to take part in his first 24-hour race at the famous French track. There he was to be partnered by German, Jochen Neerpasch, in a Ford GT40 Mk1 with a 4.7-litre engine entered by the American team of Essex Wire. Ickx had been asked to join the 'Ford Family' that weekend as the American company had no less than fourteen cars running in the race and were looking for top drivers to fill the seats. Although the sponsoring company was American, the Essex Wire team was actually managed by David Yorke, an Englishman. Essex Wire & Cable was a major supplier to the Ford Motor Company and had for several years been sponsoring a Ford racing team with Skip Scott as its leading driver. Starting from their qualifying position of fourteenth, Ickx and Neerpasch worked their way to seventh overall before retiring in the night after one hundred and fifty-four laps due to engine problems. The Essex Wire team were rewarded by having another GT40 – this a Mk2 with a 7.0-litre engine – come home in third place driven by the Americans, Ronnie Bucknum and Dick Hutcheson.

In the month of July, Ickx had seven starts in different cars. He drove a Formula Two at Reims and Rouen, a Formula Three at Silverstone, the Alan Mann Lotus Cortina at the Nürburgring, a BMW at Spa and a Group 7 sportscar at Brands Hatch. He did not finish the Formula Two races but he did come third at Silverstone where he started at the back of the grid and, in conditions of pouring rain, sliced through the field to come an astonishing third. A broken bearing forced Ickx – who was partnered on that occasion by Paul Hawkins – to retire at the 6-hour race at the Nürburgring, but he had more success at Spa where he was partnered by Hubert Hahne in a works BMW 2000 TI for the 24-hour race.

Grand Prix de Monaco 1966, Matra MS5

— 21 —

24 Heures du Mans 1966, Ford GT40

Grand Prix de Reims 1966, Matra MS5 - BRM n°26

24 Heures du Mans 1966, Ford GT40 n°60 (rechts / on the right)

Noch viel mehr Power bekam Ickx in Brands Hatch zu spüren. Im Rahmenprogramm des britischen F1-Grand-Prix fuhr er den McLaren Elva von Alan Brown. Obwohl es für Ickx der erste Start in dem brutalen Sportwagen mit V8-Chevrolet-Motor war, wurde der Belgier bemerkenswerter Fünfter – und das trotz eines Drehers zu Beginn. Wenige Wochen später bestritt Ickx seinen ersten richtigen Grand Prix. Am Großen Preis von Deutschland auf dem Nürburgring durften neben den Formel-1-Autos auch Formel-2-Boliden an den Start gehen. Der Veranstalter traf diese Entscheidung, damit die Tausenden Fans entlang der Nordschleife mehr Autos zu sehen bekamen. Obwohl der Matra von Ickx nur mit einem Ein-Liter-Motor bestückt war, platzierte der Belgier seinen Wagen in der fünften Startreihe. In der ersten Runde war Ickx jedoch in einen tragischen Zwischenfall verwickelt. John Taylor kollidierte mit Ickx, wobei Taylors Brabham-BRM in Flammen aufging. Der 33-jährige Engländer erlitt schwere Verbrennungen und starb einen Monat später in einem deutschen Krankenhaus.

Nach der GP-Premiere reiste Ickx erneut nach Amerika, um am Trans-Am-Rennen in Maryland teilzunehmen. Sein Partner im Lotus Cortina von Alan Mann Racing war auch diesmal Hubert Hahne. Das deutsch-belgische Duo sah bei dem 12-Stunden-Rennen nicht das Ziel, sie mussten nach 105 Runden mit Motorschaden aufgeben. In Europa waren Ickx und der Lotus Cortina dagegen erfolgreicher: Gemeinsam mit Staepelaere holte der Brüsseler beim Marathon de la Route auf dem Nürburgring den Gesamtsieg. Das Langstreckenrennen führte jetzt über volle drei Tage, sprich 84 Stunden!

Im Monoposto ging es dagegen wechselhaft weiter: In Brands Hatch landete Ickx nur auf Platz 13, in Zandvoort wurde er Zweiter hinter Chris Irwin. Nicht ganz so gut schnitt er beim Lauf zur Tourenwagen-EM ab, der am selben Wochenende ausgetragen wurde. Im belgischen Lotus Cortina wurde er im Windschatten der Alan-Mann-Ford von Frank Gardner und John Whitmore Fünfter. Ein Doppelprogramm erwartete Ickx auch am Rennwochenende im belgischen Zolder, wo er sich im Formel-3-Rennen erneut Chris Irwin geschlagen geben musste, beim Tourenwagen-Lauf aber den Sieg holte.

Die abschließenden Rennen zur Formel 2 und 3 in Frankreich und England brachten Ickx wenig Grund zur Freude. Er holte zwei vierte sowie einen siebten Platz und fiel einmal aus. Danach endete die Saison so, wie sie begonnen hatte: Im Ferrari der Ecurie Francorchamps, und mit einem Ausfall. Bei den 9 Stunden von Kyalami in Südafrika teilte sich Ickx den 250 LM erneut mit Leon Dernier und diesmal besiegelte eine defekte Zylinderkopfdichtung das vorzeitige Ende.

Für Ickx ging damit ein hektisches und ereignisreiches Jahr zu Ende. Innerhalb von elf Monaten hatte er an fast 50 Autorennen auf drei Kontinenten teilgenommen und dabei ganz unterschiedliche Fahrzeuge bewegt. Und er hatte die Weichen für die Zukunft gestellt: 1967 blieb er im Team von Ken Tyrrell, für die er jetzt nur noch in der Formel 2 starten sollte und die zur neuen Saison stark umgekrempelt wurde. Die FIA schuf eine neue Formel-2-Europameisterschaft, in der fortan seriennahe 1,6-Liter-Motoren zugelassen waren. Außerdem zeigte ein gewisser John Wyer Interesse an Ickx, er wollte den jungen Belgier für sein neues Ford-Sportwagen-Team gewinnen.

They led the race from pole position and took a convincing victory in the process of which they covered over 2,500 miles at an average speed of 105 mph.

That summer, Ickx got a taste of real power, when he drove the McLaren Elva of Alan Brown at Brands Hatch in one of the supporting races at the Formula One Grand Prix weekend. The brutish V8 Chevrolet-powered car was new to the Belgian but he finished a remarkable fifth overall even after spinning the car in the early laps. A few weeks later, Ickx made his first appearance in a Grand Prix. The organisers of the German Grand Prix at the Nürburgring had decided to allow Formula Two cars on the grid alongside the Formula One cars. They made that decision since, with a larger grid, the hundreds of thousands of eager fans round the long track would be able to see more racing. Although Ickx's Matra only had a one-litre engine, the Belgian managed a qualifying time that gave him a place on the fifth row of the grid. Unfortunately, during the course of the very first lap, his car was hit by John Taylor driving a Brabham-BRM. Both cars were forced to retire but Taylor's also caught fire and the 33-year old Englishman was badly burned in the accident. Regrettably, he died one month later in a German hospital.

Ickx went back to America to race in another Trans Am event driving an Alan Mann Lotus Cortina where his partner in this enterprise was again Hubert Hahne. The event was the 12-hour race at the Marlboro circuit in Maryland, but after just one hundred and five laps, the engine broke and they were out. However, more Lotus Cortina success awaited Ickx in Europe since, together again with Staepelaere, they emerged as the victors at the – slightly increased in length – 84-hours of the Marathon de la Route at the Nürburgring.

The single-seater programme continued with a rather disappointing thirteenth overall at Brands Hatch but things were better at Zandvoort where Ickx finished second to Chris Irwin. That same day at the Dutch track, Ickx also drove the Belgian Lotus Cortina in an ETC race in which he finished fifth, chasing home the Alan Mann Lotus Cortinas of Frank Gardner and John Whitmore. A few weeks later at Zolder in Belgium, Ickx again had a double race weekend where he was beaten by Chris Irwin in the Formula Three race, but this time won the touring car race.

The final Formula Two and Three races in France and England did not give Ickx a lot of satisfaction since the results can be summarised as a retirement, two fourth places and a seventh place. To finish the year, Ickx drove an Ecurie Francorchamps Ferrari for the second time with Leon Dernier though this time the venue was down in South Africa for the 9 Hours of Kyalami. Again the team did not finish and this time a faulty head gasket was the cause of their retirement.

For Ickx the year was over. In eleven hectic months, he had driven almost fifty motor races in all kinds of machines and on three continents. The arrangement for 1967 was that he would stay and race for Ken Tyrrell, but now only in Formula Two, a category that was to have new regulations allowing 1.6-litre production based engines and a new European Championship. In addition, as far as sportscars were concerned, John Wyer was interested in hiring the young Belgian to be part of his new Ford team.

Großer Preis von Deutschland 1966, Nürburgring, Matra MS5 - SCA

Großer Preis von Deutschland 1966, Nürburgring, Matra MS5 - SCA

Marathon de la Route 1966, Nürburgring, Ford Lotus Cortina

1967

Erfolge in der Formel 2 und im Sportwagen
Worldwide success both in Formula Two and sportscars

Als Jacky Ickx am 1. Januar 1967 seinen 22. Geburtstag feierte, stand ihm ein viel versprechendes neues Lebensjahr bevor. Ken Tyrrell hatte erneut angefragt, ob der junge Belgier für ihn im Matra in der Formel 2 starten würde, und John Wyer wollte Ickx als Verstärkung für sein Mirage-Team bei Sportwagenrennen. Darüber hinaus sollte Ickx für Ford im Tourenwagen sitzen, wann immer sich die Möglichkeit bot.

Zu Beginn der Saison 1967 stellte Ford USA sein Motorsportprogramm ein. Also gründete Rennleiter John Wyer nach drei erfolgreichen Jahren mit Ford Advance Vehicles und dem GT40 sein eigenes Sportwagenteam. Mit finanzieller Unterstützung seines Freundes John Willment übernahm Wyer die Rennsportabteilung von Ford UK und begann mit dem Einsatz eigener Sportwagen. Im Herbst 1966 war außerdem Grady Davis an Wyer herangetreten. Der Vizepräsident von Gulf Oil, selbst Besitzer eines GT40, suchte eine Plattform, um seine Firma weltweit zu vermarkten.

On January 1st, 1967 Jacky Ickx celebrated his twenty-second birthday. He had a bright season in prospect since Ken Tyrrell had once again asked the young Belgian to drive his Matra Formula Two cars while the young star had also been approached by John Wyer to join his Mirage sportscar team in endurance racing. In addition, Ickx would continue to drive Ford touring cars whenever an opportunity presented itself.

After three years of successful working with Ford Advanced Vehicles and the GT40 programme, Ford USA stopped racing and their team manager, John Wyer, started up his own sportscar team. With financial help from his friend John Willment, Wyer took over the British racing division of Ford and started racing their own-design sportscars. At the same time, late 1966, Grady Davis, a vice president of Gulf Oil, approached Wyer. The American had a GT40 himself and was looking for worldwide promotion for Gulf Oil and associated products.

24 Hours of Daytona 1967, Daytona Beach, Ford GT40 n°11

Copyright: From the collections of The Henry Ford.

Dem Vorstand von Gulf gefielen Sportwagenrennen besser als die Formel 1 und sie sahen in Wyer und seinem Team geeignete Partner.

John Wyer behielt die meisten Angestellten bei, die schon während seiner Zeit bei Ford USA für ihn gearbeitet hatten, und verpflichtete zwei neue Führungskräfte: John Horsman als Technischer Direktor und David Yorke als Teamchef. Wyer setzte zwei Autos in der Internationalen Markenmeisterschaft ein. Dabei handelte es sich um modifizierte Ford GT40, bei denen die Karosserie dank des neuen Reglements leicht verändert wurde. Len Bailey war für das „Facelift" des drei Jahre alten Wagens verantwortlich. Zudem gab es bei Chassis und Motor – jetzt mit fünf Liter Hubraum – ein Update. Ford wollte nicht, dass der neue Wagen die Bezeichnung Ford trägt, also musste sich Wyer einen Namen ausdenken. Zusammen mit Gulf Oil entschieden sie sich für „Mirage". Die erste Ausfahrt des orangeblauen Prototypen namens „M1" fand am 21. März 1967 in Snetterton statt, wo Formel-2-Pilot Alan Rees den Mirage bewegte. Der Brite war der erste Fahrer, den Wyer unter Vertrag genommen hatte.

Bevor er den Mirage in Europa einsetzte, wollte er das Team aber noch einem letzten Test unterziehen. Dafür wählte er die 24 Stunden von Daytona – eine Veranstaltung, die er sehr gut kannte. In Florida setzte das neue Team „John Willment Automotive", kurz JWA, den privaten GT40 von Grady Davis ein. Dr. Dick Thompson und Jacky Ickx fungierten als Fahrer. Thompson war hauptberuflich Zahnarzt, aber auch ein versierter Rennfahrer, der viele Jahre auf Shelby Cobra unterwegs gewesen und auch den GT40 von Davis schon bei zahlreichen SCCA-Läufen in den USA gefahren war. Er war also eine offensichtliche Wahl.

▪ *John Horsman: „Als wir Grady Davis sagten, dass Jacky Ickx unser Fahrer ist, fragte er: ‚Wer ist dieser Mister X?'"*

Wyer versicherte Grady, dass der junge Belgier genau der richtige Mann für den Job war. Ickx sollte das JWA-Team aber nicht nur in Daytona verstärken, sondern auch für den Rest der Saison. Ickx hatte 1966 mit guten Leistungen bei Formel-2-Rennen in Europa auf sich aufmerksam gemacht und war in Le Mans einen Ford GT40 gefahren. Bei Ickx' Premiere an der Sarthe war der Sportwagen von Essex Wire unter der Leitung von David Yorke eingesetzt worden. Der Teamchef kannte Jackys Fähigkeiten also genau. Eine Rolle spielte auch, dass Ickx 1966 einen Ferrari 250 LM beim 24-Stunden-Rennen in Daytona bewegt hatte und die Strecke kannte. Man darf aber auch nicht von der Hand weisen, dass Ickx einen so guten Draht zu Ford Belgien hatte, dass der Importeur ebenfalls einen Beitrag zur Verpflichtung von Ickx leistete.

Für JWA diente das Rennen in Daytona vor allem als Generalprobe, die junge Mannschaft war auf dem Speedway in Florida nicht unbedingt auf Erfolge aus. Thompson und Ickx spulten das Training ohne Probleme ab und platzierten den GT40 mit einer Rundenzeit von 2.01 Minuten auf der 13. Position – hinter den leistungsstärkeren Prototypen von Ferrari und Chaparral sowie den Ford MkII mit Sieben-Liter-Motoren! Der Gulf-Ford hielt sich einen Großteil des Rennens in den Top Ten und wurde nur durch ein Elektrikproblem und einen überhitzenden Motor eingebremst. Nach 24 Stunden kam das Team auf einer respektablen sechsten Position ins Ziel – hinter drei Ferrari und zwei Porsche, aber vor den mächtigen Ford MkII. Zudem gewannen Ickx/Thompson die Sportwagenklasse. Zwei Monate später wurde das Auto auch bei den 12 Stunden von Sebring eingesetzt. Hier teilte sich Thompson das Cockpit mit Ed Lowther, schied aber zur Halbzeit durch Motorschaden aus.

Their board of directors preferred sportscar racing to Formula One and thought that by joining Wyer and his team, both organisations would benefit from the association. John Wyer kept most of his employees from his Ford USA years and added John Horsman as technical director and David Yorke as his team manager. The plan was to run two slightly updated Ford GT40s in the endurance championship. The new cars would be based on the existing GT40s but, with the new regulations, the car could be reshaped. The original GT40 was now three years old and Len Bailey designed a new 'greenhouse' for the car. Also the engine would be upgraded – up to five litres – and several chassis adjustments would be implemented. Ford did not want their name on the new cars, so Gulf Oil asked Wyer to come up with a name. Together they came up with Mirage. The car would be painted in the blue and orange colours of Gulf Oil. The first car was ready to run on March 21st, 1967 when Alan Rees drove it at Snetterton. Rees, a British Formula Two regular, was the first driver to have been signed by the new team.

However, prior to racing with the Mirage in Europe, Wyer wanted to have a dry run with his team. He chose to go to the Daytona 24-hour sportscar race, an event that he personally knew well. Run by the new team – John Willment Automotive or JWA for short – Grady Davis's own GT40 was entered with Dr. Dick Thompson and Jacky Ickx nominated as the drivers. Thompson was by profession a dentist and an accomplished club driver who, after years driving Shelby Cobras, had also driven Davis's GT40 at several SCCA events in the United States and was thus an obvious choice.

▪ *John Horsman: "When we told Grady Davis that Jacky Ickx was our driver, he said 'Who is this Mister X'."*

Wyer convinced Grady that the young Belgian was a perfect choice and reassured him that Ickx was the man for the job. Indeed Ickx had been asked to join Wyer not just for this race but also for the remainder of the season. Ickx had made a good impression by scoring good points in Formula Two races in Europe and had also driven a GT40 at Le Mans on which occasion his car had been entered by the Essex Wire Company and had had David Yorke as its team manager, who was thus fully aware of Ickx's abilities. Also in the equation was the fact that Jacky Ickx had been to Daytona before when he drove the Belgian Ferrari 250 LM in the 1966 24-hour race. Of course, it also helped things along that Ford Belgium and Ickx had such a good relationship and that they were able to make a contribution to the contract.

The Daytona race was a final test for the operation of the new organisation and thus the team was not out to set any records at the famous speedway. Neither Thompson nor Ickx encountered any difficulties in practice and with a qualifying time of 2m 01s started from the thirteenth position, behind the more powerful Ferrari and Chaparral prototypes and the big seven-litre Ford Mk IIs. The blue and orange car ran in the top ten for most of the race and was only delayed by an electrical problem and – later in the race – some overheating. After twenty-four hours, the car finished a respectable sixth overall, behind the winning Ferraris and two Porsches but, notably, ahead of the big Ford Mk IIs. It also won the sportscar class and would run again two months later at Sebring for the annual 12-hour race where Thompson shared it with Ed Lowther but they retired with engine failure after half distance.

Für Ickx begann die Europa-Saison Mitte März im englischen Brands Hatch, wo er einen Matra beim „Race of Champions" steuerte. Bei den Läufen im Südosten Englands waren Formel-1- und Formel-2-Autos zugelassen, insgesamt kamen 18 Wagen zusammen. Im Qualifying sicherte sich Dan Gurney in seinem neuen Eagle-Westlake die Bestzeit. Der Amerikaner gewann auch den ersten Heat über zehn Runden, wo Ickx Zwölfter wurde, was gleichzeitig seine Startposition für den zweiten Heat war. Während Gurney erneut siegte, wurde Ickx diesmal Zehnter. Der Eagle-Pilot triumphierte auch beim Finale über 40 Runden, welches für Ickx wegen einer defekten Benzinpumpe vorzeitig endete. Nach dem Rennen blieb Ickx in England, denn an Ostern standen gleich zwei Formel-2-Rennen auf dem Programm. Bei den Guards 100 in Snetterton fiel Ickx durch Zündungsprobleme aus. Er absolvierte nur zwei Runden im ersten Heat und konnte weder im zweiten Heat noch im Finale wieder eingreifen. Die Rennen bildeten den Auftakt zur Formel-2-Europameisterschaft, es war also ein denkbar schlechter Start für Ickx. In Silverstone lief es dagegen etwas besser. Ickx beendete beide Heats über 20 Runden auf der achten Position und wurde insgesamt als Siebter gewertet. Da Formel-1-Piloten nicht punktberechtigt waren, rückte Ickx im Klassement auf und fuhr dadurch seine ersten EM-Punkte ein. In beiden Rennen holte Alan Rees – Ickx' Teamkollege bei Mirage – die meisten Zahler.

Ein Wochenende später nahm Ickx sein drittes Formel-2-Rennen in Angriff. Diesmal ging es auf dem Straßenkurs von Pau zur Sache. Im Training war Ickx nicht glücklich, er drehte sich zweimal und beschädigte dabei seinen Matra. Am Ende der Trainings- und Qualifyingsessions stand für den Belgier die vierte Reihe zu Buche. Im Rennen hatte der Matra MS5 den schnellen Brabham BT23 von Winkelmann Racing erneut nichts entgegenzusetzen, und Jochen Rindt erwies sich wieder als unschlagbar. Ickx beendete das Rennen mit vier Runden Rückstand auf Rang fünf. Die Formel-2-Saison ging nur eine Woche später in Barcelona weiter. Auch im Montjuïc Park hatte Ickx kein Glück: Nach 21 von 60 Runden streikte der Ford-FVA-Motor: Das Aus für Jacky. Am selben Wochenende fanden auch die Vortests in Le Mans statt. Da Ickx und Rees beide in Spanien waren, verhalfen Richard Attwood und David Piper dem neuen Mirage zu seinen ersten Runden an der Sarthe. Für Ickx stand derweil zwei Wochen später das nächste Formel-2-Rennen auf der Agenda. Das „Eifelrennen" auf der Südschleife des Nürburgrings fand im Schneetreiben statt und hier holte Ickx sein bisher bestes Saisonergebnis: Er wurde Dritter hinter Rindt und John Surtees.

Das „Rennwochenende" war für Ickx damit aber noch nicht vorbei. Am Montag nahm er am 1000-Kilometer-Rennen von Monza teil, das damals immer am 25. April ausgetragen wurde, dem „Tag der Befreiung Italiens".

Beim Europa-Auftakt der Int. Markenmeisterschaft nahmen nicht weniger als 54 Autos das Training auf. Neben Ferrari und Porsche war auch der texanische Sportwagenbauer Chaparral vor Ort, Ford hingegen verzichtete auf einen Einsatz des MkII. Die Marke mit dem blauen Oval war nur durch einige private GT40 vertreten. Darüber hinaus stand die Rennpremiere von Mirage bevor. Die beiden Gulf-Autos wurden von Thompson/Piper (Chassis 1002) sowie Ickx/Rees (Chassis 1001) pilotiert. Beide Mirage waren mit V8-Motoren bestückt, deren Hubraum auf fünf Liter vergrößert worden war. Das Rennen fand auf der kombinierten Strecke des Autodromo di Monza statt, beinhaltete also den Highspeed-Abschnitt mit der berühmtberüchtigten Steilkurve. In der Qualifikation stellten Mike Spence und Phil Hill ihren Chaparral auf Pole, gefolgt von drei Ferrari. Ickx war der schnellste der Mirage-Fahrer, er reihte sich auf Platz fünf ein.

The European season for Ickx started in mid-March at Brands Hatch in England where he drove the Matra at the 'Race of Champions'. This race was open to Formula One and Formula Two cars and a total of eighteen cars participated in the heats at this circuit in the south-east of England. The fastest man in qualifying was the American Dan Gurney in his new Eagle-Westlake. In the first heat of ten laps that was won by Gurney, Ickx finished twelfth which would thus be his starting position for the second heat. Again the heat was won by Gurney with Ickx finishing tenth. The American was also victorious in the forty-lap final but Ickx did not finish thanks to a faulty fuel pump. Ickx stayed in Great Britain, since over the Easter weekend there were Formula Two races at both Snetterton and Silverstone. At the Guards 100 at Snetterton, Ickx did not finish because of ignition problems. In fact, he only completed two laps in his first heat and did not start in either the second heat or in the final. This race was the first event counting for the European Championship, so it was a poor start with no points for Ickx. The race at Silverstone was, however, slightly better. Ickx finished seventh on aggregate after finishing eighth in both the twenty-lap heats and this meant that, as a non-graded driver, he would earn points for the championship since regular Formula One drivers, the graded drivers, could not score points. In both these races, it was Alan Rees – Ickx's team-mate at Mirage – who collected the most points.

The weekend after that, Ickx started in the third Formula Two race of the season, this time on the street circuit of Pau in the south of France. He was not happy in practice since he spun twice and damaged his Matra. At the end of practice and qualifying, he managed to make it to the fourth row of the grid. In the race, his Matra MS5 was once again no match for the fast Brabham BT23s of Winkelmann Racing. And again it was Jochen Rindt who was unbeatable. Ickx did finish the race, but four laps down on the Austrian in fifth place overall. The busy Formula Two schedule next took the drivers to Barcelona for a race in the historic Montjuïc Park. And again Ickx was out of luck for, after just twenty-one of the sixty laps, his Ford FVA engine broke and he retired. That same weekend the annual tests at Le Mans were being held. With both Rees and Ickx competing in Spain, Richard Attwood drove the new Mirage together with David Piper. The next Formula Two race on the calendar was to be at the Nürburgring, two weeks later. In snowy conditions, the annual 'Eifelrennen' were held on the Südschleife of this famous track and Ickx scored his best finish so far of the year with third overall behind Rindt and John Surtees.

All things being considered, it was a good start to the weekend, since on the Monday immediately afterwards, the Monza 1,000-kilometre race would be run as this Italian event is always held on the Italian National Holiday of April 25th.

No less than fifty-four cars arrived for this first European endurance race of 1967. Of course, Ferrari was there with several prototypes as was Porsche. The American Chaparral also came to Monza but Ford did not send any of their Mk IIs though a number of customer GT40s did attend. It would be the first time that Mirage would race and the two Gulf cars were to driven by Thompson and Piper in car 1002 and Ickx with Rees in car number 1001. Both cars now had the enlarged five-litre V8 engine and were well-prepared by the JWA team. The race would be run on the combined layout of the Autodromo di Monza, which thus included the high-speed part of the track with its formidable banking. At the end of qualifying, Mike Spence and Phil Hill had their Chaparral on pole ahead of three Ferraris.

Guards "100" 1967, Snetterton, Matra MS5 - FVA

Eifelrennen 1967, Nürburgring, Matra MS5 - FVA

1000 km de Spa-Francorchamps 1967, Mirage M1 - Ford

Seine Teamkollegen folgten mit einer Sekunde Rückstand auf Rang sechs, damit standen beide M1 in Startreihe drei. Für Ickx dauerte das Rennen nur 13 Runden, dann brannte der Zündverstärker durch. Der andere Mirage wurde nach kleineren Problemen abgeschlagen Neunter, mit acht Runden Rückstand auf den siegreichen Ferrari.

Wenige Tage später waren dieselben Autos wieder im Einsatz, und zwar bei den 1000 Kilometer von Spa. Für den Klassiker in den Ardennen bekam Wyer einen neuen 5,7-Liter-V8-Ford-Motor aus Amerika. Das berühmte Ford-Stockcar-Team Holman & Moody aus Charlotte hatte das Triebwerk speziell für ihn gebaut. Einer dieser Motoren wurde direkt in einen neuen Mirage, Chassis 1003, verbaut. Ickx war in dem neuen Wagen während des Trainings und Qualifyings extrem schnell und stellte Chassis 1003 auf den zweiten Startplatz, zwischen dem Chaparral und einem Ferrari 330 P4. Bis zu diesem Rennen hatte Alan Rees den Eindruck, er wäre die Nummer eins im Team. Entsprechend unzufrieden war er, dass Ickx in Spa den Start fahren sollte und dass er sich als Lieblingsfahrer von David Yorke herauskristallisierte. Rees war so sauer, dass er die Strecke noch vor dem Rennen verließ. Also blieben nur noch drei Fahrer für die beiden Mirage-Cockpits übrig.

Das 71-Runden-Rennen begann bei typischem Spa-Wetter: Es schüttete wie aus Eimern. Ickx erwischte einen guten Start und ging als Erster durch die Eau Rouge. Der andere Mirage war dagegen schon früh weg vom Fenster. Wegen eines defekten Stoßdämpfers hatte David Piper einen heftigen Unfall, den er zum Glück unverletzt überstand. Dick Thompson stand also plötzlich ohne Auto da und konnte sich daher das Cockpit des 5,7-Liter-Mirage mit Ickx teilen. Nach dem Piper-Unfall hatte Thompson kurz die Strecke verlassen und so ging das Team auf hektische Suche nach ihm. Der Amerikaner schaffte es zurück an die Box, doch bis dahin hatte Ickx die maximal erlaubte Fahrzeit von drei Stunden schon überschritten. Das hätte eine Strafe zur Folge haben sollen. Wyer und Yorke rannten zu den Rennkommissaren, die den Regelverstoß aber einfach ignorierten. Thompson hatte in der Zwischenzeit das Auto von Ickx übernommen und versuchte, die Führung zu verteidigen, was bei diesen Bedingungen nicht leicht war. Der Zahnarzt war pro Runde zwar 30 Sekunden langsamer als Ickx, machte aber keine Fehler und behauptete die Spitze. Nach einer Stunde übergab er das Steuer wieder an Ickx, der die letzten 13 Runden abspulte und mit einem Umlauf Vorsprung auf den Porsche von Hans Herrmann/Jo Siffert siegte. Für Jacky war es ein fantastischer Triumph bei seinem zweiten Einsatz im Mirage. Gulf-Vizepräsident Grady Davis war in Spa live dabei und von diesem Resultat natürlich begeistert. Nach dem Rennen versuchte Ford, die Punkte für den Sieg in der Internationalen Markenmeisterschaft anerkannt zu bekommen, doch die FIA lehnte ab. Die Begründung: In der Bezeichnung des Autos auf dem Nennformular stand nichts von „Ford", sondern nur „Gulf Mirage".

Zwei Wochen nach Spa saß Ickx wieder in seinem Formel-2-Matra. Bei der Guards Trophy im Mallory Park in Zentralengland gewann Ickx seinen Heat und wurde beim Finale über 75 Runden Vierter. Während des Rennens hatte Ickx vier Dreher (!) und im Ziel vier Runden Rückstand auf den Sieger John Surtees. Eine Woche später stand Ickx' nächstes Heimrennen an: der „Grote Prijs van Limburg" in Zolder. Auf der Strecke im Norden Belgiens war für Ickx in der Formel 2 früh Feierabend. Im ersten Heat zerstörte sich der Motor nach fünf Runden von selbst, während der Lotus 48 von Jim Clark im Feld von nur 17 Autos zum Sieg fuhr. Am selben Wochenende nahm Ickx auch an einem Tourenwagenrennen teil, und hier war er erfolgreicher. Im Lotus Cortina wurde er Vierter in seiner Division hinter den stärkeren Alfa Romeo GTA.

Jacky Ickx was the best Mirage driver and recorded the fifth fastest time. The other Mirage was about a second slower and would start sixth with both cars on the third row of the grid. However, once the race got under way, Ickx could only manage thirteen laps before the ignition amplifier on his car burned out. The other Mirage, after some lesser problems, finished a distant ninth, eight laps behind the winning Ferrari.

Only a few days later, the same cars would go to Spa for its 1,000-kilometre sportscar classic and for this race, Wyer had obtained new 5.7-litre Ford V8 engines from America. Holman & Moody, the famous Ford stock car team from Charlotte, North Carolina, had built these especially for him. One of these engines was immediately fitted into a new Mirage, chassis 1003. In practice and qualifying, Ickx was very fast on his home circuit and eventually he put the brand new car in the middle of the front row, between the Chaparral and the works Ferrari prototype. Until this race, Alan Rees had been under the impression that he was the number one driver in the team. The English driver was far from happy about Ickx being chosen to start the race plus the fact that he was emerging as the favourite driver of David Yorke. Rees got very annoyed and left the track just before the race. This left only three drivers who had qualified in the Mirages to drive the two cars. The seventy-one lap race started in typical Spa-Francorchamps weather with rain falling in profusion. Ickx made a good start and was away first up the hill from Eau Rouge. In the bad weather, David Piper crashed his Mirage after breaking a shock absorber and badly damaged the car but without Piper being hurt. The upshot was that Dick Thompson was available to share the driving with Ickx in the 5.7-litre car. However, after the Piper accident, Thompson had temporarily left the circuit and the team frantically went looking for him. The American driver made it to the pits ready to drive, but by then Ickx had already exceeded the maximum three-hour driving stint and the car should have been penalised. Wyer and Yorke rushed up to see the race officials and got this rule infraction ignored. Meanwhile Thompson had taken over the leading car from Ickx and tried to keep it in the lead, which was not easy in such conditions. However Thompson, circulating some thirty seconds a lap slower than Ickx, made no mistakes, retained the lead and, after his obligatory one-hour driving stint was finished, he handed the car back to Ickx. The Belgian did the final thirteen laps and finished with a one-lap advantage over the Porsche of Hans Herrmann and Jo Siffert. This was simply a wonderful win in only its second race for the Mirage. Grady Davis, the Vice-President of Gulf Oil had been with the team for the race and was of course delighted with the result. After the race, Ford tried to claim the points for winning, but the FIA refused since there was no 'Ford' mentioned on the entry form in the description of the car, merely 'Gulf Mirage'.

Two weeks after the Spa race, Ickx was back behind the wheel of his Matra Formula Two car for the Guards Trophy at Mallory Park in central England. After winning his heat, Ickx finished fourth in the seventy-five lap final. He had had no fewer than four spins on this small circuit and, in the end, finished four laps behind the eventual winner, John Surtees. The following weekend it was back to Belgium for the 'Grote Prijs van Limburg', the Grand Prix of Limburg, held at the Zolder track. Only seventeen cars ran in the first heat, which was won by Jim Clark in his new Lotus 48. Ickx managed only five laps before his engine self-destructed and his day was over as far as Formula Two was concerned. However, he did drive in the touring car race with a Lotus Cortina where he finished fourth in his division behind the powerful Alfa Romeo GTAs.

Beim 1000-Kilometer-Rennen auf dem Nürburgring setzte Mirage Chassis 1001 und 1003 ein, die jetzt beide mit den 5,7-Liter-Motor von Holman & Moody ausgerüstet waren. Nach dem Abgang von Alan Rees verpflichtete JWA Richard Attwood als neuen Partner von Jacky Ickx. Im anderen Auto saßen Piper und Thompson. Letzterer legte seinen Mirage im Training aufs Dach, nachdem der Wagen auf einer der vielen Kuppen abgehoben war. Der Schaden an dem Mirage war so groß, dass JWA das Auto nicht mehr rechtzeitig zum Rennen reparieren konnte. Ickx erzielte in der „Grünen Hölle" die neuntbeste Zeit hinter dem neuen Lola T70 Mk3, dem Chaparral und zahlreichen Porsche. Im Rennen lieferte der Belgier anfangs eine Meisterleistung ab: Als er das Steuer an Attwood übergab, lag der Mirage auf Platz zwei. Als Ickx in der 30. Runde an der Box bereit stand, um das Auto von Attwood zu übernehmen, tauchte der Mirage aber plötzlich nicht mehr auf. Attwood war über einige Trümmerteile gefahren und hatte sich dabei die Reifen an der Vorder- und Hinterachse aufgeschlitzt – und das an einer Stelle, die so weit von der Box weg war wie irgend möglich. Attwood hatte zwar ein Ersatzrad dabei, aber das reichte nicht, um mit dem Auto über die Strecke zu humpeln, ohne schwerwiegende Schäden zu verursachen. Damit war das Rennen vorbei.

Von Deutschland flog Ickx direkt nach London, wo einen Tag später die Formel 2 in Crystal Palace gastierte. Da viele Top-Fahrer wegen der Indianapolis 500 noch in Amerika verweilten, waren die Läufe sehr offen. Surtees und Bruce McLaren galten als Favoriten, doch die Matra-Piloten stahlen ihnen die Show. Jean-Pierre Beltoise gewann den ersten Heat, im zweiten Lauf landeten die Tyrrell-Matra von Jean-Pierre Jaussaud und Ickx auf den Plätzen zwei und vier. Im Finale zeigte Ickx einige großartige Überholmanöver, ging an McLaren, Surtees und Beltoise vorbei und gewann zum ersten Mal in seiner Karriere ein Formel-2-Rennen.

Nach einigen Monaten voller Rennen hatte Ickx jetzt ein Wochenende frei, ehe es nach Le Mans ging. 1967 sollte das letzte Rennen in der Geschichte des 24-Stunden-Klassikers sein, bei dem es keine Hubraumgrenze gab. Es sah nach einem Jahrhundertrennen aus, bei dem so viele starke Werksteams an den Start gingen wie noch nie zuvor. Ford, Ferrari, Chaparral, Lola, Mirage und Porsche kämpften alle um den Sieg. Ickx bestritt das Rennen mit dem australischen Tourenwagenspezialisten Brian Muir, da Richard Attwood – Ickx' neuer Partner bei Mirage – schon Maranello Concessionaires zugesagt hatte, einen ihrer Ferrari zu fahren. Mirage reiste voller Hoffnung auf ein gutes Ergebnis an die Sarthe. Der neue 5,7-Liter-Motor hatte sich bei den zurückliegenden Rennen als konkurrenzfähig erwiesen, außerdem hatten die Mirage-Fahrer in Le Mans schon gute Leistungen gezeigt. John Wyer hatte den Klassiker sogar schon gewonnen, 1959 mit Aston Martin. Die 1967er-Ausgabe sollte für JWA aber nicht erfolgreich enden. Im Training hatte eines der neuen Triebwerke einen Kolbenschaden, woraufhin Wyer vorsichtshalber die alten Fünfliter-Motoren einbauen ließ. Durch den Leistungsverlust schafften es die Mirage in der Qualifikation nur auf die Plätze 15 und 16, beide waren mehr als zwölf Sekunden langsamer als die Siebenliter-Ford. Das erwies sich als schlechtes Omen für das Rennen. Ickx schied nach 29 Runden mit defekter Zylinderkopfdichtung aus, Piper rollte nach 59 Runden mit gebrochenem Einlassventil aus. Alles in allem ein sehr enttäuschendes Ergebnis für JWA, Mirage und Gulf Oil.

In den folgenden Wochen nahm Ickx an drei weiteren Formel-2-Rennen teil, dort konnte der Belgier aber nicht mehr den süßen Duft des Sieges genießen. In Reims wurde er Sechster, während Rindt erneut gewann.

For the Nürburgring 1,000-kilometre race, Mirage entered cars 1001 and 1003, but now both equipped with the more powerful 5.7-litre Holman & Moody engines. With Alan Rees having left the team, Richard Attwood was asked to partner Jacky Ickx while the other car had its regular team of Piper and Thompson. The latter however crashed his car in practice after getting airborne on one of the many humps. Sadly, the Mirage landed on its roof and the damage was such that the car could not be repaired in time for the race. On this twisty and demanding track, Ickx set the ninth best time in qualifying behind the new Lola, the Chaparral and several Porsches. He drove a magnificent first part of the race and, when he handed over to Attwood, the Mirage was in second position. However, when Ickx was waiting to take over from Attwood on lap thirty, the Mirage did not return to the pits. Attwood had driven over some debris and had punctures on both front and rear tyres at a location that was the furthest possible from the pits on what was a long track. Although one wheel could be replaced by the spare carried in the car, it was simply impossible to return all the way to the pits without seriously damaging the car and they were out.

The next day after the Nürburgring race was a Bank Holiday in Great Britain and Jacky Ickx flew to London to race at the Crystal Palace circuit in South London. With many of the top racing drivers still in America to drive in the Indianapolis 500, it was a very open race with Surtees and Bruce McLaren starting as favourites. However the Matras had a great day with Jean-Pierre Beltoise winning the first heat and Jean-Pierre Jaussaud finishing second in the second heat with Ickx fourth. In the final, Ickx made some great moves to pass McLaren, Surtees and Beltoise and thus won the first Formula Two race of his career.

After a couple of months full of racing, Ickx got a weekend off before going to Le Mans. The 1967 edition of Le Mans was the last race where cars could run with unlimited engine capacity and thus seemed destined to be the race of the century. It would have the strongest and most powerful entry in its forty year history with works teams from Ford, Ferrari, Chaparral, Lola, Mirage and Porsche all going flat out for the win. Jacky Ickx was partnered by the Australian touring car specialist, Brian Muir. The reason for this was that his new companion at Mirage, Richard Attwood, had already promised Colonel Hoare of Maranello Concessionaires to drive their Ferrari at Le Mans. Mirage had high hopes for a good result since the new 5.7-litre engines had showed themselves to be competitive in their last races and the Mirage drivers all had a good record at the French event. And of course, John Wyer had been the winning team manager in 1959 with Aston Martin. But it turned out to be less successful than anticipated for the JWA team. In practice, one of the new engines developed a holed piston so, as a precaution, both cars were fitted with their older and less powerful five-litre motors. Down on power, the cars ended up fifteenth and sixteenth on the starting grid with both of them more than twelve seconds a lap slower than the mighty seven-litre Fords. The bad omens turned out to foreshadow reality since Ickx retired after only twenty-nine laps with a blown head gasket while Piper could only manage fifty-nine laps before an inlet valve broke. In all, this was a very disappointing result for JWA, the Mirage and Gulf Oil.

In the weeks that followed, Ickx drove another three Formula Two races but, after the sweet taste of victory at Crystal Palace, they provided less than satisfying results. In Reims, he finished sixth in a race that was won yet again by Rindt. At the Hockenheimring, Ickx retired in the first heat with a broken clutch but then won the second race thus finishing tenth on aggregate.

ADAC-1000-km-Rennen 1967, Nürburgring, Mirage M1 - Ford

— 35 —

ADAC-1000-km-Rennen 1967, Nürburgring, Mirage M1 - Ford

24 Heures du Mans 1967, Mirage M1 - Ford n°15

Am Hockenheimring schied Ickx im ersten Heat mit Kupplungsschaden aus, dafür gewann er den zweiten Lauf, was ihm Gesamtrang zehn einbrachte. Als nächstes folgte das Flugplatzrennen in Tulln-Langenlebarn, wo Ickx den neuen Matra MS7 pilotierte und nach einer problemlosen und konstanten Fahrt Fünfter wurde.

Nach ihrem Sieg bei den 24 Stunden von Spa-Francorchamps 1966 traten Jacky Ickx und sein deutscher Freund Hubert Hahne auch dieses Jahr wieder zusammen an. Diesmal steuerten sie aber einen Ford Mustang von Alan Mann Racing. Im Training fuhr das Muscle-Car dem restlichen Feld auf und davon. Ickx/Hahne waren acht Sekunden schneller als ihre ersten Verfolger Chris Tuerlinx/Pat Gautot in einem weiteren Mustang, dem ehemaligen Ickx-Auto. Die wiederum hatten ein Polster von sechs Sekunden auf den drittplatzierten Mustang aus Frankreich. Der Leistungsunterschied zwischen den schnellsten und langsamsten Tourenwagen auf dem Highspeed-Kurs war gigantisch: Der Mini Cooper der Niederländer Frans Lubin und Han Akersloot brauchte für die 14 Kilometer rund sechseinhalb Minuten, also über zwei Minuten länger als Ickx. Der Start des 24-Stunden-Rennens fand bei dem Wetter statt, wofür die Ardennen-Achterbahn berüchtigt ist: Regen! Die Vorjahressieger führten das Rennen in den ersten Stunden an. Der Vorsprung von Ickx und Hahne war zwar nicht beträchtlich, aber komfortabel – und wenn alles glatt gegangen wäre, hätte das deutsch-belgische Duo sicher wieder gewonnen. Als die Nacht einsetzte, machte das Getriebe des Mustang jedoch Probleme und das Team verlor durch die Reparatur 16 Minuten. Drei Runden später schleppte Ickx den Ford mit Differenzialschaden an die Box zurück. Nach 56 Runden war das Rennen für Ickx und Hahne gelaufen.

Beim Formel-2-Rennen in Zandvoort eine Woche später war Ickx dafür erfolgreicher. Im altbewährten Matra MS5 gewann er den Vorlauf über 15 Runden sowie das mit 30 Umläufen doppelt so lange Finale, zudem erzielte er mit einer Zeit von 1:27.9 Minuten die schnellste Rennrunde. Besonders bemerkenswert an dieser Leistung war, dass Ickx eine schnellere Rundenzeit in den Asphalt brannte als Jim Clark einen Monat vorher beim Großen Preis der Niederlande – und das im deutlich stärkeren Dreiliter-Lotus! Nach sieben von elf Läufen führte Jacky Ickx die Formel-2-Europameisterschaft erstmals an. Er hatte 26 Zähler auf dem Konto, Frank Gardner einen weniger.

Die Nürburgring-Nordschleife ist mit 22 Kilometern eine der längsten Rennstrecken der Welt, eine Runde dauerte selbst mit einem Rennwagen bis zu acht Minuten. Um den Zuschauern in der Eifel mehr Action zu bieten, ließ der Veranstalter beim Großen Preis von Deutschland neben der Formel 1 auch wieder Formel-2-Autos starten. Diese mussten sich in der Startaufstellung für das 15-Runden-Rennen aber hinter den F1-Boliden einreihen. Im Qualifying erzielte Jim Clark mit einer Zeit von 8:04.1 Minuten die Pole Position vor Denny Hulme (8:13.5 Minuten), Jackie Stewart (8:15.2 Minuten) und Dan Gurney (8:19.9 Minuten). Gleichzeitig sorgte Formel-2-Fahrer Jacky Ickx für eine gewaltige Überraschung. Der Belgier umrundete die Nordschleife in 8:14.0 Minuten – das war die drittbeste Gesamtzeit und damit war er 20 Sekunden schneller als der zweitbeste Formel-2-Pilot Jackie Oliver. Jo Bonnier, damals Vorsitzender der Grand Prix Drivers Association (GPDA), wollte nicht, dass Ickx mit seinem Formel-2-Matra zwischen den ganzen Formel-1-Autos startet, da er es für zu gefährlich hielt. Also startete Jacky hinter der kompletten F1-Armada an der Spitze des Formel-2-Feldes. Dort erwischte er einen guten Start und zog schon in der ersten Kurve an Bonnier (!) vorbei. Nach sechs Runden lag der Belgier schon auf dem vierten Gesamtrang!

The third race, the Flugplatzrennen at Tulln-Langenlebarn outside Vienna, was where Ickx drove the new Matra MS7 for the very first time. He finished the race without problems and claimed a steady fifth overall.

After winning the 1966 edition of the Spa-Francorchamps 24-hour race, Ickx was back with his German friend Hubert Hahne. This time however they were to drive a Ford Mustang entered by Alan Mann Racing. In practice, this powerful and well-prepared car was much quicker than its competitors and this was borne out in qualifying where Ickx was no less than eight seconds faster than his nearest rival, another Mustang – the older Jacky Ickx/Alan Mann car – driven by Chris Tuerlinx and Pat Gautot. In their turn, they had a slightly lesser gap of six seconds over the third fastest car, a French-entered Ford Mustang. To emphasise the large speed difference between the fastest and the slowest cars at the ultra-fast Belgian track, a Mini Cooper driven by Dutchmen Frans Lubin and Han Akersloot needed six and a half minutes to cover the fourteen-kilometre lap and this was two minutes slower than Ickx's Mustang. In the race, after a solid start, Ickx led for the first four hours of a race that was being held in typical conditions for that part of the Ardennes – rain! His lead was not considerable, but sufficient, if accompanied by well executed pit stops throughout the night to have ensured success. However at the beginning of the night, the Mustang's gearbox gave problems and the team lost over sixteen minutes to fix the problem. But it was only three laps later that Ickx limped back to the pits with a broken differential so that, after fifty-six laps, the race was over for Ickx and Hahne.

Happily, there was more success the weekend after when Ickx won the Formula Two race at Zandvoort. He drove his trusted Matra MS5 again and won the fifteen-lap 'qualifying' heat as well as the thirty-lap final during which he posted the fastest lap of the race in 1m 27.9s. What was particularly satisfying was that this meant that he was even quicker round the Zandvoort track than Jim Clark had been in the three-litre Lotus a month earlier at the Dutch Grand Prix! After seven races and with four to go, the European Formula Two Challenge now showed that Jacky Ickx was leading with twenty-six points, one point ahead of Frank Gardner.

With its twenty-two kilometres, the Nordschleife of the Nürburgring is a circuit which needs up to eight minutes to complete in a racing car. To give the spectators more cars to watch during the fifteen-lap German Grand Prix, the Formula Two cars were again invited to join the Formula One racers. The smaller cars had their own grid behind the slowest of the Formula One cars. The front row of this German Grand Prix comprised Jim Clark on pole with a lap of 8m 4.1s with Denny Hulme next with 8m 13.5s, Jackie Stewart on 8m 15.2s and Dan Gurney with 8m 19.9s. However, there was a big surprise in store since Jacky Ickx covered the twenty-two kilometres in just 8m 14s! This would give him the third time overall and he was twenty seconds faster than the second best Formula Two car driven by Jackie Oliver. Jo Bonnier, who at that time was head of the Grand Prix Drivers Association, did not want Ickx to start at the front with a Formula Two car in the middle of the Formula One cars as he thought it would be too dangerous. Thus Ickx started at the back of the Formula One grid and at the head of the Formula Two cars. After a good start, he worked his way up to the front and was able to sweep past Bonnier already at the first corner! After only six laps he was fourth overall. Unfortunately he had to retire on the twelfth lap with broken suspension. But by then, Jacky Ickx had made his point. He belonged with the big boys.

24 Heures du Mans 1967

24 Heures de Spa-Francorchamps 1967

Großer Preis von Deutschland 1967, Nürburgring, Matra MS5 - FVA

Sveriges Grand Prix 1967, Karlskoga

Gran Premio d'Italia 1967, Monza, Franco Lini (Ferrari-Rennleiter / Ferrari team manager) & Jacky Ickx

Sveriges Grand Prix 1967, Karlskoga, Matra MS5 - FVA

Im zwölften Umlauf endete der Auftritt leider durch einen Aufhängungsschaden. Bis dahin hatte Jacky Ickx aber längst seine Duftmarke hinterlassen. Er gehörte jetzt zu den großen Jungs! Eine Woche später reiste Ickx zum Großen Preis von Schweden. Trotz der Bezeichnung „Grand Prix" wurde in Karlskoga aber kein Formel-1-Rennen ausgetragen, im hohen Norden duellierten sich die Piloten in F2-Boliden und Sportwagen. Beim Formel-2-Rennen fuhr Jackie Stewart im neuen Matra MS7 einen schönen Sieg heraus, sein Teamkollege Ickx wurde im bewährten MS5 Sechster. Dann stand für den jungen Belgier die nächste Herausforderung an: John Wyer schickte ihn beim 20-Runden-Rennen für Sportwagen in einem Mirage an den Start. Damit bedankte sich Wyer bei Gulf Schweden für die große Unterstützung des Sportwagenprogramms – und Ickx bedankte sich mit einem Sieg vor Teamkollege Jo Bonnier im zweiten Mirage. Von Schweden ging es für Ickx nach Sizilien, wo eine Woche später der GP del Mediterraneo stattfand. Zum F2-Rennen in Enna-Pergusa kam ein starkes Feld zusammen, das von Matra-Piloten auf den Plätzen eins bis fünf dominiert wurde. Während Stewart beide Heats gewann, wurde Ickx einmal Zweiter und einmal Vierter, das bedeutete zusammengerechnet Platz drei. Zu den Zuschauern zählte an jenem Tag auch Ferrari-Teamchef Franco Lini. Lini fragte bei Ickx an, ob er im kommenden Jahr für die Scuderia fahren wollen würde. Es war der erste Kontakt zwischen Ickx und Ferrari. Im Herbst reiste Jacky mehrere Male nach Modena und einigte sich letztlich mit Enzo Ferrari für die Saison 1968.

■ *Jackie Stewart: „Jacky Ickx bekam meinen Platz bei Ferrari. Als wir in Enna waren, kam ich gerade aus Maranello und Jacky fragte mich: ‚Wie lief es in Maranello?' Woher wusste er das? Dann erzählte er mir von seinem Kontakt zu Ferrari durch Franco Lini, und ich riet ihm: ‚Du solltest dahin wechseln.'"*

Am Wochenende nach Sizilien erwartete Ickx ein ganz anderes Rennen: Beim Marathon de la Route auf dem Nürburgring teilte er sich einen Ford Mustang mit Gilbert Staepelaere und Pat Gautot. Das belgische Ford-Team musste mit defekter Kraftübertragung aber früh die Segel streichen. So fuhren Hans Herrmann, Vic Elford und Jochen Neerpasch nach 84 Stunden, 323 Runden und 9.901 Kilometern zum Sieg.

Am letzten August-Wochenende gab es in England einen Feiertag und so bot sich für Ickx die Möglichkeit, ein Doppelprogramm zu absolvieren mit Rennen im F2-Boliden und im Tourenwagen. Den Formel-2-Matra brachte Ickx in seinem Heat auf Platz acht ins Ziel, das Finale beendete er als Fünfter. Bei den Tourenwagen eroberte er im werkseingesetzten Lotus Cortina Platz zwei hinter Jackie Oliver im Ford Mustang.
14 Tage später feierte Jacky Ickx dann sein heiß ersehntes Formel-1-Debüt. Da sich Pedro Rodriguez beim Rennen in Enna-Pergusa verletzt hatte, bekam Ickx beim Großen Preis von Italien die Chance, für Cooper zu starten. Ken Tyrrell hatte Teamchef Roy Salvadori den

The week after Germany, Ickx went to Sweden for the Swedish Grand Prix. Although this race had the title of 'Grand Prix' it was actually a race weekend for Formula Two cars with an accompanying race for sportscars. In the Formula Two race, Jackie Stewart drove the new Matra MS7 to a fine win while his team-mate Ickx – driving his trusted MS5 – ended up sixth. For the sportscar race, John Wyer had entered both of his Mirages. It was a twenty-lap race with only a few top drivers entered. However, Gulf Oil Sweden was always a great supporter of the Mirage effort and it was a nice gesture to run the cars there. Ickx won the race with Jo Bonnier second in the other Mirage. From Sweden, Ickx went to the south of Europe the week after for the Mediterranean GP at the Enna Pergusa track in Sicily. This turned out to be a strong race in which the Matras took the top five places. Jackie Stewart won both the heats while Ickx came second and fourth thus giving him the third place on aggregate. One interested spectator that day was Franco Lini, the racing manager of Ferrari. He asked Ickx about possibly driving for Ferrari the following year and it was thus that the first contact was made between Ickx and Ferrari. Later that autumn, Ickx went to Modena several times and eventually he and Enzo Ferrari came to an agreement for 1968.

■ *Jackie Stewart: "Jacky Ickx actually took my place with Ferrari. When we were in Enna, I had just came back from Maranello and Jacky asked me 'How was Maranello?' How did he know? He told me about his contact with Ferrari through Franco Lini and I told him 'You should go to them'."*

It was to be a totally different kind of race that Jacky drove the weekend after being in Sicily. Together with Gilbert Staepelaere and Pat Gautot, he shared a Ford Mustang in the 84-hour Marathon de la Route in which the eventual winners – Porsche drivers Hans Herrmann, Vic Elford and Jochen Neerpasch – covered a total of 9,901 kilometres that included 323 laps of the Nürburgring. Unfortunately, a transmission failure brought about an early retirement for the Belgian Ford team.

The final weekend of August, another Bank Holiday weekend in England, gave Ickx the opportunity to have two races at Brands Hatch. One was a Formula Two race and the other a touring car race. In the Formula Two race, Ickx finished eighth in his heat and fifth in the final while in the touring car race he finished second in a works Lotus Cortina behind Jackie Oliver in a Ford Mustang.

Fourteen days later, Jacky Ickx made his long anticipated Formula One debut. With regular driver Pedro Rodriguez having been injured during the Enna Pergusa race, the Cooper team invited Jacky Ickx to drive alongside Jochen Rindt at the Italian Grand Prix. It was Ken Tyrrell who had suggested to Roy Salvadori of Cooper that he should give the Belgian driver this chance. Although totally unfamiliar with the Cooper T81B-Maserati, Ickx accepted. After a careful practice,

— 43 —

jungen Belgier empfohlen. Obwohl er noch nie im Cooper T81B-Maserati gesessen hatte, stimmte Ickx zu. Im Training war der Debütant recht vorsichtig unterwegs, trotzdem war er mit einer Zeit von 1.33 Minuten nur anderthalb Sekunden langsamer als Cooper-Stammpilot Jochen Rindt. Obwohl der T81B weder das schnellste noch das zuverlässigste Auto war, brachte Ickx den Wagen als Sechster über die Distanz von 66 Runden – eine in vielerlei Hinsicht beindruckende F1-Premiere des Belgiers. Da sich Enzo Ferrari bei seinem Heim-Grand-Prix persönlich das Training und Qualifying anschaute, betrieb Ickx zudem gute Eigenwerbung.

Genau wie in Brands Hatch einige Wochen zuvor war Ickx auch im Oulton Park doppelt im Einsatz. Am Gold-Cup-Wochenende fuhr er sowohl den Formel-2-Matra als auch den Lotus Cortina, leider schied er in beiden Rennen nach Unfällen aus. In Albi im Südwesten Frankreichs lief es dagegen besser für den Belgier: Bei dem Lauf zum französischen Formel-2-Championnat wurde er Vierter. Danach bekam Ickx die zweite Gelegenheit, sich in der Formel 1 zu beweisen. Beim Großen Preis der USA in Watkins Glen – ein Kurs, der für Jacky komplett neu war – vertrat er erneut den verletzten Rodriguez. Seine Zeiten im Training und in der Qualifikation waren nicht berauschend, aber sicherlich im Rahmen der Möglichkeiten des Cooper. Das Rennen endete aber nach 45 Runden wegen eines Motorschadens.

Anschließend stand das große Finale der Formel-2-Europameisterschaft auf dem Programm: Ickx durfte zum zweiten Mal den neuen Matra MS7 bewegen und zeigte, wie gut er mit dem Auto umgehen konnte. Ickx gewann beim „Gran Premio di Roma" in Vallelunga beide Heats – und sicherte sich damit den Titel in der Formel-2-EM.

Um Gulf Oil einen Gefallen zu tun, setzte John Wyer bei den 1000 Kilometern von Paris in Montlhéry und den 9 Stunden von Kyalami in Südafrika jeweils einen Mirage ein. Beide Rennen gehörten nicht der Internationalen Markenmeisterschaft an und beide Male bekam es Ickx mit neuen Teampartnern zu tun. In Frankreich teilte er sich das Cockpit mit Paul Hawkins, in Südafrika mit Brian Redman. In Montlhéry nahm Ickx das Rennen von der Pole aus in Angriff und fuhr auf der anspruchsvollen Strecke nach über sieben Stunden zum Sieg. In Südafrika machten Ickx und Redman den Doppelpack für Mirage perfekt: Der M1 führte das Feld zwei Drittel der Renndistanz (239 von 360 Runden) an und überquerte die Ziellinie am Ende mit 13 Runden Vorsprung auf Hawkins im Lola T70. Diese beiden Siege markierten den Schlusspunkt der bemerkenswerten Debütsaison von Mirage. Das JWA-Team um Wyer, Yorke und Horsman konnte optimistisch in die Zukunft blicken, zumal die FIA das Sportwagen-Reglement umgekrempelt hatte. Das Gulf-Team würde 1968 den mittlerweile gut aussortierten GT40 einsetzen.

Für Jacky Ickx war die Saison aber noch nicht ganz vorbei, er bestritt in Jarama bei Madrid noch ein letztes Rennen. Die Spanier bereiteten sich mit einem gemischten Rennen für Formel-1- und -2-Autos auf den im nächsten Frühjahr stattfindenden Großen Preis von Spanien vor, der ebenfalls in Jarama ausgetragen werden sollte. Jim Clark gewann die Generalprobe im Formel-1-Lotus vor Teamkollege Graham Hill. Ickx landete im „alten" Matra MS5 mit einer Runde Rückstand auf Platz sechs.

Im Laufe des Jahres 1967 hatte Jacky Ickx an 36 Rennen teilgenommen und dabei von Formel-1- und Formel-2-Autos bis hin zu Sport- und Tourenwagen alles bewegt. Ickx hatte die F2-Europameisterschaft und einige große Sportwagenrennen gewonnen. Und schon zwei Monate später sollte die neue Saison beginnen, und damit auch ein neuer Abschnitt in Ickx' Karriere: Der Belgier war jetzt Formel-1-Fahrer bei Ferrari!

he set a time of 1m 33s that was just a second and a half slower than Cooper's regular driver, Jochen Rindt. Although his was neither the fastest nor the most reliable car in the race, Jacky nursed it for sixty-six laps at this high-speed track to finish sixth overall that, in many ways, was a remarkable Formula One debut for the Belgian driver. With Enzo Ferrari himself attending the practice and qualifying for his home Grand Prix, it was also excellent exposure for Ickx.

Just as at Brands Hatch some weeks before, Ickx had double duty at Oulton Park for the Gold Cup weekend where he drove the Formula Two Matra as well as the Lotus Cortina. Unfortunately in both races he had to retire due to accidents. His efforts had a better result down in Albi in south-western France where he finished fourth in a Formula Two race counting towards the French Formula Two Championship. Before going to Rome for the last race for the European Formula Two Challenge, Ickx had a second opportunity with Cooper in a Grand Prix. Again, he was substituted for Rodriguez and entered in the American Grand Prix at Watkins Glen, a circuit with which he was completely unfamiliar. His practice and qualifying times were not very competitive but were clearly within the Cooper's abilities. But then after forty-five laps of the race, the engine broke and Ickx was forced to retire.

Ickx was given his second opportunity to drive the Formula Two Matra MS7 and he immediately showed how much he liked it by winning both heats at the Rome Grand Prix held on the Vallelunga circuit near the Italian capital. By doing so, the Belgian driver clinched victory in the European Formula Two Challenge.

To please Gulf Oil, John Wyer entered a Mirage at both the 1,000 Kilometres of Paris at Montlhéry and the 9 Hours of Kyalami in South Africa. For both these events – neither of which had championship status – Ickx had new partners with Australian Paul Hawkins joining him in France and Englishman Brian Redman in South Africa. Starting from pole, after seven hours of gruelling racing on the demanding Montlhéry track, the Mirage took another deserved victory. In South Africa, Ickx drove 220 laps and his new partner 140. In all, the Mirage led for 239 of the scheduled 360 laps and crossed the finishing line to win the race with a 13-lap advantage over Hawkins in his own Lola T70. These two wins provided a very positive end to a remarkable season with Mirage so that now the JWA team of Wyer, Yorke and Horsman could make great plans for 1968. The FIA had changed the rules for sportscar endurance racing and the Gulf team could look forward to campaigning the now well-sorted GT40.

Ickx had one more race before the year was over and this was at Jarama, near Madrid. The Spanish organisers had laid on a mixed race for Formula One and Two cars that was designed to be a try-out for next spring's official Spanish Formula One GP that was also to be held at Jarama. The race was won by Jim Clark in a Formula One Lotus with his team-mate Graham Hill second. Ickx finished sixth overall in his old F2 Matra MS5, one lap down on the winners.

During the year of 1967 Jacky Ickx had participated in thirty-six races encompassing Formula One, Formula Two, sportscars and touring cars. He was crowned Formula Two champion and had won several major sportscar races. In less than two months, the 1968 season would start and, as it did so, a new career would commence for Ickx, this time as a Ferrari Formula One driver.

Gran Premio d'Italia 1967, Monza, Cooper T81B - Maserati

United States Grand Prix 1967, Watkins Glen, Cooper T86 - Maserati n°21 (ganz hinten rechts / at the back, on the right)

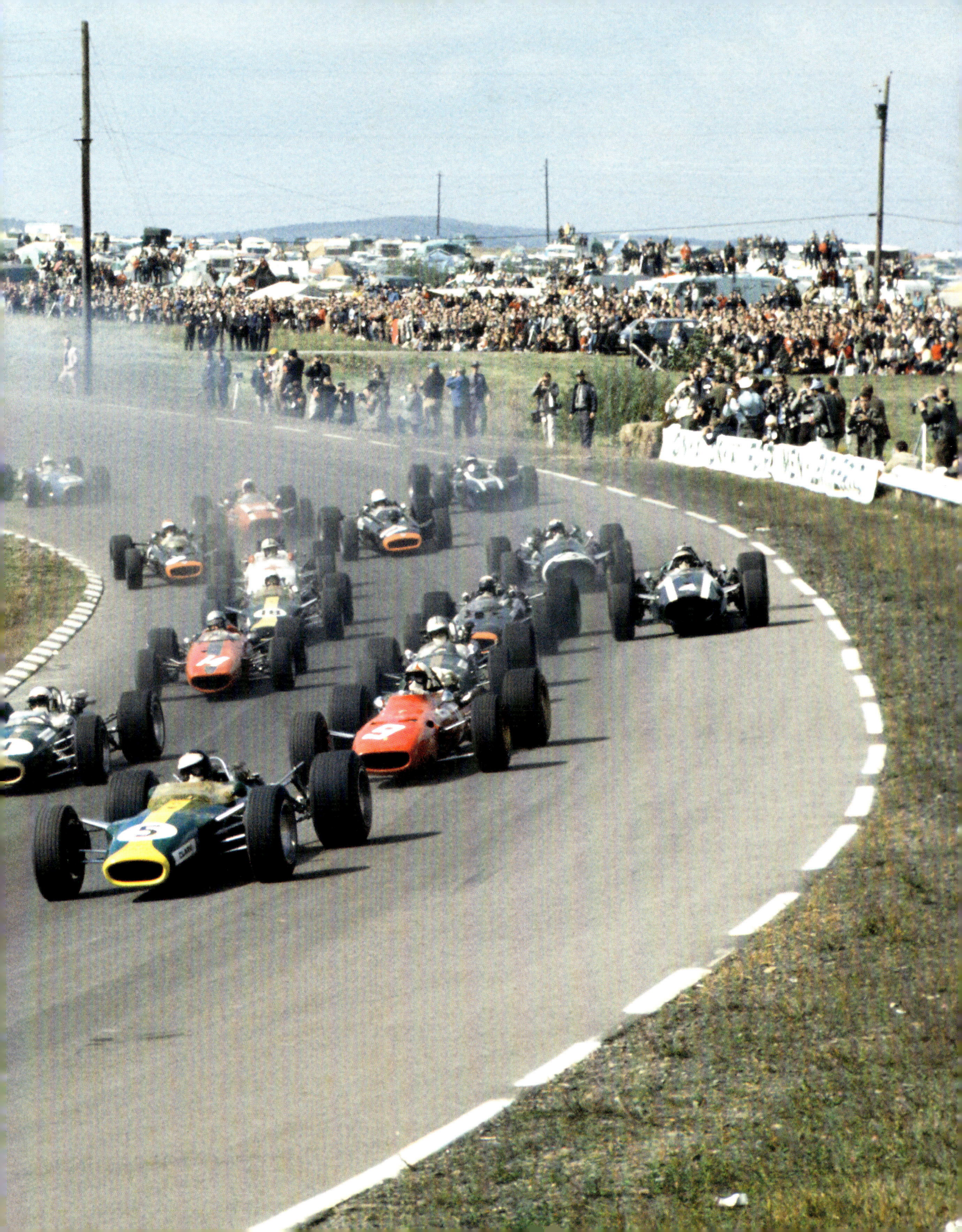

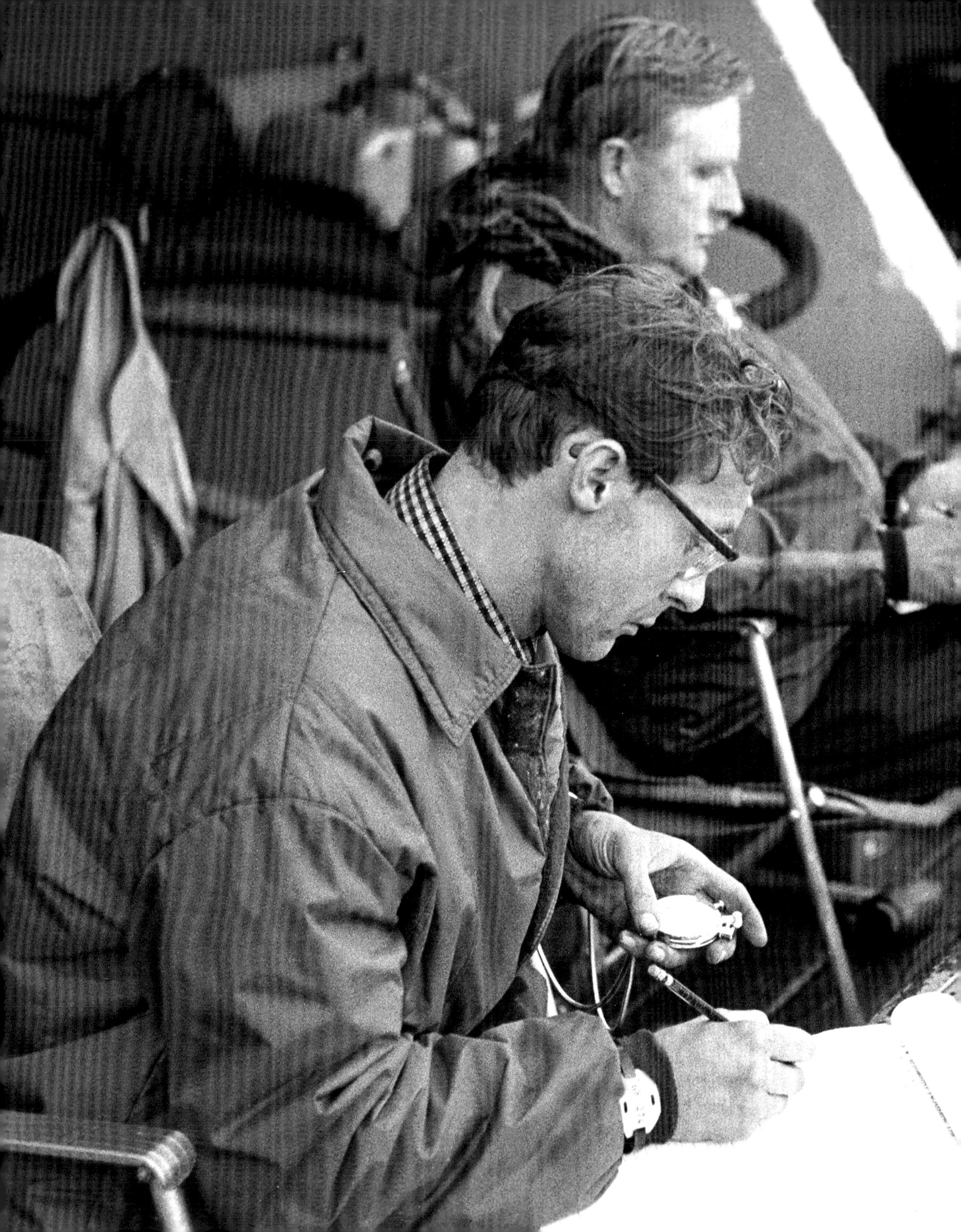

John HORSMAN

Ingenieur bei Gulf Racing
Team engineer with Gulf Racing

„Als wir 1967 zum 24-Stunden-Rennen von Daytona geflogen sind, haben wir Jacky Ickx als Fahrer mitgenommen. Wir hatten gerade einen Vertrag mit Gulf Oil unterzeichnet und wollten vor dem Start der Europa-Saison in Daytona testen. Mein Boss John Wyer und Teamchef David Yorke fragten Grady Davis, den Chef von Gulf Oil, ob sie dessen GT40 mit Ickx als Fahrer einsetzen dürften. Davis war etwas überrascht, als er hörte, dass ein 22-Jähriger mit dem Namen ‚X' sein Auto fahren sollte. Er bestand darauf, dass Dick Thompson am Steuer sitzt und so kamen wir überein, dass sich Thompson und Ickx am Steuer abwechseln sollten. Das funktionierte gut, wir beendeten das Rennen auf dem guten sechsten Platz – vor den Werks-Ford mit sieben Litern Hubraum."

„Wenige Monate später demonstrierte Jacky in Spa sein großes Talent. Wir hatten den neuen Mirage weiterentwickelt und mit einem starken Motor bestückt, daher hofften wir auf dem schnellen Kurs auf ein gutes Ergebnis. Ickx erzielte im Qualifying die Bestzeit und fuhr im Rennen auf und davon. Schon nach der ersten Runde war sein Vorsprung immens. Wir haben gewonnen, und danach war auch Grady Davis von unserem jungen Fahrer überzeugt. Ein Jahr später sind wir in Spa im Regen gefahren – und Ickx ist wahrlich geflogen! In der ersten Runde hat er sich ein Polster von 39 Sekunden herausgefahren."

„Und dann gab es natürlich noch den großartigen Le-Mans-Sieg 1969. Als Ickx beim Start zu seinem Auto geschlendert ist, hat er uns Angst gemacht. In der ersten Runde lag er am Ende des Feldes und war dadurch zumindest nicht in den Unfall von John Woolfe verwickelt. Am Ende siegten Ickx und Oliver knapp. Für diese großartige Fahrt in einem so alten Auto muss ich ihnen wirklich Tribut zollen!"

„John Wyer liebte Jacky Ickx. In den drei gemeinsamen Jahren hatten wir fantastische Ergebnisse. Die Zeit mit Gulf war großartig, aber es gab auch Spannungen im Team. Ich weiß noch, dass Mike Hailwood kein großer Fan von Ickx war. Den zehnfachen Motorrad-Weltmeister nervte Jackys Arroganz. Und auch David Hobbs hatte seine eigene Meinung über ihn. Aber wir haben die Erfolge gefeiert, die wir uns erhofft hatten – allen voran natürlich die beiden Siege in Le Mans."

"When we came to Daytona for the 24-hour race in 1967, we brought Jacky Ickx as one of our drivers. We had just signed a contract with Gulf Oil and, before the European season started, we were thinking of doing the Daytona race. My boss John Wyer and team manager David Yorke asked Grady Davis – the boss of Gulf Oil – to let us enter his personal GT40 and have Ickx as the driver. Davis was a bit of surprised to hear that a 22-year old with the name of 'X' was to drive. He insisted that Dick Thompson should drive and we agreed to let Dick share the driving duties with Ickx. It worked well since the team finished a respectable sixth overall. We had even beaten all the works seven-litre Ford GTs."

"A few months later, Jacky showed his immense talent at Spa. We had the new Mirage well sorted out and now fitted with a strong engine so we hoped to do well at this fast circuit. Ickx had already set the fastest time in qualifying and in the race he just ran off into the distance. After the first lap, he had an immense gap to the next car. We won that event and even Grady Davis was now convinced about the young driver. When we were back at Spa a year later, again we had to race in the rain. And again Ickx just flew. When he came past the pits after the first lap, he had a margin of no less than 39 seconds!"

"And then of course there was the great Le Mans win in 1969. He scared us all by walking to his car at the start but got away safely. By being at the back of the field in that first lap, he certainly missed the John Woolfe accident. In the end, he and Oliver won by a tiny margin. A great tribute to a great drive by both of them in such an old car."

"John Wyer loved Jacky Ickx and in those three years, we had some marvellous results. It was great time to be with Gulf although there were sometimes some frictions within the team I remember that Mike Hailwood was not a great fan of Ickx. The ten-times World Champion on two wheels was sometimes annoyed by the arrogance of Jacky. And David Hobbs had his own thoughts about him. But we had the results for which we were hoping of which the two Le Mans victories stand out as good examples."

1968

Der erste Formel-1-Sieg und ein Beinbruch
A Formula One victory but also a major injury

Jacky Ickx feierte seinen 23. Geburtstag in Südafrika, wo am Neujahrstag die neue Formel-1-Saison begann. Für Ickx war es erst der dritte F1-Grand-Prix und das erste Rennen als Ferrari-Werksfahrer. Es sollte der Auftakt eines aufregenden Jahres mit zahlreichen Siegen werden. Eine Verletzung zeigte Jacky aber auch die Schattenseiten des Motorsports auf.

Zwischen Belgien und Ferrari gab es schon lange eine enge Bindung. Als der italienische Hersteller mit dem Bau von Sportwagen anfing, gehörte Jacques Swaters zu den ersten Händlern. Der Brüsseler verkaufte in seiner Garage Francorchamps aber nicht nur Straßenautos, sondern setzte die Ferrari auch bei Rennen ein. 1951 pilotierte mit Johnny Claes ein anderer Belgier einen Ferrari 340 America bei den 24 Stunden von Le Mans, 1956 schickte die Équipe Nationale Belge das Duo Lucien Bianchi/Alain de Changy in einem Ferrari Testa Rossa an den Start.

On New Year's Day 1968, Jacky Ickx celebrated his twenty-third birthday in South Africa. That was also the day that he would start his third Formula One Grand Prix and his first as a Ferrari works driver. It heralded what would turn out to be an exciting year with several victories, though these were later to be overshadowed somewhat by an injury sustained in an accident during the qualifying of the Canadia GP.

There had long been a strong relationship between Belgium and Ferrari. When the Italian manufacturer first started selling its cars, Jacques Swaters from Brussels was among its very first dealers. Through his Garage Francorchamps, he not only sold road-going Ferraris, but also ran them in races. Another Belgian, Johnny Claes, drove a Ferrari 340 America at the 24 Hours of Le Mans in 1951 while in 1956 a Ferrari Testa Rossa was entered by the Équipe Nationale Belge for Lucien Bianchi and Alain de Changy.

South African Grand Prix 1968, Kyalami, Ferrari 312

Ein Jahr später nahm Swaters den Circuit de la Sarthe mit einem 290 MM selbst unter die Räder. Im Laufe der Jahre gingen viele belgische Ferrari-Piloten in die Geschichte des Langstreckenklassikers ein: Olivier Gendebien triumphierte vier Mal in Le Mans, 1960 sogar zusammen mit Landsmann Paul Frère. Willy Mairesse wurde 1961 bei seinem Debüt im Ferrari Zweiter. Und 1963 gelang den Belgiern Leon Dernier (alias Elde) und Jean Blaton (alias Beurlys) in einem Ferrari 250 GTO der dritte Platz. Letzterer ging nicht weniger als 15 Mal in Le Mans an den Start. Einige dieser Fahrer fuhren auch in der Formel 1 für Ferrari und so war es keine große Überraschung, dass Enzo Ferrari für die Saison 1968 ein belgisches Nachwuchstalent für die Formel 1 und Formel 2 unter Vertrag nahm.

1967 hatte Ferrari eine Saison mit Höhen und Tiefen erlebt. Die Scuderia setzte große Hoffnungen in ihren neuen Fahrer Chris Amon, welcher Teamkollege von Lorenzo Bandini wurde. Das Duo startete mit zwei großen Sportwagensiegen in die Saison, doch dann kam Bandini bei einem Feuerunfall während des GP von Monaco ums Leben. Seinen Platz im Team nahmen Mike Parkes und Ludovico Scarfiotti ein, die zwar routinierte Sportwagenpiloten waren, aber nur wenig Formel-1-Erfahrung hatten. Beim Großen Preis von Belgien ereilte Ferrari dann der nächste Schicksalsschlag: Parkes erlitt in Spa-Francorchamps einen schweren Unfall, der ihn fast ein Jahr außer Gefecht setzte. Parkes und Scarfiotti bestritten 1967 nur zwei Grand Prix für Ferrari, in den Niederlanden und in Belgien. Bei den restlichen Rennen setzte die Scuderia nur das Auto von Chris Amon ein, der die Weltmeisterschaft auf Platz vier beendete. Zur Saison 1968 waren Enzo Ferrari und sein Team daher bemüht, einen neuen Fahrer zu finden. Erst sprachen sie mit Jackie Stewart, doch der Schotte konnte sich nicht mit der Scuderia einigen. Daraufhin verhandelte Ferrari-Teamchef Franco Lini mit Jacky Ickx, der einen Vertrag für das Jahr 1968 unterzeichnete. Der Kontrakt, der Ickx 30.000 US-Dollar einbrachte, beschränkte sich aber auf Formel-Rennwagen. In der Markenmeisterschaft für Sportwagen ging Ickx weiterhin für John Wyer an den Start.

■ *Jackie Stewart: „Zwischen Ferrari und mir hat es nicht geklappt. Enzo bezeichnete mich immer als Engländer, und ich erwiderte: ‚Ich bin kein Engländer, ich bin Schotte.'"*

Beim ersten Grand Prix 1968 trat Ferrari mit drei Formel-1-Autos des Typs 312 an: Einer war für Nummer-Eins-Pilot Chris Amon, einer für Jacky Ickx und einer für den 26 Jahre alten Italiener Andrea de Adamich. In der Qualifikation war Ickx der Langsamste des Trios, er nahm das Rennen aus der fünften Reihe in Angriff. Während Amon ein für ihn wenig ereignisreiches Rennen auf Platz vier beendete, verunfallte de Adamich nach 13 Runden. Ickx verbesserte sich bis auf die fünfte Position, ehe er nach 51 von 80 Umläufen wegen eines defekten Ölschlauchs aufgeben musste.

Vier Wochen später flog Ickx nach Florida, um den ersten Saisonlauf für John Wyers JWA-Team zu bestreiten. Durch die Einführung einer Hubraumobergrenze wurden die leistungsstärksten Prototypen zur 1968er-Saison aus der Internationalen Markenmeisterschaft für Sportwagen verbannt. Prototypen durften ab sofort maximal drei Liter Hubraum haben, Sportwagen fünf. Für die Anerkennung als Sportwagen mussten von einem Typ mindestens 50 Exemplare innerhalb eines Jahres gebaut werden. Damit war der Mirage außen vor, und John Wyer sattelte auf den Ford GT40 um, der in der Sportwagenklasse startete. Für die zwei in den Gulf-Farben orange und hellblau lackierten GT40 verpflichtete Teamchef David Yorke das Fahrerquartett Brian Redman, David Hobbs, Paul

Jacques Swaters himself drove a 290 MM in 1957 at the Circuit de la Sarthe and for many years it was Belgian drivers who set the pace in this endurance race. Olivier Gendebien won Le Mans four times, his first in 1958 while in 1960 he was joined on the top of the podium by Paul Frère, another Belgian. Willy Mairesse debuted for Ferrari in 1961 and finished second. In 1963, 'Elde', the alter ego of Leon Dernier, finished third overall sharing his Ferrari 250 GTO with Jean Blaton, known as 'Beurlys'. The latter participated in Le Mans no less than fifteen times. But some of these drivers also drove occasionally for Ferrari in Formula One. So it was not such a surprising thing that Enzo Ferrari should choose a young talented Belgian to drive his Formula One and Formula Two cars for 1968.

Ferrari had experienced something of a mixed season in 1967. They had started out with high hopes of their new driver, Chris Amon, who joined the experienced Lorenzo Bandini in their line-up. Early in the year, they notched up two major sportscar victories, but everything changed when Bandini died in a fiery crash at the second Grand Prix of the season in Monaco. His place in the team was taken by Mike Parkes and Ludovico Scarfiotti both of whom were well-known sportscar drivers, but who had limited Formula One experience. To make things even worse for Ferrari, Mike Parkes had an awful accident during the Belgian Grand Prix at Spa-Francorchamps and as a result would be unable to drive for almost a year. Indeed, he and Scarfiotti only drove twice in grands prix for Ferrari in 1967, namely Holland and Belgium. For the remainder of the season, Ferrari ran just one car for Chris Amon who finally finished fourth in the World Championship of that year. Enzo Ferrari and his team were anxiously looking for a new driver and had offered Jackie Stewart a position for 1968, but the Scot could not come to terms with the Italians and did not sign. Ferrari's race manager, Franco Lini, then offered the drive to Jacky Ickx and thus for 1968, Ickx would drive the red Formula One and Two cars. However, he would not drive sportscars for Ferrari since he would stay with John Wyer for another year. The deal with Ferrari was that Ickx got a contract for $30,000 a year.

■ *Jackie Stewart: "It did not work out with Ferrari and me. Enzo kept calling me an Englishman, but I kept telling him 'I am not English, I am a Scot'."*

For the first grand prix of 1968, Ferrari came to South Africa with three Formula One 312s. One was for Chris Amon who would be their number one driver, one for Jacky Ickx and one for a twenty-six year-old Italian, Andrea de Adamich. Of the three, Ickx was the slowest in qualifying and started from the fifth row. Amon ran an unexciting race and ended up fourth while De Adamich crashed his car after thirteen laps. Ickx gradually worked his way up to lie fifth but had to retire after fifty-one of the eighty laps when an oil pipe broke.

Four weeks later, Jacky travelled to Florida for the first race in the JWA sportscars. The change in the rules for endurance racing meant that prototypes with unlimited engine capacity could no longer take part. There was a three-litre prototype class and a five-litre sportscar class. To qualify for the latter, at least fifty had to be built within one year. With the Mirage now ruled out, Wyer chose to run Ford GT40s in the sportscar class. Again the cars would be painted in the Gulf Oil colours of orange and blue and the JWA team manager, David Yorke, contracted four drivers. These were Brian Redman, David Hobbs, Paul Hawkins and Jacky Ickx. It is fair to say that the young Belgian driver was David Yorke's favourite and generally got

Hawkins und Jacky Ickx. Wobei man ruhig sagen kann, dass Ickx der Lieblingspilot des Teamchefs war. Der Belgier durfte sich unter anderem den Teamkollegen aussuchen, er wählte Redman. Das Duo war im November in Kyalami gemeinsam angetreten und hatte eine gute Arbeitsbeziehung. In Daytona erzielten Ickx/Redman im Qualifying die Bestzeit und starteten von der Pole. Sie waren zwei Sekunden schneller als der zweite Gulf-Ford, der noch vor den vier Werks-Porsche lag. Anfangs sah es gut aus für die wunderschönen orange-blauen GT40, doch dann schieden beide durch Probleme mit der Kraftübertragung aus. Ickx/Redman schafften gerade einmal 58 Runden, das Schwesterauto 431. Der siegreiche Porsche sah nach 673 Umläufen die Zielflagge.

▪ **Brian Redman: „Ickx war der Liebling des Teams und hatte daher freie Hand bei der Wahl seines Partners. Ich war froh, dass er mich gewählt hat. So konnte ich Rennen gewinnen."**

Die Europa-Saison begann für Ickx wie im Vorjahr mit dem Race of Champions in Brands Hatch. Bei dem Formel-1-Rennen ohne WM-Status schickte Ferrari dasselbe Trio an den Start wie in Südafrika. Während de Adamich seinen 312 im Training zerlegte und nicht am Rennen teilnehmen konnte, war Chris Amon erneut der schnellste Ferraristi. Bruce McLaren gewann das Rennen über 40 Runden im neuen McLaren-Ford, Amon wurde Vierter und Ickx abgeschlagener Achter. Wieder ein Resultat, das weder den Ansprüchen von Ickx noch denen des Teams entsprach.

Von London aus jettete Ickx direkt nach Sebring, um dort den zweiten Lauf zum Sportwagen-Championat zu bestreiten. JWA hatte die in Daytona aufgetretenen Probleme mit den ZF-Getrieben gelöst und rechnete mit einem guten Resultat. Ickx nahm das Rennen neben dem Porsche von Jo Siffert/Hans Herrmann von Platz zwei aus in Angriff, übernahm aber schnell die Führung und behauptete diese bis zum Ende seines Stints. Dann ruinierte Redman die Kupplung und musste den GT40 nach 34 Runden abstellen. Der andere Ford lag in den Top Ten, bis Paul Hawkins nach zwei Dritteln der Distanz mit dem AMC Javelin von Liane Engemann kollidierte und ausschied. Nach vier Ausfällen bei zwei Rennen sah es nicht gut aus für Wyers Team.

Eine Woche später saß Jacky Ickx zum ersten Mal im Ferrari-Formel-2-Auto, dem Dino 166 V6. Kurz nach dem Start des Rennens im Montjuïc Park von Barcelona krachte Jacky in den Lotus von Jim Clark, woraufhin beide Autos durch Aufhängungsschaden ausfielen. Möglicherweise hatte dieser Unfall dramatische Folgen: Clark fuhr dasselbe Auto eine Woche später beim Formel-2-Rennen in Hockenheim, wo er nach einem ungeklärten Defekt am Auto in den Wald abflog und starb.

Während des Hockenheim-Wochenendes war Ickx in Brands Hatch und Le Mans im Einsatz. Am Freitag nahm er in England an der Qualifikation zum Sportwagenrennen, den BOAC 500, teil und flog von dort aus nach Frankreich, um bei den Le-Mans-Vortests seine Runden zu drehen. Der Belgier absolvierte 44 Umläufe, ehe er wieder in den Flieger Richtung England stieg. In Jackys Abwesenheit hatte Redman die Zeit seines Teampartners egalisiert und den GT40 in der dritten Startreihe neben dem Howmet-TX-Turbinenwagen von Dick Thompson platziert. In Brands Hatch setzte das JWA-Team nur einen Wagen ein, da die kurvige Strecke eher den kleineren Porsche entgegen kam. Wyers Hauptaugenmerk lag also eher auf den Le-Mans-Tests als auf dem Rennen in Brands Hatch.

the best deal. For example, Ickx wanted to have Redman as his driving partner. They had driven together in South Africa the previous November and the two possessed a good working relationship. In Daytona, this duo set the fastest time in qualifying and thus started from pole. They were two seconds faster than the other Wyer Ford and had an even wider margin to the four works Porsches. Although from the start it looked good for the beautifully prepared Fords, their race would be over rather too soon for their driver's liking since both cars had to retire with transmission problems. The Ickx/Redman car was out already after fifty-eight laps and the other after four hundred and thirty-one laps. The winning Porsche covered six hundred and seventy-three.

▪ **Brian Redman: "Ickx was the team's favourite and thus he was free to choose a partner. I was happy that he chose me. That gave me the possibility to win races."**

The European racing season started in the middle of March with the non-championship 'Race of Champions' at Brands Hatch in England and Ferrari sent three 312s for the same drivers that ran in South Africa. Again Amon was fastest in practice but only two cars made it to the grid because Andrea de Adamich crashed his car in practice and could not start. The fifty-lap race was won by Bruce McLaren in his new McLaren-Ford with Chris Amon fourth and Ickx a somewhat distant eighth. Again, this was not the result for which Ickx – or the team – had been hoping.

Jacky Ickx flew from London direct to Sebring for the second endurance championship race. The Daytona problems with the ZF gearboxes had been solved and the team was looking for a good result. After starting from second position behind the Jo Siffert/Hans Herrmann Porsche, Ickx took an early lead and kept it during his stint. Unfortunately, Redman made an error and ruined the clutch, which meant that they had to retire after only thirty-four laps. The other Ford ran in the top ten until Paul Hawkins collided with Dutchman Liane Engemann's AMC Javelin at about two-thirds distance and the damage caused resulted in retirement for him. It was not looking good with two races of the championship gone and four retirements.

Jacky got his first opportunity to drive the Dino 166 V6 Formula Two car a week later in the streets of Barcelona. However, right after the start of the Montjuïc Park race, Jacky ran into Jim Clark's Lotus and both cars had to retire with suspension damage. It is possible that this accident had a very serious outcome since Jim Clark drove his same car a week later at the Hockenheim Formula Two race where, after an unidentified failure on the car, the Scot crashed the Lotus into some trees and was killed.

The same weekend as that Hockenheim race, Ickx was back at Brands Hatch. This time he was there to drive in the BOAC 500 sportscar race. For him it was a busy weekend since, after qualifying on Friday, Ickx flew to France on Saturday to test a GT40 during the Le Mans test days. The Belgian drove forty-four laps before flying back to Brands Hatch. Meanwhile, Brian Redman had equalled Jacky's practice times and put the car on the third row alongside the Howmet Turbine car of Dick Thompson, the American dentist who was having another season in sportscar racing. Wyer only ran one car at Brand Hatch as the JWA team thought that the twisty circuit was more suited to the smaller Porsches. Thus their main concentration for that weekend was actually on the Le Mans test sessions and not at Brands Hatch.

24 Hours of Daytona 1968, Daytona Beach, Ford GT40 n°8

Race of Champions 1968, Brands Hatch, Ferrari 312

Race of Champions 1968, Brands Hatch, Mauro Forghieri (Ferrari) & Jacky Ickx

Internationales ADAC-Eifelrennen 1968, Nürburgring, Ferrari Dino 166 V6 n°3

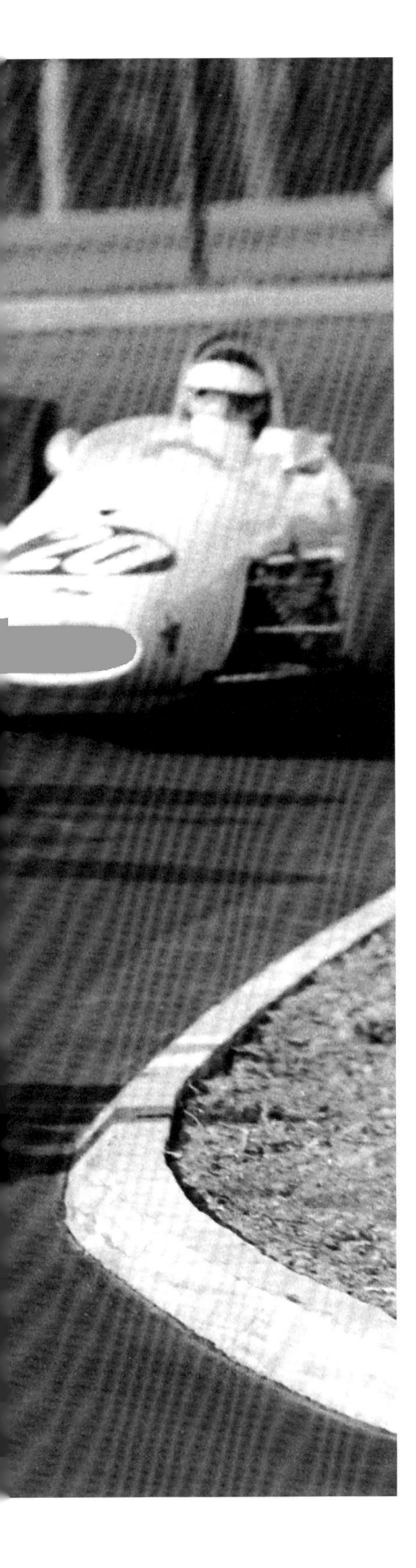

Nach dem Start an einem kalten, nebligen Morgen übernahmen die Porsche sofort das Kommando und zogen ihren Gegnern auf und davon. Doch dann mussten die 907er außerplanmäßige Boxenstopps einlegen, um die Bremsbeläge zu wechseln, und so ging Brian Redman – der gerade das Steuer von Ickx übernommen hatte – in Führung. Nach dem zweiten Fahrerwechsel hatte der Gulf-Ford immer noch ein komfortables Polster, allerdings holte Ludovico Scarfiotti im Porsche schnell auf. John Wyer gab diese Info per Boxentafel an Ickx weiter, woraufhin der Belgier einen Zahn zulegte, um den Vorsprung zu bewahren. Mit Erfolg: Ickx überquerte die Ziellinie 22 Sekunden vor dem Porsche von Gerhard Mitter und Scarfiotti. Die Freude über den Sieg war aber nur allzu schnell verflogen, als die traurige Nachricht von Jim Clarks Tod die Runde machte.

In den folgenden Wochen fanden zahlreiche Formel-2-Rennen statt. Ickx nahm aber nur am Eifelrennen auf dem Nürburgring teil, wo seine Vorstellung wegen eines defekten Kühlers nach fünf Runden endete. Bei der International Trophy in Silverstone – einem Formel-1-Rennen ohne WM-Status – feierte Ickx dann seine zweite Zielankunft im Ferrari. Er wurde Vierter hinter zwei McLaren und Ferrari-Teamkollege Chris Amon. Am folgenden Tag, dem 25. April, war Ickx in Monza im Einsatz, um dort das 1000-Kilometer-Rennen zu bestreiten. Trotz der Bestzeit in der Qualifikation gingen die Gulf-Ford-Piloten Redman und Ickx erneut mit leeren Händen nach Hause, nachdem der Auspuff des Ford GT40 gebrochen war – möglicherweise eine Folge der vielen Unebenheiten in der Steilkurve von Monza. Dafür holten ihre Teamkollegen Hawkins und Hobbs den Gesamtsieg! Am 5. Mai konnte Ickx erstmals als Ferrari-Werksfahrer in seiner Heimat antreten, wenn auch nur im Formel-2-Monoposto. Beim Grote Prijs van Limburg in Zolder wurde Ickx nach beiden Heats zusammengerechnet auf Platz vier gewertet, Teamkollege Amon wurde Zweiter. Immerhin konnte Ickx den zweiten Heat für sich entscheiden.

1968 fand der Große Preis von Spanien erstmals auf der neuen Rennstrecke von Jarama vor den Toren von Madrid statt. Der Kurs war ein Jahr zuvor eröffnet worden und hatte schon zwei Formel-Rennen beherbergt. Für Ickx war Jarama kein Neuland, er hatte hier im November im Formel-2-Matra den sechsten Platz belegt. Im Qualifying erzielte Amon die Bestzeit und startete folglich von der Pole Position. Ickx war knapp zwei Sekunden langsamer als der Neuseeländer und fuhr aus der dritten Reihe los. Das Rennen endete für beide Ferraristi vorzeitig: An Jackys Auto ging nach 13 Runden die Zündung kaputt, Amon rollte nach 44 Runden mit einem Problem bei der Benzinzufuhr aus.

From the start of the race, on a very cold and foggy morning, the Porsches took the lead and pulled out a large margin over their competitors. However, the German cars had to come in for unscheduled pit stops in order to change brake pads and Brian Redman – who just had taken over from Ickx – went into the lead. When Jacky took over again from Redman, they still possessed a healthy lead although Ludovico Scarfiotti in one of the Porsches was gaining on the Gulf Ford. By means of pit signals, John Wyer passed that information to Ickx and the Belgian consequently went a bit faster so as to retain his advantage. At the chequered flag, Ickx had a twenty-two second margin over the Porsche of Gerhard Mitter and Scarfiotti and thus won the race. After the podium ceremonies, the joy of victory changed to sorrow after the news came through about Jim Clark's accident in Germany.

There were several Formula Two races during the weeks that were to follow but Jacky Ickx only drove in the 'Eifelrennen' at the Nürburgring where a cracked radiator ended his race after five laps. At the International Trophy at Silverstone, Ickx completed his second race in a Ferrari. He finished fourth behind two McLarens and Chris Amon in the other Ferrari. The next day, April 25th, Ickx went to Monza to compete in the 1,000-kilometre sportscar event. Although the powerful Ford out-qualified the Porsches in practice, the race saw Ickx and Redman leave empty-handed after a cracked exhaust – probably the result of the bumps on the infamous Monza banking – forced them to retire. The good news however was that the other Wyer Ford, driven by Hawkins and Hobbs, won the race outright. On May 5th, Jacky could finally drive a Ferrari in front of his local fans when he participated in the Formula Two Grand Prix of Limburg at Zolder. Both Ickx and Amon finished the two-heat race and, on aggregate, were classified as fourth and second respectively. However, Jacky did have the pleasure of winning the second heat.

For the first time, the Spanish Grand Prix was to be run at the new Jarama circuit outside the Spanish capital. The track had opened a year earlier and already two formula races had been held there and it may be recalled that Jacky finished sixth at Jarama in November the previous year driving a Matra Formula Two. In qualifying, Amon made the fastest time and could start from pole while Jacky could not equal the New Zealander's time and, with a lap some two seconds slower, started from the third row. In the race, after thirteen laps the ignition broke on Jacky's car and at forty-four laps Amon had to retire with fuel problems.

— 55 —

1000 km di Monza 1968

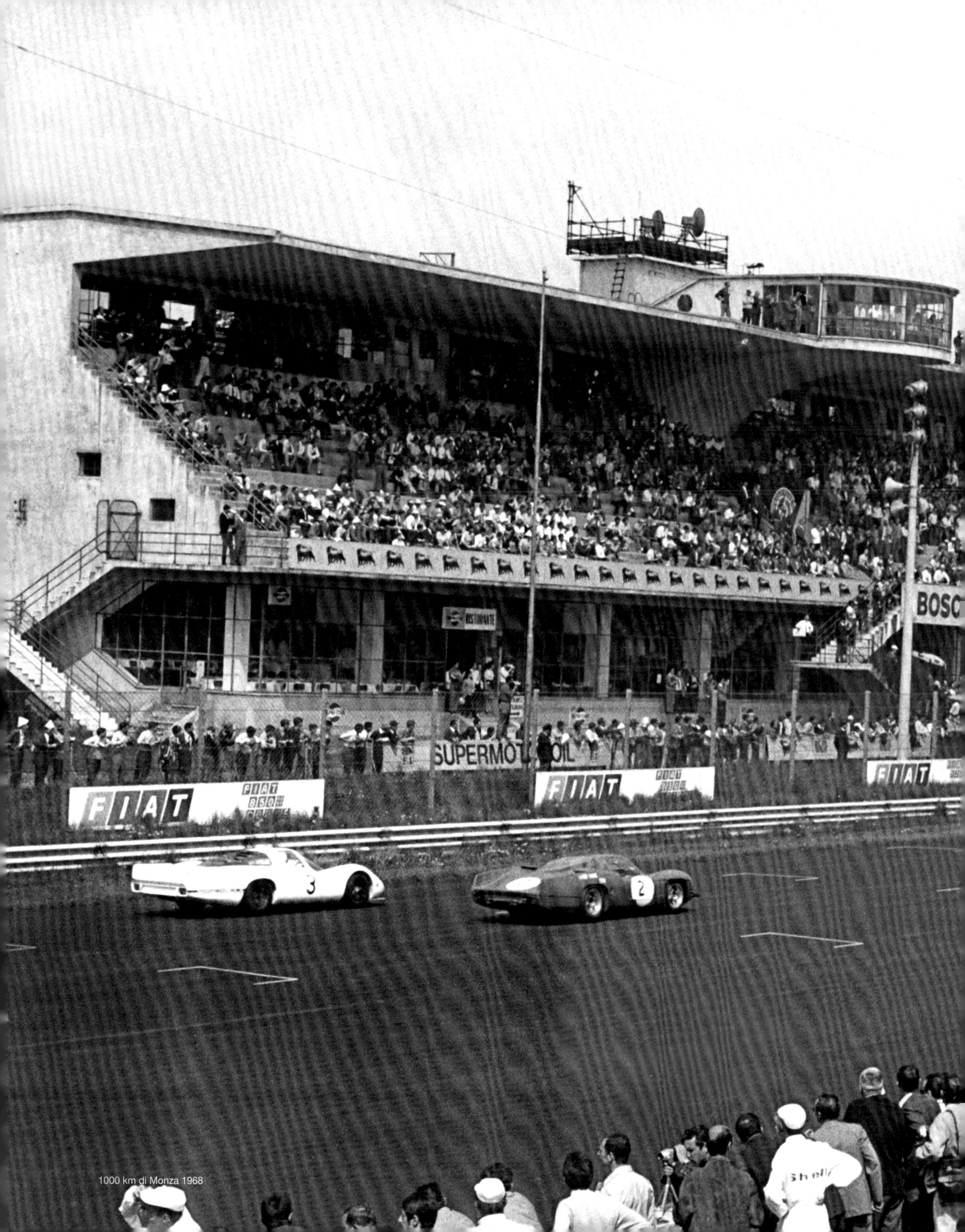

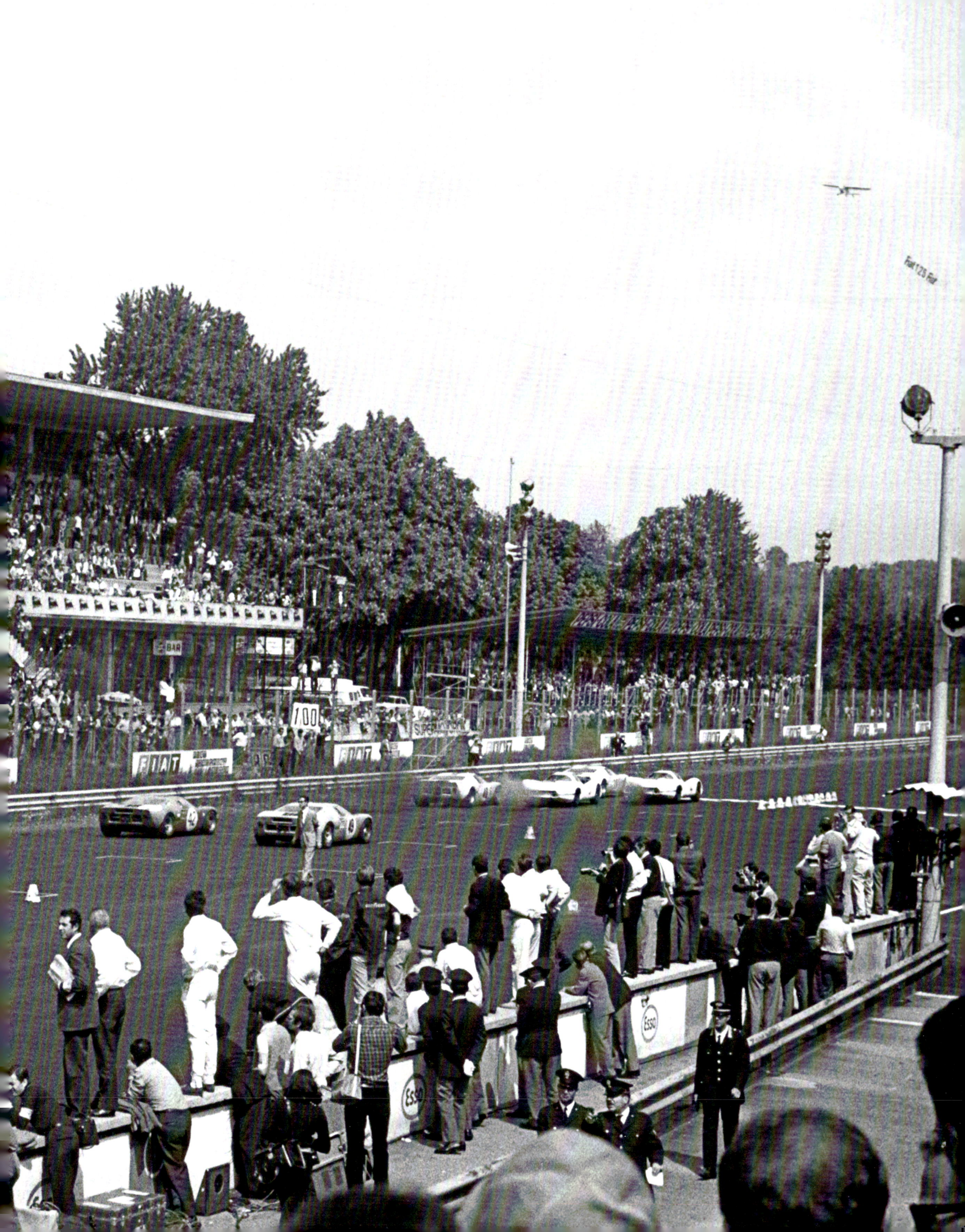
BAR
100
FIAT
FIAT
Esso
Esso

Gran Premio de España 1968, Jarama

Nach dem Spanien-GP folgten zwei Langstreckenrennen im Ford GT40: Bei den 1000 Kilometer auf dem Nürburgring teilte sich Ickx das Cockpit mit Paul Hawkins, dem John Wyer und David Yorke auf der anspruchsvollen, 22 Kilometer langen Strecke mehr zutrauten als Brian Redman. Wyer entschied sich für den Fahrerwechsel, da sich der Brite in Sebring und Monza einige Male gedreht hatte. Porsche holte wie erwartet die Pole Position, dahinter sorgte Ickx mit der zweitbesten Zeit für eine große Überraschung! Beim Le-Mans-Start nahm sich Ickx viel Zeit, seinen Gurt anzulegen und büßte dadurch einige Plätze ein. Daraufhin zeigte er aber eine gute Leistung und blieb bis zum Ende seines Stints in Sichtweite der Führenden. Hawkins war anschließend aber fast 25 Sekunden pro Runde langsamer als Ickx und verlor wertvollen Boden auf die Porsche. Als Ickx das Steuer wieder übernahm, hatte er fünf Minuten Rückstand auf die Spitzenreiter – diese Lücke war einfach zu groß. Letztendlich erreichten Ickx/Hawkins als Dritte das Ziel, der andere Gulf-Ford wurde Sechster. Es ist durchaus möglich, dass noch mehr möglich gewesen wäre, wenn Wyer nicht den Fahrerwechsel vollzogen hätte.

■ *Brian Redman: „Ich war überrascht, dass Ickx am Nürburgring zusammen mit Hawkins fuhr. Am Ende hat es nicht funktioniert, weil Hawkins so viel langsamer war. Wenn ich im Auto gewesen wäre, hätten wir das Rennen gewinnen können. Nach dem Lauf hat sich Yorke für die Fahrerwahl mehr oder weniger bei mir entschuldigt."*

Für die Sportwagenszene gab es keine Zeit zum Verschnaufen, denn eine Woche später standen die 1000 Kilometer von Spa auf dem Programm. Jeder erwartete ein spannendes Rennen. Der Ford GT40 sollte auf der Highspeed-Strecke eigentlich einen Vorteil gegenüber den Porsche haben, gleichzeitig wurden der neue Matra und der Dreiliter-Prototyp von Ford von Rennen zu Rennen schneller. Dass Ickx in Spa starten konnte, obwohl das Rennen am selben Tag stattfand wie der GP von Monaco, hatte er Enzo Ferrari zu verdanken. Nach dem tödlichen Unfall von Lorenzo Bandini im Vorjahr schickte er diesmal keine Autos ins Fürstentum. Beim Training in Spa setzte Frank Gardner im Ford-Prototypen F3L P68 überraschend die Bestzeit:

For two weekends in a row, Ickx would race the GT40 in endurance racing. At the Nürburgring 1,000 Kilometres, Paul Hawkins partnered Jacky since John Wyer and David Yorke thought this would be a better pairing for the challenging twenty-two kilometre race track. Redman had had some spins – at Sebring and Monza – so Wyer thought that it would be an idea to change the drivers round. As was to be expected, Porsche took pole position, but Ickx surprised everybody by setting second fastest time in the Ford. At the Le Mans-type start, Ickx took time to secure his harness and left the grid late. He did a good job and kept in sight of the leaders for most of his stint. But then, Hawkins turned out to be almost twenty-five seconds a lap slower than Ickx and the team lost valuable ground to the Porsches. When Ickx took over for the final stint, the Ford was five minutes behind the leading Porsches and that was simply an impossible gap to close in the remaining distance. In the end, their Ford finished a respectable third with the other Wyer Ford in sixth place. It is quite likely that if Wyer had not made that change of driver pairing, things could have worked out better.

■ *Brian Redman: "I was surprised that Hawkins drove with Ickx at the Nürburgring. In the end it did not work out since Hawkins was so much slower. If I was in the car we could have won that race. After the event, Yorke more or less excused himself to me about his choice."*

There was no time to rest, since a week later was the 1,000 Kilometres of Spa. This would be an interesting race since the high-speed track would give the Fords some advantage over the Porsches, but the new Matra as well as the Ford three-litre prototypes were getting faster with every race. Jacky Ickx was able to drive at Spa even though on the same day there was to be the Monaco Grand Prix. The reason for this was that, following Lorenzo Bandini's fatal accident at that race a year earlier, Enzo Ferrari did not want to send any of his cars to the Principality. Back in Spa, it was the Alan Mann Ford F3L prototype that surprised everybody with Frank Gardner setting the fastest qualifying time. He was four seconds faster than Ickx and seven seconds faster than Willy Mairesse, who was driving a Belgian-entered GT40.

— 58 —

ADAC-1000-km-Rennen 1968, Nürburgring, John Horsman, Paul Hawkins & Jacky Ickx

1000 km de Spa-Francorchamps 1968, Ford GT40 n°33

Er war vier Sekunden schneller als Ickx und sieben schneller als Willy Mairesse in einem belgischen GT40. Ford hatte also die komplette erste Startreihe inne, dahinter folgten die Werks-Porsche.

Am Morgen vor dem 1000-Kilometer-Rennen fand im Beiprogramm ein Lauf für Tourenwagen statt, den Ickx in einem Ford Mustang bestritt. Er deklassierte die Konkurrenz und siegte mühelos. Viel wichtiger war jedoch: Er wusste ganz genau, wie die Bedingungen auf der Strecke waren. In der Nacht hatte es angefangen zu regnen und bei Nässe war es auf einem schwierigen Kurs wie Spa, der auch über öffentliche Straßen führte, enorm wichtig, die Verhältnisse zu kennen. Beim Sportwagenrennen setzte sich Gardner anfangs an die Spitze, nur um eine halbe Runde später auszurollen. Das Problem: Wasser war in die Elektrik eingedrungen und legte den Motor lahm. Ickx hatte nach der ersten Runde im strömenden Regen 39 (!) Sekunden Vorsprung auf den zweitplatzierten Mairesse im Ford. Als Redman das Wyer-Auto von Ickx übernahm, hatte er zwar einige „Big Moments", er behauptete aber die Führung. Nach 71 Runden unter den schlimmsten Bedingungen, die man sich für ein Highspeed-Rennen vorstellen kann, fuhren Ickx/Redman als Sieger ins Ziel – mit einem Schnitt von 197 km/h (trotz Boxenstopps). Mit einer Runde Rückstand folgte der beste Porsche.

Nach zwei Formel-2-Rennen in Crystal Palace und Hockenheim, die für Ickx mit einem Ausfall und einem fünften Platz endeten, standen drei Formel-1-Grand-Prix in Folge an. Den Anfang machte der Große Preis von Belgien in Spa.

■ **Derek Bell: „Shell sagte mir, dass Ferrari mich für den Test eines Formel-2-Autos haben wollte. Also haben sie einen Test in England angesetzt. Doch dann hat Jacky das Auto in Crystal Palace zerstört und ich musste nach Modena fliegen, um einen anderen Wagen zu fahren."**

Anders als beim Sportwagenrennen 14 Tage zuvor zeigte sich das Wetter in den Ardennen diesmal von seiner guten Seite. Und Ferrari war mit dem 312, der erstmals einen hohen Heckflügel hatte, vorn dabei. Amon holte die Pole, Ickx gesellte sich zu ihm in der ersten Reihe. Dazwischen stand nur der Matra von Stewart. Amon erwischte einen guten Start und ging in Führung, schied aber nach acht Runden mit einem Loch im Kühler aus. Ickx schaffte es ins Ziel und wurde mit Platz drei belohnt, nachdem Stewart wenige hundert Meter vor dem Ziel stehen geblieben war. Während des Rennens hatte Redman – Jackys Teamkollege bei Ford – einen schweren Unfall, als die Vorderradaufhängung kaputt ging. Der Engländer brach sich den Arm und musste einige Wochen pausieren.

Zwei Wochen später ging es mit dem Großen Preis der Niederlande weiter. Amon fuhr wieder auf die Pole, Ickx landete mit einer Sekunde Rückstand in Reihe drei. Amon konnte aus seiner Startposition wieder kein Kapital schlagen. Bei einsetzendem Regen wählte er die falschen Reifen, musste einen Boxenstopp einlegen und wurde Sechster. Ickx, dessen Ferrari 312 jetzt auch mit einem Heckflügel ausgestattet war, wurde Vierter. Schlechtes Wetter bestimmte auch das Geschehen beim GP von Frankreich in Rouen-Les Essarts. Im Qualifying war Ickx diesmal schneller als Amon und startete aus der ersten Reihe. Nachdem der berühmte „Toto" Roche das Rennen eröffnet hatte, stürmte Ickx – dank der Firestone-YB10-Regenreifen – direkt an die Spitze und behauptete sie bis ins Ziel. Ickx' Sieg wurde aber von einem tödlichen Unfall überschattet. Routinier Jo Schlesser hatte endlich die Chance bekommen, ein Formel-1-Auto zu bewegen, nachdem sich Honda-Stammpilot John Surtees geweigert hatte, das Experimentalauto mit Magnesiumkarosse zu fahren.

Thus there was an all Ford front row with the works Porsches right behind them.

Before the sportscar race there was a touring car race held in the morning in which Jacky Ickx drove a Ford Mustang. He easily outclassed the competition and won the race, but more importantly still, he knew the precise nature of the track conditions. It had started raining overnight and, in the wet, the Spa-Francorchamps circuit that comprises roads normally open to the public became very demanding and good knowledge of the track was essential. At the start of the 1,000-kilometre race, Gardner immediately took the lead and went away up the hill only to stop halfway round the first lap. The problem was rainwater getting into his electronics and stopping the engine. After the first lap in the pouring rain, Ickx had a thirty-nine second lead over the second-placed man, Mairesse, driving the yellow Ford. After Redman took over from Ickx, he kept the car in first position although he did have his moments. After seventy-one laps in some of the worst possible conditions for high speed racing, the team won the race having averaged 197 kph (123 mph), which included pit stops. At the end of the race, they had a one-lap advantage over the nearest Porsche.

After two Formula Two races, in Crystal Palace and at Hockenheim, in which Jacky could only score a fifth-place finish at the German race, there were three Grand Prix in a row beginning with the Belgium Grand Prix at Spa.

■ **Derek Bell: "I was told by Shell that Ferrari wanted me to test as a Formula Two driver. So they set up a test in England. But when Jacky shunted the car at Crystal Palace, I had to fly down to Modena to test in another one."**

Unlike at the sportscar race, the weather was fine in the Belgian Ardennes and Ferrari was back in full force. Amon took pole in a 312 that was for the first time sporting a high-slung rear aerofoil. Jacky joined him on the front row, with Stewart in the middle between them. Amon made a good start and took the lead only to retire after eight laps when a stone punctured his radiator. Ickx, however, did make it to the end of the race and was rewarded by being elevated to third place when Stewart stopped a few hundred yards before the finish line. During the race, Ickx's Ford team-mate, Brian Redman, had a big accident when his front suspension failed. The Englishman broke an arm and was out of racing for some weeks.

A fortnight later, at the Dutch GP, Amon again took pole and this time Ickx was a second slower in row three. Again, Amon did not capitalise on his starting position. A wrong tyre choice – it came on to rain during the race – forced him to pit and lose valuable time. He ended up sixth while Ickx, who now also had a rear aerofoil on his Ferrari 312, came in fourth. The French Grand Prix was held on the Rouen-Les Essarts track amid miserable weather conditions. During qualifying, Ickx was faster than Amon and consequently he started from the front row. As soon as the infamous Toto Roche dropped the French national flag, Ickx took the lead that – thanks to his Firestone YB10 rain tyres – he kept for the entire race. His victory was overshadowed by a fatal accident. The veteran French driver, Jo Schlesser, had finally got an opportunity to drive a Formula One car, albeit a very underdeveloped experimental Honda. The regular Honda driver, John Surtees, had refused to drive this car but Schlesser, who knew the circuit well, was more than willing to have a go. The Frenchman crashed on the third lap, the car caught fire and the high proportion of magnesium in its construction made it almost impossible to extinguish.

— 61 —

Coupes de Spa 1968, Spa-Francorchamps, Ford Mustang n°3

Grand Prix de Belgique 1968, Spa-Francorchamps

Grand Prix de Belgique 1968, Spa-Francorchamps, Ferrari 312

Grand Prix de Belgique 1968, Spa-Francorchamps, Ferrari 312 n°23

Grand Prix de France 1968, Rouen-Les-Essarts, Ferrari 312

Schlesser, der die Strecke von Rouen sehr gut kannte, willigte ein, den RA302 zu fahren. Der Franzose verunfallte jedoch in der dritten Runde, wobei der Wagen Feuer fing und durch den hohen Magnesiumanteil komplett ausbrannte.

■ *Bernard Cahier: „Ickx hatte immer ein gutes Gefühl für das Wetter. In Rouen war er der einzige, der richtige Regenreifen aufzog. Das zahlte sich aus."*

Die Formel-1-Saison war jetzt zur Hälfte rum. Graham Hill führte die WM-Tabelle an, Jacky Ickx lag auf Platz drei.

Spannend ging es auch in der Markenmeisterschaft für Sportwagen zur Sache. Von den ersten sieben Rennen hatte Porsche vier und Ford drei gewonnen. Und jetzt ging es nach Watkins Glen im Bundesstaat New York. Wegen seines Armbruchs wurde Redman in den USA von Lucien Bianchi vertreten. Der routinierte Belgier war ein alter Freund von John Wyer und hatte einen guten Ruf als Rallye- und Rennfahrer. Im Training war der Ford von Ickx/Bianchi nur etwas langsamer als der schnellste Porsche, es sah also gut aus. Von Platz zwei aus gestartet, übernahm Ickx schon bald die Führung. Hawkins zeigte im zweiten Gulf-Ford einige gute Überholmanöver und eroberte Platz zwei. Die Porsche wurden durch kleinere Zwischenfälle zurückgeworfen und versuchten sich danach mit wilden Fahrerwechseln zu verbessern, aber es nützte nichts. Nach sechs Stunden siegte das belgische JWA-Ford-Duo vor dem Schwesterauto von Hawkins und Hobbs.

■ *David Hobbs: „Wir führten das Rennen in Watkins Glen an, Ickx war Zweiter. Dann schrieb uns David Yorke vor, langsamer zu fahren und Ickx gewinnen zu lassen. Ich war total sauer. Die Gulf-Ford waren Erster und Zweiter, warum sollten wir die Plätze tauschen? In der Markenmeisterschaft machte das punktemäßig keinen Unterschied!"*

Für John Wyer war es ein tolles Ergebnis: Mit je vier Siegen lagen Ford und Porsche in der Markenmeisterschaft jetzt gleichauf. Als Nächstes ging es nach Zeltweg, wo wegen der kurzen Distanz von 500 Kilometern nur halbe Punkte vergeben wurden. Hawkins fuhr in Österreich den einzigen JWA-Ford alleine und wurde hinter zwei Porsche Dritter. Die Titelentscheidung in der Markenmeisterschaft 1968 musste also beim Saisonfinale fallen, bei den 24 Stunden von Le Mans. Die fanden wegen der politischen Unruhen in Frankreich aber erst Ende September statt. Die Terminverschiebung vom Hochsommer musste sich beim Wetter nicht unbedingt bemerkbar machen, sie bedeutete aber sicherlich mehr Dunkelheit für die Piloten. Für Ickx standen im Sommer zunächst drei Formel-1-Rennen im Kalender: die Großen Preise von Großbritannien und Deutschland sowie der Gold Cup in Oulton Park, der nicht zur WM zählte. Beim Britischen Grand Prix in Brands Hatch erlebte Ferrari ein großartiges Wochenende. Amon wurde Zweiter, Ickx Dritter. Der Sieg ging überraschend an Jo Siffert im privat eingesetzten Lotus 49 von Rob Walker. Mit diesem Ergebnis verbesserte sich Ickx in der Formel-1-Weltmeisterschaft auf die zweite Position. Zwei Wochen später stellte Ickx seinen Ferrari auf dem Nürburgring sogar auf die Pole – und das im Regen! Auf der nassen Piste waren die Rundenzeiten etwa eine Minute langsamer als ein Jahr zuvor. Das Rennen selbst fand bei Regen und dichtem Nebel statt und war sehr gefährlich. Ickx hatte ein paar kleinere Probleme – einmal steuerte er die Box an, um seine beschlagene Brille zu wechseln –, sodass er das Ziel auf dem vierten Platz erreichte.

■ *Bernard Cahier: "Ickx always had a good feeling for the weather since he was the only driver to choose full wets in Rouen, and it paid off."*

The Formula One season was now at the halfway point and Graham Hill was leading with Jacky Ickx third.

The sportscar championship was exciting as ever and the next race was scheduled for the Watkins Glen track in upstate New York. After seven races, Porsche had four wins and Ford three. Due to his broken arm, Redman could not drive in America, so Lucien Bianchi stepped in alongside Ickx. The experienced Belgian sportscar driver had long been a friend of John Wyer and had a good reputation in rallies and races. In practice, their Ford was only marginally slower than the fastest Porsche and the prospects looked favourable. Ickx took the start from the second position and soon led the race. In the other Ford, Hawkins made some great passes and joined the head of the field. A number of small incidents slowed the Porsches and switching drivers between cars to try and gain an advantage did not work out well for the Germans. After six hours, the Belgian couple won the race closely followed by the other JWA Ford crewed by Paul Hawkins and David Hobbs.

■ *David Hobbs: "We were leading the Watkins Glen race with Ickx second. Then David Yorke told us to slow down and let Ickx win. I was totally annoyed, the Gulf Fords were first and second so why let us change position. It would not make any difference in the points for the manufacturers championship."*

It was a great result and now Ford and Porsche were neck-and-neck in the championship. The next championship race on the calendar was held in Austria at Zeltweg, but because of its short distance compared with the other races, only half points were awarded. Hawkins drove solo in the only Ford sent there and was rewarded by third place behind two Porsches. Thus it would be the final race that would decide the 1968 sportscar championship and there were still two months before that event, the 24 Hours of Le Mans, would take place. The race was to be held in late September thanks to the political unrest in France that had occurred in spring. An interesting change from its normal date in mid-summer since, though the weather would probably be all right, the darkness would come earlier on the Saturday night.

For Ickx that summer there were three Formula One races in which he was due to compete. These were the British and German Grands Prix and the non-championship Gold Cup race at Oulton Park. Ferrari had a great race at Brands Hatch with Amon finishing second and Ickx third. The winner however was Jo Siffert, thus giving private entrant Rob Walker his first win for seven years. With this result, Ickx now moved up into second position in the Formula One World Championship rankings. At the Nürburgring, two weeks later, Ickx finally got his Ferrari on pole, which was a remarkable achievement as he set his time in the rain. The wet track had resulted in the qualifying times being over a minute slower than at the same time the year before. In the race too, it rained and a dense fog made the event very dangerous. Jacky Ickx finished fourth after experiencing a few problems of which one of the most serious was that, early on, he had to make a pit stop to replace his goggles as they were misting up. A fourth place under these circumstances was the best result he could manage. At the Gold Cup race, Ickx had to retire with ignition problems and, as at the Nürburgring, Stewart won again.

Grote Prijs van Nederland 1968, Zandvoort, Ferrari 312

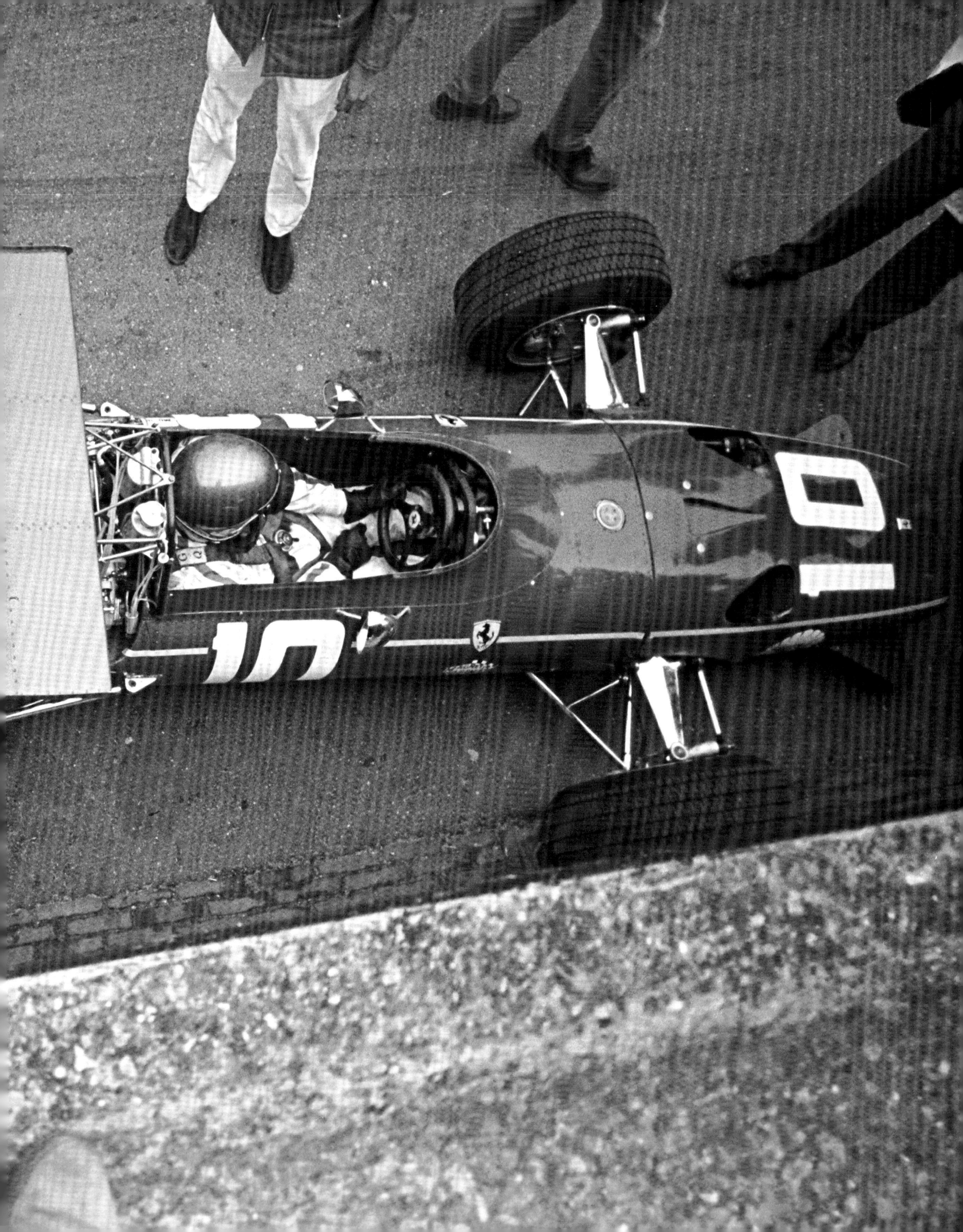
10

Unter diesen Umständen war mehr einfach nicht drin. Beim Gold Cup schied der Belgier mit Zündungsproblemen aus – und Stewart fuhr wie am Nürburgring zum Sieg.

Beim Gran Premio del Mediterraneo auf Sizilien ging Ferrari gleich mit vier Formel-2-Autos an den Start. Neben Ickx saßen die Italiener Ernesto Brambilla und Mario Casoni sowie der Engländer Derek Bell in den Dino 166 V6. Wie so oft gewann Jochen Rindt das Rennen. Brambilla wurde Dritter, Bell Fünfter und Ickx Sechster. Nach den zuletzt so guten Formel-1-Ergebnissen reisten Ickx, Ferrari und die Tifosi voller Hoffnung zum Großen Preis von Italien nach Monza, wo Derek Bell das Ferrari-Aufgebot verstärkte. Zur Freude der Fans startete Amon aus der ersten Reihe, das war aber der einzige Lichtblick. Im Rennen schied Bell durch Probleme mit der Benzinzufuhr nach fünf Runden aus, Amon verabschiedete sich nach neun Umläufen in die Bäume, blieb aber zum Glück unverletzt. Ickx konnte nie in den Kampf um den Sieg eingreifen, lag aber bis kurz vor Schluss auf Kurs zu Platz zwei hinter Denis Hulme im McLaren. Wenige hundert Meter vor dem Ziel begann der Ferrari-Motor jedoch zu stottern, sodass Johnny Servoz-Gavin im Matra MS10 noch an Ickx vorbeiziehen konnte. So musste sich der Belgier mit Platz drei begnügen. Das Fahrerlager platzte aus allen Nähten, weil die US-Stars Mario Andretti und Bobby Unser in Monza waren, um für Lotus bzw. BRM zu fahren. Der Automobil Club d'Italia gab den Amerikanern aber keine Starterlaubnis, weil diese nach dem Freitagstraining in die USA zurückflogen, um dort am Samstag ein Rennen zu bestreiten, ehe sie am Sonntag wieder nach Italien zurückkehrten. Nach dem Regelwerk der Formel 1 war es verboten, innerhalb von 24 Stunden vor einem Grand Prix an einem anderen Rennen teilzunehmen, daher wurden sie disqualifiziert.

Beim Großen Preis von Kanada starben alle Hoffnungen auf einen möglichen Formel-1-Weltmeistertitel von Jacky Ickx schon beim Training. Vor einer Highspeed-Kurve blieb das Gas stecken und Ickx flog über eine Böschung in einen Zaun. Der Ferrari-Pilot kam mit einem Beinbruch davon, seine Sicherheitsgurte verhinderten Schlimmeres. Damit war Ickx allerdings mehr als einen Monat außer Gefecht gesetzt. Er verpasste die Grands Prix von Kanada und den USA sowie die 24 Stunden von Le Mans.

■ **Jacky Ickx: „Während der Trainingssitzungen bin ich mehrmals an die Box gefahren und habe Borsari, meinem Chefingenieur, gesagt, dass etwas nicht stimmt. Er sagte jedes Mal, dass alles in Ordnung sei. Naja, das war es nicht."**

Da Redman und Ickx beide verletzungsbedingt für Le Mans ausfielen, heuerte John Wyer für den Klassiker neben Lucien Bianchi auch Pedro Rodriguez an. Die beiden Routiniers waren ihr Geld wahrlich wert: Sie siegten souverän vor den Porsche und Alfa Romeo und sicherten Ford dadurch die Krone in der Internationalen Markenmeisterschaft mit drei Punkten Vorsprung auf Porsche.

Anfang November bestritt Ickx sein erstes Rennen nach der Verletzungspause. Beim GP von Mexiko fuhr Jacky unter Schmerzen und mit Stahlstiften im Unterschenkel oberhalb des Knöchels. Die Qualifikation beendete er auf Platz 15, beim Rennen war schon nach drei Runden Feierabend, als der Ferrari auf halber Strecke mit Zündungsproblemen strandete. Dort musste der Belgier das ganze Rennen ausharren, weil er wegen seines verletzten Beins nicht an die Box zurückgehen konnte. Graham Hill siegte und feierte seinen zweiten F1-Titel nach 1962. Ickx landete in der Endabrechnung auf Rang vier. Für Hill und das leidgeplagte Lotus-Team, das im April den Tod von Jim Clark hinnehmen musste, war es ein sehr emotionaler Moment.

Ferrari sent no less than four Formula Two cars to the island of Sicily for the Mediterranean Grand Prix at Enna. Joining Ickx in the team were Ernesto Brambilla from Monza, another Italian, Mario Casoni, and Englishman Derek Bell. As so often Jochen Rindt won the race with Brambilla third, Bell fifth and Ickx sixth. With his good results this summer, Ickx – and certainly all the Italian fans – had high hopes for him and Ferrari at the Italian Grand Prix at Monza where Derek Bell had now joined the Ferrari regulars. To everyone's delight, Amon would start from the front row but that was as good as it got. In the race, Bell was out after five laps with fuel problems while Amon could only manage a total of nine laps before crashing into the trees from which he fortunately emerged unhurt. Ickx was never in contention for the lead but it did look as though he would finish second behind Denny Hulme's McLaren. But with only a few hundred metres to go, his Ferrari engine sputtered and Johnny Servoz-Gavin in the Matra MS10 overtook him. Thus Ickx had to be content with third. The Monza paddock had been buzzing with the possibility of seeing Mario Andretti and Bobby Unser driving in the Grand Prix. The two American stars were down to drive for Lotus and BRM, only to see their participation being refused by the Italian Automobile Club. The reason given was that, after practice on Friday, they flew back to America to race there on Saturday and then be back on Sunday for the Grand Prix. But the regulations forbade a driver to take part in any other race within the twenty-four hours preceding a grand prix.

All hopes of a possible Ferrari World Championship in Formula One vanished when Ickx crashed during practice for the Canadian Grand Prix. The throttle stuck open entering a high-speed corner and Ickx charged over a bank and into a wire fence. His safety harness saved him from serious harm and he escaped with a fractured leg. But this meant that he was out of racing for more than a month, missing the US Grand Prix and the 24 Hours of Le Mans.

■ **Jacky Ickx: "During practice, I came into the pits several times to tell Borsari, my chief engineer, that something was wrong. And each time he said it was OK. Well, it was not."**

With both Redman and Ickx injured and unable to race at Le Mans, Wyer asked Pedro Rodriguez to join Lucien Bianchi for this important race. These two experienced drivers did for what they were paid to do and won the race comfortably ahead of the Porsches and Alfa Romeos. This result was enough to crown Ford as World Champion Manufacturer by three points from Porsche.

Ickx was back behind the wheel in early November to race at the Mexican Grand Prix, but – still in pain and with steel pins inserted above his ankle – he did not enjoy the event. His qualifying time only put him fifteenth on the starting grid and his race was over after only three laps when the Ferrari coasted to a halt with ignition problems. The car stopped halfway round the circuit and Ickx was forced to wait with it until the race was over since he could not walk back to the pits because of his injured leg. Graham Hill won the event and thus secured his second World Championship title while Ickx ended up fourth in the final Formula One standings. For Hill and the Lotus team it was an emotional result after having lost Jim Clark in April.

To wrap up the season, Jacky Ickx joined David Hobbs in the old 1967 Mirage M1 for the 9 Hours of Kyalami in South Africa. Like the year before, Ickx won this event and with a convincing twelve-lap margin over Tony Dean/Basil van Rooyen's Dino. Hawkins in his own Ferrari was third and Brian Redman, now fully recovered from his accident at Spa, came fourth in a Chevron.

Großer Preis von Deutschland 1968, Nürburgring

Großer Preis von Deutschland 1968, Nürburgring

Großer Preis von Deutschland 1968, Nürburgring, Franco Gozzi (Ferrari Rennleiter / Ferrari sporting director) & Jacky Ickx

Zum Abschluss des Jahres nahm Ickx zusammen mit David Hobbs im alten 1967er-Mirage-M1 an den 9 Stunden von Kyalami teil. Wie im Vorjahr gewann Ickx souverän, im Ziel hatte er 12 Runden Vorsprung auf den Ferrari Dino von Tony Dean/Basil van Rooyen. Hawkins wurde in einem weiteren Ferrari Dritter und Redman, der nach seinem Unfall in Spa wieder vollständig genesen war, im Chevron Vierter.

So ging die Saison 1968 zu Ende. Es war ein sehr bitteres Jahr für den Motorsport mit einigen tragischen Verlusten. Jim Clark, Ludovico Scarfiotti, Jo Schlesser, Leo Cella, Chris Lambert und Mike Spence hatten ihre Passion mit dem Leben bezahlt. Chris Irwin und Willy Mairesse beendeten ihre Karriere nach schweren Unfällen am Nürburgring bzw. in Le Mans, und auch Redman und Ickx hatten sich bei heftigen Unfällen verletzt.

Im Laufe der 1968er-Saison nahm Jacky Ickx an 28 Rennen teil, von denen er sechs gewann. Sein Formel-1-Vertrag bei Ferrari wurde nicht verlängert, allerdings baute die Scuderia einen neuen Sportwagen und wollte Ickx dafür gewinnen. Gleichzeitig bemühte sich John Wyer um eine Verlängerung des Vertrags. Ickx empfand die Kombination Wyer/Ford als bessere Option. Und was die Formel 1 anging, so kam der Belgier im Team von Jack Brabham unter, welches jetzt auch von Gulf Oil gesponsert wurde.

The 1968 season was finally over. It had been a tough year for motor sport with a great deal of sadness to bear. The deaths of Jim Clark, Ludovico Scarfiotti, Jo Schlesser, Leo Cella, Chris Lambert and Mike Spence had taken a heavy toll on the sport. In addition, there were the severe accidents of Redman and Ickx plus the career ending accidents of Chris Irwin at the Nürburgring and Willy Mairesse at Le Mans.

In the 1968 season, Jacky Ickx did twenty-eight races of which he won six. For 1969, his contract with Ferrari was not extended. Ickx wanted to drive again for John Wyer, while Ferrari was building a new sportscar and wanted Ickx to drive that as well. But for Ickx, the Ford seemed to be the best option. For Formula One, he would drive alongside Jack Brabham in his Formula One team who got additional sponsorship from Gulf Oil.

Gran Premio d'Italia 1968, Monza.

1969

Ickx schreibt Geschichte in le Mans
Making history at Le Mans

Für viele Top-Rennfahrer begann die Saison 1969 im Schweizer Skiort Villars-sur-Ollon. Der französische Journalist Bernard Cahier veranstaltete hier den Grand Prix of the Snow – ein Spaß-Wochenende mit Veranstaltungen auf den Skipisten und auf dem Eishockeyfeld. Es gab keine Sieger oder Preise, es ging einfach nur darum, eine schöne Zeit zu verbringen, ehe die neue Rennsportsaison anfing.

Da die Formel 1 erst im März loslegte, begann das neue Jahr für Jacky Ickx mit den 24 Stunden von Daytona. John Wyer hatte ihn gebeten, weiterhin die von Gulf gesponserten Ford GT40 zu fahren. Und das tat er auch. Brian Redman kehrte Ford dagegen den Rücken und heuerte beim Erzrivalen Porsche an. Seinen Platz an der Seite von Ickx nahm der britische Formel-1-Fahrer Jackie Oliver ein. Im Qualifying von Daytona erzielten Ickx/Oliver nur die achte Zeit – ein Vorzeichen, dass sich die Karriere des GT40 langsam dem Ende neigte. Es war nur der Arbeit von JWA zu verdanken, dass das Auto überhaupt noch so konkurrenzfähig war. Im Rennen fielen die neuen Dreiliter-Porsche mit Motorschäden aus, sodass Ford nach vorsichtigem Beginn in Führung ging. Doch nach zwei Dritteln der Distanz baute Ickx in Turn One einen Unfall.

The 1969 motor racing season started very pleasantly for many of the top drivers in Villars-sur-Ollon in Switzerland. The French journalist, Bernard Cahier, had organised an event that he titled the 'Grand Prix of the Snow' that was basically a weekend of fun on the ski slopes and at the ice hockey rink. There were no prizes to be won since the whole idea was just to have a relaxing weekend before the racing season got under way.

With the Formula One season starting in March, Jacky Ickx's first race of the year was the 24 Hours of Daytona. John Wyer had asked him to stay with his Gulf Oil-supported team to drive in their Ford GT40s. Ickx's former co-driver, Brian Redman, had left the Ford squad and gone to their main competitor, Porsche, and he was replaced by British Formula One driver, Jackie Oliver. In qualifying, their Gulf Ford had only managed to post the eighth fastest time. It was clear that the big Ford was getting towards the end of its racing career and it was only the fact that it was being run by JWA that kept it competitive. After a careful start, the Ford team eventually got in the lead after all the new three-litre Porsches retired with engine problems. But after completing two-thirds of the race distance, Ickx crashed at Turn One.

24 Hours of Daytona 1969, Daytona Beach, Ford GT40 n°1

— 74 —

BRDC International Trophy 1969, Silverstone, Brabham BT26 - Ford

So wurde aus einem sicher geglaubten Sieg eine Niederlage. Nach dem Rennen blieb der Belgier in Florida, wo er in einem von Holman & Moody aufgebauten Mercury Cyclone die berühmten Daytona 500 bestreiten durfte. Beim Training zum Nascar-Rennen krachte Ickx in Turn Four in eine Mauer und zerstörte das Stockcar so stark, dass es zum Rennen nicht rechtzeitig repariert worden konnte.

■ *David Hobbs: „Mike Hailwood mochte die Einstellung von Ickx nicht – besonders, weil David Yorke den jungen Belgier schützte. Hailwood hatte schon zehn WM-Titel errungen und einen gewissen Status. Er dachte sich: Wer ist dieses kleine arrogante Kind?"*

Am 1. März bestritt Ickx in Kyalami sein erstes F1-Rennen für Brabham. In der Quali war er mehr als drei Sekunden langsamer als Teamchef Jack Brabham und startete daher aus Reihe fünf. Bei seinem Brabham BT26 handelte es sich prinzipiell um das 1968er-Chassis, das jetzt nicht mehr mit einem Repco-Motor, sondern mit einem Ford-Cosworth V8 ausgestattet war. Beide Brabham hatten vorn und hinten große Spoiler, die aber zu zerbrechlich waren und während des Rennens brachen. Beim Saisonauftakt sah kein Brabham das Ziel. Die Europa-Saison begann wie üblich mit dem Race of Champions in Brands Hatch. Obwohl das Rennen nicht der WM angehörte, kamen 14 F1-Autos zusammen. Ickx war in der Quali erneut langsamer als sein Teamchef und musste nach 23 Runden wegen eines fehlerhaften Benzindosiersystems aufgeben. Zwei Wochen später zur International Trophy in Silverstone erhielten die Brabham ein kleines Update, welches sich auszahlte. Ickx und Brabham starteten aus der ersten Reihe. Brabham siegte, Ickx wurde Vierter.

This was another defeat snatched from the jaws of victory. After the race, the Belgian stayed in Florida since he was invited to drive a Holman & Moody-prepared Mercury Cyclone in the famous Daytona 500 Nascar race. However in practice, he drove the stock car into the wall at Turn Four and demolished the big American car, putting it beyond immediate repair and thus he was not able not take part in the race.

■ *David Hobbs: "Mike Hailwood did not like Ickx's attitude. Especially as David Yorke was protecting the young Belgian driver. Hailwood already had ten world championships and had achieved a status, so who was this arrogant little kid?"*

On March 1st at Kyalami in South Africa, Jacky Ickx drove his first Formula One race of the new season in a Brabham. In qualifying, he was over three seconds slower than his team boss, Jack Brabham, and started from the fifth row. The Brabham BT26 was basically the same chassis as in 1968, but it now had a Ford Cosworth V8 engine rather than the Repco motor. Both of their cars had big spoilers front and rear, but these turned out to be too fragile. They broke during the race and both drivers were eventually forced to retire. Back in Europe, the Formula One season kicked off at Brands Hatch with the Race of Champions. Although a non-championship race, twelve cars took the start. Again Ickx was out-qualified by his team boss and then had to retire after twenty-three laps due to a faulty fuel metering unit. Two weeks later, at the Daily Express meeting at Silverstone, the cars were slightly updated and both Ickx and Brabham started from the front row. Brabham won the race with Ickx coming in fourth.

Zwischen diesen beiden F1-Rennen nahmen Ickx und Oliver an den 12 Stunden von Sebring teil, wo sich Chris Amon im neuen Ferrari 312P die Pole sicherte. Der Gulf-Ford von Ickx/Oliver landete in der Startaufstellung trotz des brandneuen AAR-Motors von Dan Gurney nur auf Platz zwölf. Der schlechte Fahrbahnbelag auf dem Flugplatz von Sebring und die große Anzahl an Fahrzeugen sorgten für viele Probleme. Der Ferrari von Amon und Mario Andretti lag lange Zeit in Führung, überhitzte aber und wurde gegen Ende erheblich langsamer. Dadurch konnte Ickx die Lücke schließen und kurz vor Schluss am roten Ferrari vorbeiziehen und so den Sieg holen. Im englischen Brands Hatch nahmen Ickx und Oliver dann erstmals ein Rennen im neuen Mirage M2 mit Dreiliter-BRM-Motor in Angriff. Im Training zu den BOAC 500 platzierte Ickx den Wagen auf Platz elf – hinter einigen Porsche und Lola, dem neuen Ferrari sowie zwei Ford-F3L-Prototypen. Ickx arbeitete sich auf die achte Position vor, ehe er mit gebrochener Antriebswelle aufgeben musste. Da der Mirage M2-BRM offensichtlich noch nicht konkurrenzfähig war, ließ JWA die 1000 Kilometer von Monza aus. Das eröffnete Ickx die Möglichkeit, im belgischen Zolder einen Ford Escort TC zu fahren. In der Klasse über 1,3 Liter qualifizierte sich Ickx auf Platz drei hinter den Porsche von Toine Hezemans und Gijs van Lennep. Im Rennen schied Ickx nach sieben Runden durch Getriebeschaden aus.

▪ *Jackie Oliver: „Ickx war einer der schwierigsten Teamkollegen, die ich je hatte. Ickx war definitiv die Nummer eins im Team. Ich war zufrieden damit, ich wollte keine Probleme haben. Nach der 1969er-Saison war ich aber so sauer, dass ich keine Langstreckenrennen mehr fahren wollte."*

Als nächstes stand der Große Preis von Spanien an, der diesmal im Montjuïc Park von Barcelona ausgetragen wurde. 14 Autos gingen an den Start, von denen acht ausfielen. Ickx blieb zwar sieben Runden vor Schluss mit Aufhängungsschaden liegen, wurde aber als Sechster gewertet und holte damit seinen ersten WM-Punkt. Der Sieg ging an Jackie Stewart.

In between these two Formula One races, Ickx and Oliver drove in the 12-hour sportscar race at Sebring. Chris Amon achieved the fastest qualifying time with the new Ferrari 312P spyder and got pole position. The Ickx/Oliver Ford, although with a brand new AAR engine built by Dan Gurney, could only manage twelfth fastest. The surface of the old airport of Sebring and the big number of slow cars allowed in the race caused many problems for the competitors. Although it was overheating, the Ferrari kept going, but near the end both Mario Andretti and Amon slowed considerably. This allowed Ickx to close the gap and just before the end, the Ford passed the red Ferrari and took the victory. Back in England, Ickx and Oliver had their first race in the new three-litre Mirage M2 BRM sportscar in the BOAC 500 at Brands Hatch. Ickx qualified the car eleventh behind a number of Porsches, the new Ferrari, some Lolas and two of the Alan Mann Ford prototypes. Ickx got to eighth position but then had to retire with a broken drive shaft. Since the JWA team did not have the Mirage BRM running competitively yet, they skipped the 1,000 Kilometres of Monza. This gave Ickx the opportunity to drive a Ford Escort TC at Zolder in Belgium. Running in the over 1.3-litre class, Ickx qualified third behind the two Porsches of Toine Hezemans and Gijs van Lennep. But then in the race Ickx had to retire after seven laps when the gearbox failed.

▪ *Jackie Oliver: "Ickx was one of the most difficult teammates I ever had. Ickx was definitely the number one in the team. But I was happy about that, I did not want any problems. After the 1969 season, I did not want to do any more endurance racing, I was totally pissed off."*

Next on the calendar was the Spanish Grand Prix, this time held at Montjuïc Park in Barcelona. With only fourteen cars at the start and with eight retirements, Ickx got his first championship point by finishing sixth, although his race ended seven laps from the finish due to suspension failure. Jackie Stewart survived and won the race.

Sebring 12-Hour Endurance Race 1969, Sebring, Ford GT40

BOAC 500m 1969, Brands Hatch, Mirage M2/300 - BRM

76

BOAC 500m 1969, Brands Hatch, Mirage M2/300 - BRM

Gran Premio de España 1969, Montjuïc,
Brabham BT26 - Ford n°4

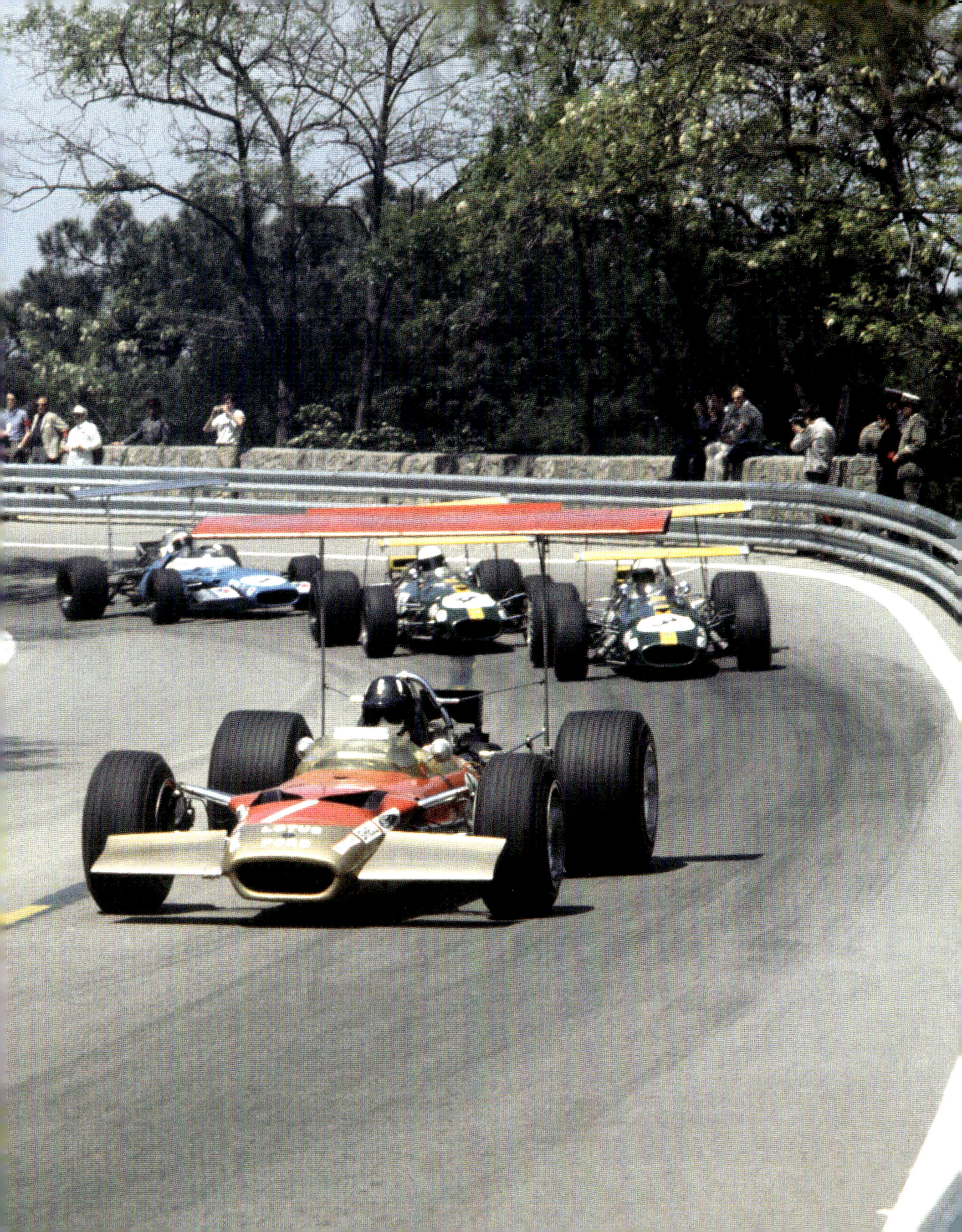
LOTUS
FORD

24 Heures du Mans 1969, Jacky & Catherine

Bei den 1000-Kilometer-Rennen in Spa und am Nürburgring war das JWA-Team wieder am Start. In Belgien sah es zunächst gut aus. Ickx nahm das Rennen von Platz zwei aus in Angriff, doch nach zehn Runden streikte die Benzinpumpe und Ickx schied aus. Auch in der Eifel kam der Mirage nicht ins Ziel. Mit Oliver am Steuer brach nach wenigen Runden die Aufhängung. Es sollte der letzte Einsatz des Mirage M2 unter der Leitung von Wyer sein. Direkt nach dem Rennen verkaufte er die Autos an Jo Siffert. In Spa konnte sich Ickx zumindest mit einem Sieg in einem von Alan Mann Racing vorbereiteten Ford Falcon bei einem Tourenwagenrennen trösten, das samstags vor den 1000 Kilometern stattfand.

Da die F1-Fahrer wegen der Instabilität der hohen Flügel immer größere Sicherheitsbedenken hatten, schritt die FIA ein und verbot sie nach dem ersten Training zum Monaco-GP. Auch dieses Rennen endete für Ickx vorzeitig. Zur Halbzeit lag der Belgier auf Platz zwei, als die Aufhängung des Brabham brach. Beim ersten F2-Lauf im Brabham BT23C hatte er mehr Glück. In Zolder beendete er beide Heats auf Platz zwei und wurde so im Gesamt als Zweiter gewertet. Der Sieg ging an Jochen Rindt. An jenem Wochenende fuhr Jacky erstmals für das kleine englische Team von Frank Williams.

Bei den 24 Stunden von Le Mans setzte Wyer auf die Zuverlässigkeit des Ford GT40. Ickx und Oliver saßen im Auto mit der Chassisnummer 1075. Dieser GT40 hatte im März in Sebring (Ickx/Oliver) und 1968 in Le Mans (Lucien Bianchi/Pedro Rodriguez) gewonnen. Die einzigen Unterschiede zum Vorjahr bestanden im neuen Motor von AAR/Gurney und in breiteren Reifen an der Hinterachse. Im Qualifying hatte der GT40 den neuen Porsche 917 nichts entgegenzusetzen. Die beiden werkseingesetzten 917 LH waren in den Trainings- und Qualifikationssitzungen mit Abstand am schnellsten. Ickx gelang im GT40 nur die 13. Zeit. Doch das Rennen von Le Mans ist lang und Zuverlässigkeit ein entscheidender Faktor. Dass ein 24-Stunden-Rennen nicht in der ersten Runde entschieden wird, dachte sich auch Jacky Ickx, als er beim Start gemächlich zu seinem Auto ging, während die anderen Piloten von der linken Straßenseite los spurteten. Ickx hatte sein Auto gerade erst erreicht, da waren die anderen Wagen schon im Vorwärtsgang und fuhren den Belgier fast über den Haufen. Die Gurte schnallten sie erst im Laufe der ersten Runde fest, was häufig zu schweren Unfällen führte. Im Vorjahr verunfallte Willy Mairesse beim Anlegen seines Gurts. Diesmal baute John Woolfe in Maison Blanche einen Crash, bei dem er aus seinem Porsche 917 geschleudert wurde und verstarb.

The JWA team was back at both Spa and the Nürburgring for the 1,000-kilometre races. Spa looked promising when Ickx started the race from the front row, but after ten laps the fuel pump of the Mirage failed and Ickx had to retire. At the Nürburgring, the team did not finish either. After a few laps, the suspension broke while Oliver was behind the wheel. This was the last race of the Mirage M2 for JWA and the cars were sold to Jo Siffert right after the race. There was however success for Ickx as he easily won the touring car race in an Alan Mann Ford Falcon at Spa on the Saturday before the 1,000-kilometre event.

Since the Formula One drivers were more and more concerned about the safety of their cars due to the instability of the large wings, the FIA outlawed them right after the first practice of the Monaco Grand Prix. In this race, once again Ickx did not finish. While lying second at halfway, the suspension of his Brabham broke. However, he had more success at Zolder when he finished second in his first Formula Two race of the season. In both heats, he finished second behind – as usual – Jochen Rindt. It was Jacky's first event driving a Brabham BT23C for the small English team of Frank Williams.

For the 24 Hours of Le Mans, Wyer chose to count on the reliability of the Ford GT40s. Ickx drove with Oliver in the Sebring winning car, the '1075'. This was also the car that Lucien Bianchi and Pedro Rodriguez had driven to victory in Le Mans the previous year. The only difference from 1968 was the AAR/Gurney engine and wider rear wheel rims. In practice, the Ford GT40 was no match for the new Porsche 917s. The team from Zuffenhausen had entered two works cars and they were by far the fastest in practice and qualifying. Ickx's GT40 could only manage to be thirteenth fastest. But the Le Mans race is a long one and reliability is an important issue. With the thought in mind that the race cannot be won in the first lap and remembering Willy Mairesse's accident the year before – the Belgian driver crashed heavily when trying to put on his safety harness – Jacky Ickx walked to his car on the start grid rather than ran. He barely made it to his car as the first cars were streaming away and almost collected him. The whole question of Le Mans starts where the drivers struggle into their safety belt during the first lap was thrown into sharp relief at this race. The reason was simply that on the first lap John Woolfe crashed his Porsche 917 at Maison Blanche, was thrown out of his car and died instantly.

24 Heures du Mans 1969

24 Heures du Mans 1969

24 Heures du Mans 1969

24 Heures du Mans 1969, Ford GT40

Nach der ersten Stunde lag Ickx auf Platz 15 – und damit voll im Zeitplan, den sich das Team gesteckt hatte. Die Porsche von Siffert (908), Gerhard Mitter (908) und Vic Elford (917) gingen an der Spitze ein zu hohes Tempo. Der GT40 lief dagegen wie ein Uhrwerk, sodass Ickx und Oliver am Sonntagmorgen schon auf Platz drei lagen. Als Elfords 917 ausschied, lag der Ford von Ickx knapp vor dem verbliebenen Porsche 908 von Hans Herrmann und Gérard Larrousse. Die letzten Stunden sollten zu einem legendären Zweikampf werden, den Ickx knapp für sich entschied. Nach 24 Stunden hatte der Belgier gerade einmal 100 Meter Vorsprung, doch das reichte für den vierten Ford-Sieg in Serie.

■ *John Horsman: „Beim letzten Boxenstopp haben wir Ickx im Auto gelassen. Er hatte einen guten Rhythmus. Das war der winzige Vorteil gegenüber den Porsche."*

Eine Woche später fuhr Ickx den Brabham beim Großen Preis der Niederlande auf den fünften Platz. Beim Formel-2-Rennen in Reims schied er dagegen aus. Dafür lief es beim Frankreich-GP in Clermont-Ferrand wieder besser. Auf dem „kleinen Nürburgring" wäre Ickx um ein Haar Zweiter hinter Stewart geworden, wenn er in der letzten Runde keinen Fehler begangen hätte, durch den Jean-Pierre Beltoise an ihm vorbeiziehen konnte.

After the first hour, Ickx was in fifteenth position, running to a schedule planned by the team. The Porsches were going way too fast and Siffert (908), Gerhard Mitter (908) and Vic Elford (917) were the ones setting the pace at the front. The GT40 ran flawlessly and by Sunday morning Ickx and Oliver were lying third. When the Elford 917 retired, Ickx took the lead marginally ahead of the remaining Porsche 908 of Hans Herrmann and Gérard Larrousse. The final hours of the race turned out to be a legendary battle between the two cars in which Ickx just prevailed. At the finish, he had a hundred metres advantage after 24 hours of racing. It was the fourth Ford victory at Le Mans in as many years.

■ *John Horsman: "At the last pit stop, we left Ickx in the car. He was in a good rhythm. That gave us just that little advantage over Porsche."*

A week later Ickx drove his Brabham to fifth place at the Dutch Grand Prix in Zandvoort. During the following weeks, he drove at Reims in the Formula Two race, where he retired, and in the French GP at Clermont-Ferrand. At this 'Little Nürburgring' of a circuit, Ickx finished third after an error by him on the last lap had given Jean-Pierre Beltoise an opportunity to get through and take second behind Stewart.

24 Heures du Mans 1969, Jackie Oliver & Jacky Ickx

— 85 —

SOLEX
SOLEXINE
ANTAR
molygraphite
AUTO-LITE BATTERIES
GENERAL - INCENDIE
elf
Castrol
DUNLOP
64

24 Heures du Mans 1969

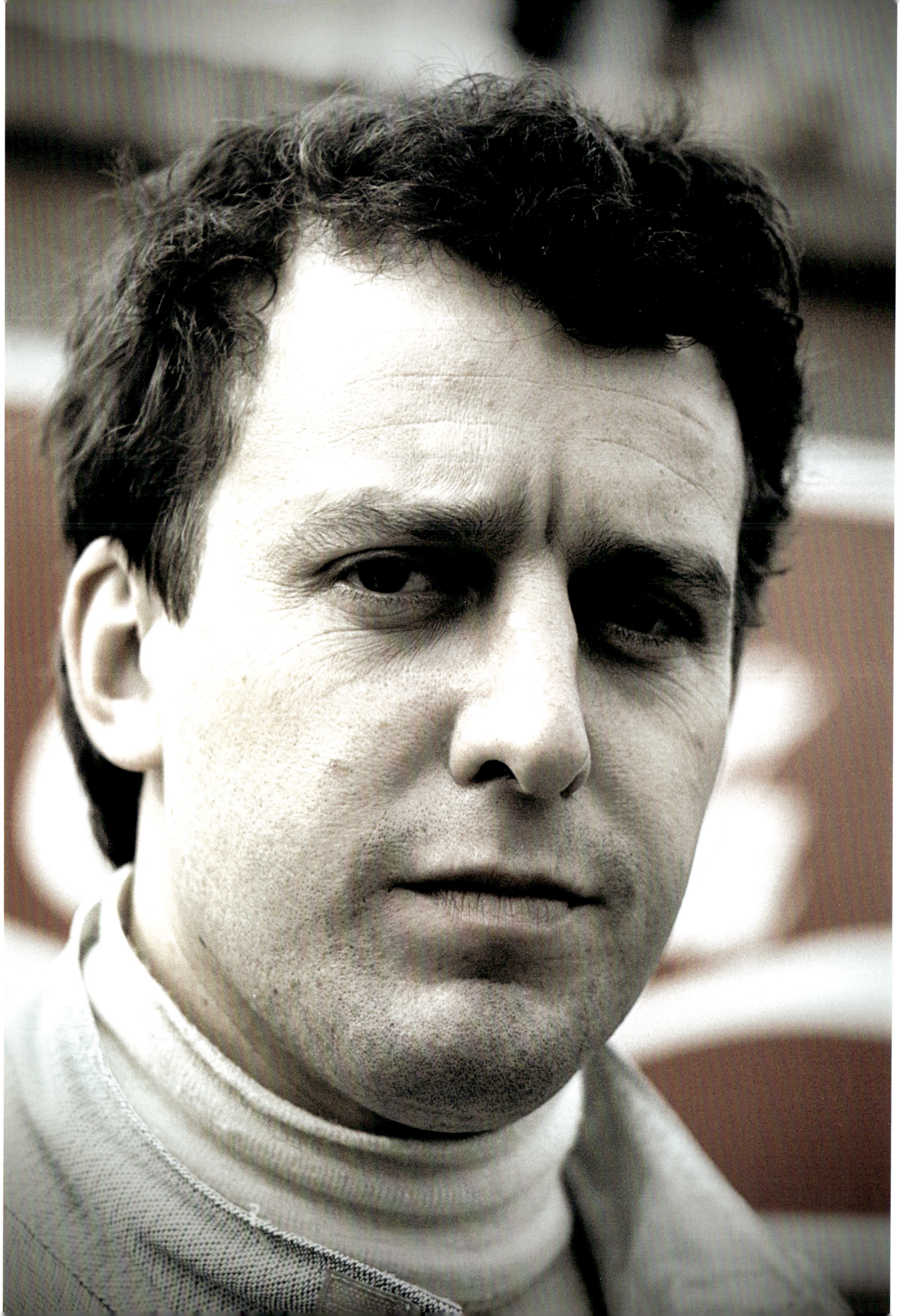

Jackie OLIVER

1969 Le-Mans-Sieger mit Ickx
Winner of Le Mans 1969 with Jacky Ickx

Das Duo Jacky Ickx und Jackie Oliver wird man immer mit dem großen Sieg in Le Mans 1969 in Verbindung bringen. „Wir galten nicht als Favoriten, da wir ein altes Auto gefahren sind und mit Porsche einen starken Gegner hatten. Doch das Wyer-Team hat bei der Vorbereitung des Ford einen großartigen Job gemacht – und in Le Mans geht es ja um Ausdauer. Ickx war nicht nur bei uns im Auto, sondern in der gesamten Wyer-Operation die Nummer eins. Er war John Wyers Liebling und so hat er sich auch verhalten. Jacky war drei Jahre jünger als ich, hatte aber mehr Le-Mans-Erfahrung. Ich bin schon 1968 für Wyer in Le Mans gefahren, da hat Brian Muir aber schon in Runde zwei die Kupplung des Ford GT40 ruiniert, als er sich in der Mulsanne aus dem Sand befreien wollte. 1969 ging Brian Redman zu Porsche und ich wurde Partner von Ickx. Wir gewannen den zweiten Lauf, die 12 Stunden von Sebring, hatten danach aber Pech mit unserem Mirage-Prototypen."

„In Le Mans starteten wir im Ford GT40. Es war dasselbe Auto, mit dem Lucien Bianchi und Pedro Rodriguez ein Jahr zuvor gewonnen hatten. Wir einigten uns darauf, dass Jacky den Start fährt – er war ja auch die Nummer eins im Team. Wir wussten, dass er zum Auto gehen und nicht sprinten würde. Das war eine berühmte Szene. Am Ende musste er aber doch laufen, sonst hätten ihn die ersten Autos abgeräumt. Das Resultat ist ja bekannt. Wir haben mit knapp über 100 Metern Vorsprung gewonnen." Der GT40 war ohne Probleme gelaufen und hatte am Sonntag die Führung geerbt, nachdem die schnelleren Porsche 917 kaputt gegangen waren. „Wir sind sehr besonnen gefahren, haben vorsichtig gebremst und sind ein beständiges Tempo gegangen, das uns David Yorke vorgegeben hat. In der Nacht war ich schneller als Jacky und habe viele Plätze gutgemacht. Ab Sonntagmorgen haben wir dann um den Sieg gekämpft."

„Ich fand es recht schwierig, mit Jacky zu arbeiten. Er war sehr egoistisch und selbstgefällig. Er war schnell, aber eine echte Primadonna. Bei Langstreckenrennen muss man schnell sein und auf das Auto aufpassen, das hat gut funktioniert. Ich habe meine Rolle als Nummer zwei akzeptiert, weil ich keine Probleme haben wollte, denn schon damals hatte ich meine Lektion in puncto Diplomatie gelernt."

„Am Jahresende 1969 wollte ich keine Sportwagenrennen mehr bestreiten und erhielt einen guten Vertrag von BRM für die Formel 1. Trotzdem habe ich 1970 im Ferrari am Sportwagenrennen in Brands Hatch teilgenommen. Wieder mit Ickx. Wir haben aber nur ein Top-Ten-Ergebnis erzielt. 1971 stand ich ohne F1-Cockpit da, also kehrte ich zu Wyer zurück mit Rodriguez als Partner. Das funktionierte gut, er war ein guter Kollege. Nach seinem Tod stellte sich das Team neu auf und ich hatte genug. Ich bin gegangen, da mir Shadow ein sehr attraktives Angebot für die Can-Am gemacht hatte. Die Mannschaft um John Wyer war sehr wütend, als ich das Team verlassen habe. Aber ich hatte eben andere Pläne."

British driver, Jackie Oliver, will always be remembered as being Ickx's partner when they won Le Mans in 1969. "We were not favourites as we were driving an old car and the Porsche opposition was fierce. But the Wyer team did a great job in preparing the Ford and Le Mans is all about endurance. Ickx was the number one driver within our pairing but also within the Wyer organisation. He was the favourite of John Wyer himself and behaved appropriately. He was three years my junior, but already had more Le Mans experience than I did. I drove for Wyer in a Ford GT40 in the 1968 Le Mans but only did two laps after Brian Muir had killed the clutch trying to get out of the sand at Mulsanne. For 1969, I had a contract with Wyer to join Ickx after Brian Redman had left for Porsche. Ickx and I won the second round, the 12 Hours of Sebring, but were unlucky after that since we were driving the unsorted Mirage prototype."

"For Le Mans, we had a Ford GT40 again, actually the same car with which Lucien Bianchi and Pedro Rodriguez won the year before. We agreed that Jacky would start the race – he was the number one driver – and we knew he intended to walk to the car rather than sprint. It was a famous sight with everybody running and Jacky just walking. Although he had to run in the end otherwise the first cars leaving the grid would have hit him. Well, the result is well-known and we won by just over 100 metres." The Ford had run without problems and when the fast Porsche 917s broke down, the blue and orange car was at the front on Sunday. "We drove very sensibly, careful on the brakes and at a steady pace set by David Yorke. During the night, I was faster than Jacky and gained a lot of positions. Then from Sunday morning on we were fighting to win."

"I found Jacky quite a difficult person to work with, very selfish and sure about himself. Yes, he was fast but a real prima donna. But in endurance racing you must be both fast and look after the car. And that worked. I fully accepted to be the number two driver, I did not want any problems for by then I had learned my lessons about diplomacy in racing."

"At the end of 1969, I didn't want to do sportscar racing and I got a good contract with BRM in F1 for the next year. However, I did the Brands Hatch sportscar race with a Ferrari in 1970. That was with Ickx, but we only managed a top-ten result. In 1971, without a regular F1 drive, I was back with Wyer, now partnering Rodriguez. That worked well since Rodriguez was a good partner but, after his death, the team was being reshuffled and I had had enough. So I just left and went to Canada to do Can-Am as I had received a very attractive offer from Shadow. The Wyer team were very angry when I walked out, but I had other plans."

Grand Prix de France 1969, Charade, Brabham BT26 - Ford

Canadian Grand Prix 1969, Mosport Park, Brabham BT26 - Ford

Beim nächsten Sportwagenrennen in Watkins Glen saß Ickx im neuen Mirage M3 – ein offener Prototyp mit Ford-Cosworth- statt BRM-Motor. Ickx nahm das Rennen von Platz fünf in Angriff, schied aber zur Halbzeit durch Motorschaden aus. Beim Finale der Markenmeisterschaft, den 1000 Kilometern von Zeltweg, sorgte Ickx für eine faustdicke Überraschung: Er stellte den Mirage auf die Pole vor den Lola und Porsche 917. Leider endete sein Rennen auch hier zur Halbzeit, schuld war eine gebrochene Lenksäule.

Mit dem Brabham BT62 lief es für Ickx dagegen immer besser. Der Belgier wurde beim Grand Prix von Großbritannien Zweiter, gewann am Nürburgring und dominierte auch den nicht zur Weltmeisterschaft zählenden Gold Cup in Oulton Park. In der WM-Tabelle hatte Ickx zwar auf den Führenden Jackie Stewart aufgeholt, doch der Schotte lag vier Rennen vor Schluss noch immer komfortabel in Führung. Bevor er das nächste F1-Rennen in Monza unter die Räder nahm, bestritt Ickx den Gran Premio del Mediterraneo auf Sizilien in einem De Tomaso. Im ersten Heat erlitt der neue Formel-2-Renner jedoch einen Motorschaden, sodass Ickx am zweiten Lauf nicht teilnehmen konnte. Beim Italien-GP waren die Hoffnungen auf ein gutes Ergebnis schon nach dem Training hinüber, als Ickx' Motor seinen Geist aufgab. Für das Rennen bekam er von Frank Williams ein Ersatztriebwerk, das aber weniger Leistung hatte. Außerdem musste Jacky am Ende des Feldes starten, weil er nicht die geforderten fünf Qualifikationsrunden zurückgelegt hatte. Ickx war also ohne Chance und schied letztlich mit einem Problem an der Benzinzufuhr aus. Er blieb in Italien, um den Mirage bei den 500 Kilometern von Imola zu fahren. Bei dem nicht zur Markenmeisterschaft zählenden Rennen hatte der Belgier gegen die Werkswagen von Alfa Romeo leichtes Spiel: Er sicherte sich die Pole und gewann das wegen Regens verkürzte Rennen.

Jetzt standen für Ickx nur noch drei Grands Prix in Amerika im Terminkalender. Im kanadischen Mosport holte Ickx die Pole und siegte nach einem packenden Duell mit Stewart. In Runde 32 fuhren die beiden Kontrahenten Seite an Seite in die erste Kurve, dabei berührten sich die Autos. Während Ickx weiterfahren konnte, drehte sich Stewart und schied aus. Zwei Wochen später endete das Rennen in Watkins Glen für Ickx durch einen Ölverlust am Ford-Motor vorzeitig. Dann stand der letzte GP des Jahres bevor und Ickx' letztes Rennen für Brabham: Beim Mexiko-GP startete Ickx aus der ersten Reihe und lag zwischenzeitlich in Führung, musste sich am Ende aber Denis Hulme geschlagen geben.

Damit war die Saison 1969 für Ickx vorüber. Er hatte die 24 Stunden von Le Mans gewonnen und war in der Formel 1 Vizeweltmeister geworden. Zudem hatte er Siege in Sebring, Oulton Park, Zeltweg, Imola, Mosport, Spa sowie am Nürburgring errungen. Der Belgier hatte aber auch einige Enttäuschungen erlebt. 1970 lockte Ickx eine alte, neue Herausforderung: Nach einjähriger Pause kehrte der Belgier zu Ferrari zurück. Diesmal sollte er für die Mannschaft aus Maranello aber nicht nur in der Formel 1 antreten, sondern auch im Sportwagen.

For the next sportscar race at Watkins Glen, Ickx was reunited with a Mirage that was now a spyder and had its BRM engine replaced by a Ford Cosworth. After starting from the fifth spot, behind several Porsches, the car retired due to engine failure halfway through the race. At the final endurance race of the year, the 1,000-kilometre race at the new Zeltweg track, Ickx surprised everybody by putting the Mirage on pole, ahead of the powerful Lolas and Porsche 917s. Unfortunately, round about halfway Ickx came into the pits to retire with a broken steering column.

In contrast, Ickx had a good summer with the Brabham BT26. He was second at the British GP, won at the Nürburgring and also dominated the non-championship Gold Cup race at Oulton Park. The Brabham driver was gaining on Stewart in the Formula One championship, but the Scottish driver still had a healthy advantage with four races left. Before going to Monza for the Italian Grand Prix, Ickx drove a De Tomaso Formula Two car at the Mediterranean Grand Prix at Sicily. In the first heat the engine broke on the new car and therefore Ickx did not drive in the second heat. The chances of getting a good result at the Monza GP were reduced when the engine of Ickx's Brabham broke in practice. For the race, Frank Williams lent them an engine but it was down on power. Since Ickx had not completed the five practice laps required he was only allowed to start from the back of the grid. Chasing the entire field, Ickx had no chance and eventually had to retire when the fuel supply failed. Ickx stayed in Italy to drive the Mirage at the non-championship 500-kilometre race at Imola. With only works cars from Alfa Romeo as opposition, Ickx put the Mirage on pole and then won the rain-shortened event.

There were now only three races left in the 1969 season, all grand prix events in America. In Canada at Mosport, Ickx took pole and won after a fierce battle with Stewart during which, at one point, the two men drove side by side into the first turn and their cars touched. Stewart spun off and had to retire while Ickx was able to continue and eventually win the race. Two weeks later Ickx had to retire at Watkins Glen when the Ford engine lost its oil pressure. For the final race of the year, and his final race with Brabham, Ickx was on the front row for the Mexican Grand Prix. After leading for some laps, Denny Hulme overtook him and they finished in that order.

The 1969 season was over for Ickx. He had come second in the Formula One World Championship and won the 24 Hours of Le Mans. He also won individual races at Sebring, Oulton Park, Nürburgring, Zeltweg, Imola, Mosport and Spa. But to counteract those, he had also had some disappointing outings. Enzo Ferrari contacted the Belgian driver for the next season and after a one year absence, he would be back in a Ferrari for 1970. And this time not just in Formula One for he would also drive for Ferrari in sportscar events.

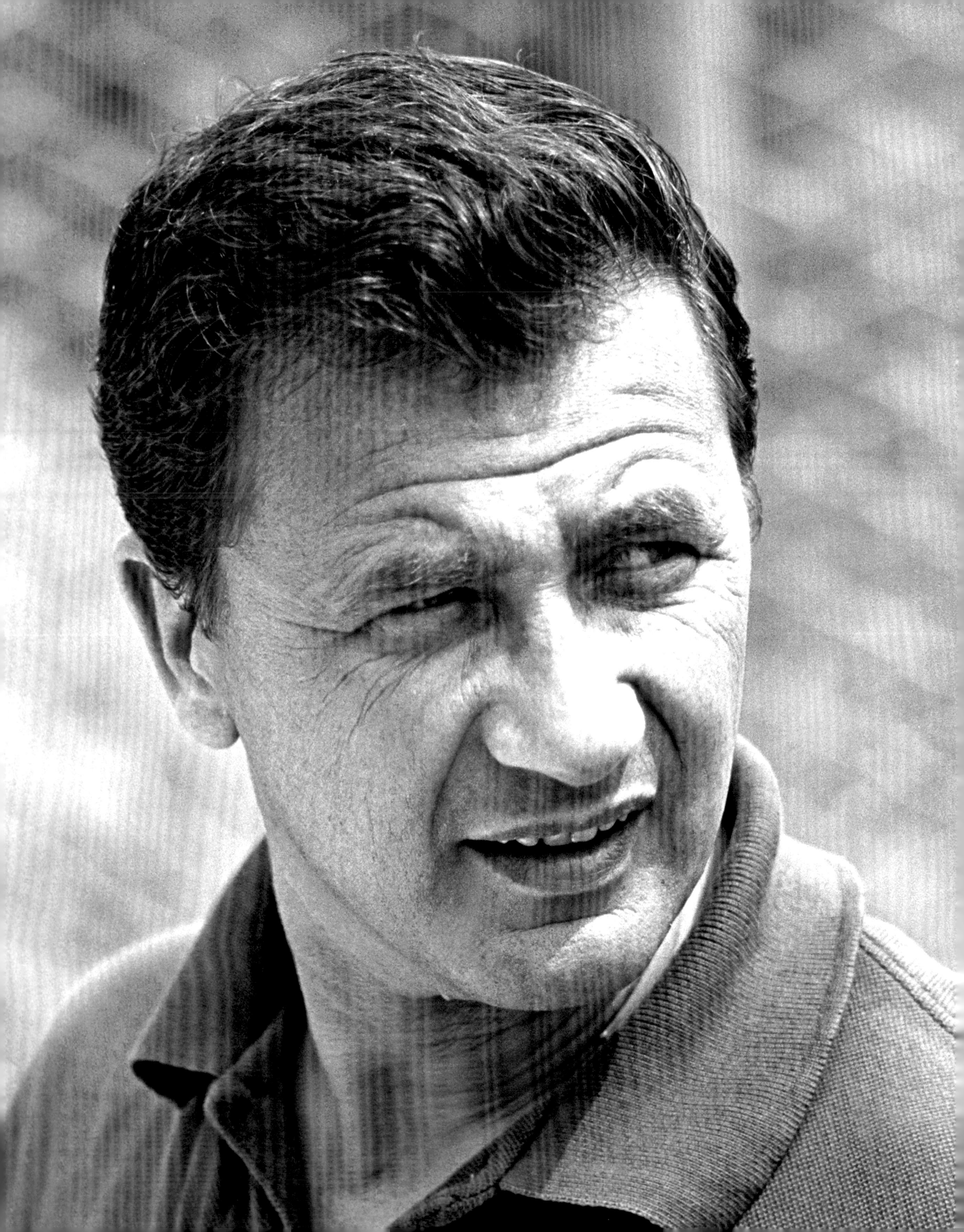

Hans HERRMANN

Fast-Teamkollege von Ickx bei Mercedes
Almost a colleague in a Mercedes-Benz

Die deutsche Rennfahrerlegende Hans Herrmann ist oft gegen Jacky Ickx gefahren. Bei den 24 Stunden von Le Mans 1969 zum Beispiel, als Ickx' Ford GT40 im Ziel gerade einmal 120 Meter Vorsprung auf Herrmanns Porsche 908 LH hatte. Das Cockpit geteilt haben sich die Sportwagen-Spezialisten indes nur fast …

„Jackys Bruder kannte ich aus meiner Zeit bei Abarth in den frühen 60ern. Pascal fungierte in der Rennabteilung als eine Art Berater. Mit Jacky bin ich nie zusammen gefahren, wobei es einmal fast so weit gewesen wäre."

„Ein paar Tage nach unserem Duell in Le Mans waren Jacky und ich am Hockenheimring, um einen Mercedes 300SEL zu testen. 14 Jahre nach dem Ende der Silberpfeile wollte Mercedes in den Rennsport zurückkehren und hatte sich dazu durchgerungen, bei den 24 Stunden von Spa zwei Autos einzusetzen. Ich weiß noch genau, dass es 1969 war, weil das ganze Team im Fahrerlager die Mondlandung von Neil Armstrong verfolgt hat. Der Tourenwagen mit 6,9-Liter-Motor war sehr stark und lief auf den langen Geraden des Hockenheimrings hervorragend. Wir sind damals noch auf der alten Strecke ohne Schikanen gefahren, die war ganz anders als der kompakte Kurs, der heute genutzt wird. Unsere einzige Sorge waren die Reifen. Das schwere Auto hat das Gummi sogar auf den Geraden verschlungen."

Einen Monat später reiste das Mercedes-Team nach Belgien, um das 24-Stunden-Rennen in Angriff zu nehmen. In der Qualifikation erzielten Ickx/Herrmann die zweitschnellste Zeit. Vor dem Rennen entschieden die Ingenieure jedoch, dass es zu unsicher war, auf der Highspeed-Strecke zu fahren. Spa unterschied sich vom Charakter her zu sehr von Hockenheim. Selbst mit neuen Reifen, die extra aus England eingeflogen worden waren, wollten sie das Risiko nicht eingehen. „Im Regen wäre es okay gewesen, aber im Trockenen hätte der Reifenhersteller nicht garantieren können, dass das Gummi hält. Daher sind wir wenige Wochen nach unserem Kampf in Le Mans doch nicht zusammen gefahren. Das ist schade, denn Jacky war ein netter Mensch. Es hätte sicher viel Spaß gemacht, mit ihm in Belgien zu fahren." Zwei Jahre später gingen die 300SEL übrigens in Spa an den Start, dann jedoch ohne Ickx und Herrmann.

German racing legend Hans Herrmann never drove with Jacky Ickx, but they competed against one another in many events. The most famous of these was the 1969 24 Hours of Le Mans when they finished first and second, just 120 metres apart.

"I knew Jacky's brother Pascal from when I was with Abarth in the early sixties where he had some kind of advisory function in the racing department. But I never drove with Jacky. Except that, one day, I almost did."

"Just a few days after we had that famous fight at Le Mans, Jacky and I went to the Hockenheimring in Germany to test a Mercedes-Benz 300SEL touring car. Mercedes wanted to return to racing, fourteen years after the Silberpfeile and they had chosen to enter the 24 Hours of Spa-Francorchamps. The 6.9-litre touring car was very powerful and the team had two cars ready. I remember it was 1969 since the whole team was watching television in the paddock to see the first moon landing by Neil Armstrong. We were all in good spirits and the cars ran beautifully on the long straights of the Hockenheimring. In those days, it was the old circuit without the chicanes and was definitely not the short circuit that they use today. However, the only concern we had were the tyres since the heavy car was eating them up even on this straightforward circuit."

A week later the Mercedes-Benz team went to Belgium to compete in the 24-hour race. But after practice and qualifying, where they got second fastest time, the engineers decided it was unsafe to drive at this high-speed track. Its nature was completely different to the track on which they had tested and it was decided that the cars would not start. Even using special new tyres flown in from England they would not take the risk. "In the rain it would be OK, but in the dry the tyre manufacturer could not guarantee that the tyres would last. So a few weeks after our beautiful battle at Le Mans, we did not drive together in a race. A pity, since Jacky was a nice person and it would have been a great joy to drive with him in Belgium." The Mercedes cars came back two years later, but without either Ickx or Herrmann.

1970

Die Rückkehr zu Ferrari
Back with Ferrari

Jacky Ickx kehrte 1970 zu Ferrari zurück, nachdem Fiat – als neuer Besitzer der Marke Ferrari – dem Belgier ein sehr attraktives Angebot unterbreitet hatte. Anders als 1968 sollte Ickx für die Scuderia aber nicht nur in der Formel 1 starten, sondern auch im neuen Sportwagen namens 512S. Die Italiener wollten Porsche herausfordern, deren 917 genau wie der 512S als Sportwagen und nicht als Prototyp lief. In der Formel 1 blickte Ferrari auf ein schwaches Jahr zurück, doch dank Fiat hatte die Scuderia jetzt ein gesundes Budget, um einen neuen F1-Renner mit Zwölfzylinder zu bauen. Neben Ickx starteten Gianclaudio „Clay" Regazzoni und Ignazio Giunti für Ferrari.

Für Ickx begann das Jahr wie so oft mit den 24 Stunden von Daytona, wo Ferrari nach erfolgreichen Vorsaison-Tests voller Optimismus antrat. Die Mannschaft aus Maranello schickte drei 512S an den Start. Jacky Ickx teilte sich seinen Sportwagen mit dem Schweizer Peter Schetty, der 1969 die Europa-Bergmeisterschaft auf Ferrari gewonnen hatte. Im Qualifying erzielten ihre Teamkollegen Mario Andretti und Arturo Merzario die Bestzeit, dahinter folgten drei Porsche sowie der 512S von Ickx auf Platz fünf. Nach einem Sechstel der Renndistanz musste das belgisch-schweizerische Team jedoch nach einem Mauerkontakt mit Aufhängungsschaden aufgeben. Ickx erhielt daraufhin Merzarios Platz neben Andretti.

Jacky Ickx re-joined Ferrari for the 1970 season after Ferrari's new owners, Fiat, had made a very attractive financial offer to the Belgian ace. But this year, Ickx was not just contracted to drive in Formula One, he also would drive the new 512S sportscar in endurance races. The Italian manufacturer was keen to challenge Porsche, whose 917 would race in the same class as the new sportscar from Maranello. After a poor year for results in 1969, Ferrari now had – thanks to Fiat – a healthy budget to build a new Formula One car, powered by a flat 12-cylinder engine. Also in the team with Ickx were Swiss driver, Gianclaudio 'Clay' Regazzoni, and a young Italian talent, Ignazio Giunti.

The season started as usual with the 24 Hours of Daytona and, after some pre-season testing at the Florida speedway, the Ferrari team was optimistic about its chances. The Italian factory had entered three 512S sportscars and Jacky Ickx was partnered with Peter Schetty, the Swiss driver who had won the European Hillclimb Championship for Ferrari in 1969. In qualifying, Mario Andretti, sharing his Ferrari with Italian, Arturo Merzario, was fastest and beat all the Porsches while Ickx managed fifth fastest time. After one-sixth of the race distance, the Belgian-Swiss team had to retire with suspension damage after hitting a wall and Ickx was then given Merzario's place with Andretti.

BARC Thruxton 1970, BMW 270 n°30

Unfortunately, this car lost over an hour in the pits to repair yet more suspension damage and thus had no chance to win. Ickx and Andretti finally finished third behind the two John Wyer Gulf Porsches.

On March 17th in Kyalami, Ickx got back into a Formula One Ferrari. At the South African Grand Prix, Ickx was on the second row and from the start he moved up into second position. Unfortunately, after sixty laps the engine broke and he had to retire. A week later, Schetty again partnered Ickx for the 12 Hours of Sebring. After setting the fourth qualifying time – again Andretti was on pole – Ickx drove a good race and challenged Andretti for the lead several times. But at halfway, a broken valve forced him to retire. Andretti won the race, though not in his own car. Some hour and a half before the end, he encountered gearbox problems and had to retire. He then joined Giunti and Nino Vaccarella in the third works 512S and they took it to victory.

Back in Europe, Ickx drove a BMW Formula Two car at Thruxton. In his heat, Ickx was second behind Jochen Rindt while in the final Ickx finished sixth overall, two laps down on Rindt. Meanwhile, Ferrari had made some improvements to the 512S sportscar and, for the BOAC 1000 at Brands Hatch, Ickx was reunited with Jackie Oliver. They would start from the front row alongside Chris Amon, who had replaced Andretti in the Ferrari team here. The race was run in cold and rainy weather and in the race the Ferraris were no match for the Porsche 917s. Ickx and Oliver finished eighth. It was a busy weekend for Ickx, since he also found time to test the long-tail 512S at Le Mans.

■ *Vic Elford: "Strange that I never drove in the same team with Jacky, although our careers more or less covered the same period. I do remember his driving capabilities in the rain as at Brands Hatch in 1970. Together we had a great dice, but neither of us could catch Pedro (Rodriguez) in the Gulf Porsche."*

For Ickx the Spanish Grand Prix at Jarama was over after only a few hundred metres. In the second corner, Jackie Oliver lost the brakes on his BRM and hit Ickx's Ferrari 312B, damaging its fuel tank and resulting in both cars catching fire. While both drivers got out of their cars, Oliver was unharmed but Ickx received burns to his arms and legs. He had to rest for a few weeks and thus could not start in Monza for the 1,000-kilometre sportscar race. Ickx was back for the Monaco Grand Prix but, when a drive shaft failed, he was an early retirement. For the 1,000-kilometre race at Spa-Francorchamps, Ickx found John Surtees as his partner. The Englishman was back with Ferrari for the first time in four years and he had substituted for Ickx in Monza while for the Belgian race, he took Peter Schetty's place alongside Ickx. Starting from the second row, the newly formed team had a great race and finished second to the Gulf Porsche of Jo Siffert and Brian Redman and finished just three minutes behind them. On the morning before the sportscar race, Ickx drove a Ford Mustang in a touring car race but unfortunately had to retire. A week later, still in Belgium, Ickx was at Zolder for the annual Formula Two race, but his visit lasted only two laps when his BMW engine broke in the first heat.

■ *Jochen Mass: "Jackie Stewart had lost many friends in racing accidents and always wanted more safety. Ickx was young and a little detached, he did not see any reason for things like bigger run-off areas."*

— 95 —

Gran Premio de Espana 1970, Jarama. Direkt nach dem Start versagten an Jackie Olivers BRM die Bremsen und er krachte in den Ferrari von Jacky Ickx (der auf der Innenseite zum Stehen kam). Beide Autos fingen Feuer und Ickx zog sich dabei Verbrennungen zu / Just after the start Jackie Oliver's BRM lost its brakes completely and it T-boned the Ferrari of Jacky Ickx. Both cars caught fire and Ickx, whose car was on the inside, was partly burned.

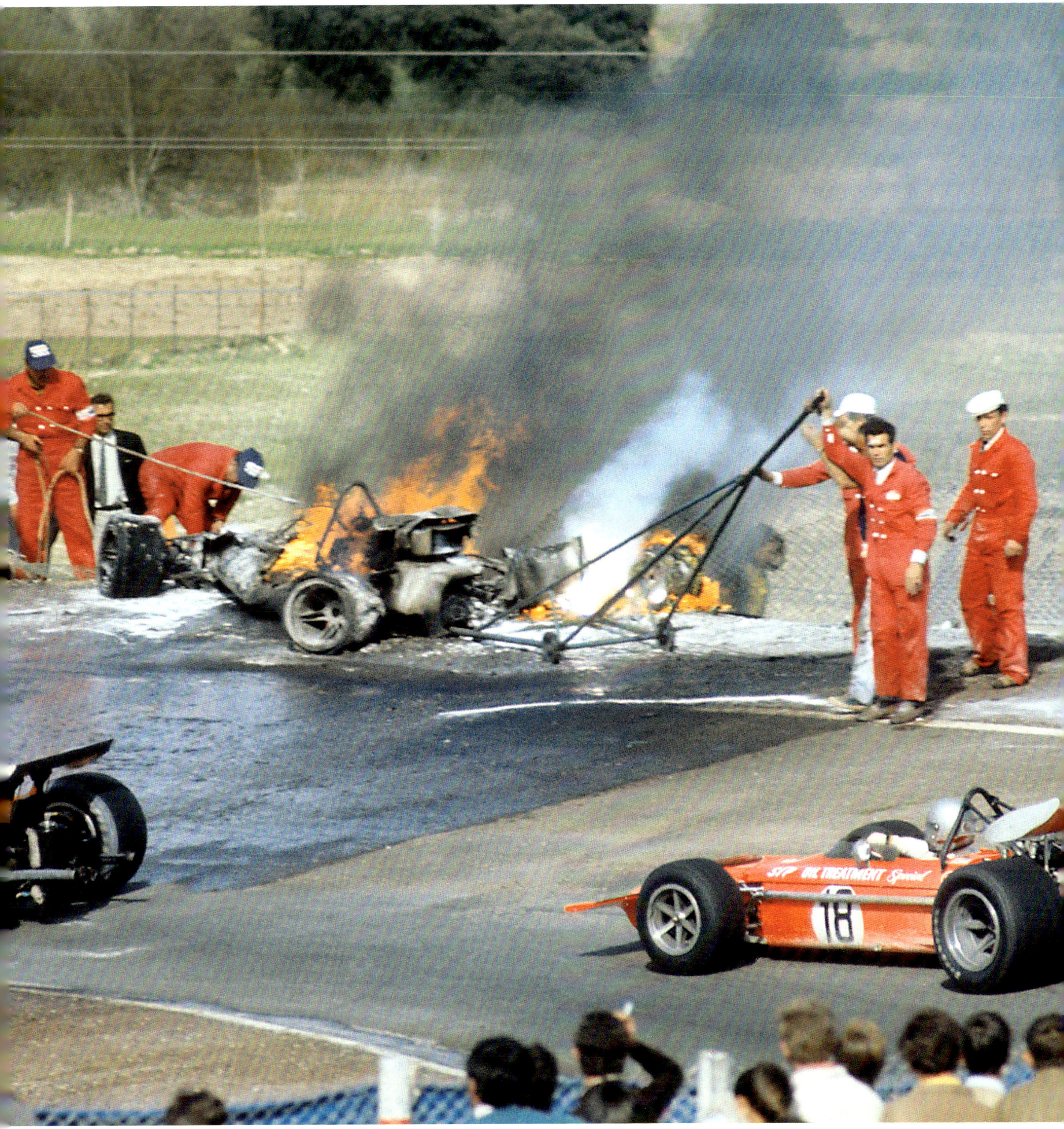
STP OIL TREATMENT Special
18

ADAC-1000-km-Rennen 1970, Nürburgring, Ferrari 512S, Peter Schetty

Grand Prix de Belgique 1970, Spa-Francorchamps, Ferrari 312B

Grand Prix de Belgique 1970, Spa-Francorchamps

24 Heures du Mans 1970, Ferrari 512S

An den 1000 Kilometern Nürburgring konnte Ickx nicht teilnehmen, weil Schetty den Ferrari im Training zerstört hatte. Für Jacky war das aber nicht weiter tragisch: Er war kurz zuvor eine Treppe heruntergefallen und hatte sich an den Handgelenken verletzt. Nach ein paar Trainingsrunden wusste er, dass er wegen der Schmerzen ohnehin nicht fahren konnte. Bei seinem Heim-GP in Spa war Ickx wieder fit, hatte aber kein Glück. Nach 22 Runden musste er wegen eines Benzinlecks die Box ansteuern und verlor einige Plätze. Ickx wurde letztlich als Achter gewertet.

Bei den 24 Stunden von Le Mans rollten nicht weniger als elf Ferrari 512S an den Start, darunter vier Werkswagen. Ickx wurde auch hier mit Schetty zusammengespannt. Die Ferrari waren aber nur zahlenmäßig überlegen, im Training und Qualifying erzielte jeweils ein Porsche 917 die Bestzeit. Die 917er gingen auch nach dem Start in Führung und ließen nie eine andere Marke an die Spitze. Für Ferrari wurde das Rennen zum Albtraum. In Runde sieben schied Vaccarella mit Motorproblemen aus, nach drei Stunden krachten drei 512S ineinander (!) und fielen ebenfalls aus. Beim Versuch, den Unfall zu umfahren, überdrehte Derek Bell den Motor seines Ferrari und musste auch aufgeben. Einige Stunden später dann die nächste schlechte Nachricht: Ickx verunfallte auf Platz zwei liegend wegen eines Bremsdefekts. Bei dem Crash in der Ford-Schikane kam ein Streckenposten ums Leben und das Auto brannte komplett aus. Für Ferrari war es wahrlich ein Wochenende zum Vergessen.

At the Nürburgring a week later, Ickx did not take part in the 1,000-kilometre race after a practice accident by Schetty had damaged their Ferrari 512S. In fact, he was not planning to drive anyway since he had fallen down some stairs and had hurt his wrists. After a few practice laps, he decided that driving at the Nürburgring would be too painful. He came back for his home GP at Spa-Francorchamps, but again was out of luck. After twenty-two laps, he had to come into the pits to repair a fuel leak that cost him some places and he eventually finished eighth.

There were no fewer than eleven Ferrari 512S entered for the 24 Hours of Le Mans. Four were works entries and Ickx was in one of them partnered again by Peter Schetty. Although the Ferraris outnumbered the Porsches, the 917s were fastest in practice and qualifying. From the start Porsches took the lead and never let anybody else in front. For Ferrari, the race turned into a nightmare. After seven laps, Nino Vaccarella had to retire with engine problems and, after three hours, almost unbelievably three 512Ss crashed into one another. Derek Bell, in trying to avoid this accident, over-revved the engine of his Ferrari and also retired. Ickx was running in second position when he crashed at the Ford chicane some hours later. A broken rear brake sent the five-litre sportscar out of control and off the track. A marshal was killed in this tragic accident and, in addition, the car burst into flames. This was truly a race to forget for the Scuderia.

24 Heures du Mans 1970,
Ferrari-Werkstatt / Ferrari workshop

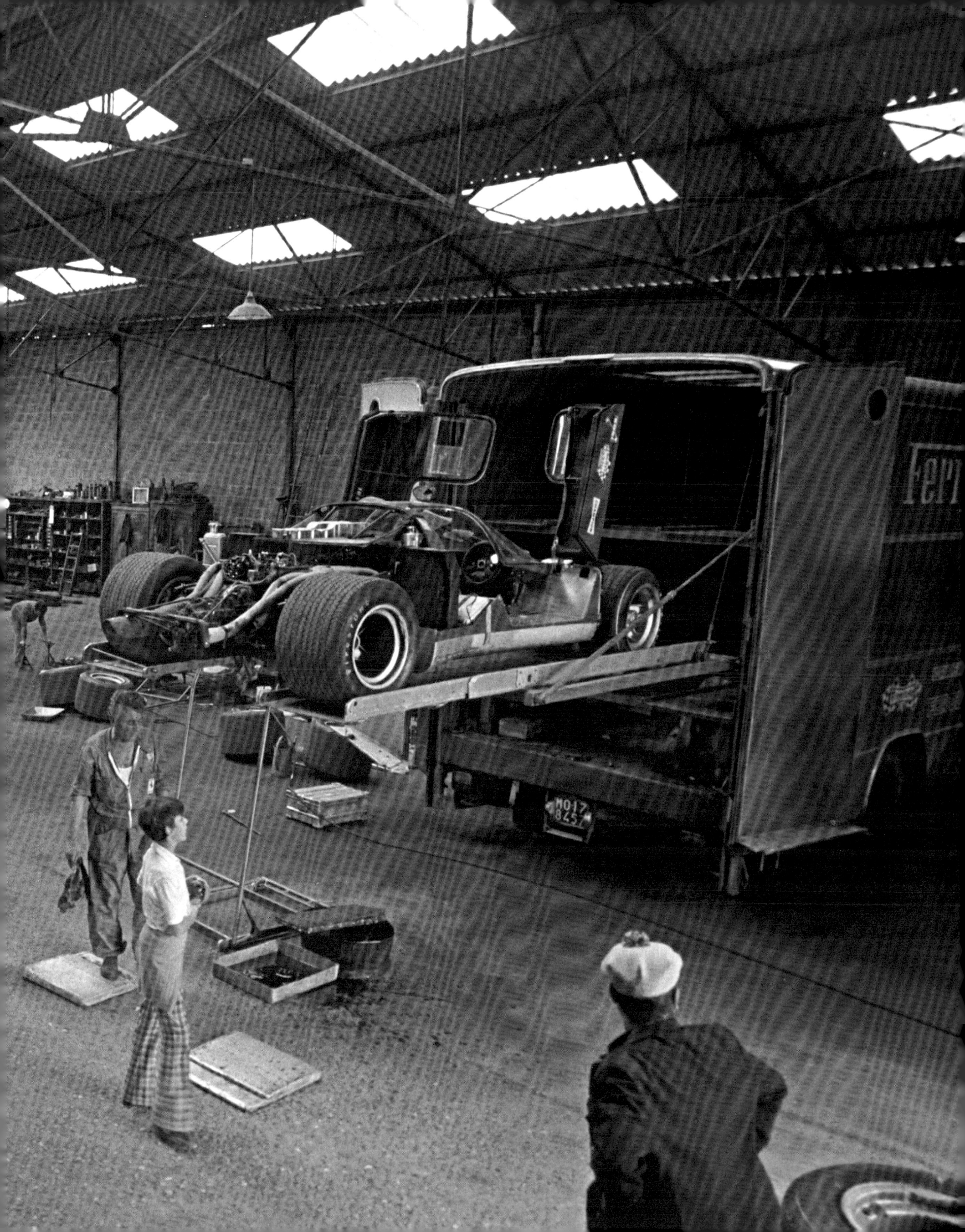

24 Heures du Mans 1970, Ferrari 512S

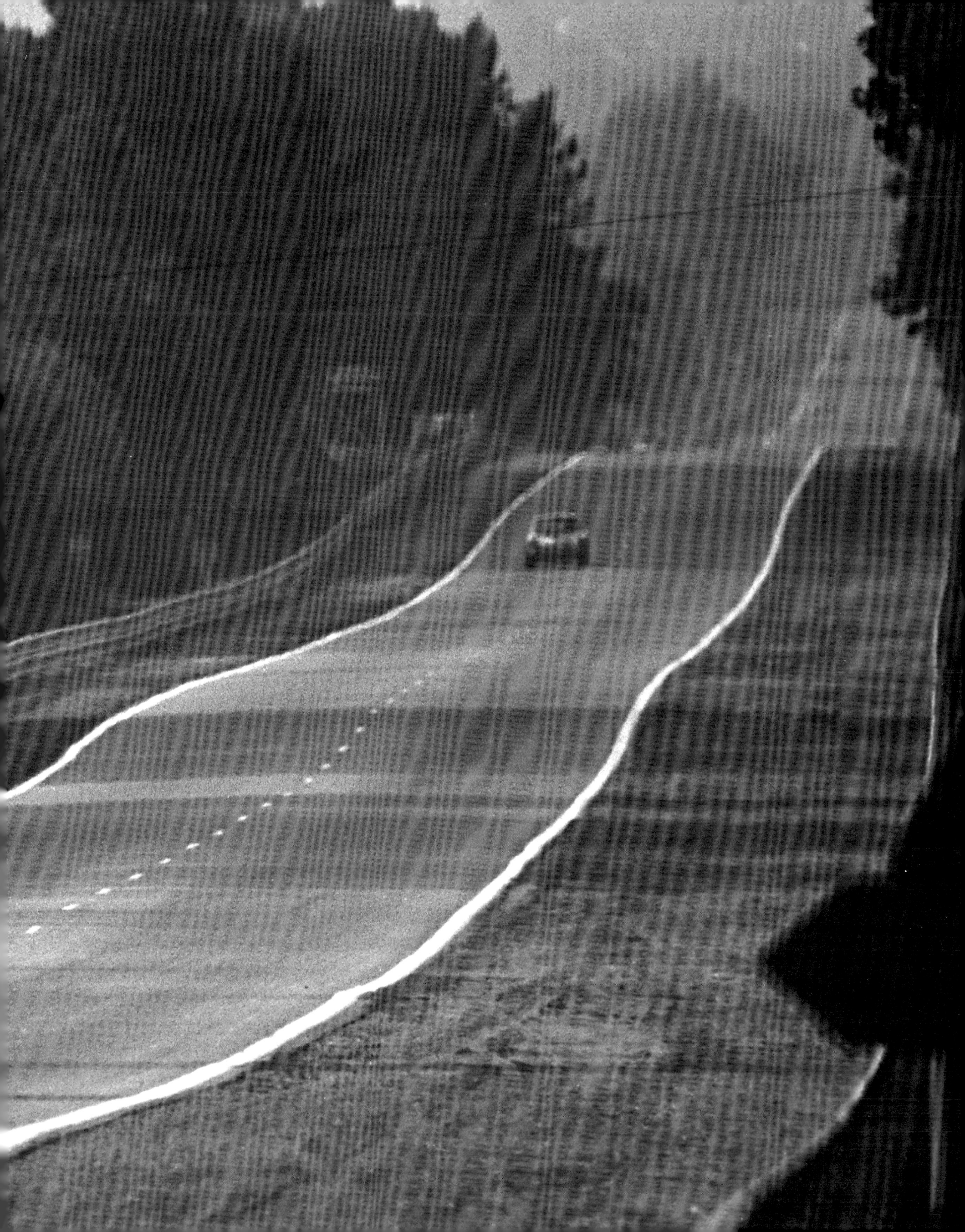

British Grand Prix 1970, Brands Hatch, Ferrari 312B

Beim GP der Niederlande gelang Ickx der erste Podestplatz in der laufenden F1-Saison, die Freude über Rang drei wurde aber durch den tödlichen Unfall von Piers Courage getrübt. Eine Woche später wurde Ickx beim Formel-2-Rennen in Rouen Vierter, beim F1-GP in Clermont-Ferrand schied er wiederum durch Motorschaden aus. Am folgenden Wochenende absolvierte Ickx in Watkins Glen ein Doppelprogramm: Den Lauf zur Int. Markenmeisterschaft über sechs Stunden beendete er auf Rang fünf. Bei dem am Sonntag stattfindenden Can-Am-Rennen schied er durch einen Unfall aus. In beiden Fällen steuerte Ickx einen 512S Spyder. Jackys Pechsträhne setzte sich auch beim GP von Großbritannien fort, wo sein Ferrari nach sieben Runden mit Getriebeschaden strandete. Beim Formel-2-Rennen in Le Castellet sackte dafür der Öldruck in den Keller und zwang Ickx zur Aufgabe.

Bis zu diesem Zeitpunkt hatte Ickx an 20 Rennen teilgenommen und kein einziges gewonnen.

■ **Vic Elford: „Ich bin nie mit Jacky Ickx gefahren, aber oft gegen ihn. Er war ein echter Gentleman, immer höflich und respektvoll. Ich erinnere mich noch an das 1000-Kilometer-Rennen von Brands Hatch 1970. Er fuhr im Ferrari, ich im Porsche 917. Ich habe ihn in der Paddock Bend überholt, danach wollte er mich in Druids ausbremsen. Im letzten Moment hat er gemerkt, dass er es nicht packt. Heutzutage fahren die Piloten dem anderen ins Auto. Jacky war anders. Er wusste, dass er es nicht schafft. Also steuerte er aufs Gras, sodass beide weiterfahren konnten. Er war ein anständiger Fahrer."**

1970 fand der Deutschland-GP erstmals auf dem Hockenheimring statt. Der Kurs in Baden-Württemberg ersetzte den Nürburgring, den viele Fahrer für zu gefährlich hielten. Hockenheim hatte durch den Tod von Jim Clark zwei Jahre zuvor zwar auch einen schlechten Ruf, war durch zwei Schikanen aber sicherer gemacht worden. Ickx und Jochen Rindt nahmen das Rennen aus der ersten Reihe in Angriff und lieferten sich bis ins Ziel ein atemberaubendes Duell. Letztlich behielt der Österreicher mit weniger als einer Sekunde Vorsprung die Oberhand. Zwei Wochen später dominierte Ferrari das erste Formel-1-Rennen auf dem neu gebauten Österreichring. Regazzoni, Giunti und Ickx lagen alle unter den ersten vier, bis Giunti wegen eines Reifenschadens an die Box musste. Im Ziel lag Ickx vor Regazzoni und feierte seinen ersten Triumph im Jahr 1970! Österreich

At the Dutch Grand Prix at Zandvoort, Ickx finally managed to finish third but even this good result was overshadowed by a fatal accident to Piers Courage. In Rouen a week later, Ickx finished fourth in a Formula Two race and, in the French GP again held at Clermont-Ferrand, he had to retire with engine failure. Ickx drove two races at Watkins Glen the week after. The 6-hour race counting towards for the World Championship and on Sunday there was the third round of the Can-Am Series. In both events he was at the wheel of a 512S spyder. He was fifth in the 6-hour race, but he crashed in the Can-Am event. Back in Europe, his run of bad luck continued when he retired with gearbox problems after only seven laps of the British GP and then a lack of oil pressure was the reason for his retirement at the Le Castellet Formula Two race on July 26th.

Up to that point, Ickx had driven twenty races in 1970 and he had not won one of them.

■ **Vic Elford: "I have never driven with Jacky Ickx, but a lot of times against him. He was a nice gentleman, always polite and full of respect. I remember Brands Hatch 1970 in the 1,000-kilometre race where he was in a Ferrari and I drove a Porsche 917. I overtook him at Paddock Bend and he wanted to regain the spot by out-braking me at Druids. At the last moment he realised he could not make it. Nowadays drivers crash into each other, but not Jacky. He knew he had got it wrong and steered onto the grass. We both continued the race. He was a fine driver."**

The German Grand Prix was to be held on the Hockenheimring for the first time in 1970. This circuit just south of Frankfurt was chosen to replace the Nürburgring that several Formula One drivers thought was too dangerous. The Hockenheim track had also acquired a bad reputation after Jim Clark's death two years earlier, but had now been made safer by inserting two chicanes. For the race, Jochen Rindt joined Ickx on the front row and they had an exciting race-long duel. In the end, it was the Austrian driver who crossed the finish line less than a second ahead of Ickx. Two weeks later, at the first Formula One race at the new Österreichring, Ferrari dominated the Austrian Grand Prix. Regazzoni, Giunti and Ickx all ran in the top four until Giunti went into the pits to replace a punctured tyre. In the end, Ickx won ahead of Regazzoni and could finally celebrate a win in 1970. Before going to Monza for the Italian Grand Prix, Ickx drove

Gran Premio del Mediterraneo 1970, Enna-Pergusa, Jacky Ickx & Dieter Basche

Großer Preis von Österreich 1970, Zeltweg, Jacky & Catherine

— 107 —

Großer Preis von Österreich 1970, Zeltweg, Ferrari 312B n°12

erwies sich für Ickx auch in der Formel 2 als gutes Pflaster. Nachdem er mit dem stark verbesserten BMW 270 in Enna-Pergusa Dritter geworden war, fuhr er auf dem Salzburgring zum Sieg.

Auch abseits der Strecke gab es im Hause Ickx gute Nachrichten: Anfang August heiratete Jacky seine Lebensgefährtin Catherine Blaton, die Nichte des belgischen Ferrari-Piloten Jean „Beurlys" Blaton.

Beim Italien-GP in Monza rechneten die Tifosi fest mit einem guten Ergebnis „ihrer" Ferrari. Nach dem Triumph in Österreich trauten viele der Mannschaft aus Maranello einen Heimsieg zu. Das Wochenende wurde aber überschattet durch den tödlichen Unfall von Jochen Rindt während des Samstagstrainings. Nach einem Bremsdefekt vor der Parabolica schlug der Lotus des WM-Führenden in die Streckenbegrenzung ein, Rindt starb an der Unfallstelle. Das Rennen wurde zu einer wahren Lotterie, die Clay Regazzoni im Ferrari für sich entschied, während Ickx durch Getriebeprobleme ausfiel. Kurz darauf feierte der Belgier seinen dritten Erfolg im laufenden Jahr – und das erneut in Österreich. In Tulln-Langenlebarn fuhr er im F2-BMW zum Sieg. Damit war der Bann gebrochen: Eine Woche später triumphierte er auch beim GP von Kanada in Mont-Tremblant. Ickx hatte bei den letzten vier F1-Rennen 24 Punkte geholt und rückte dadurch immer näher an den verstorbenen Rindt (45 Zähler) heran.

Das letzte Formel-2-Wochenende des Jahres in Imola wartete mit Höhen und Tiefen auf. Im ersten Heat schied Ickx mit defekter Lichtmaschine aus, das zweite beendete er auf Platz zwei. Beim US-Grand-Prix sah es anfangs sogar noch besser aus für den Belgier: Ickx fuhr im Qualifying die Bestzeit. Während des Rennens waren die WM-Hoffnungen des Ferrari-Piloten aber mit einem Schlag vorbei, als Ickx wegen einer defekten Benzinleitung die Box ansteuern musste. Er konnte weiterfahren, hatte aber keine Chance mehr den siegreichen Emerson Fittipaldi abzufangen.

Drei Monate nach den 6 Stunden von Watkins Glen fand das Finale der Int. Markenmeisterschaft im österreichischen Zeltweg statt. Hier setzte Ferrari eine modifizierte Variante seines Sportwagens namens 512M ein. Das Duo Ickx/Giunti startete aus Reihe eins und lag nach 49 Runden komfortabel in Führung, als der Ferrari wegen eines Kurzschlusses in der Elektrik ausschied. Dass Ickx' den Österreichring schneller umrundete als die Formel 1 zwei Monate zuvor und damit einen neuen Rundenrekord aufstellte, war nur ein kleiner Trost. Zusammen mit Giunti nahm Ickx auch an den 9 Stunden von Kyalami teil. In Südafrika fuhr Ickx auf die Pole und gewann – sein erster Triumph im Ferrari 512. Kurz zuvor hatten Ickx und Regazzoni beim Mexiko-GP einen Doppelsieg für Ferrari errungen. In der F1-Weltmeisterschaft landeten die Ferraristi dadurch hinter Jochen Rindt auf den Rängen zwei und drei.

■ *Jochen Mass: „Ich hatte den Eindruck, dass Ickx gar nicht Weltmeister werden wollte. Er respektierte Rindt und dachte sich: ‚Irgendwann wird mein Tag kommen.' Doch das passierte nie."*

Ickx hatte in den letzten sechs F1-Rennen 36 Punkte geholt und damit den Speed und die Zuverlässigkeit des neuen Ferrari bewiesen. Er hatte zwar nicht den Titel geholt, aber das ging für Ickx mehr oder weniger in Ordnung. Weltmeister zu werden, nachdem sein größter Gegner verstorben war, war zumindest für Jacky nicht der richtige Weg.

two Formula Two races, finishing third in Enna-Pergusa and winning at the Salzburgring. Both times he drove the now much-improved BMW 270.

It is just possible that Ickx's results became more positive following his marriage to Catherine Blaton at the beginning of August. Catherine was the niece of Belgian Ferrari driver, Jean 'Beurlys' Blaton.

The Tifosi in Monza were anticipating a strong result from the Ferraris in the Italian GP. After success in the previous races, it was assumed that a car from Maranello could definitely win again at Monza. But the weekend was overshadowed by the fatal crash of Jochen Rindt during the Saturday practice. A brake failure on his Lotus sent the car into the barriers just before the Parabolica and the leader of the Formula One World Championship died instantly. The race turned out to be a big gamble and, with Ickx retiring due to clutch problems, it was Clay Regazzoni who won for Ferrari. However, more success for Ickx came at Tulln-Langenlebarn when he won in his BMW Formula Two car and then a week later in Mont-Tremblant, he won the Canadian GP. With twenty-four points from the last four GPs, Ickx was gaining on Jochen Rindt's posthumous total of forty-five.

At Imola, Ickx drove his final Formula Two race of the season with mixed results. He retired in the first heat with a broken alternator while in the second heat he finished second. It looked good for the Belgian driver when he took pole at the American GP. However, his chances for a win in the championship were dashed when he had to come into the pits with a leaking fuel pipe. He continued after the repairs but could not catch Emerson Fittipaldi, who won his first 'Grande Epreuve'.

Three months after the Watkins Glen race, the 1970 sportscar championship had its final race at Zeltweg in Austria. Ferrari had updated its 512S and it was in a 512 Modificato that Ickx and Giunti started from the front row, took the lead and after forty-nine laps had a healthy lead. But then they had to retire when the car developed a short circuit in its electrics. They had the consolation of setting a new lap record by going even faster than the Formula One cars had done two months earlier. The same two drivers were entered for the 9 Hours of Kyalami in South Africa. Ickx claimed pole and, at the chequered flag, Ickx had finally won a race in a 512S. This success came right after winning the Mexican Grand Prix where Ickx finished ahead of Regazzoni thus resulting in second and third positions for them in the final standings of the championship at whose head was Jochen Rindt.

■ *Jochen Mass: "I got the impression, Jacky did not want to become World Champion. He respected Rindt and thought that 'eventually, my day will come'. But that never happened."*

Ickx had scored thirty-six points in the last six Formula One races thus proving the speed and reliability of the new Ferrari. It could not give him the title but he was more or less happy with that. Becoming World Champion after your main opponent had died was, for him at least, not the correct way.

109

Gran Premio d'Italia 1970, Monza, Ferrari 312B

Gran Premio d'Italia 1970, Monza, Ferrari 312B

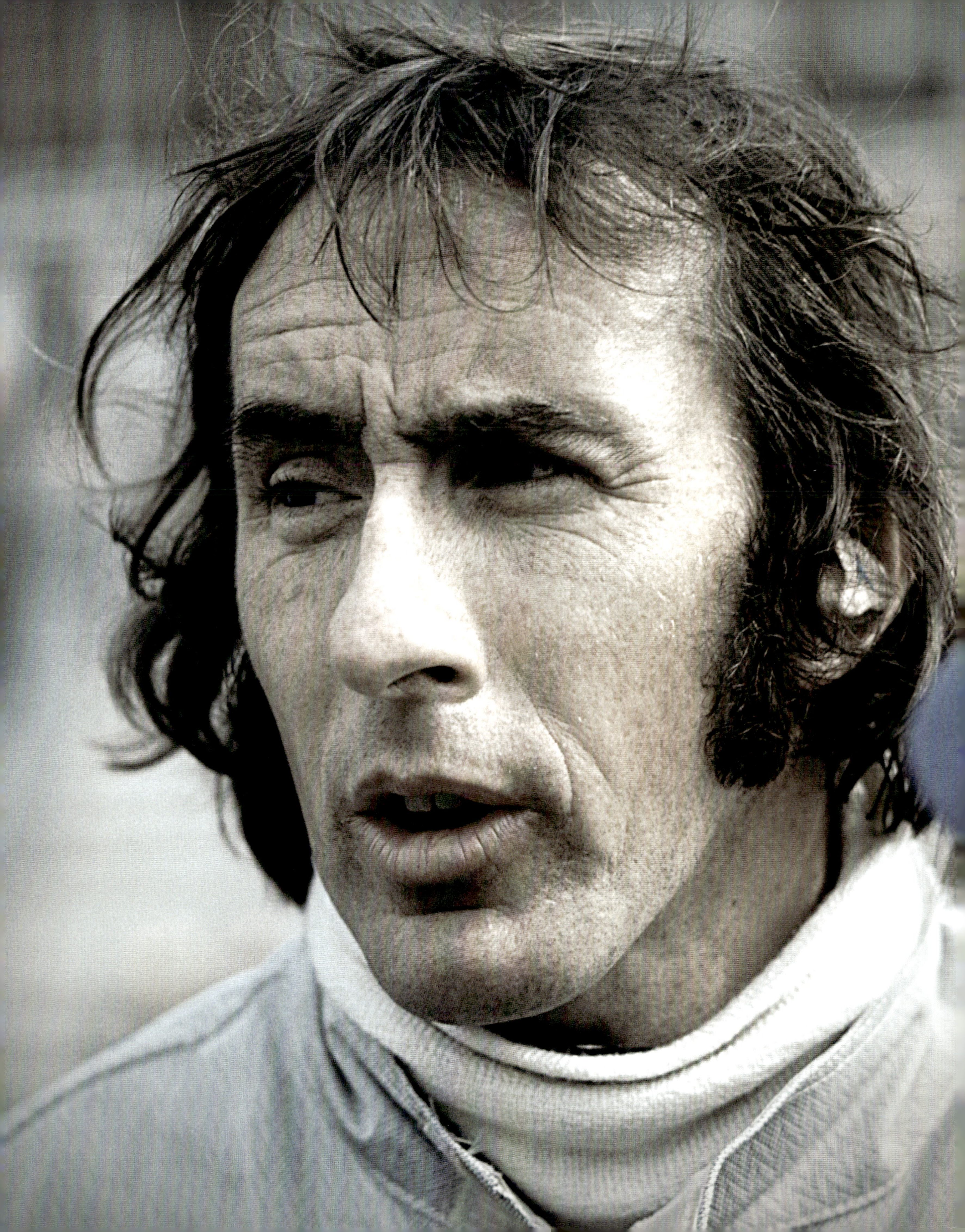

Jackie STEWART

Teamkollege von Ickx bei Tyrrell
Ickx's team-mate with Tyrrell

„Jacky Ickx wurde 1966 mein Teamkollege bei Tyrrell. Genau wie ich 1964 fuhr er für das britische Team in der Formel 3 und Formel 2, und ein Jahr später ausschließlich in der Formel 2. Ken hatte einen guten Riecher für Talente und Ickx war sicher eines davon. Er war damals ja gerade einmal 21 Jahre alt. Er war so wie Ayrton Senna im selben Alter: sehr talentiert, aber vielleicht etwas übermotiviert."

„Jacky hat sich damals keine Gedanken über die Sicherheit gemacht. Er interessierte sich nur fürs Fahren. Mit seiner Art, nur an sich und ans Gewinnen zu denken, war er so etwas wie ein Einzelgänger. In Spa ist er immer sensationell gefahren. Dort hatte ich 1966 meinen schweren Unfall und habe daraufhin eine Sicherheitskampagne gestartet. In den folgenden Jahren bin ich manchmal mit Ickx aneinander geraten. Egal, wie schlecht die Bedingungen waren, Ickx wollte immer nur fahren, während ich mir – genau wie die anderen Fahrer – Sorgen über die Sicherheit auf den Rennstrecken gemacht habe."

„1967 trat Ferrari an mich heran und fragte, ob ich im kommenden Jahr für sie fahren wollen würde. Nach einigen Treffen in Maranello ist der Deal geplatzt und Ickx bekam den Job. Während ich mit Tyrrell in die Formel 1 eingestiegen bin, hatte Jacky eine erfolgreiche Saison bei Ferrari."

„Später hat sich Ickx manchmal auch mit der Sicherheit beschäftigt – wie 1969 in Le Mans –, manchmal war er aber auch einfach nur egoistisch. Beim Spanien-GP 1975 war er einer von wenigen, die bereit waren, auf dem gefährlichen Kurs von Montjuïc zu fahren. Was mich überrascht hat, ist, dass er es in der Formel 1 nicht ganz nach oben geschafft hat. 1970 war er nah dran, hat aber nie den Titel gewonnen."

„Ickx war über einen Zeitraum von 20 Jahren ein sehr guter Fahrer. Er war ein komplizierter Charakter, aber nichtsdestotrotz ein großartiger Fahrer."

"Jacky Ickx joined me in Ken Tyrrell's team in 1966. Just as I had done in 1964, he drove in Formula Two and Three with the British team and the year after only drove in Formula Two. Ken always had a good eye for talent and Ickx was definitely in that category. He was just twenty-one at that time, very much like Ayrton Senna at that age. Very talented, fast but maybe a little over-enthusiastic."

"Jacky did not think about safety at that time, he was just interested in racing and that is all he wanted to do. He was a kind of loner only thinking about himself and trying to win races. The way he drove at Spa was always sensational, and it was at Spa that I had my big crash in 1966. It was from then on that I started my safety campaign in racing. And in the years that followed, I sometimes clashed with Ickx. He only wanted to race irrespective of the conditions, while I – and other drivers – were concerned about the safety of the tracks on which we were going to race."

"During the 1967 season, I was approached by Ferrari to drive with them for the next year. After meetings in Maranello the deal fell through and it was Ickx who got the job. I went with Tyrrell in a new F1 team while Jacky had a successful season with Ferrari."

"In later years, he occasionally got involved in safety issues – like Le Mans in 1969 – but sometimes he was behaving selfishly. He was one of the few who were prepared to drive at the dangerous Montjuïc circuit for the 1975 Spanish GP. However, I am still a bit surprised that he did not make it to the very top in F1. He came close in 1970 but never won the title."

"Ickx was a great driver over a period of some twenty years, a man with a complicated character, but a great driver nevertheless."

1971 – 1972

Höhen und Tiefen mit Ferrari
Mixed success with Ferrari

Die guten Ergebnisse in der zweiten Jahreshälfte 1970 stimmten das Ferrari-Team optimistisch für die kommende Saison, zumal die Scuderia das Formel-1-Auto über den Winter weiter verbessert und einen neuen Dreiliter-Sport-Prototypen entwickelt hatte.

In der Fahrerbesetzung gab es bei den Roten nur minimale Änderungen: Wie im Vorjahr fungierte Jacky Ickx als Nummer eins und sein Teamkollege war der Schweizer Gianclaudio „Clay" Regazzoni. Darüber hinaus sollte der Amerikaner Mario Andretti 1971 bei einigen F1-Rennen an den Start gehen. Ignazio Giunti und Arturo Merzario kamen zudem im Sportwagen zum Einsatz.

Für Ickx sollte die Saison eigentlich Ende Januar mit dem GP von Argentinien beginnen. Auf derselben Strecke fand zwei Wochen vorher mit den 1000 Kilometern von Buenos Aires der erste Lauf zur Int. Markenmeisterschaft für Sportwagen statt, wo Ferraris neuer Sport-Prototyp namens 312PB debütierte. Giunti/Merzario legten einen vielversprechenden Auftakt hin, bis Giunti in Runde 38 in den Matra von Jean-Pierre Beltoise krachte, den Beltoise gerade über die Strecke schob. Der Ferrari fing Feuer und da die Streckenposten nicht in der Lage waren, ihn zu befreien, starb der Italiener in den Flammen. Nach der Tragödie sagte die Scuderia die Teilnahme am F1-Rennen in Buenos Aires ab, das ohnehin nicht zur WM zählte.

The positive results achieved in the second part of 1970 made the Ferrari team optimistic for the new season. Ferrari further fine-tuned their existing Formula One car and also introduced a new three-litre sports prototype for the endurance championship, the 312PB.

There were minor changes in the Ferrari line-up compared to the previous season. Jacky Ickx was their number one driver with Swiss, Gianclaudio 'Clay' Regazzoni, as his partner. For a number of races, American Mario Andretti would join the Formula One team while young Ignazio Giunti would drive the new sportscar where he would race with Arturo Merzario.

For Jacky Ickx, the season was intended to have started at the end of January with the Argentinean GP. It was at the same track where the World Sportscar Championship had already kicked off two weeks earlier with the 1,000 Kilometres of Buenos Aires where Giunti and Merzario had debuted the new Ferrari sportscar and got off to a promising start. However, after 38 laps, Giunti crashed into Jean-Pierre Beltoise's Matra that Beltoise was pushing across the circuit. The Ferrari caught fire and Giunti died when the marshals were unable to rescue him. After this tragedy, the Scuderia withdrew all of its cars from the non-championship Formula One race in Buenos Aires.

BOAC 1000 km 1971, Brands Hatch

Gran Premio de España 1971, Montjuïc

Beim Auftakt der Formel-1-WM in Südafrika ging Ferrari aber wie geplant mit drei Wagen an den Start. Zum Einsatz kamen noch die 1970er-Autos, die das ganze Wochenende Probleme mit den Reifen hatten. Ickx musste während des Rennens sogar wegen eines Reifenschadens an die Box kommen. Andretti übernahm dagegen vier Umläufe vor Schluss die Führung von Denny Hulme und feierte seinen ersten GP-Sieg. Regazzoni wurde Dritter, Ickx landete mit einer Runde Rückstand auf Rang acht. Für Ferrari war es also ein guter Start in die F1-Weltmeisterschaft.

Nach der Tragödie von Argentinien verzichtete Ferrari auch auf den Start in Daytona, bei den 12 Stunden von Sebring waren die 312PB aber dabei. Ickx formte mit Andretti ein starkes Team. Nach der zweitbesten Zeit im Qualifying blieben die früheren Daytona-Sieger in der ersten Rennhälfte immer in Schlagdistanz zur Spitze, bis sie den Ferrari nach 117 Runden abstellen mussten. Das Problem war, dass der 312PB prinzipiell ein Formel-1-Auto mit einer Sportwagenkarosse war und Motor wie Getriebe nicht den Belastungen eines Langstreckenrennens gewachsen waren. Ickx blieb danach in Amerika, um am Questor Grand Prix teilzunehmen. Bei dem Rennen in Kalifornien traten die europäischen F1-Autos gegen die amerikanische Formel A an. Ferrari-Mann Mario Andretti nutzte hier seine Erfahrung in Highspeed-Ovalen und gewann beide Läufe. Ickx wurde im ersten Rennen Fünfter und schied im zweiten Heat aus.

Eine Woche später erzielte Ickx bei den 1000 Kilometern von Brands Hatch in der Quali die Bestzeit. Ickx und Regazzoni führten das Rennen über weite Strecken an, bis sie mit einem sich drehenden Chevron kollidierten und zehn Minuten an der Box verloren. Später musste auch noch der Gaszug des 312PB gewechselt werden. Dadurch wurden Ickx/Regazzoni nur Zweite, drei Runden hinter dem siegreichen Alfa Romeo Tipo 33. Beim Spanien-GP in Barcelona wurde Ickx erneut Zweiter, diesmal hinter Jackie Stewart. Ickx war von der Pole gestartet, musste den Schotten aber in Runde fünf vorbeilassen und konnte ihn danach nicht mehr abfangen.

For the first Formula One World Championship race, the South African Grand Prix, Ferrari entered three of their 1970 cars. The whole weekend the Ferrari team was plagued with tyre problems and, in the race, Ickx had to come into the pits with a flat tyre. This left him one lap down on the leaders. After a fierce battle with Denny Hulme, Mario Andretti took the lead four laps before the end of the race and eventually won his first Grand Prix. Regazzoni finished third with Ickx a lap down in eighth. For Ferrari, it was a good start to the F1 season.

After the tragic race in Argentina, Ferrari decided not to race at Daytona but entered a 312PB sports prototype for the 12 Hours of Sebring with Ickx partnering Andretti, both former winners of this legendary race. The little spyder set the second fastest time in qualifying and ran up near the front for most of the first half of the race. The new 312PB was basically a Formula One car with full bodywork and thus the engine and gearbox were not up to the strain of a long race. Consequently, the team had to retire after one hundred and seventeen laps. After the race, Ickx stayed in America to compete in the non-champion Questor Grand Prix in California. Over thirty cars were entered in this battle between Formula One cars and American Formula A cars. Mario Andretti showed his knowledge and experience of high-speed ovals by winning both heats in his Ferrari. Ickx came fifth in the first race but had to retire in the second.

A week later Ickx set the fastest qualifying lap for the 1,000 Kilometres of Brands Hatch in the 312PB sportscar. Together with Regazzoni, he led most of the race, but had to pit for a ten-minute repair after hitting a spinning Chevron. Later an accelerator cable had to be replaced and the team finished second, three laps down on an Alfa Romeo 33. At the Spanish Grand Prix in Barcelona, Ickx again finished second, this time to Jackie Stewart. Ickx started from pole but the Scottish driver took the lead after five laps and Ickx was unable to re-pass him.

1000 km di Monza 1971

Die nächsten beiden Sportwagenrennen fanden auf Highspeed-Strecken statt und hier zeigten Ickx/Regazzoni in der Quali eine sensationelle Form. In Monza startete das Ferrari-Duo aus der ersten Reihe, in Spa von der fünften Position. Leider endeten beide Rennen dramatisch. In Italien krachte Ickx in den Ferrari 512M von Merzario, nachdem sich ein Porsche 907 vor den beiden Ferrari gedreht hatte. In Belgien wurde Regazzoni bei Tempo 240 von einem Dulon-Porsche von der Strecke gedrängt. Zum Glück blieben die Ferraristi bei beiden Kollisionen unverletzt.

Ferrari ließ die Targa Florio aus, war bei den 1000 Kilometern auf dem Nürburgring aber wieder mit von der Partie. Ickx wurde seinem Ruf als Nordschleifen-Spezialist gerecht und stellte den 312PB auf die Pole – mit neun (!) Sekunden Vorsprung auf den zweitplatzierten Rolf Stommelen im Alfa Romeo. Im Rennen setzte sich die Pechsträhne von Ferrari aber fort, Ickx schied in Führung liegend mit Motorschaden aus. Der 312PB war zweifellos schnell und hielt in Normalfall auch 1000 Kilometer durch, aber wohl eher keine 24 Stunden. Aus diesem Grund ließ Ferrari Le Mans sausen. Ickx und Regazzoni mussten also bis Ende Juni warten, ehe sie wieder im Sportwagen saßen.

The next two sportscar races were to be held at high-speed tracks and both Ickx and Regazzoni showed tremendous form in qualifying. In Monza, the Ferrari pairing started from the front row and at Spa-Francorchamps they qualified fifth. Unfortunately both races ended in drama. In Italy, Ickx ran into Merzario's Ferrari 512M after Merzario found a spinning Porsche 907 in front of him. In Belgium, Regazzoni got bundled off the track by a Dulon-Porsche that put him into the barriers at 240 kph. Fortunately, on both occasions, the Ferrari drivers escaped unscathed.

Ferrari decided not to go to Sicily for the Targa Florio, so the 1,000 Kilometres of the Nürburgring was the next sportscar race. Jacky Ickx was by now known as a Nürburgring specialist and the Belgian driver delivered in style by qualifyiing on pole. He was nine seconds faster than the second-placed man, Rolf Stommelen in an Alfa Romeo. In the race, however, Ferrari's bad luck continued as the engine broke while leading. The 312PB was a fast car and could race for a 1,000 kilometres but Ferrari decided not to risk going to Le Mans for their 24-hour endurance race. Instead, Ickx and Clay Regazzoni had to wait until late June for the Austrian sportscar race at Zeltweg.

ADAC-1000-km-Rennen 1971, Nürburgring, Ferrari 312PB

ADAC-1000-km-Rennen 1971, Nürburgring, Ferrari 312PB

▶ ADAC-1000-km-Rennen 1971, Nürburgring, Ferrari 312PB

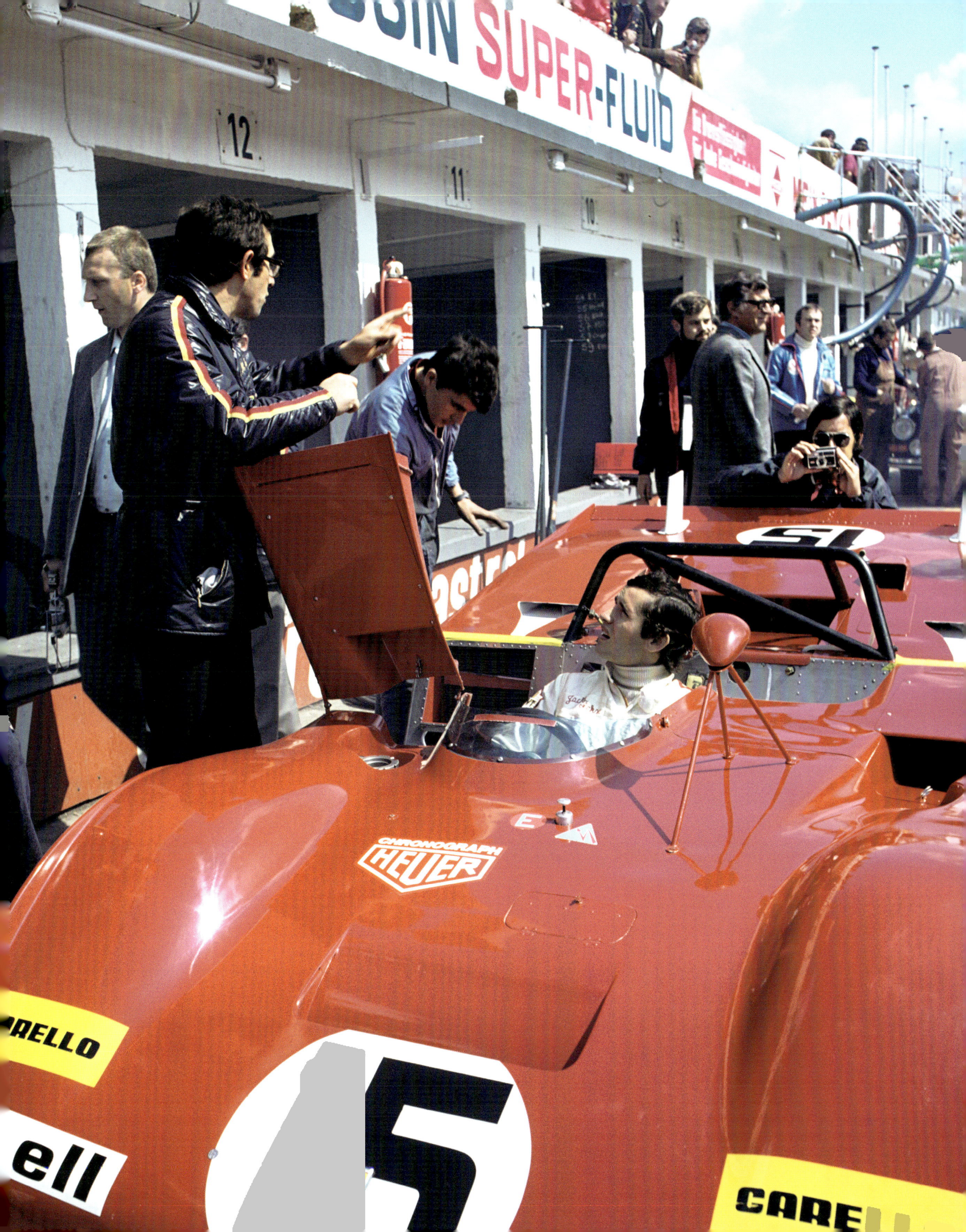
SUPER-FLUID
12
11
10
CHRONOGRAPH
HEUER
5

Beim Monaco-GP hatte zwischenzeitlich der neue F1-Renner 312B2 – eine Weiterentwicklung des erfolgreichen 312B – sein Debüt gegeben. Ickx startete aus der ersten Reihe und wurde Dritter. Da Ickx in Le Mans nicht zum Einsatz kam, nahm er stattdessen am Jochen Rindt Memorial auf dem Hockenheimring teil. Bei dem Formel-1-Rennen ohne WM-Status holte der Belgier die Pole und siegte nach 35 Runden souverän. Eine Woche später beim GP der Niederlande holte Ickx seine zweite Pole in der laufenden F1-Weltmeisterschaft. Das Rennen in Zandvoort fand bei widrigsten Wetterbedingungen statt, und Ickx fühlte sich auf der nassen Piste in seinem Element. Ickx gewann vor Pedro Rodriguez. Die beiden Regenspezialisten überrundeten im Laufe des Rennens das komplette restliche Feld. Beim Frankreich-GP, der erstmals auf dem neuen Circuit Paul Ricard bei Le Castellet ausgetragen wurde, startete Ickx aus Reihe eins, schied aber nach vier Runden durch Motorschaden aus. Der Zwölfzylinder ließ ihn auch in Silverstone im Stich, sodass Ickx schon zur Halbzeit praktisch keine Chance mehr auf den Formel-1-Titel hatte. Ickx hatte 19 Punkte auf dem Konto, Jackie Stewart schon 42.

Pech hatte Ickx auch bei den letzten zwei Sportwagenrennen: In Österreich verunfallte Regazzoni wegen eines Bremsdefekts schwer. Beim Finale in Watkins Glen, wo sich Ickx das Cockpit mit Andretti teilte, sorgte ein defekter Anlasser für das Aus.

Beim Deutschland-GP startete Ickx erneut aus Reihe eins und hoffte auf ein gutes Ergebnis, zumal der Große Preis nach dem Gastspiel auf dem Hockenheimring wieder auf der Nordschleife stattfand, die sicherer gemacht worden war. Ickx erwischte einen guten Start und fuhr als Erster auf die Nordkurve zu, doch Stewart bremste ihn aus und ging in Führung. In Runde zwei unterlief Ickx dann ein seltener Fehler: Am Wippermann drehte er sich von der Strecke in einen Zaun und fiel aus. Beim Österreich-GP war es dann wieder der Motor, der Ickx im Stich ließ. In Monza machte der Antriebsstrang nach 15 Runden auf Platz drei liegend schlapp. In Kanada war der Ferrari dagegen überraschend langsam, Ickx wurde im Mosport Park nur Achter. Beim US-Grand-Prix strandete der 312B2 wiederum mit defekter Lichtmaschine. Ickx beendete die Formel-1-Saison also mit fünf Nullnummern in Folge und belegte in der Endabrechnung der WM nur Platz vier – punktgleich mit Jo Siffert.

Ende September saß Jacky erstmals seit 1966 wieder am Steuer eines BMW-Tourenwagens. Zusammen mit Hans-Joachim Stuck nahm er an den 6 Stunden von Paul Ricard teil. Im ersten Heat des EM-Laufs erreichte ihr BMW 2800 CS nach Bremsproblemen nur den 31. Platz. Den zweiten Heat beendeten sie auf Rang zehn. Zum Abschluss des Jahres trat Ickx wie üblich bei den 9 Stunden von Kyalami an, wo er sich die verbesserte 1972er-Version des 312PB mit Andretti teilte. Bei dem Lauf zur südafrikanischen Springbok Series wurden Ickx/Andretti Zweite hinter ihren Teamkollegen Regazzoni/Brian Redman in einem 1971er-Ferrari.

Mit nur zwei Gesamtsiegen war die Saison 1971 für Ickx eher enttäuschend verlaufen. Trotz der Probleme mit der Zuverlässigkeit des Formel-1-Renners und Sportwagens blieb der Belgier der Marke mit dem springenden Pferd treu und verlängerte seinen Vertrag um ein Jahr.

Ferrari nutzte den Winter für umfangreiche Tests mit dem Sport-Prototypen 312PB und ging daher als Favorit in die Saison 1972. In der Formel 1 setzte die Scuderia die neueste Entwicklungsstufe des 312B2 ein. Und auch personell gab es bei Ferrari eine große Veränderung: Peter Schetty wurde neuer Rennleiter.

For the Monaco Grand Prix, Ferrari debuted the new 312B2, an updated version of the successful 312B. Ickx qualified for the race on the front row and finished third. Instead of being at Le Mans, Ickx went to the Hockenheimring to race in the Jochen Rindt memorial race, a non-championship Formula One race. Ickx took pole position and won the thirty-five-lap race easily. For the Dutch GP at Zandvoort a week later, Ickx got his second pole in the current Formula One World Championship. The race was held in very poor climatic conditions, but the rain suited Ickx. He was in his element and won ahead of Pedro Rodriguez. These two – both on Firestone tyres – both proved to be rain specialists and lapped all the other competitors. At the French GP, held this time at the new Paul Ricard track near Le Castellet in the south of France, Ickx started from the front row but unfortunately, the engine broke after just four laps. His engine let him down at Silverstone as well so that at the halfway point of the 1971 season after six grands prix, Ickx was already without a chance of winning the title since he had nineteen points compared with Jackie Stewart's forty-two.

Bad luck also came in the sportscar races. In Austria, Regazzoni crashed heavily due to a brake failure while at the final race in Watkins Glen – this time Ickx was partnered again by Andretti – a broken starter motor led to yet another retirement.

Ickx was on the front row for the German GP and the team was hoping for a great result. After last year's transfer to the Hockenheimring, the Nürburgring had now been completely overhauled and made much safer. Ickx made a good start and led going into the Nordkurve. However, Jackie Stewart out-braked him and took the lead. During the second lap, Ickx made a rare mistake going into Wippermann, spun and crashed into the fence to retire. For the Austrian GP, Ickx again did not finish and this time it was the engine that broke. His bad luck continued in Monza where the transmission let him down after fifteen laps while lying third while both in Canada and at Watkins Glen, Ickx failed to score points. Unusually, the Ferrari ran poorly in the Canadian race at Mosport Park while, at the US GP, the alternator packed in leaving Ickx stranded. Thus there were no points for Ickx from the final five GPs of the year and the Belgian ended the 1971 Formula One World Championship in fourth place, ex-aequo with Jo Siffert.

In late September, Jacky Ickx was back behind the wheel of an Alpina-BMW when he joined Hans-Joachim Stuck in a race for the European Touring Car Championship, the 6 Hours at Le Castellet. The pairing drove a BMW 2800 CS and finished a lowly thirty-first in the first heat due to brake problems. The following day in the second heat they finished tenth so that on aggregate they were classed as a non-finisher. Ickx ended his racing season in South Africa where he and Andretti drove the updated 1972 version of the 312PB to second place in the 9 Hours of Kyalami, a round of the South African Springbok Series. They were only beaten by their team-mates Regazzoni and Brian Redman in a 1971 Ferrari.

With only two victories, 1971 was not the best season that Ickx had experienced. But although both Ferrari's Formula One and sportscar machines had suffered many unreliability problems, the Belgian driver decided to renew his contract with the Italian manufacturer for 1972.

Ferrari did a lot of testing over the winter and their new sportscar, the 312PB, was expected to be the car to beat in 1972. In Formula One, Ferrari would start with an updated version of last year's 312B2. In addition, Peter Schetty, Ickx's ex-partner, had taken over as manager of the Maranello team.

RAC British Grand Prix 1971, Silverstone, Ferrari 312B2

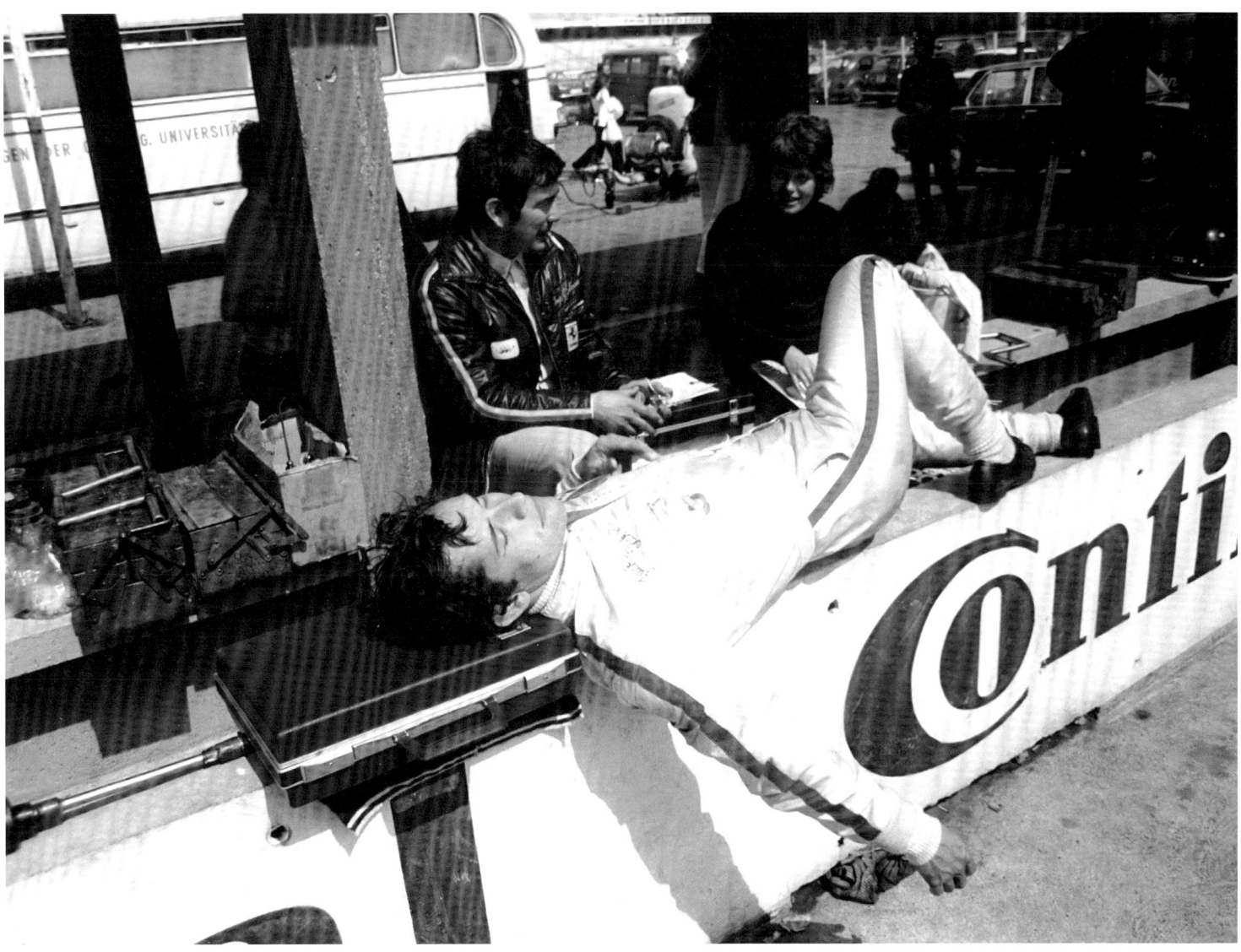

Rindt Memorial 1971, Hockenheim

— 121 —

Grand Prix de Monaco 1971

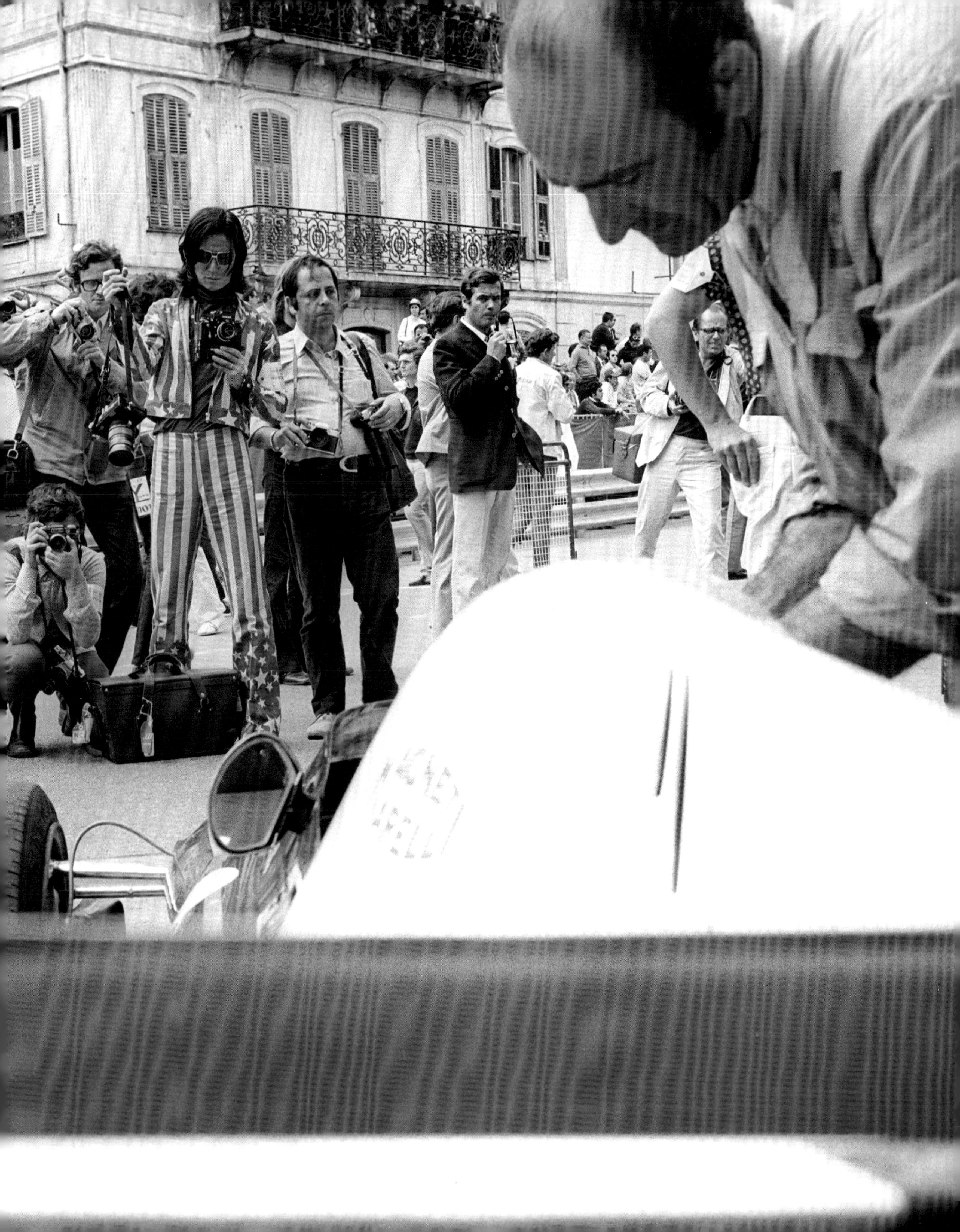

Gran Premio d'Italia 1971, Monza

BOAC 1000 km 1972, Brands Hatch, Ferrari 312PB

Ferrari reiste in voller Stärke zum Auftakt der Sportwagen-WM 1972 in Argentinien. Die drei 312PB wurden von Tim Schenken/ Ronnie Peterson, Clay Regazzoni/Brian Redman sowie Jacky Ickx/ Mario Andretti gefahren. Ihre größten Gegner in Buenos Aires waren die Dreiliter-Prototypen von Alfa Romeo sowie die von Jo Bonnier eingesetzten Lola. Nach der Qualifikation standen die Ferrari auf den Plätzen eins, drei und vier. Im Rennen fuhren die 312PB einen Start-Ziel-Sieg mit Schenken/Peterson an der Spitze ein. Ickx wurde nach Handlingproblemen an seinem Ferrari nur Zehnter. Die Motorsport-elite blieb danach in Buenos Aires, um zwei Wochen später den ersten GP des Jahres unter die Räder zu nehmen. In der Quali schaffte es Ickx im weiterentwickelten Ferrari 312B2 nur in die vierte Reihe, während die vorderen Plätze fest in der Hand von Goodyear-Piloten waren. Im Rennen verbesserte sich Ickx auf Rang drei, allerdings mit einer Minute Rückstand auf den siegreichen Jackie Stewart.

Da der 312PB vermutlich keine 24 Stunden überstehen würden, fragte Enzo Ferrari bei Bill France an, ob er das Rennen in Daytona von 24 auf sechs Stunden reduzieren könnte. Aus Angst, Ferrari zu verlieren, stimmte er dem Vorschlag zu. Genau wie in Argentinien waren die 312PB auch in Florida eine Klasse für sich. Diesmal fuhr die Starbesetzung Ickx/Andretti zum Sieg. Beim GP von Südafrika musste sich Ickx dafür wieder hinten anstellen. Ickx startete aus der dritten Reihe, hielt sich das Rennen über im Mittelfeld auf und wurde letztlich mit einer Runde Rückstand Achter. Nach Südafrika legte die Formel 1 eine zweimonatige Pause ein. Ferrari und Firestone hatten also Zeit, um Auto und Reifen zu verbessern.

Für Ickx standen drei Sportwagenrennen in Folge bevor: Sebring, Brands Hatch und Monza. Davor hatte der Belgier allerdings noch den Frühjahrstest in Le Mans im Kalender stehen, wo er die Überlegenheit des Ferrari mit der Bestzeit untermauerte. Für die 12 Stunden von Sebring hatte Ferrari ein neues Getriebe entwickelt und die Karosse im Heck verändert, um schnellere Boxenstopps zu ermöglichen. Ickx/Andretti erwiesen sich im Training und Rennen erneut als Maß der Dinge. Ferrari landete mit Ickx/Andretti vor Schenken/Peterson einen Doppelsieg. In exakt derselben Konstellation endete auch das Rennen in Brands Hatch. Bei den regnerischen 1000 Kilometern von Monza feierte Ickx den dritten Triumph in Folge. Da Andretti am selben Wochenende in den USA startete, nahm Regazzoni in Italien den Platz neben Ickx ein.

Ferrari sent a full team to Argentina for the first race of the 1972 World Sportscar Championship. Three new 312PBs with Tim Schenken and Ronnie Peterson in one car, Clay Regazzoni partnered by Brian Redman, and Jacky Ickx as in 1971 with Mario Andretti. The main opposition came from Alfa Romeo, who also entered three 3-litre sportscars, and from several Lolas run by Jo Bonnier. After practice and qualifying, Ferraris were on pole as well as in third and fourth. In the 1,000-kilometre race, Ferrari was in charge all the way and Schenken and Peterson won but Ickx ended up tenth after he was slowed by poor handling on his car. The motor sport community then stayed in Buenos Aires for the first Grand Prix of the year. Ickx had an updated Ferrari 312B2 but, in qualifying, Goodyear-shod cars were fastest and Ickx found himself on the fourth row. After a steady, uneventful race, the Belgian driver finished third, almost a minute behind the winner, Jackie Stewart.

Since their sportscars were not strong enough to compete for twenty-four hours, Enzo Ferrari asked Bill France to change the 24 Hours of Daytona into a six-hour event. The owner of the Florida speedway was afraid that Ferrari might stay away and thus agreed to the proposition. As in Argentina, the Ferraris were in a class of their own and this time the star team of Ickx and Andretti won. However, at the South African GP, they still trailed the faster Tyrrell of Stewart and Ickx could only qualify on row three. After racing mid-field, Ickx finished one lap down in eighth place. There was then a two-month gap before the Spanish Grand Prix, so this gave Ferrari and Firestone some time to improve matters.

For the sportscar team, there were three races in a row: Sebring, Brands Hatch and Monza. But before going to Sebring, the team attended the traditional spring tests at Le Mans where Jacky Ickx confirmed the superiority of Ferrari by setting the fastest lap. For the 12-hour race in Sebring, the team had a new gearbox and new rear bodywork to enable faster pit stops. Again, the Ickx-Andretti car was fastest in qualifying and in the race they were unchallenged. They won and led home a one-two for Ferrari. They gained the same result in England where Ickx-Andretti won ahead of Schenken-Peterson. The 1,000 Kilometres at Monza was run in rainy conditions and again Ickx won the race. Due to commitments in the USA, Regazzoni had taken Andretti's place in Italy and thus shared the win with him.

Vor dem ersten Grand Prix auf europäischem Boden hatte Ferrari den 312B2 in einigen Bereichen verbessert, und das zahlte sich mit der Pole Position im spanischen Jarama aus. Nach einem schlechten Start machte Ickx einige Plätze wieder gut, an Emerson Fittipaldi kam er aber nicht mehr heran. In den Straßen von Monaco stellte Ickx seinen Ferrari ebenfalls in Reihe eins. Am Renntag regnete es in Strömen. Jean-Pierre Beltoise gelang ein großartiger Start aus der zweiten Reihe. Er ging in Führung und behauptete diese über 80 Runden. Ickx wurde mit 38 Sekunden Rückstand erneut Zweiter. Zwischen diesen beiden Grands Prix bestritt Ickx zwei Rennen auf seiner Lieblingsstrecke Spa-Francorchamps: Im BMW 2800 CS von Schnitzer gewann er das Tourenwagenrennen von der Pole aus. Die 1000 Kilometer von Spa begann er auch von der Pole, musste sich am Ende aber mit Platz zwei hinter den Teamkollegen Redman/Merzario begnügen. In der Quali zum 1000-Kilometer-Rennen am Nürburgring wurden Ickx/Regazzoni bei ständig wechselnden Wetterbedingungen deklassiert. Das Duo landete hinter den anderen 312PB, den Alfa, dem neuen Gulf-Mirage und einigen anderen Autos auf Rang acht. Dem Rennen drückten die Ferrari aber ihren Stempel auf und feierten im Ziel einen weiteren Doppelsieg. Ickx war an diesem Triumph aber nicht beteiligt, nachdem Regazzoni im Kampf mit dem Gulf-Mirage abgeflogen war. Eine Woche später gastierte die Formel 1 in der Heimat von Ickx. Der Belgien-GP wurde 1972 aber nicht in Spa, sondern in Nivelles ausgetragen, weil die Fahrer wegen der schlechten Sicherheitsstandards nicht in Spa fahren wollten. Ickx hatte auf dem kleinen Kurs südlich von Brüssel kein Glück, er schied durch Zündungsprobleme aus.

For the first European GP at Jarama near Madrid, Ferrari had made several improvements to their cars and this resulted in a pole position for Ickx. After a slow start, the Belgian re-passed several cars but was unable to catch Emerson Fittipaldi. In the streets of Monaco, Ickx qualified on the front row once again. It was raining hard on race day and Jean-Pierre Beltoise made a great start from the second row. In very bad conditions, the Frenchman stayed in front for all eighty laps with Ickx finishing second, just thirty-eight seconds behind him. Between these Formula One races, Ickx drove two races at his favourite track, Spa-Francorchamps. In a touring car race, against mainly local drivers, he won from pole in a Schnitzer BMW 2800 CS. The next day, he started the 1,000-kilometre race from pole as well but, after some four hours, he and Regazzoni had to settle for second behind team-mates Redman and Merzario. Due to constantly changing weather conditions, Ickx and Regazzoni were outclassed during qualifying for the 1,000 Kilometres at the Nürburgring. That was not only by the two other Ferraris but also by Alfa Romeo and the new Gulf-Mirage. Right after the start however, the Ferraris took command and, after just over six hours, Ferrari had another double victory. Unfortunately however, Ickx was left empty-handed after Regazzoni had crashed their 312PB trying to keep ahead of the new Gulf-Mirage. The week after that, at Nivelles for the Belgian GP, Ickx again did not score as a faulty injection system on his 312B2 forced him to retire. The race was run at this little track south of Brussels for the first time because the drivers had said that they did not want to race F1 cars at Spa because of its poor safety record.

Grand Prix de Monaco 1972, Ferrari 312B2

Gran Premio de España 1972, Jarama, Ferrari 312B2 n°4

1000 km Österreichring 1972, Zeltweg, Ferrari 312PB

Gran Premio d'Italia 1972, Monza, Mario Andretti & Jacky Ickx

Da Ferrari bisher alle acht Läufe zur Sportwagen-WM gewonnen hatte – bei der Targa Florio hatten Sandro Munari und Merzario für Maranello gesiegt –, verzichtete die Scuderia auf einen Start in Le Mans. Stattdessen baute das Team neue Autos und reiste zwei Wochen später mit vier 312PB zu den 1000 Kilometern am Österreichring. Carlos Pace und Helmut Marko verstärkten das Team. Da sich Regazzoni verletzt hatte, kam es in Zeltweg zum Wiedersehen von Ickx und seinem 1968er-Teamkollegen Redman. Das Rennen hätte für Ferrari nicht besser laufen können: Die Mannschaft aus Maranello feierte einen Vierfachsieg mit Ickx/Redman an der Spitze.

Bei den F1-Rennen in Frankreich und Großbritannien lief es dagegen nicht wie gewünscht. In Charade startete Ickx aus der zweiten Reihe und war im Rennen Zweiter, als er durch einen Reifenschaden mehrere Minuten verlor. Am Ende wurde Jacky nur Elfter. In Brands Hatch markierte Ickx die Pole und führte das Rennen bis zur 48. Runde an, schied dann aber ohne Öldruck aus. Am Nürburgring präsentierten sich Ickx und der Ferrari aber wieder in Topform: Ickx fuhr in der Quali und im Rennen die schnellste Runde und siegte vor Teamkollege Regazzoni. Zwischendurch hatte die Scuderia in der Sportwagen-WM ihr nächstes Erfolgserlebnis gefeiert: Ickx hatte zusammen mit Andretti das Finale in Watkins Glen gewonnen. Für den Belgier war es der sechste Sportwagen-Sieg im laufenden Jahr.

In der Formel 1 schlug dafür wieder der Defektteufel zu: Auf dem Österreichring mussten Ickx und sein Teamkollege Regazzoni wegen Problemen mit der Benzinzufuhr aufgeben. In Monza startete der Belgier von der Pole und lag in Führung, als ihm acht Runden vor Schluss die Elektronik hängen ließ. Das Aus für Ickx. Emerson Fittipaldi fuhr in Italien seinen fünften Saisonsieg ein und krönte sich damit im Alter von 25 Jahren zum bis dato jüngsten Formel-1-Weltmeister.

Obwohl die 500 Kilometer von Imola nicht der WM angehörten, ging Ferrari mit zwei Autos an den Start. Beim Heimspiel der Scuderia fuhr Ickx als Vorbereitung auf die Saison 1973 bereits die neueste Version des 312PB Spyder. Nach der Pole in der Quali musste sich der Belgier im Rennen jedoch dem zweiten Ferrari von Merzario geschlagen geben. Die letzten beiden F1-Rennen des Jahres fanden in Übersee statt. Im kanadischen Mosport Park wurde Ickx nach einem blassen Rennen und einem Reifenwechsel nur Zwölfter. Zwei Wochen später wurde er in Watkins Glen Fünfter. In der kompletten Formel-1-Saison hatte Ickx nur 27 WM-Punkte geholt und belegte somit Platz vier. Der Sieg am Nürburgring war sein mit Abstand bestes Ergebnis gewesen.

Den Abschluss der Saison bildeten erneut die 9 Stunden von Kyalami. Ickx ging zusammen mit Brian Redman an den Start, schied aber wegen eines Motorproblems vorzeitig aus.

Damit ging das Motorsportjahr 1972 zu Ende. Zwei Monate später sollte aber schon die neue Saison beginnen, die Ickx erneut in den F1-Autos und Sportwagen von Ferrari bestritt.

Because Ferrari had won all eight sportscar races held so far in 1972 – a single Ferrari entry of Sandro Munari and Merzario had also won the Targa Florio – the Italian team chose not to go to Le Mans. This gave them time to build new cars, so that four 312PBs would be competing in the 1,000 Kilometres at the Österreichring. New to the team were Carlos Pace and Helmut Marko. Here Brian Redman, Ickx's old teammate with Gulf-Ford, replaced an injured Regazzoni thus partnering Jacky Ickx. No problems whatsoever for the Ferraris and they finished a strong 1-2-3-4 with Ickx-Redman as the overall winners.

Ickx had no success at the French and British GPs. At Charade, Ickx would start from the second row but, while lying second, he had a puncture and lost several minutes replacing the wheel and ended up eleventh. At Brands Hatch, after starting from pole, Ickx led for forty-eight laps but then had to retire with no oil pressure. However, two weeks later at the Nürburgring, Ickx was on top form. He set fastest time in qualifying, recorded fastest lap in the race and won ahead of team-mate Regazzoni. In between, the Ferrari team had travelled to America for the final sportscar race of the season, the 6 Hours at Watkins Glen. With Andretti back as his team-mate, Ickx won his sixth sportscar race of the season.

Ickx had more bad luck with his Formula One cars in Austria and Italy. At the Österreichring, the Belgian had to retire with fuel problems along with his team-mate Regazzoni. Then at Monza, despite starting from pole and leading for most of the way, the electronics let him down and he had to retire eight laps from the end. With his fifth win of the season in Italy, Emerson Fittipaldi was crowned as new World Champion, and at 25 years old, the youngest ever.

Although not counting for the World Championship, Ferrari sent two sportscars to Imola for the 500-kilometre race. In preparation for the 1973 season, Ickx drove an updated version of the successful spyder. Although Ickx started from pole, Merzario in the other Ferrari beat him. The two final Formula One races of 1972 were held overseas in Canada and the United States. At Mosport Park, Ickx drove an unexceptional race, and after a tyre change, ended a lowly twelfth. Two weeks later at Watkins Glen he finished fifth. In total, Jacky Ickx had scored twenty-seven championship points and that gave him fourth place in the championship with his victory at the Nürburgring being by far his best result.

Once again, the season would come to an end in South Africa. With Brian Redman as partner, he competed in the 9 Hours of Kyalami. However, this year an engine problem caused them to retire.

The season was now over and, in just over two months, Ickx would be back with Ferrari and, as in 1972, driving both sportscars and Formula One.

RAC British Grand Prix 1972, Brands Hatch

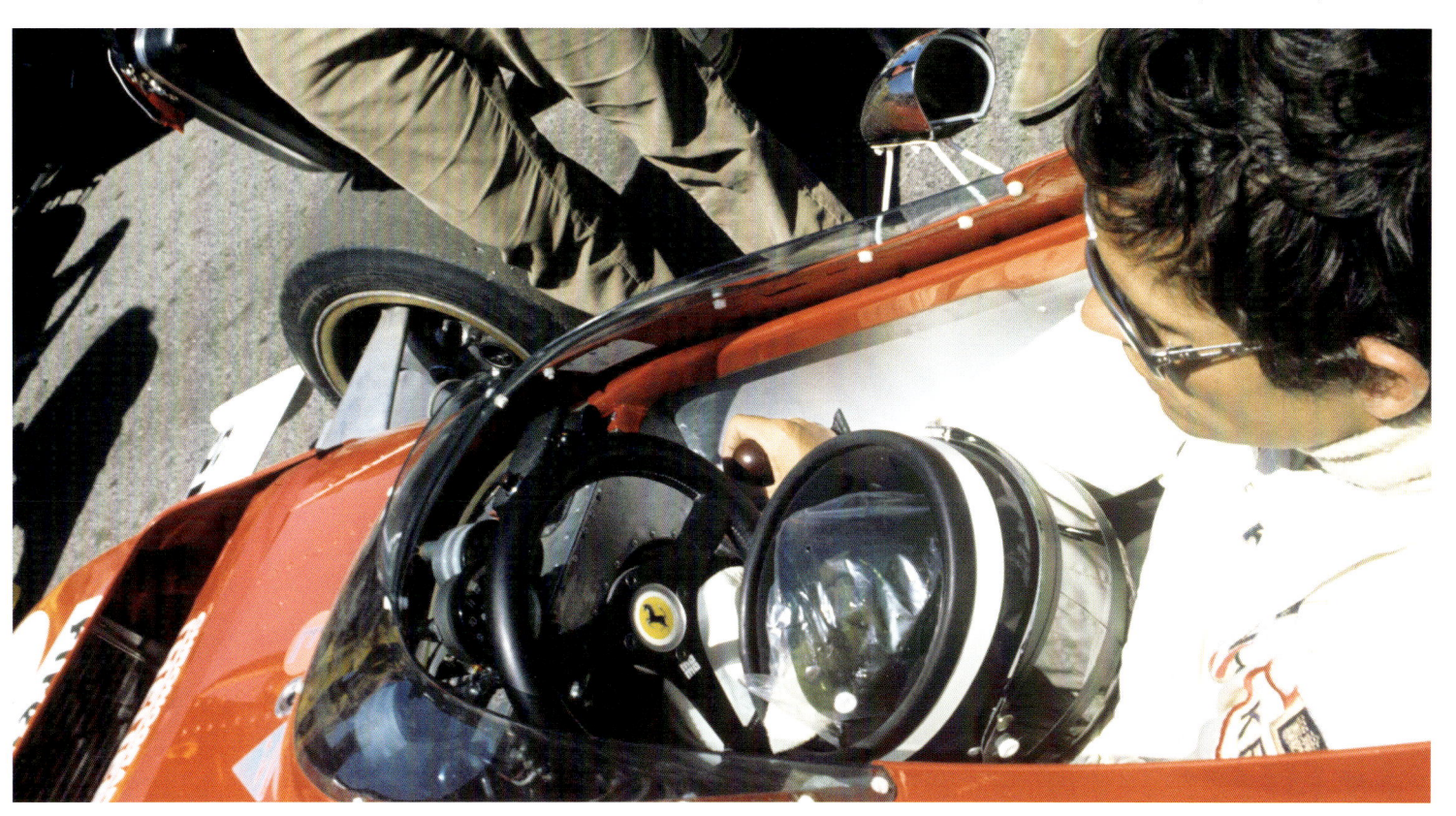

RAC British Grand Prix 1972, Brands Hatch, Ferrari 312B2

RAC British Grand Prix 1972, Brands Hatch, Ferrari 312B2

— 131 —

1973

Das letzte Jahr bei Ferrari
The final year with Ferrari

Ferrari wollte zur Saison 1973 gravierende Veränderungen an seinem Formel-1-Auto vornehmen. Beim Auftakt in Argentinien am 28. Januar war der neue 312B3 aber noch nicht fertig. Zudem hatte die Scuderia den erfolgreichen Sport-Prototyp 312PB im Detail verbessert, und dieser war auch schon zu Jahresbeginn einsatzbereit.

In der Formel 1 bekam es Jacky Ickx mit einem neuen, alten Teamkollegen zu tun. Sportwagen-Ass Arturo Merzario ging für Ferrari jetzt auch bei Grands Prix an den Start. In Argentinien war Ickx klar schneller. Der Belgier erzielte in der Quali die drittbeste Zeit und beendete das Rennen nach Problemen mit dem Gasgestänge als Vierter – mit 43 Sekunden Rückstand auf den Sieger Emerson Fittipaldi. Zwei Wochen später landete Ickx in der Qualifikation in Brasilien wieder auf Platz drei. Im Rennen behauptete der Belgier diese Position, als er wegen eines Reifenschadens – die Ferrari rollten neuerdings auf Goodyear – die Box ansteuern musste.

Ferrari was planning to make substantial changes to its Formula One car for the 1973 season. However, for the first grand prix of the year, on January 28th in Argentina, the new car was not yet ready. But their sportscar, the very successful 312PB, had only been slightly modified and was ready to go at the start of the season.

For the Argentine Grand Prix, Ickx had a new team-mate in Arturo Merzario. In qualifying, Ickx did well and set third fastest time. After an uneventful race, only slowed at one point by a broken throttle rod, he finished fourth, almost forty-three seconds behind the winner, Emerson Fittipaldi. Two weeks later in Brazil, Ickx again set third fastest time in qualifying, but this time finished fifth in the now ageing 312B2. For a long time, Ickx had held third position, but a puncture made him visit the pits. Ferrari was now using Goodyear tyres and somehow the team fitted a wheel from Merzario's car, which was an inch narrower.

Targa Florio 1973, Ferrari 312PB

Beim Wechsel montierte das Team jedoch einen von Merzarios Pneus, die einen Zoll schmaler waren. Das machte das Fahrverhalten des 312B2 nicht besser und so kam Ickx nicht über Platz fünf hinaus. Beim Südafrika-GP verunfallte Ickx in Runde zwei. Auslöser war ein Dreher von Lokalmatador Dave Charlton in der Crowthorne Corner und die folgende Kollision mit Mike Hailwood. Clay Regazzoni konnte nicht mehr ausweichen und krachte in Hailwoods Wagen, und Ickx wiederum in Regazzonis BRM, der sofort in Flammen aufging. Hailwood eilte sofort zur Hilfe, zog den bewusstlosen Regazzoni aus dem brennenden Auto und rettete ihm so das Leben.

In den sechs Wochen vor Beginn der Europasaison der Formel 1 nahm Ickx an drei Sportwagenrennen teil. Den Auftakt bildeten die 6 Stunden von Vallelunga, welche die 12 Stunden von Sebring im WM-Kalender ersetzten, da der Flugplatzkurs nicht mehr den Sicherheitsbestimmungen der FIA entsprach. Ickx fuhr dieses Jahr mit einem neuen Partner: Brian Redman kehrte nach einem Sabbatjahr auf die Rennstrecke zurück und ersetzte Regazzoni. Der Schweizer durfte die Goodyear-bereiften Ferrari 312PB nicht fahren, da sein Formel-1-BRM auf Firestone-Reifen unterwegs war. Im Training und Qualifying hatten die Ferrari Probleme mit dem Handling und waren daher langsamer als die Matra MS670B. Im Rennen landeten die Ferrari auf den Plätzen zwei, drei und vier – hinter dem MS670B von Henri Pescarolo, Gérard Larrousse and François Cevert. Matra gewann auch den zweiten WM-Lauf in Dijon-Prenois vor Ickx/Redman im Ferrari. Für die 1000 Kilometer von Monza hatte Ferrari die Karosserie im Heck geändert, um das Handling zu verbessern. Mit Erfolg: Von der Pole gestartet, gewannen Ickx/Redman mit drei Runden Vorsprung auf ihre Teamkollegen Carlos Reutemann und Tim Schenken.

Beim Spanien-GP war der neue 312B3 endlich einsatzbereit. Ferrari reiste mit zwei verschiedenen Varianten an, und Ickx entschied sich für Chassis 011 mit einem vorn liegenden Kühler. Wegen anhaltender Streiks hatte Ferrari die Monocoques in England anfertigen lassen, nur der Zusammenbau erfolgte in Maranello. Auf dem Straßenkurs im Montjuïc Park fuhr Ickx im Training die sechste Zeit und lag zur Rennmitte weiterhin auf Platz sechs. Danach musste er stoppen, um die Bremsflüssigkeit zu prüfen und verlor dadurch mehrere Plätze. So erreichte Ickx abgeschlagen als Zwölfter das Ziel. Anschließend trat Ferrari mit denselben Autos beim Belgien-GP in Zolder an. Ickx nutzte seinen Heimvorteil mit Platz drei in der Qualifikation, sein Rennen endete aber nach sieben Runden mit defekter Ölpumpe. Während des Wochenendes gab es nicht weniger als elf Unfälle, die allesamt auf den schlechten Zustand der Strecke zurückzuführen waren. In Monaco beschädigte Ickx im Freitagstraining die Aufhängung seines Ferrari und erzielte am Samstag die siebte Zeit. Doch auch hier musste der Belgier vorzeitig aufgeben, als in Runde 45 die Antriebswelle brach.

■ *George Follmer: „In Spanien hatte ich einen tollen Fight mit Ickx. Mein Shadow lief auf dem Straßenkurs richtig gut. Der Kampf endete, als bei Ickx die Bremsen hinüber waren, aber er führte zu einer langen Freundschaft."*

Im 312PB lief es für Jacky kaum besser. Das Duo Ickx/Redman erzielte in Spa die Bestzeit und führte das Rennen souverän an, schied aber wegen eines defekten Ölkühlers aus. Eine Woche später kam Ickx bei der Targa Florio nur drei Runden weit, ehe ihm die Straße ausging. So unglaublich es klingen mag für einen erfahrenen Sportwagenpiloten wie Ickx: Es war sein erster – und letzter – Start bei der Targa Florio. Vor dem Rennen wollte sich der Belgier bei seinem sizilianischen Teamkollegen Nino Vaccarella einen Rat holen.

This combination did not help the road holding and thus he was not able to climb any higher than fifth. The South African GP ended early as Ickx was involved in Clay Regazzoni's horrific accident. Local driver, Dave Charlton, had spun at Crowthorne Corner, which had then caught out Mike Hailwood who spun as well. Regazzoni ran into Hailwood and Ickx into Regazzoni. The BRM of Regazzoni caught fire and Hailwood saved the life of Ickx's former team-mate by pulling him out of the burning car. After South Africa there was a six-week break to the next GP where Ferrari was due to enter its new 312B3.

Meanwhile, the sportscar season took off for Ickx with the 6 Hours of Vallelunga. This race replaced the 12 Hours of Sebring whose track no longer conformed to the FIA's safety requirements. Ickx had a new team-mate for this series, Brian Redman. After a one-year sabbatical, the Brit was back into racing and Ickx chose him to replace Regazzoni. The Swiss had found a new home at BRM but since the British team used Firestone tyres, Regazzoni was not allowed to drive the Goodyear-shod Ferrari sportscars. In practice and qualifying, the Ferraris suffered from poor road holding and were beaten by Matra. In the race, the Ferraris finished second, third and fourth, only beaten by the Matra shared by Henri Pescarolo, Gérard Larrousse and François Cevert. The Matra team also won the second race of the championship at Dijon-Prenois where Ickx-Redman finished second. For the 1,000 Kilometres of Monza, the Ferraris got new rear bodywork that improved road holding. The Ickx-Redman team started from pole and won with a three-lap advantage over their team-mates Carlos Reutemann and Tim Schenken.

Ferrari had the new 312B3 ready for Ickx to drive in the Spanish Grand Prix at Barcelona. There were two different versions available and the Belgian chose the car with a front radiator, chassis 011. Because of constant strikes in Italy, the monocoques were built in England and the cars were completed in Maranello. Ickx managed a sixth qualifying time on the street circuit and halfway through the race was lying in sixth position. Unfortunately, he had to pit to check the brake fluid and lost several laps finally finishing a long way down in twelfth position. Ickx had the same cars to choose from for the Belgian Grand Prix, held this time at Zolder. Thanks to his home advantage, Ickx managed a third qualifying time, but after seven laps he had to retire with a broken oil pump. During the weekend there were no less than eleven accidents, all thanks to the very bad condition of the track. In the Monaco GP, Ickx damaged his front suspension during the Friday practice, and on Saturday managed to set seventh fastest time. His race ended after forty-five laps when a drive shaft broke.

■ *George Follmer: "I had a great fight with Ickx in Spain. My Shadow went well on the street circuit. The battle ended however when Ickx lost his brakes. But this battle resulted in a long friendship."*

Ickx was also out of luck with the 312PB sportscar. Although fastest in qualifying for the 1,000 Kilometres of Spa, he and Redman had to retire with a broken oil cooler while the Belgian driver was in a commanding lead. A week later in Sicily for the Targa Florio, they only managed three laps before Ickx crashed. Although Ickx was an experienced sportscar driver, this was his first – and only – visit to the Targa Florio. Before the race, he had asked advice from Nino Vaccarella, the local hero who was driving in another 312PB.

Grand Prix de Monaco 1973

Grand Prix de Monaco 1973, Ferrari 312B3

1000 km Nürburgring 1973

1000 km Nürburgring 1973

▪ Nino Vaccarella: „Jacky Ickx fragte mich, wo es hinter Cerda lang ging. Ich sagte ihm, er solle rechts abbiegen. Das tat er auch, dabei ging es links herum. Der Belgier ist zwischen ein paar Bauernhöfen gelandet, von meinem Humor war er nicht gerade begeistert."

Bei den 1000 Kilometern auf dem Nürburgring sorgte Ickx für die große Überraschung, als er in der Qualifikation nicht die Bestzeit erzielte. Dafür lief es im Rennen nach Plan. Nachdem der von der Pole gestartete Matra von Jean-Pierre Beltoise und Cevert ausgefallen war, fuhren Ickx und Redman zum Sieg. Ferrari ging in jenem Jahr auch in Le Mans an den Start, wo die Scuderia eine Langheck-Version des 312PB einsetzte. Anfangs sah es noch gut aus für Ferrari: Die 312PB standen in der ersten Startreihe und dominierten auch die ersten Stunden. Das ganze Rennen über herrschten packende Duelle zwischen Ferrari und Matra. Ickx/Redman übernahmen im Auto mit der Nummer 15 gegen Mitternacht die Führung, die sie bis zum Morgen verteidigten. Nach 19 Stunden kam Ickx mit einem Leck im Tank an die Box. Durch die Reparatur verlor er sechs Runden und die Führung. Ickx holte zwar auf den führenden Matra auf, konnte ihn aber nicht mehr einholen. Und dann war anderthalb Stunden vor Schluss plötzlich alles vorbei: Der Ferrari blieb mit defekter Ventilsteuerung liegen. Kurz nach dem Rennen in Le Mans machte die Sportwagen-WM am Österreichring halt. Zu diesem Zeitpunkt lag Ferrari in der Tabelle noch vor Matra, die in der Quali und im 1000-Kilometer-Rennen in Zeltweg klar schneller waren. Ickx und Redman mussten im Rennen wegen einer falschen Benzineinstellung einen unplanmäßigen Boxenstopp einlegen und wurden nur Dritte. Beim Saisonfinale in Watkins Glen trat Ferrari mit drei Autos an, doch auch hier waren die beiden Matra schneller und eroberten die erste Startreihe. Nach sechs Stunden fuhr der Matra von Pescarolo/Larrousse als Erster über die Ziellinie, Ickx/Redman folgten mit zwei Runden Rückstand. Durch diesen Sieg krönte sich Matra zum Sportwagen-Weltmeister.

▪ Nino Vaccarella: "Jacky Ickx asked me where to go when leaving Cerda. I told him to turn right. Which he did, although the course goes left. The Belgian driver ended among some farmhouses and he was not amused by my humour."

Although Ickx surprised everybody by not setting the fastest qualifying time for the 1,000 Kilometres at the Nürburgring, he and his partner Brian Redman did win the sportscar race in Germany. Once the pole sitting Matra of Jean-Pierre Beltoise and François Cevert had retired, Ickx took the lead and led until the end. This year, Ferrari did enter the 24 Hours of Le Mans and the team ran modified, long-tail versions of their 312PB. Everything looked good with two Ferraris on the front row and, from the start, the red cars dominated. For the whole race, it was a battle between the three Ferraris and the three Matras. Just after midnight, the number fifteen, the Ickx-Redman Ferrari, moved into the lead that they then held through until the late morning. After nineteen hours of racing, Ickx came into the pits with a leaking fuel cell. The repair cost him six laps and he went back into the race in second position. Although Ickx made up some ground, he was unable to catch the leading Matra. Then all hope was gone with an hour and a half to go when the valve gear of the Ferrari's engine broke. Right after Le Mans, the sportscars ran at the Österreichring and at this point Ferrari was still ahead of Matra in the championship. In qualifying and the race, the Matras showed their speed and it was clear that the French cars were by far the fastest. Ickx and Redman had to make an unplanned pit stop for fuel thanks to an over-rich fuel setting and they finished third. Ferrari sent three cars to the final race of the championship at Watkins Glen in America. But again the Matras were quickest and two of the French cars started from the front row. At the finish, it was the Pescarolo-Larrousse Matra that won, two laps ahead of Ickx and Redman. With this victory, Matra became World Champion.

— 137 —

Großer Preis von Deutschland 1973, Nürburgring, McLaren M23 - Ford

🟨 *Brian Redman: „Am Nürburgring gab es ein packendes Duell zwischen Merzario und Ickx. Wir hatten uns vorher geeinigt, dass jenes Team gewinnen darf, welches zur Halbzeit führt. Ickx ließ Merzario passieren. Kurz vor der Rennmitte zog er dann aber plötzlich am Italiener vorbei und führte das Rennen an. Merzario war außer sich!"*

Da die Sportwagen-WM schon Ende Juli gelaufen war, konnten sich Ickx und Ferrari anschließend voll auf die Formel 1 konzentrieren. Der 312B3 hatte viele Probleme, die gelöst werden mussten. In Schweden wurde Ickx Sechster und holte einen WM-Punkt. Der Ferrari war aber wieder langsamer als die Top-Autos mit Ford-Motoren. Im französischen Le Castellet startete Ickx nach einem Trainingsunfall aus dem Mittelfeld und schaffte es nur durch die Unfälle zweier Konkurrenten auf Platz fünf, der ihm zwei WM-Punkte brachte. In Silverstone gab es beim Start einen heftigen Unfall, den nur 19 Autos überlebten. Ickx entkam dem Getümmel nur knapp, war beim Restart also dabei und wurde Achter. Kurz darauf brachte Ickx seinen Ärger über die mangelnden Fortschritte des 312B3 in einem Interview zum Ausdruck. Ickx sagte der englischen Autosport: „Das Auto ist unfahrbar. Es ist eine Schande, dass ein so renommierter Hersteller wie Ferrari mit all seinen Ressourcen und dem Geld des Giganten Fiat kein besseres Auto bauen kann." Auf die öffentliche Kritik folgte ein Rapport bei Ferrari, der zur sofortigen Auflösung des Vertrags führte. Also suchte sich Ickx für den Deutschland-GP auf seiner Lieblingsstrecke, dem Nürburgring, ein anderes Auto. Das Yardley Team McLaren gab ihm einen McLaren M23, mit dem er sich für die zweite Reihe qualifizierte. Im Rennen wurde er mit dem für ihn neuen Auto Dritter.

Vor dem Italien-GP änderte Ferrari seine Meinung und begnadigte Ickx. Obwohl Mauro Forghieri den 312B3 weiterentwickelt hatte, qualifizierte sich Ickx in Monza nur im Mittelfeld. Auch im Rennen konnte Jacky nicht mit der Spitze mithalten und wurde nur Achter. Damit war die Ära Ferrari für Ickx aber endgültig vorbei. Für den US-Grand-Prix Anfang Oktober bot Frank Williams dem Belgier ein Cockpit an. Dessen Iso-Marlboro-Ford war nicht konkurrenzfähig und daher landete Ickx in der Quali am Ende des Feldes. Im Rennen verbesserte er sich immerhin auf Platz sieben. So ging eine unbefriedigende Saison zu Ende. Mit zwölf Punkten belegte Ickx in der F1-Weltmeisterschaft nur den neunten Platz.

Im Herbst nahm Ickx darüber hinaus an drei Rennen in BMW-Tourenwagen teil. Bei den 6 Stunden von Paul Ricard teilte er sich einen Alpina-BMW 3.0 CSL mit dem jungen Engländer James Hunt. Das Duo wurde Zweiter hinter den Routiniers und Markenkollegen Toine Hezemans und Dieter Quester. Nach dem US-GP bestritt Ickx zudem ein Rennen in seiner Heimat. Bei den 24 Stunden von Nivelles handelte es sich – anders als der Name vermuten lässt – nur um zwei Läufe über je drei Stunden, die innerhalb von 24 Stunden stattfanden. Hier schieden Ickx und Teampartner Brian Muir in beiden Rennen durch Motorschaden aus. Den Abschluss der Saison bildeten wieder einmal die 9 Stunden von Kyalami, die Ickx zusammen mit Hans-Joachim Stuck in einem BMW 3.5 CSL bestritt. In Südafrika landete ihr Werks-BMW hinter zahlreichen Sportwagen auf Rang sieben.

Das Jahr 1973 endete für Ickx also mit nur zwei Gesamtsiegen, die er beide im Sport-Prototypen 312PB erzielt hatte. Jackys Zeit bei Ferrari war vorbei, in der Zwischenzeit hatte aber Colin Chapman angerufen und den Belgier als Teamkollege von Ronnie Peterson für das F1-Team von Lotus verpflichtet.

🟨 *Brian Redman: "At the Nürburgring, there was a fierce battle between Merzario and Ickx. We had all agreed that the team who led at halfway would be allowed to win. Ickx let Merzario go and when they came up to receive the halfway flag, Ickx suddenly overtook the Italian and led the race. Merzario was furious."*

With the World Sportscar Championship over by mid-July, Ickx and Ferrari could then concentrate on Formula One. The 312B3 had shown a lot of problems that needed solutions. In Sweden, Ickx finished sixth, earning one point, but again the Ferrari was slower than the top Ford-powered entries. After a practice accident in France at the Le Castellet circuit, Ickx started mid-field and it was only because the leading cars crashed out that the Belgian driver finished fifth and added two points to his score. There was a massive start accident at Silverstone and only nineteen cars took the re-start. Ickx who had narrowly missed the pile-up was one of them and finished eighth. With the 312B3 not showing any progress, Ickx recounted his dissatisfaction to Autosport magazine. Ickx said that "the car was undriveable. A pity that a renowned manufacturer as Ferrari, with all its resources and the money of giant Fiat, can not produce a better car." Because of this criticism, Ferrari hauled him in for a discussion that ended in them releasing him from his contract immediately. Thus Ickx could pick up a drive elsewhere for the German GP to be held at his favourite circuit, the Nürburgring. Yardley Team McLaren offered him a car and Ickx qualified it on the second row. Although unfamiliar with the McLaren, Ickx drove well and finished third.

Then Ferrari changed its mind for the Italian Grand Prix so Ickx was back with the Scuderia at Monza. Although Mauro Forghieri had updated the 312B3, Ickx only qualified mid-field. During the race, he could not get on terms with the top drivers and once more finished eighth. It was the final Formula One race for Ickx with Ferrari. For the American Grand Prix in early October, Marlboro asked him to drive Frank Williams's Iso Marlboro Ford. But in this uncompetitive car, Ickx qualified at the rear of the grid and drove round to seventh place. After an unsatisfying season, Ickx had only scored twelve points and thus finished ninth in the World Championship.

In the autumn of 1973, Ickx returned to the BMW touring car works team after a two-year break. He drove an Alpina BMW at the 6 Hours of Paul Ricard, this time partnered by a young English driver, James Hunt. They finished second to the BMW of experienced touring car drivers, Toine Hezemans and Dieter Quester. After returning from the American Grand Prix, Ickx again raced for BMW, this time at a local event in Belgium. Together with Brian Muir, he contested the 24 Hours of Nivelles. In reality, this race comprised two three-hour races held over two days. However, in both races, the engine broke and they had to retire. In November, Ickx drove his final race of the season by joining Hans-Joachim Stuck in a BMW for the 9 Hours of Kyalami, the opening round of the South African Springbok Series. In a very mixed field, their works BMW finished seventh overall.

The 1973 season thus came to an end with only two victories for Ickx and both of those with the 312PB sportscar. His contract with Ferrari had ended and now, for 1974, Ickx got a call from Colin Chapman at Lotus who needed a partner for Ronnie Peterson in their Formula One team.

Grand Prix de France 1973, Paul Ricard

Großer Preis von Deutschland 1973, Nürburgring, McLaren M23 · Ford

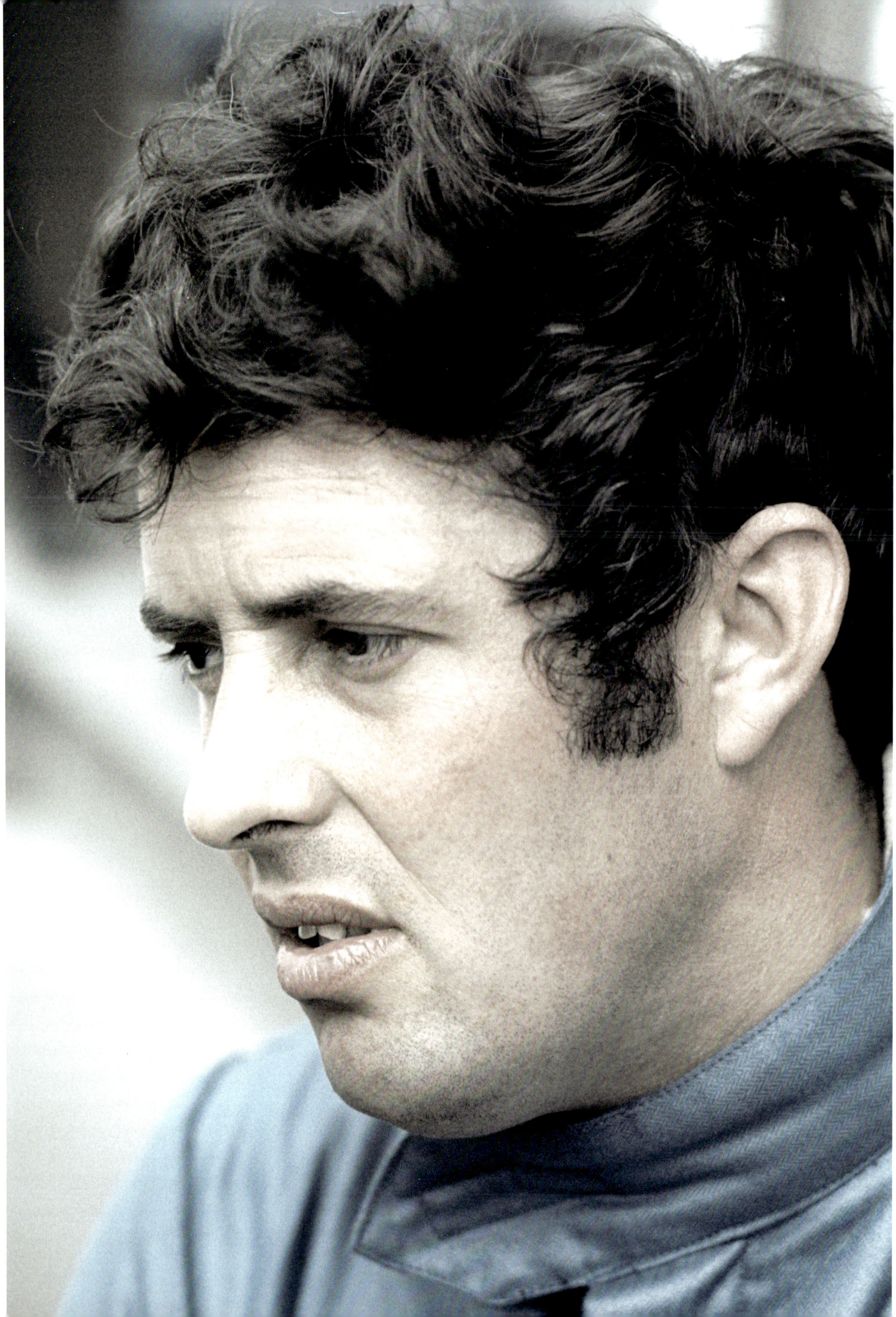

Brian
REDMAN

Partner von Ickx bei Ford und Ferrari
Partner to Ickx at Ford and Ferrari

„Jacky und ich sind viele Rennen zusammen gefahren, haben oft gewonnen und eine großartige Zeit erlebt. Ende 1967 bin ich in Kyalami erstmals für das Team von John Wyer gefahren, und 1968 wurde ich dann zweiter Fahrer neben Jacky. Beim ersten Lauf in Daytona haben wir gleich die Pole geholt. Ich wusste, dass Jacky der Lieblingsfahrer von Wyer und David Yorke war, aber ich habe mich nicht beschwert. Ich wollte Rennen fahren. Und wenn man mit dem Liebling ein Team bildet, dann hat man gute Chancen, viele Rennen zu gewinnen. Das haben wir auch geschafft. 1968 im GT40 und ein paar Jahre später im Ferrari. Leider war die 1968er-Saison für mich durch einen Unfall in Spa vorzeitig vorbei."

„Ein Rennen, das wir 1968 nicht gewonnen haben, waren die 1000 Kilometer auf dem ‚Ring'. Yorke wollte, dass Ickx mit Paul Hawkins fährt. Also bin ich ins Auto von David Hobbs gerutscht. Ein Grund für die Entscheidung war vielleicht mein Dreher in Monza, ich weiß es nicht. Wie auch immer: Am Ring haben weder Ickx noch ich gewonnen. Wenn man sich die Zeitentabellen anschaut, hätten wir aber gewinnen können, wenn wir zusammen gefahren wären."

„Jacky und ich hatten einen ganz unterschiedlichen Hintergrund. Er kam aus dem kultivierten Brüssel, ich aus Lancashire in Nordengland. Aber diese Mischung war gut. Nach meiner Porsche-Zeit bin ich 1973 zu Ferrari gegangen und fuhr wieder mit Jacky. Und wieder haben wir gewonnen, unter anderem in Spa. Ich mag den Kurs nicht besonders, obwohl ich dort einige 1000-Kilometer-Rennen gewonnen habe."

„Insgesamt war es leicht, mit Jacky zu arbeiten. Er fand es okay, wie ich das Auto abgestimmt habe, und hat sich nie beschwert. Viele Leute hatten Probleme mit ihm, ich nicht. Es war eine große Freude, mit ihm zu fahren."

"Jacky and I did many races together and we won so many that we had a great time. I joined John Wyer's team for the Kyalami race at the end of 1967 and for 1968 stayed as second driver to Jacky. We took pole at Daytona in our first championship race. I knew Jacky was the favourite of Wyer and David Yorke but I did not complain. I wanted to race and being partnered by the favourite meant that I had a good chance of winning a lot of races. And that is what we did, first in 1968 with the GT40 and then some years later with Ferrari. However, a F1 accident at Spa ended my 1968 season prematurely that spring."

"A race we did not win that year was the 1,000 Kilometres at the 'Ring'. Yorke wanted Paul Hawkins to drive with Ickx, so I ended up with David Hobbs. Maybe that choice was as a result of a spin I had at Monza, I don't know. Anyway, Ickx did not win and neither did I. Looking at the timesheets, if Jacky and I had been together, we could have won."

"We came from different backgrounds. He was from sophisticated Brussels and I was from Lancashire in the north of England. But the mix worked well. After the Porsche period, I came back with Ferrari and in 1973 was again driving with Jacky. And again we won races. Among them was Spa that is a circuit I don't like very much but nevertheless over the years I have won several 1,000-kilometre events there."

"In general, Jacky was easy to work with. He accepted the way I set up the car and never complained. A lot of people had some issues with him, but I was fine. It was a great pleasure to race with him."

1974

Ein Neustart als Nummer zwei bei Lotus
A new start as second driver at Lotus

Zur Saison 1974 heuerte Jacky Ickx als zweiter Fahrer beim „John Player Team Lotus" an. Die von Colin Chapman geführte Mannschaft hatte im Vorjahr die Konstrukteurs-WM gewonnen. Der Lotus 72 war erwiesenermaßen noch immer ein schnelles Auto, dennoch sollte zu Beginn der Europa-Saison ein neuer Bolide fertig sein.

Die Quali zum Argentinien-GP lief für Ickx nicht gut. Während Ronnie Peterson seinen Lotus auf die Pole stellte, startete Ickx nur aus Reihe vier. Beim Start verbesserte sich Ickx um einige Plätze und lag später lange auf Platz drei, als er wegen eines Reifenschadens die Box ansteuern musste. Kurz darauf ging die Kupplung kaputt, das Aus für Ickx. Die Ferrari – die jetzt unter der Leitung von Luca di Montezemolo eingesetzt wurden – landeten hinter Denny Hulme auf den Rängen zwei und drei. In Brasilien war Ickx in der Quali zwar besser, aber immer noch langsamer als Peterson. Ickx fuhr ein fehlerfreies Rennen, erbte durch Petersons Ausfall Platz drei und behauptete diesen bis ins Ziel. Clay Regazzoni wurde im Ferrari Zweiter hinter Emerson Fittipaldi und übernahm die WM-Führung.

For 1974, Jacky Ickx had signed up as second driver with 'John Player Team Lotus' run by Colin Chapman. The previous year, they had won the constructors championship and the type 72 was still a quick car. Additionally, the team had said that they would have a new car for the start of the European season.

At Buenos Aires for the Argentine GP, in qualifying Ickx set a time that gave him a spot in the fourth row, while team-mate Ronnie Peterson got pole. Right after the start, Ickx gained several places and was in third position for a long time until he got a puncture and had to pit. A few laps later the clutch broke and he was forced to retire. The Ferraris, who were now being run by Luca di Montezemolo, finished second and third behind the winner, Denny Hulme. Ickx qualified better for the second race in Brazil, but was still behind Peterson. Ickx drove a faultless race and after the retirement of Peterson took third place which he held to the end. Clay Regazzoni was second in his Ferrari behind Emerson Fittipaldi thus inheriting the championship lead.

Race of Champions 1974, Brands Hatch, Lotus 72E - Ford

Beim Race of Champions in Brands Hatch – an dem Formel-1- und Formel-5000-Autos teilnahmen – bestritt Ickx sein erstes Saisonrennen in Europa. In der Quali platzierte er den alternden Lotus 72E nur auf Startplatz elf. Das Rennen fand bei Kälte und Regen statt – die perfekten Bedingungen für Ickx. Während sich viele Gegner drehten, blieb der Belgier auf der Strecke und siegte mit einer Sekunde Vorsprung auf Niki Lauda im Ferrari. Das Resultat brachte ihm zwar keine WM-Punkte ein, dafür aber reichlich Selbstvertrauen.

Beim Südafrika-GP gab der Lotus 76 sein Debüt. Im Training und Qualifying kämpften die Piloten mit der Abstimmung des Boliden und landeten daher nur im Mittelfeld. Beim Rennstart waren Ickx und Peterson in eine Kollision mit Jochen Mass und Henri Pescarolo verwickelt, sodass jede Hoffnung auf ein gutes Ergebnis schon verflogen war. Ickx legte im Laufe des Rennens fünf Stopps ein, um sein Auto abzustimmen, und musste letztlich mit gebrochener Bremsscheibe aufgeben. In Spanien profitierte der Lotus 76 von zahlreichen Verbesserungen. Peterson startete aus der ersten Reihe, Ickx stand zwei Reihen dahinter. Im Rennen lief es dagegen nicht so gut. Peterson schied nach 23 Runden ohne Öldruck aus, für Ickx war wenig später Feierabend. Der Belgier war auf Regenreifen gestartet und hatte auf abtrocknender Piste die Box angesteuert. Bei dem chaotischen Stopp wurde nicht nur ein Rad falsch montiert, sondern auch der Feuerlöscher ausgelöst. Ickx konnte das Rennen trotz allem wieder aufnehmen, schied aber wenig später mit Bremsdefekt aus.

Mitte April nahm Ickx für BMW erneut an einem Lauf zur Tourenwagen-EM teil. Beim 4-Stunden-Rennen auf dem Salzburgring teilte sich Jacky einen BMW 3.0 CSL mit Hans-Joachim Stuck. Das Duo erzielte die Pole und fuhr nach dem Ausfall der beiden Werks-Ford-Capri zum Sieg. Vier Tage später – am 25. April, dem „Tag der Befreiung Italiens" – ging Ickx bei den 1000 Kilometern von Monza an den Start. Dort pilotierte er zusammen mit Rolf Stommelen einen werkseingesetzten Alfa Romeo 33TT12. Das Duo beendete die Quali zwar nur auf Startplatz fünf, da es aber am Renntag regnete, blickten sie den 1000 Kilometern trotzdem optimistisch entgegen. Ickx drehte sich jedoch in Runde zwei und kam nach vier Runden in die Box, um sich neue Reifen zu holen. Danach lief es besser, sodass Ickx/Stommelen noch als Zweite hinter ihren Teamkollegen Arturo Merzario/Mario Andretti die Zielflagge sahen. Wenige Tage später stand schon der nächste Lauf im Sportwagen an: die 1000 Kilometer von Spa. Während die Formel 1 die Ardennen-Achterbahn mied, gastierte die Sportwagen-WM weiterhin auf der Highspeed-Strecke, die durch eine Schikane am Anfang der Malmedy-Geraden etwas entschärft worden war. Da Alfa in Belgien nicht antrat, startete Ickx für Konkurrent Matra, wo er Jean-Pierre Beltoise vertrat, der nicht in Spa fahren wollte. Ickx erfüllte die Erwartungen und siegte gemeinsam mit Jean-Pierre Jarier.

Beim GP von Belgien, der erneut auf dem nichtssagenden Kurs von Nivelles stattfand, kam Ickx nicht mit dem Lotus 76 zurecht. Er beendete die Quali im Mittelfeld und verlor im Rennen viel Zeit durch eine Kollision mit Merzario. Zehn Runden vor Schluss endete seine Fahrt mit nachlassenden Bremsen und überhitzendem Motor. In Monaco kehrte Chapman zum bewährten Lotus 72 zurück. Für Ickx änderte sich dadurch wenig: Nach schwacher Qualifikation schied er zur Halbzeit wegen eines defekten Ölschlauchs aus. Beim GP von Schweden saß Ickx erneut im Lotus 72 und blieb erneut glücklos. In der Qualifikation musste er sich Peterson geschlagen geben, im Rennen steuerte er wegen einer leeren Batterie nach 19 Runden die Box an und schied kurz darauf ohne Öldruck aus.

Back in Europe, Ickx drove the single Lotus entry in the Race of Champions at Brands Hatch, a mixed Formula One and Formula 5000 race. In qualifying, the now out-dated Lotus 72E could only manage eleventh fastest time. But on race day it was cold and rainy, the perfect conditions for Ickx. In a race which saw many spins and crashes, Ickx stayed on the road and won it with a one second advantage over Niki Lauda in a Ferrari. This win was a great boost for Ickx. If nothing else, it gave him back a lot of confidence.

For the South African Grand Prix, JPS had its new Lotus 76 ready but the new car was not easy to set up. Thus both Lotus drivers started from the middle of the grid and, when they both ran into Jochen Mass and Henri Pescarolo at the start, any hope of a good result was gone. In fact, Ickx made a total of five pit stops to sort out his car, but eventually had to retire with a broken brake disc. With several modifications, the 76s did much better in Spain as Peterson was on the front row and Ickx two rows further back. But here, after twenty-three laps, Peterson's race was out with no oil pressure and Ickx retired some laps later. Ickx had chosen to start on wet tyres but pitted – while in the lead – as soon as the weather turned dry. However, one wheel was not properly fixed and, in the confusion, the fire extinguisher was discharged. Ickx rejoined the race, but soon had to retire with brake problems.

At the end of April, Ickx was asked to compete in the 4 Hours of the Salzburgring ETC race with Hans-Joachim Stuck in a BMW 3.0 CSL. They started from pole and won after both the works Ford Capris – their main competitors – had retired. A few days later, on April 25th, a national holiday in Italy, the sportscar championship had its first race at Monza. As a free agent, Ickx was contacted by Alfa Romeo to drive a 33TT12 sportscar with Rolf Stommelen as his partner. They set the fifth fastest qualifying time and, because the race was run on a wet track, they were able to feel optimistic. However, on the second lap, Ickx spun and two laps later came into the pits for new tyres. After 1,000 kilometres, Ickx and Stommelen finished second to their team-mates Arturo Merzario and Mario Andretti. Only a few days later came the second sportscar championship race, this time at the Spa-Francorchamps track. This was no longer in use for Formula One races but the sportscars still drove the ultra-fast track now with a chicane inserted at the beginning of the Malmedy straight. With Alfa Romeo not going to Belgium, Ickx was contacted by Matra to replace Jean-Pierre Beltoise who did not want to race at Spa. Ickx did as was to be expected, he won the race sharing his car with Jean-Pierre Jarier.

At the Belgian Grand Prix, once again held on the featureless Nivelles track, Ickx did not feel too good about his JPS Lotus. He qualified mid-field and then lost valuable time after a collision with Merzario. With fading brakes and an overheating engine, he retired ten laps from the end. For the Monaco Grand Prix, JPS once again entered their trusty Lotus 72. And once again, Ickx did not qualify well and retired halfway because of a broken oil pipe. The same cars were used for the Swedish Grand Prix and once more Ickx was out-qualified by Peterson. A dead battery forced him into the pits after nineteen laps of the race and then low oil pressure caused him to retire some laps later. For the Dutch Grand Prix at Zandvoort, JPS came with an updated version of the Lotus 76, but after practicing with it, the team opted for the older 72. This again resulted in no success for Ickx after a race he would have preferred to forget during which he lost several laps thanks to pit stops for new tyres. Following on from these disappointing Formula One races, Ickx was happy to finish the French Grand Prix at Dijon.

Grand Prix de Belgique 1974, Zolder, Lotus 76/2 - Ford

Grote Prijs van Nederland 1974, Zandvoort, Lotus 76/2 - Ford

Grand Prix de Monaco 1974, Jacky Ickx & Colin Chapman

Grand Prix de Monaco 1974, Peter Warr, Colin Chapman & Jacky Ickx

Grote Prijs van Nederland 1974, Zandvoort, Lotus 76/2 - Ford n°2

Für den GP der Niederlande brachte Lotus eine neue Version des 76 heraus, entschied sich nach dem Training aber für den alten Lotus 72. Ickx erlebte in Zandvoort wieder ein Wochenende zum Vergessen. Er musste sich zwei Mal neue Reifen holen und hatte im Ziel drei Runden Rückstand. Nach den vielen Enttäuschungen der Vorwochen war die Zielankunft beim Frankreich-GP in Dijon schon ein Erfolg. Nach konstanter Fahrt wurde er Fünfter und holte somit zwei WM-Punkte. Zwei Wochen später lief es für Ickx im englischen Brands Hatch mit Platz drei noch besser.

Obwohl Alfa Romeo bei den 1000 Kilometern auf dem Nürburgring an den Start ging, nahm Ickx das Angebot von BMW an, deren 3.0-CSL-Tourenwagen zu fahren. Ickx und sein Partner Stuck waren zwar die Schnellsten in der Klasse, der Sieg war ihnen aber nicht vergönnt, da Stuck in Runde drei mit defekter Kraftübertragung liegen blieb. Ickx kam im Rennen nicht einmal zum Einsatz. Bei den 1000-Kilometer-Rennen in Imola und am Österreichring saß Ickx dann wieder mit Merzario im Alfa. In Imola kollidierte Merzario mit dem Abarth von Nanni Galli und schied nach elf Runden aus. Ickx blieb wieder nur die Zuschauerrolle. Im österreichischen Zeltweg, wo Vittorio Brambilla als dritter Fahrer hinzu kam, war der Motor nach 152 Runden hinüber. Das Alfa-Trio hatte damit aber über 90 Prozent der Renndistanz zurückgelegt und wurde daher als Fünfter gewertet. Da Matra die Sportwagen-WM schon gewonnen hatte, verzichtete Alfa Romeo auf den Start bei den 1000 Kilometern von Paul Ricard. Ickx nutzte die Gelegenheit für ein Wiedersehen mit alten Kollegen: Der Belgier startete – mit Derek Bell als Partner – für das Gulf-Mirage-Team von John Wyer. Obwohl sich Ickx einen Platten einfing, sich einmal drehte und ein weiteres Mal von der Strecke abkam, wurde er hinter den übermächtigen Matra Dritter.

Einen Monat zuvor hatte sich Ickx schon einmal das Cockpit mit Bell geteilt. Beim Großen Preis der Tourenwagen auf dem Nürburgring hatten die beiden einen BMW pilotiert. Der EM-Lauf endete für Ickx/Bell nach Getriebeproblemen aber vorzeitig.

Beim F1-Rennen auf dem Nürburgring zeigte Ickx eine gewohnt starke Leistung, er holte im Lotus Platz fünf sowie zwei weitere WM-Punkte. Am Österreichring erlebte er im ungeliebten Lotus 76 ein Wechselbad der Gefühle: Ickx startete aus der drittletzten Reihe, arbeitete sich während des Rennens aber bis auf die vierte Position vor, ehe eine Kollision mit Patrick Depailler seinen Nachmittag ruinierte. In Monza schob Ickx dagegen wieder Frust. In der Qualifikation kam er nicht über das Mittelfeld hinaus, im Rennen musste er zwei Mal die Reifen wechseln und den Lotus 76 dann mit defekter Benzineinspritzung abstellen. In Kanada nahm Ickx wieder im alten Lotus 72 Platz, allerdings ohne Erfolg. Das Qualifying beendete Jacky neben Debütant Helmut Koinigg in einem noch älteren Surtees in der drittletzten Reihe und im Rennen kam Ickx nicht über Platz 13 hinaus. Man könnte fast meinen, dass sowohl Ickx als auch Lotus nicht allzu traurig darüber waren, dass die Saison kurz darauf mit dem US-Grand-Prix zu Ende ging, wo Ickx in Runde acht verunfallte.

Ickx' Saison im JPS-Lotus war ein Jahr zum Vergessen. Bei 15 Rennen war Jacky acht Mal ausgefallen. Im Gegenzug konnte er nur zwei dritte und zwei fünfte Plätze sowie Platz zehn in der F1-Weltmeisterschaft vorweisen. Darüber hinaus hatte Teamkollege Ronnie Peterson das Qualifikationsduell mit 13:2 für sich entschieden. Trotz der enttäuschenden Saison kam Ickx mit Colin Chapman überein, ein weiteres Jahr für Lotus zu fahren.

After a steady race, he came in fifth and scored two points. A fortnight later, at the British Grand Prix at Brands Hatch, he did even better by finishing third.

Although Alfa Romeo had entered for the 1,000 Kilometres at the Nürburgring, Ickx chose to drive a BMW 3.0 CSL in the touring car class. As before, he was partnered by Stuck. Although they were the fastest touring car, they did not win their class since Stuck retired with transmission failure on the third lap and thus Ickx did not drive at all that afternoon. For both the 1,000-kilometre races at Imola and the Österreichring, Ickx was back with Alfa Romeo sharing duties with Merzario. In Imola, Merzario had a collision with Nanni Galli and had to retire after eleven laps and once more Ickx did not have a chance to drive. At the Österreichring, Vittorio Brambilla joined Ickx and this time the engine broke after 152 laps and they failed to finish. But because they had covered 90% of the race distance, they were still awarded fifth position. As Matra had already clinched the title, Alfa Romeo did not go to Le Castellet for the 1,000 Kilometres of Paul Ricard. This gave Ickx an opportunity to be reunited for that race with the JWA Gulf Team and with Derek Bell as his partner in a Mirage. Although Ickx had a puncture, spun and also a minor off-track excursion, they finished third behind the two all-conquering Matras.

In July, Ickx had already partnered Bell for the 'Großer Preis der Tourenwagen' race at the Nürburgring that was a round of the ETC. Unfortunately they had to retire their BMW early in the race after encountering gearbox problems.

Ickx finished fifth in the German Grand Prix at the Nürburgring and picked up a couple more championship points. At the Österreichring, he did not qualify well and could only manage a place in the third-to-last row. Nevertheless at least to start with, Ickx enjoyed the race since it was his best outing with the unloved Lotus 76. It had got him up to fourth place before his afternoon was spoiled when he had a collision with Patrick Depailler. In Monza, Ickx used the same Lotus 76 again. After a qualifying in mid-field, Ickx had another miserable race during which he made two pits stops for new tyres and eventually had to retire with fuel injection problems. For Canada, Ickx used the Lotus 72 but this too did not yield success. He qualified at the rear of the field next to a debuting Helmut Koinigg in a much older Surtees. After an uneventful race, he finished a lowly thirteenth overall. It was perhaps merciful to both parties that the American Grand Prix at Watkins Glen was the final race of the F1 championship since Ickx's season came to an end when he crashed the car after eight laps. His year with JPS Lotus was not one to remember since it comprised fifteen races in which he retired eight times. With two third places and two fifth places, this gave him tenth position in the World Championship. Furthermore at no fewer than thirteen races, he had been out-qualified by his team-mate, Ronnie Peterson. Nevertheless, although this had been a very unfortunate year for him with Lotus, he was keen to stay for another year with the English team.

1000 km Nürburgring 1974, BMW 3.0 CSL

1000 km Österreichring 1974, Zeltweg, Alfa Romeo 33TT12

Großer Preis von Deutschland 1974, Nürburgring

1975 – 1976

Talfahrt in der F1, Triumphe im Sportwagen
Fewer races in F1, more success at endurance

Von dem versprochenen neuen Lotus war beim Auftakt der F1-Saison 1975 noch nichts zu sehen, stattdessen saß Jacky Ickx genau wie Teamkollege Ronnie Peterson im nochmals weiterentwickelten Lotus 72. Für die Sportwagen-WM hatte Ickx keinen festen Vertrag. Er bestritt aber einige Läufe in den Alfa Romeo 33TT12 von Willi Kauhsen. Der Deutsche hatte die Zwölfzylinder-Sportwagen nach dem Rückzug des Alfa-Werksteams gekauft und setzte sie 1975 selbst ein.

Für Ickx begann die Saison in Südamerika. Beim Argentinien-GP wurden die Alterserscheinungen des Lotus 72 im John-Player-Special-Look immer deutlicher. In der Qualifikation landeten Ickx und Peterson nur im Mittelfeld. Ickx erlebte ein ereignisloses Rennen, in dem er sich auf Rang acht verbesserte – mit einer Runde Rückstand auf den Sieger und amtierenden Weltmeister Emerson Fittipaldi. Eine Woche später zeigte sich in Brasilien das gleiche Bild. Während Lokalmatador Carlos Pace den einzigen F1-Triumph seiner Karriere feierte, landete Ickx nach glanzloser Fahrt auf Rang neun. Der Abwärtstrend setzte sich in Südafrika fort, wo Ickx nach einem mittelmäßigen Qualifying nur Zwölfter wurde.

Although Lotus had promised a new car for 1975, at the beginning of the season Jacky Ickx found himself in yet another updated version of the Lotus 72. Ronnie Peterson was again to be his team-mate. For sportscars, Ickx did not have a firm contract with anyone although Willi Kauhsen had asked him to drive one of his Alfa Romeo 33TT12s. The German team owner had bought the cars from the Italian factory at the end of 1974 after the Autodelta works team had decided to withdraw from racing.

The year started in South America with the Argentine Grand Prix. The John Player Special Lotus 72s of Peterson and Ickx were sadly out-dated and could only achieve mid-field starting positions. After an uneventful race, Ickx finished eighth, a lap down on the winner, the reigning champion Emerson Fittipaldi. Two weeks later, in Brazil, there was no change with the same cars and the same starting positions. So it was that, after a lacklustre race, Ickx finished ninth and local hero Carlos Pace won his first – and only – Grand Prix. Ickx's downward path continued in South Africa where he finished a lowly twelfth after another mediocre qualifying session.

Race of Champions 1975, Brands Hatch, Lotus 72E - Ford

Den Auftakt der Europa-Saison bildete für Ickx wie so oft das Race of Champions in Brands Hatch, wo Formel-1-Autos direkt gegen Formel-5000-Monoposti antraten. Für Ickx stand das Wochenende unter dem Motto „Vier gewinnt". Der Lotus-Pilot beendete die Quali und das nicht zur F1-Weltmeisterschaft zählende Rennen jeweils auf Rang vier – direkt hinter Teamkollege Peterson, aber mit einer Runde Rückstand auf den Shadow von Tom Pryce. Eine Woche später pilotierte Ickx bei den 1000 Kilometern von Mugello einen der beiden Kauhsen-Alfa-Romeo. Ickx und Arturo Merzario starteten zwar von der Pole, mussten sich im Rennen aber dem neuen Alpine-Renault A441 Turbo von Gérard Larrousse und Jean-Pierre Jabouille geschlagen geben.

▪ **Derek Bell: „Nach dem Rennen in Mugello fragte Ickx mich: ‚Warum tun wir uns das an? Vielleicht sollte ich aufhören.' Zehn Sekunden später lächelte er aber und sagte: ‚Ich weiß, warum: Wo sonst verdienen wir so viel Geld für so wenig Arbeit?'"**

Der erste WM-Lauf auf europäischem Boden fand Ende April im Montjuïc Park von Barcelona statt und endete in einer Tragödie. Schon bei der Inspektion der Strecke stellten die Fahrer fest, dass die Leitplanken teils schlecht oder gar nicht fixiert waren. Daraufhin weigerten sich all jene Fahrer, die Mitglieder der Grand Prix Drivers' Association (GPDA) waren, am Freitagstraining teilzunehmen. Ickx und der Niederländer Roelof Wunderink, der kein GPDA-Mitglied war, drehten als einzige ihre Runden. Erst als die Organisatoren drohten, die Autos zu beschlagnahmen, begannen die Piloten die Strecke unter die Räder zu nehmen. Emerson Fittipaldi zum Beispiel fuhr aber nur eine sehr langsame Runde. Als der Brasilianer erklärte, nicht am Rennen teilzunehmen, flammte die Debatte neu auf. Der Rest des Feldes ging am Sonntag wie geplant an den Start, bei dem es direkt zum ersten Unfall kam. Mario Andretti kollidierte nach wenigen Metern mit den Ferrari von Niki Lauda und Clay Regazzoni sowie dem Tyrrell von Patrick Depailler. Nach der ersten Runde stellten Merzario und Wilson Fittipaldi ihre Autos an der Box ab, um ihre Solidarität zu Emerson Fittipaldi zu demonstrieren. Auf der Strecke ging die Unfallorgie derweil weiter: Nach sechs Runden verunfallte James Hunt, nach 16 Runden Andretti – beide lagen zum Zeitpunkt ihrer Unfälle in Führung.

Der tragischste Unfall ereignete sich in Runde 26, als am neuen Hill GH1 von Rolf Stommelen – ebenfalls in Führung liegend – der Heckflügel brach. Der Wagen flog über eine Leitplanke hinweg in eine Zuschauermenge, dabei wurden fünf Menschen getötet und zehn weitere verletzt. Vier Runden später brachen die Organisatoren das Rennen ab. Jacky Ickx hatte nach 28 Runden kurzzeitig in Führung gelegen, wurde dann aber von Jochen Mass überholt, der somit zum Sieger erklärt wurde. Der Sieg von Mass war aber sehr umstritten, da Carlos Reutemann und Vittorio Brambilla vor dem Deutschen die Zielflagge geschwenkt bekamen. Insgesamt wurden nur acht Autos gewertet, wobei die sechstplatzierte Lella Lombardi an diesem unrühmlichen Tag Geschichte schrieb. Der Italienerin war es als erste Frau gelungen, bei einem Formel-1-Rennen in die Punkte zu fahren. Auch wenn sie nur einen halben Zähler zugesprochen bekam, da zum Zeitpunkt des Abbruchs weniger als 50 Prozent der Renndistanz absolviert worden waren.

▪ **Jochen Mass: „Beim Spanien-GP hatte ich vorgeschlagen, eher eine Parade zu fahren als ein Rennen. Alle waren damit einverstanden. Doch als die Flagge geschwenkt wurde, fuhren alle los wie die Idioten und das führte zum Unfall in der ersten Kurve."**

The first event for Ickx in Europe was the Race of Champions at Brands Hatch. Again the field of this non-championship race was a mix of Formula One and Formula 5000 cars. After setting the fourth fastest time in qualifying, Ickx could not improve and finished the forty-lap race in the same position. He finished right behind team-mate Peterson but one lap down on Tom Pryce, the 26 year-old Shadow driver. A week later, Ickx went to Italy to drive in the 1,000-kilometre race at Mugello in Italy where Arturo Merzario partnered him in one of the two Kauhsen Alfa Romeos. Although they were fastest in qualifying, the new Alpine-Renault A441 Turbo of Gérard Larrousse and Jean-Pierre Jabouille beat them in the race.

▪ **Derek Bell: "After the Mugello race, Jacky asked me: 'Why are we doing this racing, maybe I should stop.' Then ten seconds later he smiled and said: 'I know why we do this. Where else can we earn so much money for doing so little?'"**

The first European GP was held in late April in the streets of Barcelona. It turned out to be a race surrounded by tragedy. It was to be held in the Montjuïc Park but, when the drivers inspected the track on the day before practice, they found the safety barriers were either very poorly fixed or in some cases, not fixed at all. The drivers who were members of the GPDA – the Grand Prix Drivers' Association – refused to practice on Friday. Only Ickx and a Dutchman, Roelof Wunderink – who was not a GPDA member – drove any laps. The organisers reacted by threatening to impound the cars if the drivers did not start racing. Eventually most of them did so, although Emerson Fittipaldi chose to do a very slow lap. Before the start, the controversies continued as Fittipaldi refused to take part at all. As soon as the flag dropped, Mario Andretti ran into the Ferrari of Niki Lauda sending the red car into Clay Regazzoni's Ferrari and thus eliminating Ferrari's chances of a good result after a few hundred yards while Patrick Depailler was a victim of this same accident. Then after the first lap, Merzario and Wilson Fittipaldi came into the pits to retire to show solidarity with Emerson Fittipaldi. On the track, James Hunt led but after six laps he crashed. Some ten laps later, Andretti – who had taken the lead – crashed as well. In the laps to follow, more drivers crashed of which the worst was that involving Rolf Stommelen. The German driver had his rear wing break while in the lead and crashed into the barrier and then over it, landing amongst the crowd. His new Hill GH1 killed five people and injured ten more. It was four laps later that the organisers decided to stop the race with Jochen Mass in first place. Jacky Ickx, who had had an uneventful race, had been leading after twenty-eight laps only to be passed by Mass. In the end, only eight cars made it to the finish. Lying in sixth place and two laps down on the leaders, Lella Lombardi was the first lady driver to be awarded points in a Formula One GP. However, since less than 50 % of the scheduled race distance had been covered before it was stopped, she was only awarded half a point. Mass's victory was hotly disputed because both Carlos Reutemann and Vittorio Brambilla had received the chequered flag before the German crossed the finish line.

▪ **Jochen Mass: "For the Spanish GP, I had suggested a parade rather than a race. Everybody agreed but, when the flag dropped, they all went off like fools and that resulted in the first corner crash."**

1000 km di Mugello 1975, Alfa Romeo 33TT12

Gran Premio de Espana 1975, Montjuïc. Als am Hill GH1 von Stommelen der Heckflügel brach, drehte sich das Auto und flog über diese Leitplanke hinweg in die Menge. Dabei kamen fünf Zuschauer ums Leben / When the struts to the rear wing broke on Stommelen's car, it spun, hit the barrier and leapt into the crowd killing five spectators.

Gran Premio de Espana 1975, Montjuïc. Die Leitplanken sorgten schon vor dem Rennen für Aufregung. Bei der Begehung der Strecke entdeckten Fahrer wie Niki Lauda, dass einige Schrauben lose waren / The barriers had come it for much criticism from the drivers before the race and during an inspection Niki Lauda found that many bolts were loose.

— 157 —

Ickx nahm nicht an den Sportwagenrennen in Dijon oder Monza teil, erst bei den 1000 Kilometern von Spa griff er wieder ins Lenkrad des Kauhsen-Alfa-33TT12. In seiner Heimat war er in der Qualifikation überraschend vier Sekunden langsamer als das Schwesterauto von Henri Pescarolo und Derek Bell. In dieser Reihenfolge endete auch das Rennen, das wegen starken Regens nach 54 Runden abgebrochen wurde.

■ **Derek Bell: „In Spa hatten wir einen tollen Kampf. Jacky hat alles versucht, um mir das Überholen unmöglich zu machen. In der Eau Rouge habe ich aber eine perfekte Linie getroffen und ihn bergauf überholt. Nach dem Rennen sagte Jacky zu mir: ‚Es ist unglaublich, wie schmal diese Strecke ist.'"**

Nach den Unfällen von Spanien ließ der Automobil Club von Monaco zu seinem Grand Prix nur 18 Autos zu und ergänzte seinen Kurs um eine Schikane, um die Geschwindigkeit zu senken. Ickx erzielte im Training zwar nur die 14. Zeit, qualifizierte sich damit aber fürs Rennen. Beim Start war die Strecke feucht, sie trocknete aber im Laufe des Rennens ab, sodass alle Fahrer auf Slicks wechselten. Ickx, der sich zwischendurch auf Rang drei verbessert hatte, kam als Neunter aus der Box und konnte sich in den verbleibenden 50 Runden nur um einen Rang verbessern. Beim Belgien-GP in Zolder war das JPS-Lotus-Duo erneut chancenlos. Ickx schied in seiner Heimat auf Platz zehn liegend mit gebrochener Bremshalbwelle aus. In Schweden lief es nicht besser. Nach einem Boxenstopp, bei dem seine Bremsen neu eingestellt wurden, landete Ickx nur auf Platz 15.

After Mugello, Ickx did not race the Alfa Romeo at Dijon or Monza, but re-joined Kauhsen's team for the 1,000 Kilometres of Spa. Surprisingly, Ickx did not get pole position since the other Alfa Romeo 33TT12 of Henri Pescarolo and Derek Bell was four seconds faster. The race was stopped after fifty-four laps because the weather became too bad to permit racing and in that time, Ickx and Merzario were not able not catch the other Alfa Romeo and thus finished second.

■ **Derek Bell: "We had a great battle at Spa. Jacky did everything to make it impossible for me to overtake. But I got the perfect line through Eau Rouge and got him going up the hill. After the race, Jacky said to me: 'It is amazing how narrow this track is.'"**

As a reaction to the accidents in Spain, the organisers of the Monaco GP only allowed eighteen drivers to participate in their race. And they had modified their track with a chicane to keep speeds down. Ickx made it into the race by setting fourteenth fastest time in qualifying. The race started on a humid track and, as it dried out after some twenty five laps, all the cars came into the pits for slick tyres. Ickx, who had got up to third position came back into the race in ninth place and could only gain one more spot in the remaining fifty laps. The Belgian GP was once again taking place at the Zolder track and here too the JPS Lotuses were outclassed. Jacky Ickx did not make the distance as a stub axle broke when he was lying tenth. Things did not improve for the Swedish Grand Prix and this time Ickx finished fifteenth after a late pit stop to adjust his brakes.

1000 km de Spa-Francorchamps 1975, Alfa Romeo 33TT12, Arturo Merzario & Jacky Ickx

Grand Prix de Monaco 1975, Lotus 72E - Ford

1000 km de Spa-Francorchamps 1975, Alfa Romeo 33TT12

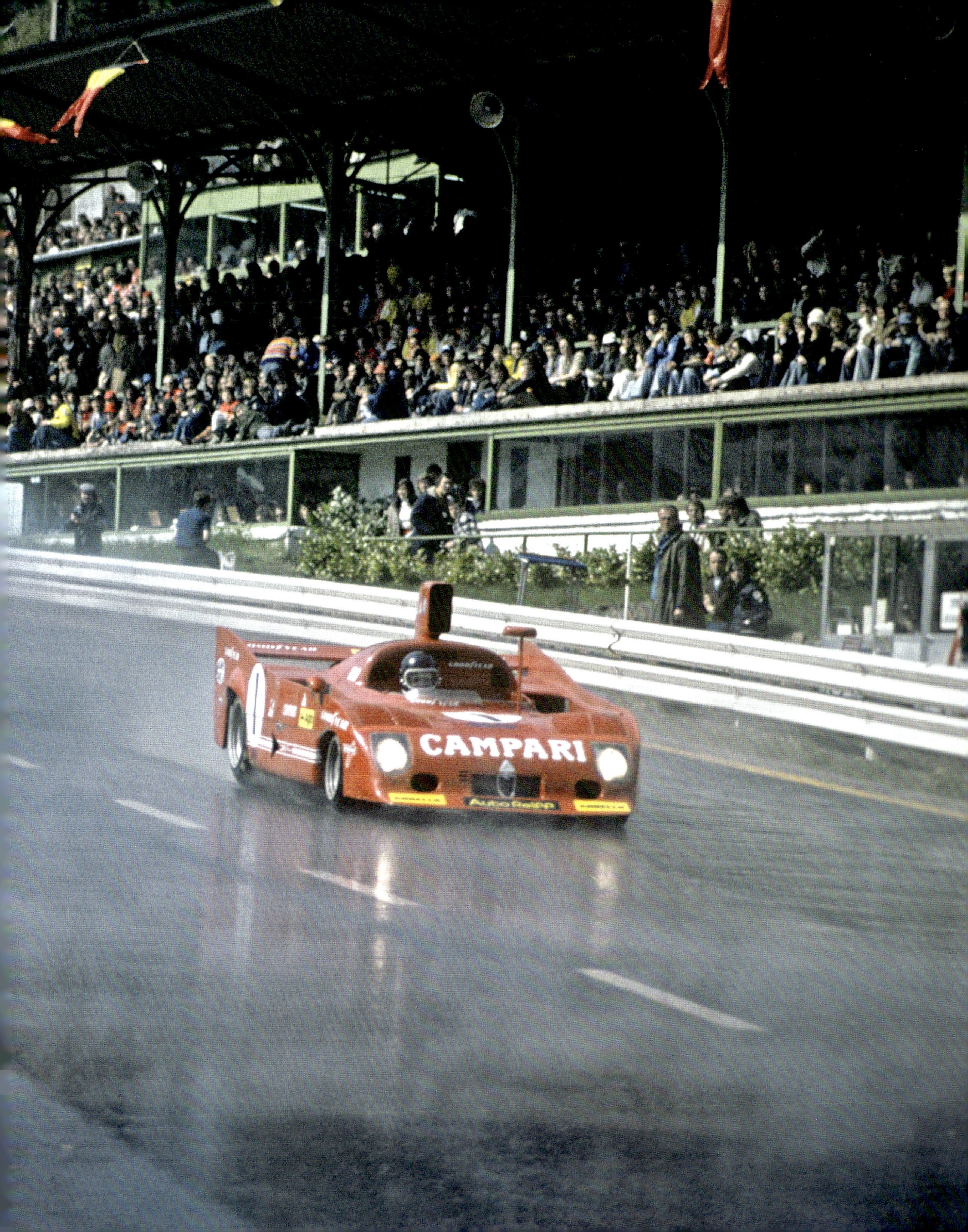
CAMPARI

Vor den 24 Stunden von Le Mans fragte Jacky Ickx seinen Freund John Wyer, ob das Cockpit im Gulf-Mirage GR8 neben Derek Bell noch frei sei. Die Antwort lautete „Ja". Obwohl der Langstrecken-Klassiker nach einem Disput mit der FIA nicht mehr der Sportwagen-WM angehörte, nahmen 55 Autos – darunter viele GT – das Rennen an der Sarthe auf. John Wyer setzte in seinem letzten Jahr mit Gulf zwei Autos ein, die sich in Le Mans mit Abstand als Maß der Dinge erwiesen.

■ **Derek Bell: „Obwohl Jacky schon in Le Mans gewonnen hatte, bot er mir an, im ersten Stint und bei der Zieldurchfahrt im Auto zu sitzen. Der Grund dafür war, dass ich die komplette Entwicklung des Autos gemacht hatte."**

Nach dem Start ging zunächst der Gulf-Mirage GR8 von Vern Schuppan und Jean-Pierre Jaussaud in Führung, doch als Ickx das Steuer des Schwesterautos übernahm, setzte er sich an die Spitze und behauptete diese bis ins Ziel. Schuppan/Jaussaud verloren wegen Zündaussetzern am Motor 20 Minuten an der Box und wurden daher nur Dritte. Ickx/Bell hatten dagegen während des gesamten Rennens nur ein Komfortproblem: Sie dachten, der Auspuff wäre kaputt.

■ **Derek Bell: „Ein Großteil des Rennens haben wir dieses Geräusch aus dem Heck des Wagens gehört. An der Box haben wir aber nie etwas gefunden. Als das Auto nach unserem Sieg auseinandergenommen wurde, haben wir dann festgestellt, dass ein Aufnahmepunkt der Aufhängung am Getriebe gebrochen war. Wenn das Auto stand, konnte man das nicht sehen."**

Beim GP der Niederlande saß Ickx wieder in „seinem" Lotus – Chassis 72/5 –, in dem er die ganze Saison bestritt. Die Negativserie setzte sich auch in Zandvoort fort, wo der Motor nach sechs Runden hinüber war. Beim Frankreich-GP schied Ickx erneut aus, als – wie schon in Belgien – die Vorderachse brach. Ickx' Enttäuschung erlebte einen neuen Höhepunkt. Nach dem Rennen erklärte er Colin Chapman, dass er nicht mehr für JPS-Lotus fahren will. Damit war die Saison für Ickx vorzeitig gelaufen.

Trotz seines zweiten Sieges bei den 24 Stunden von Le Mans blickte Jacky Ickx auf eine katastrophale Saison zurück. Nach nur 13 Rennen hatte der Belgier genug und legte für den Rest des Jahres eine Pause ein.

Zur Saison 1976 trieb Frank Williams bei Marlboro Geld auf, mit dem er Jacky Ickx für die Formel 1 verpflichtete. Nach vielen harten Jahren ging es der Mannschaft aus England nicht zuletzt wegen eines anderen Sponsors besser. Der Kanadier Walter Wolf zahlte der Rennwagenschmiede Hesketh 450.000 Britische Pfund (rund 2,4 Millionen DM) für deren 1975er-Formel-1-Autos, die fortan nicht mehr unter der Bezeichnung Hesketh 308C, sondern als Wolf-Williams FW05 antraten. Neben diesem F1-Engagement nahm Ickx für Porsche an Sportwagenrennen teil. Mit Jochen Mass als Partner startete er im 935 in der Marken-Weltmeisterschaft und im 936 in der Sportwagen-Weltmeisterschaft.

■ **Patrick Head: „Der FW05 war ein schreckliches Auto. Das Monocoque war einfach nicht steif genug. Wir haben versucht, es steifer zu machen, aber dann war es zu schwer. Außerdem war die Spur zu schmal. Wir haben alles versucht, aber wir haben es nicht geschafft, das Auto schneller zu machen. Deswegen hat sich Jacky einige Male nicht qualifiziert."**

For the 24 Hours of Le Mans, Jacky Ickx had written to John Wyer asking him whether he could get a drive with Derek Bell in the new Gulf Mirage GR8 to which the answer was 'yes'. Thanks to a falling-out with the FIA, the French race was not part of the 1975 World Sportscar Championship. However, fifty-five cars participated although most of them were entered in various GT classes. John Wyer, in his final year with Gulf, had built two cars to satisfy the new rules and the cars proved to be by far the best for an endurance race.

■ **Derek Bell: "Although Jacky was already a Le Mans winner, he offered me the chance to do the first stint as well as finishing the race. That was because I had done all the development driving on the car."**

The Gulf Mirage GR8 of Vern Schuppan and Jean-Pierre Jaussaud took the lead from the start, but as soon as Ickx took over the other Gulf Mirage, he moved into the lead and it stayed there for the remainder of the race. Because it lost time with a misfiring engine, the Schuppan-Jaussaud car spent some twenty minutes in the pits but they eventually re-joined and finished third. Ickx and Bell did not have any problems during the race other than the minor discomfort of what they thought was a broken exhaust.

■ **Derek Bell: "During most of the race, we could hear this noise at the back of the car, but when they checked it over at pit stops, they couldn't find anything. After our win, the car was taken apart and they found a broken suspension pick-up point at the gearbox. When the car was stationary, nobody could see it."**

For the Dutch Grand Prix at Zandvoort, Ickx was back with his Lotus chassis 72/5, the car he used all year. The bad results for Ickx in Formula One continued as the engine of his car broke down after just six laps. Ickx's frustration came to a climax after the French Grand Prix when the Belgian again had to retire. This time, just as had happened in Belgium, the front axle broke. After the race, Ickx told Colin Chapman that he no longer wanted to drive for JPS and that decision spelt an early end of the season for him.

Although he had won the 24 Hours of Le Mans for the second time in his career, the Belgian driver had had a miserable season. After only thirteen races, he decided to take a rest and drive no more in 1975.

For the 1976 season, Frank Williams used money from Marlboro to ask Ickx to join his new team. In addition, after many years of struggling, the British team owner had finally found a big sponsor. Between them, they had bought the 1975 Hesketh 308C Formula One cars and these came complete with engineer Harvey Postlethwaite. Canadian Walter Wolf paid Bubbles Horsley – who was Lord Hesketh's team manager – £ 450,000 and renamed the cars Wolf-Williams FW05. In addition to his F1 commitment, Ickx would race for Porsche who would enter both the sportscar championship and the endurance championship. For these races, Jochen Mass would share driving duties with him in either a Porsche 935 or a Porsche 936.

■ **Patrick Head: "The FW05 was a dreadful car. The monocoque was simply not stiff enough. We tried to make it stiffer but then the car became too heavy. Also the wheel track was too narrow. We did everything but we simply could not get that car to go faster. As a result, Jacky failed to qualify several times that year."**

24 Heures du Mans 1975, Gulf Mirage GR8 -
Ford, Jacky Ickx & Derek Bell

Sveriges Grand Prix 1975,
Anderstorp, Jacky & Catherine

Die Formel-1-Saison begann erneut in Südamerika, diesmal aber mit dem Brasilien-GP, wo der Williams FW05 nicht konkurrenzfähig war. Ickx fehlten in der Qualifikation fünf Sekunden zur Bestzeit. Von Platz 19 aus gestartet, arbeitete sich Ickx im Rennen jedoch bis auf die achte Position vor. Im Ziel hatte er eine Runde Rückstand auf den siegreichen Niki Lauda. Beim zweiten Rennen lief es nicht besser. Ickx startete von weit hinten und wurde nur 16. – mit fünf Umläufen Rückstand auf Lauda. Beim Race of Champions in Brands Hatch, das nicht der WM angehörte, kam mit Platz drei ein kleiner Hoffnungsschimmer auf. Als nächstes stand ein neuer WM-Lauf im Kalender: der GP USA-West. Für das Rennen in den Straßen von Long Beach konnten sich nur 20 Autos qualifizieren. Ickx gehörte nicht dazu, sein FW05 war zu langsam.

Das erste Sportwagenrennen des Jahres fand in Mugello statt, wo sich Ickx den Martini-Porsche-935 mit Jochen Mass teilte. In einem Feld von nur 24 Autos – darunter auch Tourenwagen wie der Ford Escort und BMW 2002 – holten Mass/Ickx souverän die Pole Position. Im Rennen fing sich Ickx zwar in Runde zwei einen Reifenschaden ein, das hinderte das Duo aber nicht am Sieg.

■ *Jochen Mass: „Ab 1976 bin ich zusammen mit Jacky für Porsche gefahren. Er war seit vielen Jahren ein Top-Fahrer und ein Vorbild für mich. Und es war einfach, mit ihm zu arbeiten. Wir waren immer ein echtes Team. Wenn ich Änderungen am Auto machen wollte, stimmte er denen meist ohne zu meckern zu."*

Die nicht zur F1-Weltmeisterschaft zählende International Trophy in Silverstone fand 1976 in Gedenken an Graham Hill statt, der am 29. November 1975 bei einem Flugzeugabsturz gestorben war. Ickx erlebte wieder ein unglückliches Wochenende: Nach Platz 15 in der Quali dauerte sein Rennen nur 21 Runden, ehe der Schalthebel brach.

As was traditional, the Formula One season started in South America, but this time in Brazil. The Williams FW05 was not competitive and in qualifying, Ickx was five seconds off the pace. From nineteenth place on the grid, Ickx worked his way up to eighth and finished one lap down on the winner, Niki Lauda. Things did not improve at the second race in South Africa. Ickx started way down the field and finished sixteenth, this time five laps down on Lauda. However, things looked brighter when Ickx finished third in the non-championship Race of Champions at Brands Hatch. Next was a race new to the Formula One calendar. This was the United States GP West that took place on the streets of Long Beach, a suburb of Los Angeles. For this race, only twenty cars could get on the grid and Jacky Ickx and the FW05 were not fast enough to be one of them.

The first endurance race of the year was held at Mugello where Ickx shared a Martini Porsche 935 with Jochen Mass. They took an easy pole position in a field of only twenty-four entries that included touring cars like Ford Escorts and BMW 2002s. Although Ickx had a puncture on the second lap, he and Mass won convincingly.

■ *Jochen Mass: "I started racing with Jacky in 1976 with Porsche. I looked up to him, as he had been a top driver for many years. But he was very easy to work with. We were always a real team and, most of the time, he accepted my suggested changes to the car without complaint."*

This year the non-championship Formula One race at Silverstone was held in honour of Graham Hill, who had died in an airplane crash on November 29th, 1975. The Williams FW05 was outclassed in qualifying with Ickx fifteenth and then his race was over after twenty-one laps when the gear lever broke.

1000 km di Mugello 1976, Porsche 935

1000 km di Mugello 1976, Porsche 935

Im Sportwagen ging es für Ickx dafür erfolgreich weiter. Im Porsche 935 gewann er die 6 Stunden von Vallelunga, danach war er in Monza im Einsatz, wo das Rennen 1976 statt der üblichen 1000 Kilometer, vier Stunden dauerte. Das Feld bestand ausschließlich aus Sportwagen, die Palette reichte aber vom 1,3-Liter-Chevron bis zum McLaren M8F aus der Can-Am. Mass/Ickx fuhren den 936 und stellten ihn vor den beiden Alpine-Renault A442 auf die Pole. Obwohl Jean-Pierre Jarier im A442 die schnellste Rennrunde markierte, ging der Sieg an Mass und Ickx. Einen Monat später feierten Mass/Ickx ihren insgesamt vierten Sieg in Italien in jenem Jahr. Im 936 Spyder triumphierten sie bei den 500 Kilometern von Imola. Kurz zuvor war es bei den 6 Stunden von Silverstone dagegen nicht nach Plan gelaufen. Beim Start ruinierte Ickx die Kupplung des 935. Nach zweistündiger Reparatur nahmen Ickx/Mass das Rennen auf und wurden Zehnte – und das, obwohl zwischendurch noch die Lichtmaschine gewechselt werden musste.

In der Formel 1 zeigte Ickx seinen Kampfgeist mit Platz sieben beim Spanien-GP in Jarama. Bei seinem Heim-Grand-Prix im belgischen Zolder und in Monaco folgte dann aber wieder die Ernüchterung, Ickx scheiterte beide Male in der Qualifikation.

The 1,000 Kilometres of Monza was on the calendar, but this year the event was called the Trofeo Filippo Caracciolo and would be a four-hour event open only to sportscars. It attracted a rather interesting field including anything from a Can-Am McLaren to 1.3-litre Italian specials. Jochen Mass again partnered Ickx and, driving a 936, they took pole ahead of two Alpine-Renaults. Although Jean-Pierre Jarier's Alpine-Renault set the fastest lap in the race, the victory went to Mass and Ickx. That was not the only success that they achieved in Italy that year. Driving a Porsche 935, they had won the 6 Hours of Vallelunga and afterwards, in a 936 Spyder, the 500 Kilometres of Imola. Then at the start of the 6 Hours at Silverstone, Ickx burned out the clutch. Replacing that cost him almost two hours in the pits while later the alternator had to be replaced. In the end, Mass and Ickx brought their Porsche 935 home in tenth place.

In Formula One, Jacky Ickx showed his old fighting spirit when he finished seventh in the Spanish Grand Prix at Jarama. But this good result was overshadowed by a failure to qualify for the Belgian Grand Prix at Zolder and the same thing happened in the narrow streets of Monaco.

Gran Premio de España 1976, Jarama, Wolf-Williams FW05 - Ford n°20

6 Ore di Vallelunga 1976

500 km di Imola 1976, Porsche 936

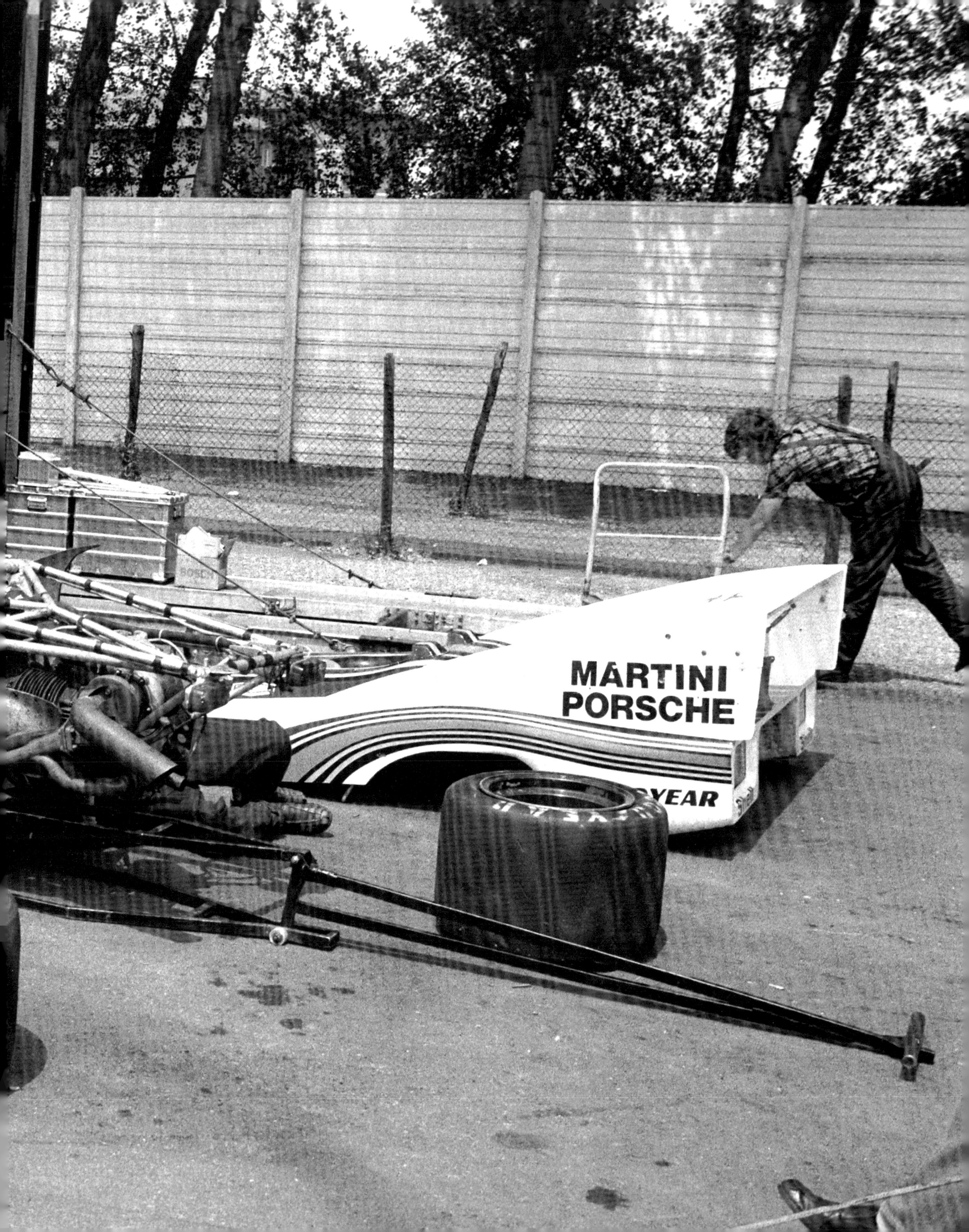
MARTINI
PORSCHE
YEAR

Die 24 Stunden von Le Mans gehörten auch 1976 keiner Weltmeisterschaft an, dennoch reiste Porsche mit einem starken Aufgebot an die Sarthe. Jochen Mass gehörte diesem aber nicht an, da er parallel am GP von Schweden teilnahm. Also nahm Gijs van Lennep, Le-Mans-Sieger von 1971, den Platz neben Ickx ein. Das belgisch-holländische Duo startete neben dem Alpine-Renault von Jabouille/Patrick Tambay aus Reihe eins, übernahm schon in der ersten Runde die Führung und behauptete diese bis ins Ziel. Für Ickx war es der dritte, für van Lennep der zweite Triumph beim 24-Stunden-Klassiker.

■ **Jochen Mass:** „Ich bin nicht gerne in Le Mans gefahren. Das Rennen an sich war anspruchsvoll, aber ich hatte immer Diskussionen mit der ACO wegen der Sicherheit. Ich habe so viele Unfälle gesehen, aber der Veranstalter wollte einfach nicht die Sicherheit erhöhen. Daher war ich froh, beim Formel-1-Rennen in Schweden zu sein."

■ **Gijs van Lennep:** „Jochen hatte keinen Vertrag mit Porsche für Le Mans, also fragte Jacky mich, ob ich mit ihm fahren würde. Abgesehen von einem kaputten Auspuff hatten wir keine Probleme. Es war ein leichter Sieg, und danach habe ich meinen Rücktritt aus dem Motorsport verkündet."

Beim Frankreich-GP landete Ickx in der Quali nur auf Startplatz 19. Im Rennen verbesserte er sich immerhin auf Rang zehn – mit einer Runde Rückstand auf den Sieger James Hunt, der 1975 noch im Hesketh gesessen hatte. Als sich Ickx nicht für den GP von Großbritannien qualifizierte, teilte er Frank Williams mit, dass er das Team verlässt. Ickx beklagte, dass das Auto keinen Grip hatte, nicht einlenkte und immer übersteuerte. Nach dem Weggang von Ickx ging Williams am Nürburgring mit nur einem FW05 an den Start, der von Merzario pilotiert wurde. Bei diesem schicksalhaften Rennen war Merzario einer der Helden, der Niki Lauda aus seinem brennenden Ferrari zog. Zwei Läufe später kehrte Jacky Ickx in die Formel 1 zurück. Da sich Chris Amon nach dem Lauda-Unfall mit sofortiger Wirkung aus dem Sport zurückzog, war das Ensign-Cockpit frei und so verpflichtete Besitzer Morris „Mo" Nunn den Belgier. Bei Ensign war zwar das Budget knapp und die Autos sahen recht simpel aus, aber die Ergebnisse stimmten.

In 1976, the 24 Hours of Le Mans still did not count for any championship, but Porsche came to France with a strong line-up. Since the event clashed with the Swedish Grand Prix, Jochen Mass could not drive in France so his place was taken by Dutchman Gijs van Lennep, the Le Mans winner of 1971. The Dutch-Belgian couple started from the front row alongside the Alpine-Renault of Jabouille and Patrick Tambay. Before the end of the first lap, the Porsche took command and kept it that way until the end. For Ickx, it was his third win and for van Lennep his second.

■ **Jochen Mass:** "I did not like to race at Le Mans. The race itself was challenging, but I always had arguments about safety with the ACO. I saw so many crashes and the organisers just did not change the safety measures. So I was happy to be in Sweden for the Formula One race."

■ **Gijs van Lennep:** "Jochen had no Porsche contract for Le Mans, so Jacky asked me to join him. Other than a broken exhaust, we did not have any problem. Actually, it was an easy win. And after the race, I announced my retirement from racing."

At Le Castellet, Ickx could only manage to qualify in nineteenth place for the French GP. In the race he finished tenth, one lap down on the winner, James Hunt, the same man who had driven the Hesketh in 1975, the car with which Ickx was now struggling. When Ickx could not qualify for the British GP, he told Frank Williams that he would leave the team. He complained that the car had no grip, would not turn in and was over-steering everywhere. With Ickx out of his team, Williams sent just one car – driven by Merzario – to the Nürburgring. At that fateful race, Merzario was one of the heroes who rescued Niki Lauda from his burning Ferrari. Two races later, at the Dutch Grand Prix, Ickx was back in Formula One. He had been asked by Mo Nunn to drive the Ensign, a car that had been driven by Chris Amon earlier that year but on witnessing Lauda's accident, Amon had retired on the spot. Although Mo Nunn's team ran on a tight budget and his cars looked simple, they were still quite fast. Ickx qualified in the Dutch Grand Prix on the sixth row, his best F1 qualification of the season. In the race, he was up to sixth place when, with seven laps to go, the electrics cut out.

24 Heures du Mans 1976, Porsche 936

Beim GP der Niederlande qualifizierte sich Ickx für die sechste Reihe – sein bester Startplatz in der laufenden Saison. Im Rennen lag er sieben Runden vor Schluss auf Punktekurs, als die Elektrik streikte.

Bei Porsche lief es dagegen weiter rund. Nach einem kurzen Tiefpunkt bei den 1000 Kilometern am Österreichring, wo Ickx und sein Interimspartner Manfred Schurti mit Motorschaden ausfielen, folgten Erfolgserlebnisse in Watkins Glen und Dijon. In Amerika komplettierten Ickx/Mass einen Porsche-Dreifachsieg, nachdem sie wegen des Wechsels der hinteren Bremsen Zeit verloren hatten. Beim Finale der Marken-Weltmeisterschaft, den 6 Stunden von Dijon, holten Ickx/Mass ihren dritten Sieg in dieser Serie und sicherten Porsche damit den WM-Titel. Einen Tag später gewannen die Schwaben auf derselben Strecke dank Ickx und Mass auch den Titel in der Sportwagen-WM. Bei den 500 Kilometern von Dijon, an denen Sportwagen und Can-Am-Autos teilnahmen, gewannen Ickx/Mass ihre Klasse. Das einzige schnellere Auto im Feld war der Can-Am-Bolide von Jackie Oliver und George Follmer, der in der WM aber nicht punktberechtigt war.

Ickx pilotierte den Ensign N176 bei drei weiteren F1-Grands-Prix, holte aber keine Punkte. In Monza landete er auf Platz zehn und im kanadischen Mosport Park auf Rang 13. In Watkins Glen lag der Belgier im Mittelfeld, als er einen schweren Unfall hatte, bei dem sich der Ensign buchstäblich in zwei Hälften teilte. Ickx erlitt bei dem Crash Knochenbrüche und Verbrennungen und hatte auf dem Weg ins Krankenhaus ein kurioses Erlebnis. Auf der 30 Kilometer langen Fahrt nach Elmira musste der Rettungswagen mit Ickx an Bord einen Tankstopp einlegen. Die Welt tickte damals noch ein wenig anders …

Für Ickx ging die Saison also mit einem schweren Unfall zu Ende. Und Jackys Formel-1-Karriere schien nach den vielen Enttäuschungen der letzten drei Jahre in eine Sackgasse zu führen. Im Sportwagen war die Welt dagegen mehr als in Ordnung. Mit Porsche hatte er sieben Gesamtsiege errungen und damit seine Stellung als erstklassiger Langstreckenpilot untermauert.

Meanwhile, everything was going much more smoothly with his career at Porsche. There was one hitch when at the Österreichring 1,000 Kilometres he and his one-off partner, Manfred Schurti, had a rare engine failure on the Zeltweg circuit. At Watkins Glen, Jochen Mass was back with Ickx and they finished third behind two other Porsches after Ickx had lost time when his rear brakes had to be changed. The final race of the manufacturer championship season was held at Dijon where Ickx won his third race of this series. And by winning that race with Mass, he brought the title to Porsche. The Stuttgart firm won the title in the sportscar championship too, for the day after winning at Dijon in the main series, Ickx and Mass won the 500 Kilometres of Dijon. In a mixed race for sportscars and Can-Am cars, Ickx won his class and was only beaten overall by the more powerful Can-Am cars of Jackie Oliver and George Follmer that were not eligible for the championship.

For the final races of the Formula One calendar – in Italy, Canada and America – Ickx drove the Ensign but was unable to score any points. He came tenth at Monza and thirteenth at Mosport in Canada. At the Glen, he had a major accident while running in the mid-field during which the Ensign literally broke in half and Ickx received several fractures plus some burns. He was taken to a local hospital in Elmira, some twenty miles from the track and, on the way, the ambulance had to make a stop for petrol. Things were different in those days and such things would not be tolerated today.

Although Ickx's season ended with a major accident, he could look back on a successful year in sportscars. With Porsche he had chalked up no fewer than seven outright victories that confirmed him as a first-rate endurance driver. By contrast, his Formula One career seemed to be at an end after so many disappointments over the last three years.

500 km de Dijon 1976, Dijon-Prenois, Porsche 936, Jacky Ickx & Jochen Mass

United States Grand Prix 1976, Watkins Glen, Ensign N176 - Ford. In Runde 15 verlor Ickx plötzlich die Kontrolle über seinen Wagen. Dabei traf er das Ende einer Leitplanke so unglücklich, dass der Ensign in zwei Hälften geteilt wurde und in Flammen aufging / On lap fifteen, Ickx's Ensign suddenly went out of control and hit the end of a guardrail head on. The effect was to cut the car in half and for both parts to catch fire.

1977 – 1978

Fokus auf Sportwagenrennen
Concentrating on sportscars

Da sich für Jacky Ickx kein Formel-1-Engagement ergab, verlängerte er den Vertrag mit Porsche und konzentrierte sich 1977 komplett auf seine Sportwagenkarriere. Für die Zuffenhausener ging er in der Marken-WM, Sportwagen-WM und der amerikanischen IMSA-Serie an den Start.

Beim ersten Lauf des neuen Jahres, den 24 Stunden von Daytona, waren Autos nach IMSA- und Le-Mans-Reglement zugelassen, daher durfte der Gruppe-5-Porsche-935 hier teilnehmen. Ickx und Jochen Mass stellten ihren Martini-Porsche in Florida mit einer Zeit von 1:48,289 Minuten auf die Pole und waren damit fast eine Sekunde schneller als der 935 von Kremer Racing. Im Rennen lieferte sich Ickx ein packendes Duell mit Danny Ongais im Porsche 911, bis sich der Belgier einen Reifen aufschlitzte und in eine Mauer krachte. Nach langer Reparatur kehrte der Martini-935 ins Rennen zurück und kämpfte sich in der Nacht bis auf Platz zwei vor, ehe er nach 16 Stunden wegen eines weiteren Reifenplatzers in der Mauer landete. Diesmal war der Einschlag endgültig.

With no Formula One involvement planned, Jacky Ickx was happy to renew his sportscar contract with Porsche. This year, there were international manufacturer and sportscar championships for them to enter while in America there was also the IMSA sportscar series.

The opening race of the season at Daytona was run according to IMSA and Le Mans rules, which allowed the Porsche 935 Group 5 car to run there. Jochen Mass partnered Jacky Ickx for the 24-hour race and their Martini-Porsche was fastest in qualifying. Jochen Mass clocked a lap of 1 minute 48,289 which was almost a second faster than the identical car entered by Kremer Racing. In the race, Ickx was battling for the lead with Danny Ongais in a Porsche 911 but after two hours of racing, Ickx cut a tyre and crashed into a wall. After extensive repairs, the Porsche came back into the race and, during the night, fought its way up to second overall. However at sixteen hours, another tyre problem sent the car into the wall again. This time it was beyond repair.

Silverstone 6 Hours 1977,
Jochen Mass & Jacky Ickx

Am Europa-Auftakt in Mugello nahm Ickx nicht teil, dafür war er bei den 6 Stunden von Silverstone mit von der Partie. Und wieder stellten Ickx/Mass das Martini-Auto vor dem Kremer-Porsche von Bob Wollek und John Fitzpatrick auf die Pole. Nach einem packenden Kampf siegten sie mit zwei Runden Vorsprung auf die Kremer-Piloten. Eine Woche später feierte Ickx beim Monaco-GP ein Kurzzeit-Comeback in der Formel 1, als er den verletzten Clay Regazzoni bei Ensign vertrat. 20 Autos durften am Rennen teilnehmen und Ickx war einer davon. Er qualifizierte seinen Ensign N177 für Startreihe neun, direkt hinter F1-Debütant Riccardo Patrese. Das Rennen beendete Ickx auf Rang zehn mit zwei Runden Rückstand auf den Sieger Jody Scheckter.

Ickx did not compete in the first European race at Mugello but he was back in action at Silverstone for the 6-hour race. Once again, Mass and Ickx set pole ahead of the Kremer Porsche. After a fierce battle, they won by two laps from Bob Wollek and John Fitzpatrick in the 935. A week later, Ickx was back in Formula One when Mo Nunn got him to substitute at the Monaco Grand Prix for the injured Clay Regazzoni in the new Ensign N177. Only twenty cars were allowed to start and this time Ickx was among them. He qualified the Ensign on the ninth row, right behind Italian, Riccardo Patrese, who was making his F1 debut. Ickx finally finished a distant tenth, two laps down on winner Jody Scheckter.

■ *Jochen Mass: „Obwohl Jacky und ich im 935 viele Rennen gewonnen haben, mochte ich den Wagen nie. Der 936 war besser, aber nicht aufregend. Und dann kamen der 956 und 962, die waren einfach magisch."*

■ *Jochen Mass: "I never liked the Porsche 935, although Jacky and I won many races with it. The 936 was different, better but not exciting. But then came the 956 and 962 – those were magic."*

Grand Prix de Monaco 1977, Ensign N177 - Ford

— 175 —

Bei den 1000 Kilometern am Nürburgring gelang Ickx/Mass die dritte Pole in Folge, im Rennen schieden sie jedoch mit defekter Benzineinspritzung aus. Als nächstes standen die 24 Stunden von Le Mans ins Haus, die keiner Meisterschaft angehörten und unter dem Reglement der ACO stattfanden. Die 55 Autos, die am Rennen teilnehmen durften, kamen aus beiden FIA-Meisterschaften und der IMSA. Porsche setzte drei Wagen ein. Die Fahrerduos Jacky Ickx/Henri Pescarolo und Jürgen Barth/Hurley Haywood pilotierten die neueste Version des 936, Rolf Stommelen/Manfred Schurti saßen im 935. Die Bestzeit in der Quali sicherten sich aber Jean-Pierre Jabouille und Derek Bell im Alpine-Renault A442. Für Ickx war das Rennen eigentlich schon nach 45 Umläufen gelaufen, dann rollte sein 936 mit Motorschaden aus. Da das Schwesterauto gleichzeitig Probleme mit der Einspritzung hatte und nur auf Platz 49 lag, kam die zusätzliche Hilfe durch Ickx gerade recht. Der Belgier verstärkte Barth/Haywood als dritter Mann und setzte in der Nacht Zeiten wie bei einem Sprintrennen. Den Rundenrekord unterbot er gleich mehrfach. Am Morgen lag der Porsche schon in Schlagdistanz zu den führenden Alpine-Renault, und als der letzte A442 durch Motorschaden ausfiel, war der Weg frei für Barth, Haywood und Ickx. Weniger als eine Stunde vor Schluss sorgte jedoch ein Kolbenschaden für einen unplanmäßigen Boxenstopp. Ein Mechaniker schaltete einen Zylinder ab und so legte Barth die letzten Runden langsam und mit einer großen Qualmwolke im Schlepptau zurück. Im Ziel hatten die Sieger elf Runden Vorsprung auf den zweitplatzierten Mirage-Renault von Vern Schuppan und Jean-Pierre Jarier.

Ickx went back to Porsche for the 1,000 Kilometres at the Nürburgring where, reunited with Mass, they were again on pole but fuel injection problems forced them to retire. Next was the Le Mans 24-hour race that was not on any championship calendar and was held under the rules of the ACO. The fifty-five cars came from several different series including IMSA and both FIA championships. Porsche entered several cars. They had updated 936s for Jürgen Barth-Hurley Haywood and Ickx-Henri Pescarolo while Rolf Stommelen and Manfred Schurti had a 935. The fastest qualifier however was the Alpine-Renault of Jean-Pierre Jabouille and Derek Bell. Right from the start, this Renault led until Sunday morning when its engine broke. Then the Barth–Haywood Porsche, now with the help of Jacky Ickx, moved into first place and kept it to the end. Ickx's 936 had only completed 45 laps before its engine had broken whereupon he joined the other Porsche. At that point, it lay in forty-ninth place after encountering injection problems. During the night, Ickx was driving as if in a sprint race. Several times he set a new lap record and by the early hours he was within striking distance of the leading Alpine-Renaults. When the last Renault retired with engine problems, it seemed that the Porsche could cruise home to a win. However, with less than an hour to go, a broken piston forced the car into the pits. A Porsche mechanic disconnected a cylinder and Jürgen Barth drove the final laps at a moderate speed with lots of oil smoke coming from the exhaust. At the finish, the 936 had an eleven-lap lead over the second-placed Mirage-Renault of Vern Schuppan and Jean-Pierre Jarier.

24 Heures du Mans 1977, Porsche 936-77

24 Heures du Mans 1977, Porsche 936-77, Jürgen Barth & Jacky Ickx

24 Heures du Mans 1977, Porsche 936-77
Jürgen Barth, Hurley Haywood & Jacky Ickx

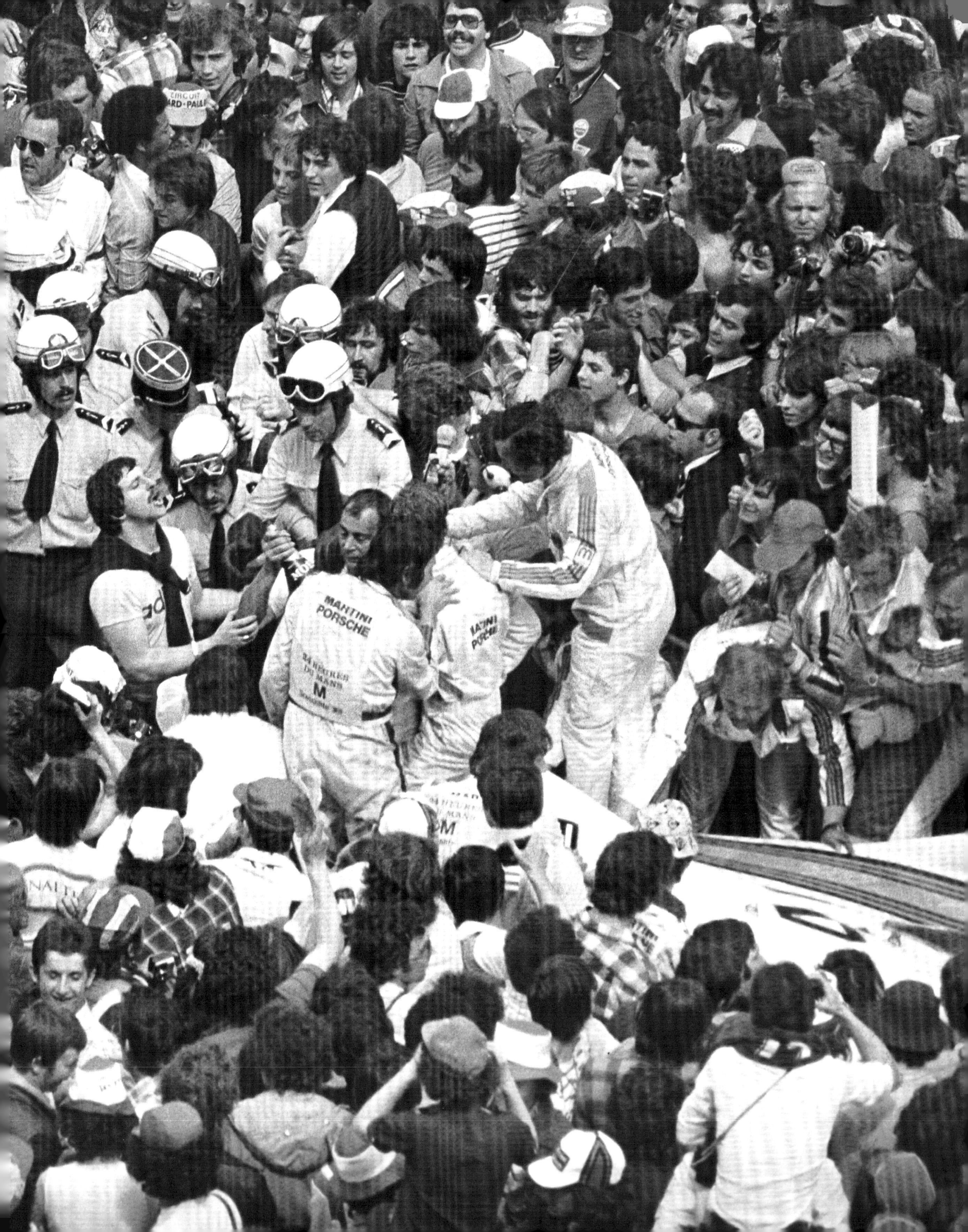
MARTINI
PORSCHE
24 HEURES
DU MANS
M
MARTINI
PORSCHE

Zwei Wochen später verfolgten 80.000 Fans das große Duell BMW gegen Porsche bei den 200 Meilen von Nürnberg. Auf dem Norisring landete der Porsche 935/77 von Ickx nach zahlreichen Problemen nur auf Rang sieben. Am Vortag hatte der Belgier zudem an einem Lauf zur Deutschen Rennsport-Meisterschaft (DRM) teilgenommen, war im Rennen über 70 Runden aber durch Elektrikprobleme ausgefallen. Nach dem Doppelprogramm am Norisring flog Ickx nach Amerika, um an den 6 Stunden von Watkins Glen teilzunehmen. Hier erwies sich der von McLaren eingesetzte BMW 320 Turbo als größter Gegner. In der Quali kam der BMW nah an den Porsche von Ickx und Mass heran, konnte eine weitere Pole des Erfolgsduos aber nicht verhindern. Im Rennen ging der Martini-Porsche in Runde 20 in Führung, als der BMW verunfallte. Ickx/Mass mussten im Laufe der sechs Stunden mehrmals stoppen, weil der Motor Öl verlor, um den Riemen der Lichtmaschine zu wechseln oder um den Turbo einzustellen. Trotz alledem fuhr das Duo mit drei Runden Vorsprung zum Sieg. Porsche belegte im Ziel übrigens die ersten zwölf Plätze! Einen Erfolg gab es auch bei Ickx' zweitem DRM-Gaststart am Hockenheimring, wo die Zweiliter-Version des Porsche 935/77 problemlos lief und Ickx vor zahlreichen BMW gewann.

 Im August und September nahm Ickx an drei Rennen in Amerika teil. Den Auftakt machte der Marken-WM-Lauf im kanadischen Mosport Park, wo Ickx zusammen mit Schurti von der Pole startete, aber nach 34 Runden mit defekter Zylinderkopfdichtung aufgeben musste. Eine Woche später lud ihn der amerikanische Porsche-Händler Vasek Polak ein, zusammen mit Skeeter McKitterick das IMSA-Rennen in Mid-Ohio zu bestreiten. Im Feld von 45 Autos war Ickx der einzige Europäer, aber er schlug sich gut und wurde im Porsche 935 Zweiter hinter Peter Gregg im Brumos-Porsche. Ickx blieb danach in den Staaten, um am ersten Lauf zum International Race of Champions (IROC) teilzunehmen. David Lockton, der Besitzer des Ontario Speedway in Kalifornien, hatte diese Serie gegründet, in der Top-Fahrer aus der NASCAR, Indy (CART) und Formel 1 in baugleichen Chevrolet Camaro gegeneinander antraten. Drei Rennen fanden im Herbst 1977 statt, das Finale im Frühjahr 1978 in Daytona. Beim Auftakt auf dem Michigan Speedway bekam es Ickx mit erfahrenen NASCAR-Piloten wie Richard Petty, Darrell Waltrip und Cale Yarborough zu tun. Während Al Unser das Rennen im Highspeed-Oval gewann, wurde Ickx nach einem Crash als Zwölfter gewertet.

 Da Porsche den Titel in der Marken-WM schon in der Tasche hatte, nahmen die Schwaben 1977 nur noch an zwei weiteren Läufen teil, das Finale in Vallelunga ließen sie aus. In Brands Hatch teilte sich Ickx das Cockpit wieder mit Mass und stellte den Porsche zum siebten Mal in diesem Jahr auf die Pole. Nach dem Unfall ihres größten Konkurrenten, des BMW 320 Turbo von Ronnie Peterson und Hans-Joachim Stuck, fuhren Ickx und Mass einen lockeren Sieg nach Hause. Bei den 6 Stunden von Hockenheim handelte es sich um zwei Rennen à drei Stunden und hier verpassten Ickx und Mass erstmals in der laufenden Saison die Pole Position. Wollek/Fitzpatrick erzielten im Kremer-Porsche die Bestzeit. Im ersten Lauf schieden Ickx/Mass kurz vor Schluss mit defekter Zylinderkopfdichtung aus, im zweiten revanchierten sie sich dafür mit dem Sieg. In der Gesamtwertung wurden sie jedoch nicht berücksichtigt.

 Danach jettete Ickx nach Kalifornien, wo die IROC-Läufe zwei und drei auf dem Programm standen. Da es sich beim Riverside International Raceway nicht um ein Oval handelte, rechnete der Belgier mit einem besseren Resultat als zuletzt. Doch auch hier hatte er den Amerikanern nichts entgegenzusetzen. Ickx beendete die Rennen auf den Plätzen acht und sieben. Die Siege gingen derweil an Al Unser und Cale Yarborough. Von Kalifornien flog Ickx direkt

Two weeks later, a crowd of 80,000 fans saw a fierce German battle between BMW and Porsche for the '200 Miles of Nürnberg' at the Norisring. Jacky Ickx encountered several problems with his two-litre Porsche 935/77 and finished seventh. The previous day, he had had to retire in a 70-lap race – counting for the Deutsche Rennsport Meisterschaft (DRM) – due to electrical problems. At Watkins Glen in America, there were forty-four cars taking part in the six-hour race. The main competitor for the Mass-Ickx Porsche was the new BMW 320 Turbo entered by McLaren. In qualifying, this new car came close to the Porsche, but once again Mass and Ickx claimed that first spot on the grid. In the race, the Martini drivers took the lead after twenty laps when the new BMW crashed. They had to stop several times to deal with a loss of oil, fit a new alternator bolt and make adjustments to the turbo but they retained their three-lap advantage. It was a Porsche fest, since the German manufacturer claimed the top twelve places. Later that summer, Ickx ran the two-litre Porsche 935/77 in another DRM race at Hockenheimring. This time the car ran flawlessly and the Belgian won ahead of several BMWs.

 Towards the end of August, Ickx entered three races in America. First there was another round of the manufacturer championship at Mosport in Canada where, together with Schurti, he claimed another pole, but after thirty-four laps a broken head gasket forced them to retire. A week later, the American Porsche dealer Vasek Polak invited Ickx to race with Skeeter McKitterick in an IMSA race at Mid-Ohio. As the only European in a field of forty-five cars, he did well in the Porsche 935 and finished second to Peter Gregg in the Brumos Porsche. Ickx stayed in America to compete in the IROC (International Race of Champions) series at Michigan. This had been created by David Lockton of the Ontario Speedway in California in which top drivers from NASCAR, Indy (CART) and Formula One would compete at four races at various circuits. They would drive identical Chevrolet Camaros set up for them by test drivers. This year, there would be three races in the fall of 1977 and one at the beginning of 1978 at Daytona, Florida. The first was to be held at Michigan Speedway where Jacky Ickx faced experienced NASCAR drivers like Richard Petty, Darrell Waltrip and Cale Yarborough. Al Unser won the race on this high-speed oval while Ickx was classified twelfth after crashing.

 Porsche decided to enter just two more races for the 1977 manufacturer championship. Since the championship was already decided, they would not bother to go the final race at Vallelunga but would go to Brands Hatch and then Hockenheimring. In England, Ickx had his regular partner Mass with him and for the seventh time they started from pole. After the BMW 320 Turbo of Ronnie Peterson and Hans-Joachim Stuck – their main competitor – had crashed, they were able to cruise to the finish and win by a large margin. The Hockenheim race was run in two three-hour sessions and, for the first time this season, Ickx failed to get on pole and it was Wollek and Fitzpatrick in the Kremer Porsche who set the fastest qualifying time. With only a few laps to go in the first heat, a head gasket failure on the Ickx car forced him and Mass to retire. However, they won the second heat, but were not classified in the combined standings.

 For the second and third IROC race, Ickx went to Riverside, California. Since this was a road course, he expected a better result than on an oval with which the American drivers are more familiar. But again, he found he could present no challenge to the Americans. In the first race, he finished eighth with Al Unser winning again while a day later, he was seventh with, this time, Cale Yarborough as the

Preis von Hessen-Hockenheim 2x3 Hours 1977, Porsche 935-77

nach Australien, um an den berühmten Bathurst 1000 teilzunehmen. Down under bekam es Ickx nicht nur mit der australischen Tourenwagen-Elite zu tun, sondern auch mit internationalen Rennsportgrößen wie Henri Pescarolo, John Fitzpatrick oder Derek Bell. Ickx teilte sich einen Ford Falcon mit Lokalmatador Allan Moffat und feierte nach sieben Stunden einen spektakulären Triumph. Das Duo siegte mit weniger als einer Sekunde Vorsprung auf Colin Bond und Alan Hamilton!

1977 hatte Jacky Ickx an nur einem Grand Prix teilgenommen, 1978 sollte er aber wieder regelmäßig für das Ensign-Team von Mo Nunn fahren. Neben der International Trophy in Silverstone sollte der Rückkehrer alle europäischen WM-Läufe bestreiten.

■ *Jochen Mass: „Jacky wollte immer Rennen fahren und hoffte natürlich auf weitere Siege. Daher nahm er im Herbst seiner Karriere verschiedene Angebote an. Mit den Siegen hat es aber nicht geklappt."*

Die Saison 1978 begann recht locker mit dem vierten und letzten IROC-Lauf auf dem Daytona Speedway in Florida, den Mario Andretti für sich entschied. Ickx wurde Sechster. Für die vier Show-Rennen im Chevrolet Camaro erhielt Ickx einen Scheck über 15.000 US-Dollar (ca. 30.000 DM), Al Unser bekam als Sieger der IROC-Gesamtwertung 50.000 US-Dollar (ca. 100.000 DM).

winner. From California, Ickx flew to Australia to compete in the famous Bathurst 1,000. He was one of several Europeans invited to drive in big Australian touring cars. He was paired with local ace, Allan Moffat, in a Ford Falcon. Also taking part were Henri Pescarolo, John Fitzpatrick and Derek Bell as were the Americans, Johnny Rutherford and Janet Guthrie. After almost seven hours, Allan Moffat and Jacky Ickx finished less than a second ahead of Colin Bond and Alan Hamilton to claim a famous win.

Jacky Ickx only drove one Grand Prix in 1977 but for 1978, he was back with the small team of Mo Nunn. After the International Trophy at Silverstone, he was scheduled to compete in the European rounds starting with the Spanish GP.

■ *Jochen Mass: "Jacky always wanted to race and, of course, hoped that he might win more races. So he accepted several offers in the later days of his career. But it did not work out for him."*

However, the 1978 season started in a relaxed way since Ickx still had to compete in the fourth and final round of the 77/78 IROC series. This last round was held on the banked speedway of Daytona, Florida, where Mario Andretti won with Ickx finishing sixth. For these four races, Ickx received a cheque for US$ 15,000 while the series winner, Al Unser, received US$ 50,000.

Preis von Hessen-Hockenheim 2x3 Hours 1977, Manfred Schurti & Jacky Ickx

182

Grand Prix de Monaco 1978, Ensign N177 - Ford

Bei der International Trophy in Silverstone gab der neue Lotus 79 sein Debüt und war auf Anhieb schnell. Ickx landete bei dem F1-Rennen ohne WM-Status mit drei Sekunden Rückstand auf die Pole im Mittelfeld. Am Renntag goss es wie aus Eimern – eigentlich die perfekten Bedingungen für Ickx, der sich diesmal aber schon in der ersten Runde von der Strecke drehte und ausfiel. Nach 40 Runden holte sich ein junger Finne namens Keke Rosberg im Theodore überraschend den Sieg. Zwei Monate später nahm Ickx im Ensign am GP von Monaco teil und qualifizierte sich für die letzte Reihe. Im Rennen legte der Belgier dafür los wie die Feuerwehr und lag innerhalb der Top Ten, ehe er wegen Bremsproblemen vorzeitig aufgeben musste.

Mitte Mai nahm Ickx zusammen mit Jochen Mass an den 6 Stunden von Silverstone teil, wo er als Test für die 24 Stunden von Le Mans eine Langheckversion des 935 pilotierte. In der Qualifikation sicherte sich das Duo mit großem Abstand die Pole Position, im Rennen zeigte sich das gleiche Bild: Ickx/Moss triumphierten mit sieben Runden Vorsprung auf Wollek und Pescarolo im älteren Porsche 935.

Seinen Heim-Grand-Prix in Zolder nahm Ickx aus der vorletzten Reihe in Angriff. Im Rennen war er lange Zeit das Schlusslicht und wurde letztlich Zwölfter mit sechs Runden Rückstand auf die dominanten Lotus 79. Beim Spanien-GP sah es ganz ähnlich aus. Während die Lotus souverän zum Sieg fuhren, mühte sich Ickx am Ende des Feldes ab, bis sein Motor elf Runden vor Schluss streikte. Als der Ensign 14 Tage später die Qualifikation für den Großen Preis von Schweden verpasste, beendete Ickx die Zusammenarbeit mit Mo Nunn. So machte er Platz für die Neulinge Derek Daly und Nelson Piquet, die im weiteren Saisonverlauf ihr F1-Debüt im Ensign geben sollten.

The International Trophy, a non-championship Formula One race at Silverstone, saw the debut of the new Lotus 79 driven by Peterson and Andretti. In practice these cars were really quick and both Lotus drivers were almost three seconds a lap faster than Ickx who qualified mid-field. On race day, it was raining hard and Ickx was one of the many drivers who spun off and he managed to do that on the very first lap. After just over an hour of racing, the young Finn, Keke Rosberg, was the surprise winner driving a Theodore. Almost two months later, Ickx was back behind the wheel of the Ensign and qualified towards the rear of the field for the Monaco GP. After a good start, Ickx was running in the top ten, but then he had to retire with brake problems.

In May, Ickx drove in the 6 Hours of Silverstone, partnered by Jochen Mass. Porsche had built a special long-tail 935 and this race would be a test for the coming Le Mans 24 Hours. Starting from pole – there was a huge time difference to the second fastest qualifier – they remained in first position and won with a seven-lap advantage over Wollek and Pescarolo in an older Porsche 935.

For his home Grand Prix at Zolder, Ickx qualified the Ensign on the second to last row and drove most of the race in last position. He finished but was six laps down on the mighty Lotus 79s. The next GP, in Spain, gave much the same result with an easy win for the Lotuses while Ickx was way back and retired with a broken engine eleven laps from the finish. A fortnight later when he could not qualify for the Swedish Grand Prix, Ickx and Mo Nunn decided that they had come to the end of their collaboration. In the GPs that followed, first Derek Daly and later Nelson Piquet made their Formula One debuts in the Ensign.

— 183 —

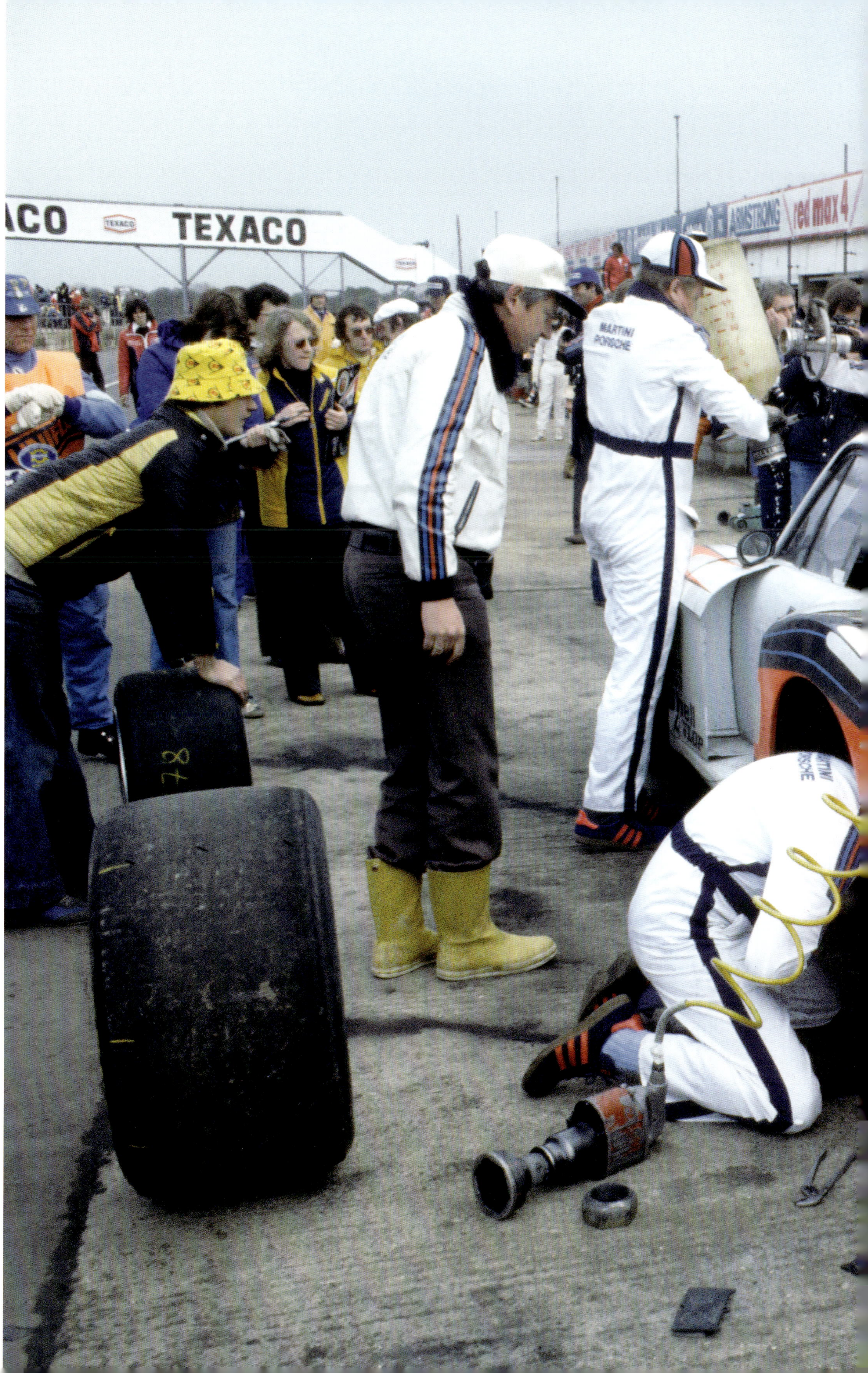
TEXACO
ARMSTRONG
red max 4
MARTINI
PORSCHE

Silverstone 6 Hours 1978, Porsche 935-78

Während die Formel 1 für Ickx nur Enttäuschungen bereithielt, konnte er im Sportwagen weitere Erfolge erzielen. Bei den 1000 Kilometern auf dem Nürburgring wurde er ebenso Zweiter wie bei den 24 Stunden von Le Mans. Bei dem Klassiker an der Sarthe nahm Ickx in zwei verschiedenen Porsche 936 Platz. In der Qualifikation stellte er sein ursprüngliches Auto, die Startnummer 5 mit Mass und Pescarolo als Partner, überraschend auf die Pole. Im Rennen hatten die Porsche den turbobefeuerten Alpine-Renault A442B aber nichts entgegenzusetzen. Die Nummer 5 hatte zunächst Probleme mit der Kraftübertragung und fiel in der Nacht durch einen Unfall von Mass in den Porsche-Kurven komplett aus. Danach wechselte Ickx in die Nummer 6 von Wollek/Barth, wo er als Ersatzfahrer eingetragen war. Am Sonntagmorgen hatte auch dieses Auto Probleme mit der Kraftübertragung und so war mehr als Platz zwei nicht drin. Nach 24 Stunden hatte der Porsche fünf Runden Rückstand auf den Alpine-Renault von Didier Pironi und Jean-Pierre Jaussaud.

Die letzten beiden Sportwagenrennen bestritt Ickx mit unterschiedlichen Partnern. In Watkins Glen schied er mit George Follmer als Fahrerkollege durch einen Motorschaden aus, im italienischen Vallelunga mussten Ickx/Schurti aufgeben, als der Riemen der Einspritzpumpe abging.

Die 24 Stunden von Spa-Francorchamps hatten zwar keinen Meisterschaftsstatus, dennoch lockten sie ein starkes Starterfeld an. Und mittendrin war Jacky Ickx, der sich mit seinem langjährigen Teamkollegen Brian Redman einen VW Scirocco teilte. Das kleine Coupé hatte gegen die deutlich leistungsstärkeren BMW und Ford Capri natürlich keine Chance, sah nach einem nächtlichen Unfall von Redman in der Malmedy-Schikane aber ohnehin nicht das Ziel.

■ **Brian Redman: „Der Einsatz im Scirocco war ein PR-Gag. Ich bin nie zuvor in einem Auto mit Frontantrieb ein Rennen gefahren. Außerdem musste ich feststellen, dass sie die Strecke geändert haben. Es gab jetzt eine Schikane in Malmedy, da bin ich im Training und im Rennen verunfallt."**

Für Ickx ging die Europa-Saison mit den 200 Meilen von Nürnberg auf dem Norisring zu Ende. Auf dem Straßenkurs stellte er seinen Porsche 935/78 in der Quali auf Platz vier. Im Rennen kam er wegen eines Motorschadens aber nicht besonders weit. Danach machte Ickx erneut in Australien halt, um wie 1977 mit Moffat in einem Ford Falcon an den Bathurst 1000 teilzunehmen. Ihren Vorjahressieg konnten sie wegen Motorproblemen aber nicht wiederholen.

Den Abschluss der Saison bildete ein „Gentlemen's Race" in den Straßen der portugiesischen Kolonie Macao. Auf baugleichen Ford Escort trat Ickx gegen berühmte Fahrer wie Stirling Moss, Dan Gurney, Jack Brabham, Toulo de Graffenried und Prinz Birabongse von Thailand an. Ickx begann das Rennen von Platz vier, zog im Laufe der zwölf Runden an der prominenten Konkurrenz vorbei und gewann.

Der Triumph beim Show-Rennen von Macao war Ickx' zweiter Saisonsieg nach den 6 Stunden von Silverstone. Insgesamt blickte der Belgier auf ein schwaches Jahr zurück. 1979 lockte jedoch eine neue Herausforderung: Für den amerikanischen Lola-Importeur Carl Haas sollte er neun Läufe zur Can-Am Series bestreiten. Darüber hinaus setzte ihn Porsche bei einigen Langstreckenrennen ein.

If F1 was a continuing disappointment for Ickx, there was more success to come in sportscars. Together with Schurti, he finished second at the Nürburgring 1,000 Kilometres and second again at the Le Mans 24 Hours. At the French classic, Ickx drove in two cars sharing first with Pescarolo and Mass and then with Barth and Wollek. The Belgian had surprised everybody by snatching pole ahead of the Alpines but, in the race, the 936 Porsches were no match for the Renault-Alpine Turbos. With the car he shared with Mass, they encountered transmission problems and lost time as a result. Finally, in the night, Mass crashed the car at the Porsche Curves and Ickx joined the other car for which he had been designated as reserve driver. But on Sunday morning, there were also long delays for this car with transmission problems. The French cars dominated the race and Ickx could not do better than second in the Wollek-Barth car. At the finish, the Porsche was five laps behind the Renault-Alpine of Didier Pironi and Jean-Pierre Jaussaud.

For the final two endurance races, Ickx found himself with George Follmer at Watkins Glen and with Manfred Schurti at Vallelunga. In America, engine problems forced the team to retire, while in Italy a broken injection pump belt meant another 'DNF'.

The 24 Hours of Spa-Francorchamps was not part of any championship, but it had a strong field in which Jacky Ickx made an appearance. Together with his long-time partner Brian Redman, he drove a Volkswagen Scirocco. This small car was no match for the BMWs and Ford Capris, all of which had much larger and more powerful engines. The race ended for these two celebrated sportscar drivers when Redman crashed at the Malmedy Chicane during the night.

■ **Brian Redman: "The Volkswagen Scirocco was a PR thing. I had never raced a front-wheel drive car. Also, I discovered that they had changed the track. There was now a chicane at Malmedy. Both in practice and in the race, I crashed there."**

Ickx completed his final European race of the year in Nürnberg when he drove in a Porsche 935/78 in the 200 Miles at the Norisring where he qualified fourth. However, it was after only a few laps that he had to retire thanks to engine failure. Next, Ickx returned to Australia for the Bathurst 1,000. Partnered once again by Moffat and driving a similar Ford Falcon, engine problems meant that they were unable to finish.

His racing season came to an end in Macau, the Portuguese colony off the Chinese coast that every year hosts races on a street circuit. Ickx was invited to compete in a 'Race for Gentlemen' with everyone driving identical Ford Escorts. Ickx qualified fourth for this twelve-lap race in which famous drivers such as Stirling Moss, Dan Gurney, Jack Brabham, Toulo de Graffenried and Prince Birabongse of Thailand took part. By the finish, he had outdriven them all and won the race.

Winning in Macau gave Ickx only his second victory of the year after Silverstone. All in all, it had been a poor season. For 1979, Ickx was contacted by Carl Haas to compete in the Can-Am Series. Haas was the American importer for Lola cars and he had a seat for the Belgian to drive in nine races. Additionally, Martini Porsche would give Ickx a number of endurance races beginning at the Daytona 24 Hours in early February.

24 Heures du Mans 1978, Porsche 936-78

LES BALS
FAURE
BUVETTE
SNACK
ORCHESTRE
AMBIANCE
Steak Frites

24 Heures du Mans 1978, Porsche 936-78

24 Heures du Mans 1978

24 Heures du Mans 1978

24 Heures du Mans 1978

1979 – 1981

Abenteuer in Amerika und Afrika
Adventures in America and Africa

Nach einer weiteren schwierigen Saison in der Formel 1 kam das Angebot von Carl Haas, einen Lola T333CS in der Can-Am zu fahren, zur rechten Zeit. In der Formel 1 war Jacky Ickx nach dem Weggang von Lotus 1975 von einem Tief ins nächste geschlittert. Ickx wurden nur zweitklassige Cockpits offeriert, in denen er nicht mit guten Ergebnissen auf sich aufmerksam machen konnte. Im Sportwagen war die Welt dagegen in Ordnung. Neben dem Can-Am-Programm bestritt er 1979 erneut einige Rennen für Porsche.

Für Ickx begann die Saison 1979 mit den 24 Stunden von Daytona, wo Georg Loos einen 935 einsetzte, den Ickx zusammen mit Peter Gregg und Bob Wollek pilotierte. Das Trio kämpfte in Florida zwar um den Sieg, schied gegen Mitternacht aber mit Motorschaden aus. Der Loos-Porsche hatte trotz zweimaligem Turboladerwechsels mehrmals in Führung gelegen, ehe das Triebwerk nach 342 Runden streikte. Einen Monat später saß Ickx bei den 6 Stunden von Mugello wieder im Loos-Porsche und teilte sich das Cockpit erneut mit Wollek. Während des Rennens setzten immer wieder Schauer ein. Bei ständig wechselnden Streckenbedingungen fiel die Entscheidung

After enduring another difficult Formula One season, Jacky Ickx was happy to accept Carl Haas's offer to drive for him in the American Can-Am Series. After leaving Lotus in 1975, the Formula One career of the Belgian had gone into rather a steep decline. As a result, he only got a chance to drive second-rate cars, which meant that he got no results. Driving sportscars, however, gave Ickx more satisfaction and, in addition to the Can-Am offer, Porsche would arrange some drives for him in 1979.

The season started in late January with the Daytona 24-hour race. Georg Loos had sent a 935 to Florida and Ickx was to be teamed with Peter Gregg and Bob Wollek. Although they were one of the contenders for the win, their race ended around midnight when the engine failed. They had covered 342 laps and had been in the lead several times even though they had to change turbochargers twice. A month later, Ickx drove his first event in Europe, the 6 Hours of Mugello, at the wheel of a Loos Porsche and partnered by Wollek as well as Manfred Schurti. The race was run in bad conditions with intermittent rain constantly changing the condition of the track.

24 Heures du Mans 1979, Porsche 936-78 n°12

— 192 —

Can-Am 1979, Watkins Glen, Lola T333CS - Chevrolet

über Sieg und Niederlage an der Box. Ickx und Wollek hatten bei dieser Lotterie nicht so viel Glück und wurden nur Zweite. Bei den 1000 Kilometer von Dijon wiederholten Ickx und Wollek – diesmal mit Verstärkung von Manfred Schurti – dieses Ergebnis.

Das Auftaktrennen zur Can-Am fand 1979 in Road Atlanta im Bundesstaat Georgia statt. Die Meisterschaft hatte viel von ihrem alten Glanz verloren. Zum Saisonstart versammelten sich nur 22 Autos und in der Nennliste tauchten wenige international bekannte Fahrer auf. Drei davon landeten in Road Atlanta auf dem Podium: Keke Rosberg gewann vor Ickx und dem Amerikaner Elliott Forbes-Robinson. Bei den nächsten beiden Saisonläufen gelang Ickx sogar der Sprung auf die oberste Stufe des Treppchens. In Charlotte und Mosport waren seine größten Gegner erneut Rosberg und Forbes-Robinson sowie der Engländer Geoff Lees.

In Le Mans setzte Porsche mit Unterstützung des amerikanischen Ölkonzerns Essex zwei überarbeitete 936er ein. Diese wurden von Bob Wollek/Hurley Haywood sowie Jacky Ickx/Brian Redman pilotiert. Beide Essex-Porsche starteten aus der ersten Reihe und dominierten das Rennen zu Beginn. Redman fing sich nach drei Stunden einen Reifenschaden ein, durch den die Karosserie in Mitleidenschaft gezogen wurde. Nach der Reparatur lief der 936 problemlos und ging wieder in Führung. In der Nacht sprang dann der Riemen der Benzinpumpe ab. Ickx konnte den Schaden auf der Strecke beheben, nahm dabei aber fremde Hilfe in Anspruch und wurde daher einige Zeit später disqualifiziert.

■ *Brian Redman: „Obwohl sie wussten, dass wir disqualifiziert waren, ließen sie uns bei schrecklichsten Bedingungen noch gut eine Stunde weiterfahren."*

Victory was gained or lost in the pits and Ickx had to be content with second place behind the other 935 entered by Georg Loos. The third round of the World Championship was the 1,000 Kilometres at Dijon where Ickx again shared a Porsche 935 with Wollek and Schurti and once more finished second.

The 1979 Can-Am Series started in May at Road Atlanta in Georgia. Twenty-two cars took part in this first race of the season and they were mostly American drivers. The series had lost most of its status and there were only a few top drivers in the entry list. First, second and third places were taken by three of these drivers with Keke Rosberg ahead of Ickx and the American, Elliott Forbes-Robinson. Within a month, Ickx had driven two more Can-Am events in Charlotte, North Carolina and at Mosport in Canada and he won both these races. Again the main competition came from Rosberg, Forbes-Robinson and – at Mosport – from Englishman, Geoff Lees.

For the 24 Hours of Le Mans, Porsche entered two updated 936s with financial support from Essex, an American oil company. Bob Wollek drove with Hurley Haywood and Ickx was reunited with Brian Redman. The two Porsches started from the front row and were leading comfortably. Then at the three-hour mark, Ickx's car lost time when Redman had a puncture that damaged the bodywork. This was repaired in the pits after which he and Redman ran faultlessly and got back into the lead. During the night, the fuel pump belt broke and Ickx replaced it out on the track but this was achieved with outside help and some time later his car was disqualified.

■ *Brian Redman: "Even though they knew we were to be disqualified, we were allowed to race on for another hour in those horrible conditions."*

An Pfingstsonntag hatte sich Patrick Depailler beim Drachenfliegen verletzt und konnte daher nicht mehr für Ligier in der Formel 1 fahren. Daraufhin fragte Guy Ligier seinen alten Freund Jacky Ickx, ob er für den jungen Franzosen einspringen würde. Ickx nahm das Angebot an und bestritt in Dijon sein erstes Rennen. Beim Frankreich-GP landete er in der Quali auf Platz 14, schied im Rennen aber durch Motorschaden aus. Zwei Wochen später lief es für Ickx in Silverstone viel besser. Jacky belohnte sich für seine starke Vorstellung mit Rang sechs und einem WM-Punkt. Es war sein erster Zähler seit dem zweiten Platz beim Spanien-GP 1975.

In den folgenden F1-Rennen wechselten sich Höhen und Tiefen ab. Beim Deutschland-GP am Hockenheimring schied er zur Halbzeit auf Platz sieben liegend durch einen Reifenschaden aus. In Österreich läutete ein Motorschaden den vorzeitigen Feierabend ein. Beim GP der Niederlande in Zandvoort lief es dagegen wie am Schnürchen, Ickx wurde in Zandvoort mit einer Runde Rückstand auf den siegreichen Alan Jones Fünfter. In Monza machte ihm allerdings erneut der Motor einen Strich durch die Rechnung.

Zwischen den Grands Prix kam Ickx seinen Verpflichtungen in der Can-Am nach und flog daher immer wieder über den großen Teich. Das Can-Am-Rennen in Watkins Glen beendete er auf der sechsten Position. In Road America und Brainerd waren dann aber die Saisonsiege Nummer drei und vier fällig. Die Zahl der Fahrzeuge hatte sich dahin zwar auf 30 erhöht, internationale Topstars blieben aber Mangelware. Anschließend folgte im kanadischen Trois Rivieres der einzige Ausfall im Lola wegen eines Crashs. Die Entscheidung in der Can-Am musste daher bei den beiden Schlussläufen in Kalifornien fallen. In Laguna Seca gewann Bobby Rahal, während Ickx nicht über Platz acht hinauskam. Beim Finale in Riverside holte der Belgier dafür den Sieg und den Can-Am-Titel.

Ickx' Formel-1-Saison nahm dagegen ein unschönes Ende. In Kanada schied er mit defekter Kraftübertragung aus, beim WM-Finale in Watkins Glen rutschte er im strömenden Regen von der Bahn. Bei den acht F1-Läufen im Ligier hatte Jacky zwar nur zweimal die Zielflagge gesehen, in diesen beiden Rennen aber jeweils Punkte mitgenommen. Drei WM-Zähler bedeuteten in der Endabrechnung Platz 15. Damit ging die Grand-Prix-Karriere des mittlerweile fast 35-jährigen Belgiers endgültig zu Ende.

Earlier in the year, Patrick Depailler had been injured in a hang glider accident and he was unable to race for Ligier in F1. Guy Ligier approached his old friend Jacky Ickx and asked him if he could replace the young Frenchman. Ickx was happy to accept and, in Dijon for the French GP, he qualified fourteenth but then retired with an engine failure. Two weeks later, Ickx did much better in England where, after a strong drive, he finished sixth at Silverstone. He scored one point, his first in F1 since finishing second in Spain in 1975.

Because Ickx was committed to drive for Carl Haas in Can-Am, between the two European GPs the Belgian drove at Watkins Glen where he finished eighth. Right after the British GP, Ickx won the Road America Can-Am race at Elkhart Lake. By now there were thirty competitors in this series, but it was still lacking sufficient top international drivers. Meanwhile in Europe, Ickx failed to finish at both the German and the Austrian GPs. At the Hockenheimring, he had a puncture halfway through the race while lying seventh. In Austria, it was once again an engine failure that sidelined him. At Zandvoort, for the Dutch GP, Ickx had a trouble free run and finished fifth, although he was one lap down on the winner Alan Jones. But then engine trouble forced him to retire during the Italian GP at Monza.

He had mixed fortunes also in Can-Am for, after winning at Brainerd, he crashed at Trois Rivieres in Canada so that it came down to the fact that the final two races in California – at Laguna Seca and Riverside – would decide who won the 1979 series. In Laguna Seca, it was Bobby Rahal who won his first of these Can-Am races with Ickx eighth. But in the final round at Riverside, Ickx took the win and also the championship.

However, his woes continued in Formula One. At the Canadian GP in Montreal, the transmission of his Ligier JS11 broke while in Watkins Glen, at the final F1 race of the year, he slid off the track in pouring rain. Out of eight Formula One races he had had just two finishes, but it has to be said that, when he finished, he earned points. With three championship points, Ickx was credited as being fifteenth in the 1979 World Championship. For Ickx, who was by now almost thirty-five years old, these had been his final Formula One races.

Grote Prijs van Nederland 1979, Zandvoort, Ligier JS11 - Ford

Großer Preis von Deutschland
1979, Hockenheim

British Grand Prix 1979, Silverstone, Ligier JS11 - Ford

24 Heures du Mans 1980, Porsche 908-80

Für die Saison 1980 erhielt Jacky Ickx kein Angebot. Seine Formel-1-Ambitionen waren im Sande verlaufen und in der Can-Am wurde er durch Patrick Tambay ersetzt. Darüber hinaus beteiligten sich die Hersteller nur sehr begrenzt an der Marken-WM. Das einzige echte Werksteam war das von Lancia, das in der Gruppe 5 startete. Ickx wurde von Porsche immerhin für die 24 Stunden von Le Mans angeheuert. An der Sarthe sollte er zusammen mit Reinhold Joest einen offenen Porsche 908-80 pilotieren, der auf dem Chassis des 936 basierte. Das deutsch-belgische Duo lag lange Zeit in Führung, trat diese jedoch am Sonntagmorgen wegen eines Problems mit der Kraftübertragung an den Rondeau M379 von Jean Rondeau und Jean-Pierre Jaussaud ab. Durch den Defekt verloren sie 30 Minuten an der Box und als dann auch noch Joest am frühen Nachmittag in eine Leitplanke einschlug, war das Rennen endgültig verloren. Ickx musste sich mit Platz zwei begnügen und durfte sich (noch) nicht über seinen fünften Le-Mans-Sieg freuen.

Einige Monate zuvor hatte Jacky Ickx bei einem Urlaub in den französischen Alpen eine neue Idee aufgeschnappt. Der Schauspieler Claude Brasseur, ein Freund von Ickx, hatte ihm von der Rallye Paris–Dakar erzählt, die Thierry Sabine 1978 als ultimative Herausforderung für Mensch und Material ins Leben gerufen hatte. Die Wüstenrallye begann in Paris und endete drei Wochen später in Senegals Hauptstadt Dakar. Ickx sehnte sich nach einer neuen Herausforderung und da kam ihm das Abenteuer Dakar gerade recht.

Ickx und Brasseur nahmen die Wüstenrallye, die am Neujahrstag 1981 – Ickx' 36. Geburtstag – in Paris begann, in einem Citroën CX mit 2,4-Liter-Motor in Angriff. Die große, frontgetriebene Limousine erwies sich jedoch als völlig unpassend. Ickx/Brasseur meisterten auf ihrem Weg durch die Sahara viele Schwierigkeiten, beschädigten den CX bei einem Unfall aber letztlich so stark, dass sie aufgeben mussten.

For 1980, Jacky Ickx had no offers to drive. His ambition for success in Formula One had fizzled out and Patrick Tambay was to be his replacement for Carl Haas in the Can-Am Series. In sportscar racing, there was little participation from the manufacturers and in Group 5, it was just Lancia who took the championship seriously. However, when Ickx was approached by Porsche to drive at Le Mans, he accepted. Together with Reinhold Joest, he was entered in an updated 908 spyder that used the chassis of a 936. Although leading for most of the race, they lost their top position early on Sunday morning to Jean-Pierre Jaussaud in the French Rondeau M379 when the Porsche had a transmission problem. That cost them half an hour in the pits and then, in the early afternoon, Joest collided with the barriers and more time was lost repairing that damage. Eventually they finished in second place two laps behind the Rondeau. No fifth victory – yet – at Le Mans for Ickx.

Earlier that year, during holidays in the French Alps, Jacky Ickx had talked with his friend, the actor Claude Brasseur, about the Paris-Dakar Rally. This was an event created by Frenchman Thierry Sabine in 1978 when he organised the ultimate challenge for car and driver, a rallye-raid starting in Paris and ending three weeks later in Dakar, the capital of Senegal. Ickx felt he needed a new challenge, and this event – which would next be held in January 1981 – could give him some new motivation.

Ickx and French movie star Brasseur entered a Citroën CX 2.4-litre in this gruelling event, which started in Paris on New Year's Day 1981. The Citroën, a large front-wheel drive limousine, was totally inappropriate for such an event. After overcoming several difficulties along the route in Africa, the team had to retire after an accident damaged their car too much to continue.

24 Heures du Mans 1980

24 Heures du Mans 1980, Porsche 908-80, Jacky Ickx & Reinhold Joest

— 197 —

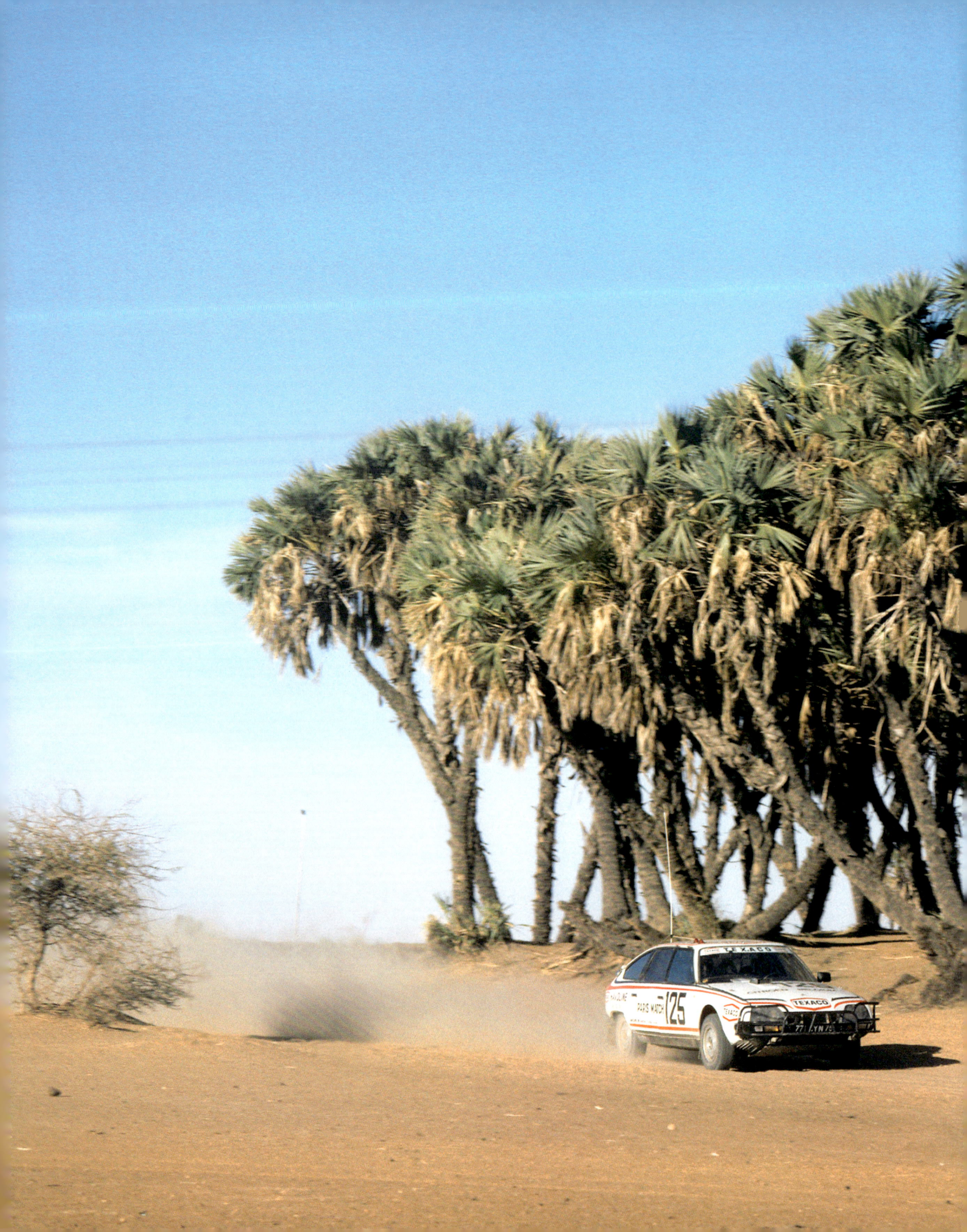
TEXACO
PARIS MATCH
125
TEXACO
TEXACO

Paris-Dakar 1981, Citroën
CX 2400 GTI, Jacky Ickx &
Claude Brasseur

24 Heures du Mans 1981, Porsche 936-81, Jacky Ickx & Derek Bell

Ein knappes halbes Jahr nach dem Wüstenabenteuer wagte Ickx den nächsten Versuch bei den 24 Stunden von Le Mans. Zusammen mit Derek Bell fuhr er einen Porsche 936, der von Jules gesponsert wurde, einer Marke des französischen Parfümherstellers Dior. An dem Klassiker durften die unterschiedlichsten Sportwagen teilnehmen, sogar NASCAR-artige Chevrolet. Die größten Rivalen von Ickx waren der Porsche 936 von Jochen Mass, Vern Schuppan und Haywood sowie zahlreiche 908er und 935er. Im Rennen gingen Ickx/Bell nach drei Stunden in Führung und dominierten das Geschehen bis ins Ziel. Nach 24 Stunden hatten sie 14 Runden Vorsprung auf den Rondeau von Jean-Louis Schlesser, Philippe Streiff und Jacky Haran. Mit seinem fünften Le-Mans-Sieg stellte Ickx einen neuen Rekord auf. Vorher hatte er sich die Bestmarke mit Landsmann Olivier Gendebien geteilt.

■ *Derek Bell: „Ich bin als letzter Fahrer zu dem Le-Mans-Projekt dazugestoßen. Als ich an der Strecke ankam, habe ich das Auto erstmals gesehen. Das Rennen war wunderbar, wir mussten kein einziges Mal die Hauben öffnen. Wir haben Öl nachgefüllt, das war's. Nach dem Rennen fragte Porsche mich, ob ich Teil ihres 1982er-Programms sein wollte."*

In Zuffenhausen arbeiteten die Ingenieure schon an der Entwicklung eines neuen Sportwagens. Der 956 würde dem zur Saison 1982 neu eingeführten Gruppe-C-Reglement entsprechen. Jacky Ickx sollte dem neuen Werksengagement ebenso angehören wie Jochen Mass und Derek Bell.

Competing in Paris-Dakar gave Ickx sufficient lift that, in the summer of 1981, he was prepared to give Le Mans another try. He was reunited with Derek Bell and they drove a Porsche 936, sponsored by Jules, a brand of the French perfume house, Dior. The race was open to all kind of sportscars, even American NASCAR-style Chevrolets. The main competitor for Ickx was a similar Porsche driven by Jochen Mass, Vern Schuppan and Hurley Haywood as well as several 908s and 935s. After three hours, Ickx got into the lead and for the remainder of the race he and Bell dominated the event. At the finish, they had a large margin over a Rondeau driven by Jean-Louis Schlesser, Philippe Streiff and Jacky Haran. By winning this Le Mans race, Ickx became the most successful driver with five wins, which was one more than his famous compatriot Olivier Gendebien.

■ *Derek Bell: "Mine was the last name to come out of the hat to drive this car at Le Mans. I only saw the car for the first time when I arrived at the circuit. But in the race, it was wonderful. They never needed to open the body panels at all, just added some oil for the engine and that was it. After the race, Porsche asked me if I wanted to join them in a new programme for 1982."*

In Stuttgart, Porsche had already started developing a new sportscar to be designated the 956. The FIA would introduce a new championship class for 1982 called Group C and the new Porsche was built to meet the requirements of these regulations. Ickx was invited to be part of their team for 1982 together with Jochen Mass and Derek Bell.

24 Heures du Mans 1981, Derek Bell & Jacky Ickx

— 201 —

1982 – 1985

Zum Abschluss im Rothmans-Porsche
The Rothmans Porsches

Porsche verpflichtete Jacky Ickx zur Saison 1982 als Werksfahrer für das neu gegründete Rothmans Porsche Team. Die Mannschaft nahm mit dem neuen Gruppe C Sportwagen namens 956 an der Langstrecken-Weltmeisterschaft teil.

Bevor Ickx das Testprogramm des neuen Porsche 956 aufnahm, wagte er sich zum zweiten Mal an das Abenteuer Rallye Paris–Dakar. Diesmal steuerte Ickx aber keine frontgetriebene Limousine, sondern einen Mercedes 280GE. Ickx und Beifahrer Claude Brasseur hätten die Rallye im Allrad-Geländewagen gewinnen können, wenn sie nicht eine Zeitkontrolle ausgelassen und 300 Minuten Strafzeit kassiert hätten. Den Sieg holten sich daher Bernard und Claude Marreau in einem stark modifizierten und mit Allradantrieb ausgerüsteten Renault 20.

Nach monatelangen Tests, die hauptsächlich im französischen Le Castellet stattfanden, setzte Porsche den von Ingenieur Norbert Singer entworfenen 956 bei den 6 Stunden von Silverstone erstmals ein. Beim Debüt landete der Wagen von Ickx und Derek Bell auf Platz zwei hinter dem Lancia LC1.

Porsche signed up Jacky Ickx to be part of their new Rothmans Porsche Team for the 1982 season. They would enter the World Endurance Championship for the all-new Group C sportscars and they would use the 6 Hours of Silverstone as a prelude to the 24 Hours of Le Mans in June.

But before Ickx started months of testing with the new Porsche, he entered the Paris-Dakar again though this time he did not choose an ordinary front-wheel drive car but a Mercedes 4x4. Co-driven again by Claude Brasseur, Ickx finished fifth in a 280GE pickup. They lost their chance of winning after missing a time control that cost them 300 minutes of penalty. The French Marreau brothers Bernard and Claude driving a highly modified Renault 20 prototype 4x4 won the event outright.

After extensive testing in the spring of 1982, most of it carried out at Le Castellet in France, Porsche entered the new 956 designed by Norbert Singer for the 6 Hours of Silverstone in May. On their debut, Ickx partnered by Derek Bell finished second behind a Group C Lancia LC1.

Paris-Dakar 1982, Mercedes 280GE, Jacky Ickx & Claude Brasseur

Silverstone 6 Hours 1982

■ *Derek Bell: „Porsche war kein großer Freund des neuen Gruppe-C-Reglements. In Silverstone mussten wir die letzten Runden im fünften Gang fahren, um Benzin zu sparen und das Ziel mit der erlaubten Spritmenge zu erreichen."*

Bei den 24 Stunden von Le Mans setzten die Zuffenhausener drei 956er ein, die von Ickx/Bell, Jochen Mass/Vern Schuppan und Hurley Haywood/Al Holbert/Jürgen Barth pilotiert wurden. Nach einem problemlosen Rennen feierte das Porsche-Werksteam einen überragenden Dreifachsieg und Ickx seinen sechsten Sieg beim Klassiker an der Sarthe. Nach Le Mans waren die Rothmans-Porsche bei vier weiteren Sportwagenrennen – nämlich Spa, Fuji, Brands Hatch und Kyalami – im Einsatz. Ickx gewann alle vier Veranstaltungen, drei davon mit Mass und eine mit Bell als Partner.

Das umfangreiche Testprogramm im Frühjahr 1982 hatte großen Anteil an dieser unglaublichen Siegesserie. Die Porsche-Ingenieure hatten das Gruppe-C-Reglement besser interpretiert als alle anderen und konnten zudem auf ihren großen Erfahrungsschatz bei Sportwagenrennen setzen. Da war es nur logisch, dass Porsche am Jahresende Marken-Weltmeister und Ickx Fahrer-Weltmeister wurden.

■ *Jochen Mass: „Der 956 und später der 962 ließen sich sehr gut fahren und waren besonders bei langen Rennen sehr angenehm. Sie waren einfach besser als alle anderen. Ich fand es toll, mit Jacky zusammen zu fahren. Er war nie egoistisch und wir hatten nie Streit. Nicht einmal über die Position unserer Namen auf dem Auto. Auf einer Seite stand sein Name oben, auf der anderen meiner."*

■ *Derek Bell: "Porsche was never actually in favour of these new Group C regulations. At Silverstone, in order to comply, we had to drive the final laps in fifth gear just to save fuel and make it to the end on the fuel allowed."*

The German manufacturer then sent three new 956s to Le Mans where Ickx was partnered by Bell, Jochen Mass had Vern Schuppan as his partner and a third car was driven by Hurley Haywood, his fellow-American Al Holbert and Porsche test driver, Jürgen Barth. After a trouble-free run, the three cars finished 1-2-3 and for Ickx it was his sixth win in the French classic. After Le Mans, Rothmans Porsches were entered in four other events, namely Spa, Fuji, Brands Hatch and Kyalami. Ickx won all these events, three with Mass and the one at Brands Hatch with Bell as his partner.

Porsche's development programme during the spring of 1982 had given the team their amazingly good results. The German engineers had interpreted the new Group C regulations to the best advantage and this, together with their long history in sportscar racing, proved to be the critical factor. It was good enough to give Ickx the driver title and Porsche the manufacturer title.

■ *Jochen Mass: "The 956 and later the 962 were very good to drive and particularly comfortable in long races. They were just better than anything else. And I loved to share the car with Jacky. He was never egoistic and we never had arguments. Not even about our names on the car. On one side his name was on top while on the other side, my name was above his."*

24 Heures du Mans 1982, Norbert Singer, Jacky Ickx & Manfred Jantke

1000 km de Spa-Francorchamps 1982, Porsche 956

Brands Hatch 1000 km 1982, Porsche 956 n°11

— 205 —

1983 setzte sich die Porsche-Dominanz in der Gruppe C fort. Die Marke gab den 956 zwar auch an Privatiers weiter, dennoch waren die Werkswagen diejenigen, die es zu schlagen galt. Für Ickx begann das Jahr aber mit einer anderen Herausforderung: der Paris–Dakar. 1983 steuerten Ickx/Brasseur erneut einen Mercedes 280GE durch die Sahara und waren erfolgreich. Sie hatten keine größeren Probleme und gewannen die Wüstenrallye. Nach der Rückkehr aus Afrika hatte Ickx erst einmal vier Monate Pause, ehe der erste Lauf zur Langstrecken-Weltmeisterschaft bevor stand.

Bei den 1000 Kilometern von Monza stand überraschend kein Porsche, sondern der Lancia LC2 von Piercarlo Ghinzani auf der Pole Position. Im Rennen drehten die 956er aber den Spieß rum: Thierry Boutsen und Bob Wollek siegten im Joest-Auto vor den Werksfahrern Ickx/Mass. Einen Monat später fiel das Rothmans-Duo in Silverstone durch einen Unfall aus. Auf einer von Ickx' Lieblingsstrecken, dem Nürburgring, wendete sich das Blatt mit dem ersten Saisonsieg aber zum Guten. Die Pole hatten sich aber die Teamkollegen Derek Bell und Stefan Bellof gesichert.

Die 24 Stunden von Le Mans bestritt Ickx zusammen mit Derek Bell. Spätestens nach der Bestzeit in der Quali galt das Duo als Favorit auf den Sieg, im Rennen mussten sich Ickx/Bell aber ihren Rothmans-Teamkollegen Holbert, Schuppan und Haywood geschlagen geben. Beide Porsche legten 371 Runden zurück und lagen im Ziel nur 64,3 Sekunden auseinander. Diesen Rückstand fing sich Ickx schon in der zweiten Runde ein, als ihm der Canon-Porsche von Jan Lammers ins Auto fuhr. Der Niederländer hatte vor der Mulsanne-Kurve den Bremspunkt verpasst. Die anschließende Reparatur kostete Ickx genau die eine Minute, die ihm am Ende fehlte.

Im Laufe der 24 Stunden hatten Ickx/Bell aber auch noch andere Probleme: Am Sonntagmorgen verloren sie durch ein Problem mit der Kraftübertragung mehrere Runden. Wenig Später blieb Bell mit Zündungsproblemen liegen und konnte erst weiterfahren, nachdem er am Straßenrand die Motorsteuerung gewechselt hatte. Insgesamt wurde das Rennen zu einem großen Porsche-Fest: In den Top Ten standen am Ende neun 956er. Einziger Eindringling war der neuntplatzierte Sauber C7-BMW.

In 1983, Porsche continued to be dominant in Group C races. Although the new 956 was now available to customers, the works cars were the ones to beat. However for Ickx, the year would once again kick off with the Paris-Dakar. For the 1983 edition, Ickx was co-driven by Claude Brasseur and a Mercedes 280GE was again their chosen transport. This year, the team did not encounter any problems and won the gruelling event. After returning from Africa, Ickx had a four-month break before he would drive his first endurance race.

It came as a surprise to find that, at the 1,000 Kilometres at Monza, it was the new Lancia LC2 driven by Piercarlo Ghinzani that was fastest in qualifying ahead of all the Porsches. In the race, the private 956 of Joest Racing, driven by Thierry Boutsen and Bob Wollek, won with Ickx and Mass second. A month later Ickx and Mass failed to finish the Silverstone race after being involved in an accident. But then fortune smiled on them at one of Ickx's favourite circuits, the Nürburgring, where they won outright. Pole position that day went to their team-mates, Bell and Stefan Bellof.

For the 24 Hours of Le Mans, Ickx was paired with Derek Bell. They set fastest time in qualifying and were favourites to win but after 24 hours, they had to be content with second place behind the other Rothmans Porsche driven by Holbert, Schuppan and Haywood. Both teams covered 371 laps and the margin at the finish was a mere minute. The race got off to a rough start for Ickx as already in the second lap, his Porsche was hit by the Canon Porsche of Jan Lammers. The Dutchman missed his braking point at the Mulsanne corner and ran into Ickx. Repairs cost Ickx just over a minute and at the finish it was that minute – actually 64.3 seconds – that cost him victory.

But Ickx's 956 had also lost a number of laps due to a transmission problem early on Sunday morning. Later still, Bell was stopped at the trackside with ignition problems that were solved by changing the ECU and the Englishman was able to continue. Porsche's domination was evidenced by the final results that showed nine 956s in the top ten. Breaking the monotony was a Swiss Sauber that finished ninth. One of its drivers was Diego Montoya, the uncle of Juan Pablo Montoya.

Silverstone 1000 km 1983,
Porsche 956-83 n°1

Paris-Dakar 1983, Mercedes 280GE

Paris-Dakar 1983, Mercedes 280GE, Jacky Ickx & Claude Brasseur

1000 km di Monza 1983

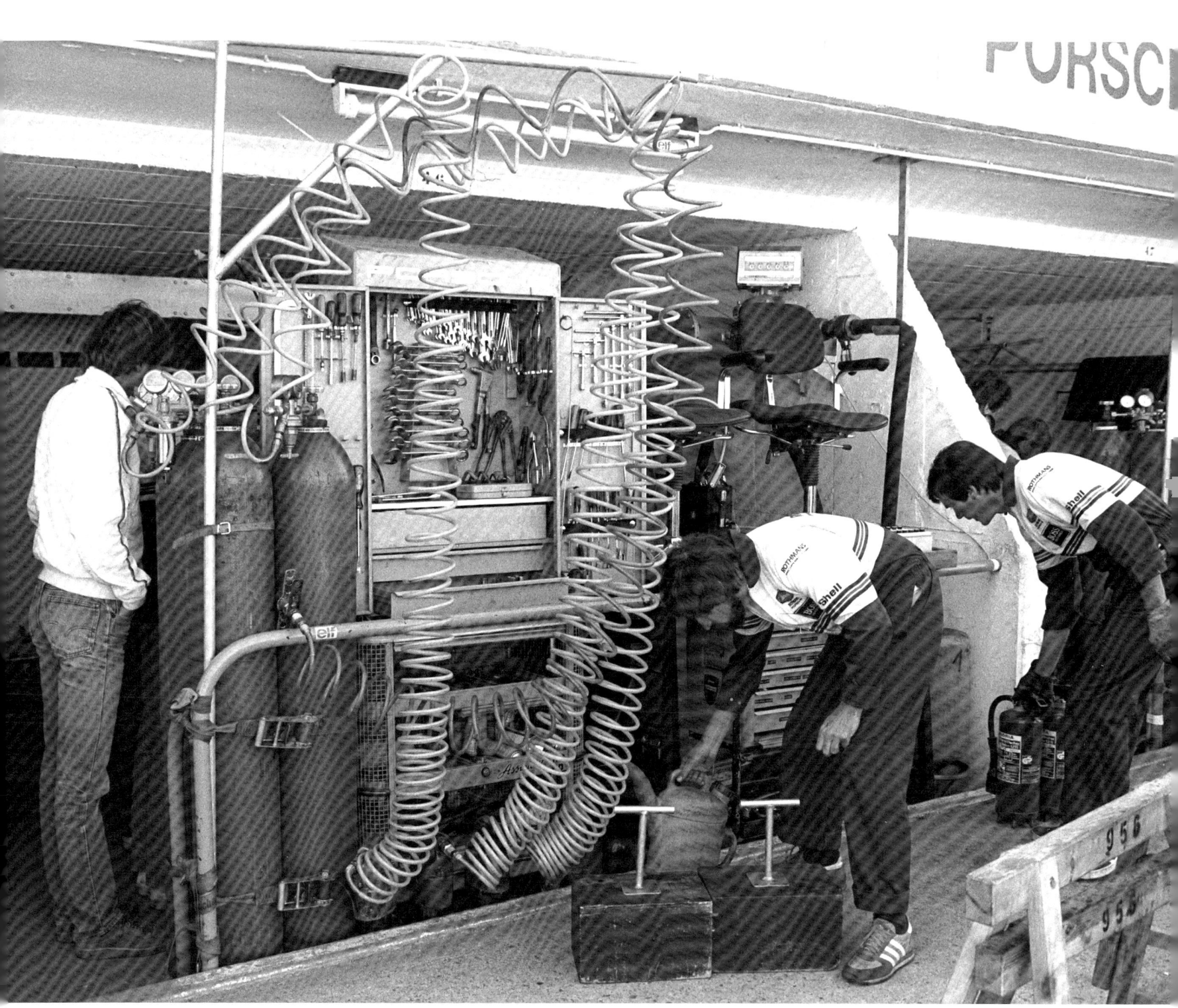

24 Heures du Mans 1983

1000 km de Spa-Francorchamps 1983, Jacky Ickx & Norbert Singer

▪ Jan Lammers: „In der zweiten Runde lagen Jacky und ich ganz dicht beieinander, als wir zur Mulsanne-Kurve kamen. Er hat zuerst gebremst und ich war etwas spät dran. Wir haben uns berührt und beide gedreht. Nicht besonders clever, wenn einem so etwas in der zweiten Runde eines 24-Stunden-Rennens passiert. Zumindest konnten wir beide weiterfahren."

▪ Derek Bell: „Jacky und ich hatten eine ganz besondere Beziehung, die bei Langstreckenrennen gut funktioniert hat. Die Ingenieure und Mechaniker liebten ihn. Da er sich für den Besten hielt, wurde er auch am besten behandelt. Das zahlte sich für uns beide aus. Nach dem Unfall mit Lammers und der Reparatur haben wir 14 Stunden gebraucht, um die Führung zu erobern. Am Sonntagmorgen war ich gerade dabei, Schuppan zu überholen, als der Motor ausging und ich das Auto am Straßenrand reparieren musste. Am Nachmittag waren unsere Bremsen hinüber, aber wir wollten gewinnen und daher bin ich so schnell gefahren wie ich konnte. Wir haben den Sieg nur knapp verpasst."

Im September gewann Ickx zusammen mit Mass die 1000 Kilometer von Spa. Im japanischen Fuji sowie bei dem nicht zur WM zählenden Rennen in Brands Hatch landete das Duo jeweils auf Platz zwei. Das WM-Finale in Südafrika beendeten Ickx und Mass auf Rang drei. Diese Ergebnisse reichten Jacky Ickx, um sich zum zweiten Mal in Folge zum Langstrecken-Weltmeister zu krönen.

▪ Jan Lammers: "At the second lap of the 24 Hours of Le Mans, Jacky and I came to Mulsanne and were almost together. He used his brakes first and I was a little late. We touched and both spun. Not very clever in the second lap of a 24-hour race. But we were both able to continue."

▪ Derek Bell: "Jacky and I had a special relationship that worked well in endurance racing. Also, the engineers and mechanics loved him. Because he thought he was the best, he got the best treatment. And that paid off for both of us. After Jacky's accident with Lammers and repairs it took us fourteen hours to get back to the top. When I wanted to pass Schuppan on the Sunday morning, the engine just quit, which meant I had to do some trackside repairs. In the afternoon, our brakes were gone but, trying to win, I ran as fast as I could and we only missed the win by a tiny margin."

Reunited with Jochen Mass, Jacky Ickx won the 1,000-kilometre race at Spa-Francorchamps in September. Then in Fuji, the Japanese circuit, Mass/Ickx could only manage second place behind their team-mates Bell and Bellof. They achieved the same result at the non-championship race in Brands Hatch while at the end-of-season race in South Africa they finished third. However, all these results were sufficient for Jacky Ickx to be crowned as the 1983 Endurance Champion.

1000 km de Spa-Francorchamps 1983, Porsche 956-83 n°1

Nach dem Triumph bei der Paris–Dakar nahm Ickx – diesmal mit Jean da Silva als Beifahrer – auch an der Pharaonen Rallye in einer Mercedes G-Klasse teil. In Ägypten konnte Ickx aber den Erfolg, den sich Jean-Claude Briavonne im Lada Niva sicherte, nicht wiederholen.

Zur Saison 1984 wurde die Langstrecken-Weltmeisterschaft von sieben auf elf Läufe erweitert, den Auftakt bildeten aber nach wie vor die 1000 Kilometer von Monza. Jacky Ickx ging ein weiteres Jahr mit Jochen Mass für Porsche an den Start. Vorher zog es Ickx jedoch wieder in die Wüste. Bei der Paris–Dakar fuhr der Belgier diesmal einen Porsche 953, das war vom Prinzip her ein 911 mit Allradantrieb. Nach einigen Problemen erreichten Ickx/Brasseur einen respektablen sechsten Gesamtrang.

Ende April begann die Sportwagensaison in Monza, wo es zum ersten Kräftemessen der beiden Porsche-Werksteams kam: Ickx/Mass gegen Bell/Bellof. In Italien behielt das deutsch-britische Duo die Oberhand. Der Sieg stand nach dem Rennen aber auf der Kippe, da der Bell/Bellof-Porsche angeblich zu leicht war. Erst als Porsche dem Veranstalter bewiesen hatte, dass deren Waage nicht richtig funktionierte, war das Ergebnis offiziell. In Silverstone hatten die 956/83 Schwierigkeiten mit der neuen Einspritzung von Bosch. Porsche löste das Problem durch die Senkung des Verdichtungsverhältnisses, was aber zu einem Leistungsverlust führte. Ickx/Mass gingen daher erst nach dem Ausfall des Porsche von Lammers und Jonathan Palmer in Führung und fuhren zum Sieg.

Anfang Juni sorgte Ickx abseits der Piste für Schlagzeilen, als er beim Monaco-GP als Rennleiter fungierte. Bei sintflutartigen Regenfällen stoppte er den Grand Prix nach 31 von 77 Runden mit der roten Flagge. Umstritten war dabei der Zeitpunkt des Abbruchs. Alain Prost lag noch in Führung, aber Stefan Bellof und Ayrton Senna kamen dem Franzosen immer näher. Kurz bevor sie Prost eingeholt hatten, beendete Ickx das Rennen und erklärte Prost zum Sieger. Die Entscheidung warf viele Fragen auf, da Prosts McLaren von einem TAG-Porsche-Motor angetrieben wurde und Ickx bekanntermaßen Porsche-Werksfahrer war.

After his success in the Paris-Dakar, Ickx who was on this occasion navigated by Jean da Silva drove a Mercedes-Benz G-wagen in the Pharaohs Rallye-Raid in Egypt. The event was won by Jean-Claude Briavonne in a Lada Niva.

For 1984, the FIA World Endurance Championship got a boost by having eleven rounds compared with just seven in 1983. Porsche asked Ickx to drive for them together with Jochen Mass. The season would start in April with the 1,000 Kilometres at Monza. But before that, Ickx entered another Paris-Dakar and this time he had a Porsche. The factory had asked the Belgian to drive a 953 that was a prototype 4x4 of the car that Porsche hoped to homologate into Group B. After encountering a few problems, they managed to finish a very respectable sixth.

The 1984 sportscar championship started with the 1,000 Kilometres of Monza in late April where Ickx was with Mass while Bell drove with Bellof. After just over five hours, the Anglo-German crew finished first ahead of Ickx and Mass. Then the winning car was penalised for being underweight and it needed Porsche to show the organisers that their scales did not work properly for the win to be reinstated. At Silverstone Porsche had some problems with their new Bosch electronic injection. By reducing the compression ratio, the problem was solved but the engine delivered less horsepower. After an oil line broke on the leading Porsche of Lammers and Jonathan Palmer, Ickx and Mass took the lead and won the race.

Ickx made headlines that spring when he was appointed Clerk of the Course for the Monaco GP. Because of torrential rain, Ickx decided to red flag the race after only 31 of the scheduled 77 laps. However, the moment he chose to do so was contentious as Alain Prost was leading in a McLaren but both Stefan Bellof and Ayrton Senna were closing on him rapidly. It was just before they caught him that Ickx stopped the race and Alain Prost was declared the winner. His decision raised a few eyebrows since Prost's McLaren was powered by an engine designed by Porsche and Ickx was Porsche's driver.

FIA-Siegerehrung / FIA prize-giving 1983

1000 km di Monza 1983, Porsche 956-83

Paris-Dakar 1984

Paris-Dakar 1984, Jacky Ickx, Roland Kussmaul & René Metge

Paris-Dakar 1984, Porsche 911, Jacky Ickx & Claude Brasseur

Porsche war mit der neuen Regel, dass die Autos in Le Mans nochmals 15 Prozent weniger Sprit verbrauchen durften, nicht einverstanden und nahm daher nicht werksseitig am Rennen teil. Ickx und Bell reisten stattdessen in die USA, um am ersten Lauf zum International Race of Champions (IROC) teilzunehmen, wo genau wie sieben Jahr zuvor auf baugleichen Chevrolet Camaro Z28 gefahren wurde. Gegen die amerikanischen Oval-Spezialisten tat sich Ickx schwer. Auf dem Michigan Speedway ging der Sieg an NASCAR-Pilot Neil Bonnett, Ickx wurde nur Neunter. Drei Wochen später landete Ickx auf dem Flugplatzkurs von Cleveland auf Rang zwölf, während NASCAR-Mann Cale Yarborough siegte.

Das ADAC 1000-Kilometer-Rennen fand 1984 nicht mehr auf der Nordschleife, sondern auf dem Grand-Prix-Kurs des Nürburgrings statt. Ickx/Mass wurden auf der hochmodernen Strecke nur Siebte. Von der Eifel reiste der Belgier direkt nach Amerika, wo der dritte IROC-Lauf sowie der kanadische Lauf zur Langstrecken-WM bevorstanden. Auf dem ultraschnellen Superspeedway von Talladega dominierten erneut die NASCAR-Piloten. Darrell Waltrip feierte den Sieg, Ickx wurde nur Zehnter. In Mosport bekamen es Ickx und Mass mit recht wenig Konkurrenz zu tun und fuhren ihren zweiten Saisonsieg ein.

■ *Jochen Mass: „In der Nacht vor dem Rennen in Mosport ist Jacky einen Marathon oder so etwas gelaufen. Er war so müde, dass ich den Großteil gefahren bin. Ich habe die Zeitungen gehasst, die am nächsten Tag schrieben: ‚Großartige Fahrt von Ickx!'"*

Das Finale des IROC fand wie schon der Auftakt auf dem Michigan Speedway westlich von Detroit statt. Während sich die NASCAR-Piloten gegenseitig im Windschatten durch das Oval zogen, war Ickx erneut chancenlos und wurde nur Zwölfter. Der Sieg ging an Bonnett. In der Gesamtwertung belegte Ickx den zwölften Platz und bekam dafür 20.000 US-Dollar (ca. 57.000 DM). Cale Yarborough wurde für den Gesamtsieg beim IROC mit 150.000 US-Dollar (ca. 430.000 DM) entlohnt.

Nach der Rückkehr nach Europa wurden Ickx und Mass bei den 1000 Kilometern von Spa Zweite. Nach 144 Runden hatten sie etwas weniger als eine Minute Rückstand auf ihre Teamkollegen Bell/Bellof. Die 1000 Kilometer von Imola waren neu im Kalender und Porsche setzte hier nur ein Auto zum Testen ein. Ickx fuhr zusammen mit John Watson einen 956 mit Automatikgetriebe. Ohne Erfolg: Das Rennen endete wegen eines Kupplungsschadens schon in der zweiten Runde.

Zum Abschluss der Saison nahm Porsche an zwei von drei Übersee-Läufen teil. Im japanischen Fuji und im australischen Sandown Park mussten sich Ickx/Mass jeweils hinter ihren Teamkollegen Bell und Bellof einreihen. Bellof holte sich damit den Fahrertitel in der Langstrecken-WM vor Mass und Ickx – und Porsche wurde in der Markenwertung erneut souverän Meister.

Für Ickx begann auch die Motorsportsaison 1985 am Neujahrstag in Paris. An seinem 40. Geburtstag fiel der Startschuss zur seiner fünften Paris–Dakar mit Claude Brasseur als Beifahrer. Die beiden Freunde saßen erneut im Porsche, diesmal aber in einem 959. Eine gebrochene Aufhängung verhinderte jedoch ein weiteres gutes Resultat beim Wüstenmarathon.

In der Langstrecken-WM trat Ickx mit dem gewohnten Team und Teamkollegen, aber mit einem neuen Auto an, dem Porsche 962C. Das Champions bestand aus zehn Läufen und begann Ende April in Mugello. Zur neuen Saison hatte die FIA die Regeln für die Gruppe C

Unhappy with the new endurance rules that included another 15 % fuel restriction, Porsche did not enter any works cars for Le Mans. Both Bell and Ickx went to the USA that weekend to participate in an IROC – International Race of Champions – race in which the cars used were, as before, identical Chevrolet Camaro Z28s. In a field of American speedway racers, Ickx finished ninth at Michigan Speedway while NASCAR driver Neil Bonnett won the race. Three weeks later on a temporary circuit at Cleveland Airport, Ickx finished twelfth. Even here it was the NASCAR drivers who were the best with Cale Yarborough winning.

For the first time, the new Grand Prix layout of the Nürburgring was used for the ADAC 1,000-kilometre race, where Ickx and Mass finished seventh overall. Right after the Nürburgring, Ickx went back to the USA for the third IROC race as well as competing at Mosport for the fourth race in the endurance championship. At Talladega in Alabama, on the very fast NASCAR Superspeedway, Ickx finished tenth in a race dominated by NASCAR drivers with this time Darrell Waltrip as the winner. There was not a strong sportscar field at Mosport thus Ickx and Mass won their second endurance race of the year.

■ *Jochen Mass: "The night before the Mosport race, Jacky ran a marathon or something like that, he was so tired that I did most of the driving. So I hated the newspapers that said the next morning 'Great drive by Ickx!'"*

The fourth and final IROC race was back at the Michigan Speedway, just west of Detroit. Again Ickx had no chance against the NASCAR drivers who were all drafting one another round the oval and he ended up twelfth in a race that was once again won by Bonnett. In the final standings after four races, Ickx found himself twelfth for which he received a check of US $ 20,000. Cale Yarborough was the overall winner of the series for which he collected a handy US $ 150,000.

Back in Europe, Ickx and Mass could only finish second at the 1,000 Kilometres of Spa where, after 144 laps, they were just under a minute behind their team-mates, Bell and Bellof. The 1,000 Kilometres of Imola in Italy was a new race in the championship and Porsche only sent one car, an experimental 956 with an automatic gearbox. Ickx was the nominated driver and he was paired with John Watson. However, clutch problems ended their race already on the second lap.

Porsche competed in two of the last three overseas races of the World Championship in Fuji, Japan, and Sandown Park, Australia. In both races Ickx and Mass finished behind Bell and Bellof. Consequently it was Bellof who won the driver championship with Mass and Ickx second and third while Porsche won the manufacturers.

For 1985, as was almost a tradition by now, Ickx would start his competition year on New Year's Eve in Paris. On his 40th birthday, he would begin his fourth participation in the Paris-Dakar with Claude Brasseur. They were still in a Porsche but this time it was a 959. However, a broken suspension prevented them from repeating their good performances of the previous years.

For the sportscar championship, Ickx was down to drive with Mass in a Rothmans Porsche, the new 962C. The championship comprised ten races and would start in late April at Mugello. The FIA had tightened the rules for the Group C cars and allowed only 510 litres of fuel for a 1,000-kilometre race. This meant that some races would be won by fuel conservation rather than by speed. In

1000 km of Sandown Park 1984, Porsche 956-83

Paris-Dakar 1985, Porsche 959, Jacky Ickx & Claude Brasseur

weiter verschärft, ein Auto durfte bei einem 1000-Kilometer-Rennen nur noch 510 Liter Sprit verbrauchen. Das hieß, dass einige Rennen nicht mehr durch Speed, sondern auch durch sparsames Fahren entschieden werden. In Mugello nutzten Ickx und Mass diesen Umstand und siegten, da ihre Gegner kurz vor Schluss Tempo rausnehmen mussten. Der zweite WM-Lauf in Monza wurde nach 138 von 173 Runden abgebrochen, weil in den Lesmo-Kurven Bäume umgestürzt waren und die Strecke blockierten. Da es keinen Restart gab, gewannen die Porsche-Privatiers Manfred Winkelhock und Marc Surer, die ihren letzten Stopp noch nicht absolviert hatten. Ickx und Mass wurden mit weniger als einer Runde Rückstand Vierte.

Einen Monat später gab es bei den 1000 Kilometern von Silverstone keine Dramen. Ickx/Mass gewannen den letzten richtigen Test vor den 24 Stunden von Le Mans souverän in ihrem Rothmans Porsche. Beim Klassiker an der Sarthe kam es noch mehr als bei den anderen Läufen auf den richtigen Spritverbrauch an. Um Benzin zu sparen lag Ickx, der neben dem Porsche von Derek Bell/Hans-Joachim Stuck aus Reihe eins gestartet war, nach der ersten Stunde nur auf Rang acht. Nach zwei Stunden gab es erstmals Probleme am 962C von Ickx/Mass, die Hinterradaufhängung musste gecheckt werden. Nach drei Stunden gab es einen Elektronikdefekt. Ickx musste in der Tertre Rouge stoppen, um die Motorsteuerung zu tauschen. Danach verlor das Duo auch noch wegen eines defekten Getriebekühlers Zeit, denn dadurch musste in der Folge der komplette Antriebsstrang gewechselt werden. Ickx und Mass lagen nach sechs Stunden auf Rang 30 und hatten keine Chance mehr auf den Sieg. Trotzdem gaben sie nicht auf und wurden am Ende Zehnte.

■ *Jochen Mass: „Ich bin oft mit Jacky im Sportwagen gestartet, aber wir haben nie zusammen in Le Mans gewonnen. Anfangs hatte ich Le Mans nicht in meinen Vertrag stehen, weswegen Jacky oft mit Derek (Bell) dort gefahren ist. Ich habe die fehlende Sicherheit gehasst. Jedes Jahr ist jemand umgekommen, entweder ein Fahrer oder ein Streckenposten."*

Das ADAC 1000-Kilometer-Rennen, das erstmals auf dem Hockenheimring stattfand, endete für Ickx und Mass nach 25 Runden wegen eines Turboschadens. Ihre Rothmans-Teamkollegen Bell und Stuck fuhren unterdessen zum Sieg. Das deutsch-britische Duo gewann auch den WM-Lauf in Mosport, wo Ickx und Mass mit etwas mehr als einer Minute Rückstand Zweite wurden. Beim Rennen in Kanada kam es jedoch auch zu einem tragischen Unfall, als Manfred Winkelhocks aus ungeklärter Ursache gegen eine Betonmauer prallte. Dabei wurde der Porsche so schwer beschädigt, dass die Rettungskräfte 25 Minuten brauchten, um den sympathischen Schwaben aus dem Wrack zu befreien. Winkelhock wurde per Helikopter ins Krankenhaus von Toronto geflogen, wo er einen Tag später seinen schweren Kopfverletzungen erlag. Es war der erste tödliche Unfall eines Gruppe-C-Piloten in dreieinhalb Jahren.

Drei Wochen später ereilte die Motorsportwelt der nächste Schock: Stefan Bellof starb als sein Porsche nach einer Kollision mit Ickx frontal in eine Mauer krachte. Nach dem letzten Boxenstopp hatten sich Ickx und Bellof drei Runden lang einen erbitterten Zweikampf geliefert. Nach der La Source versuchte Bellof seinen Kontrahenten zu überholen, doch in der Eau Rouge berührten sich die beiden Autos. Ickx' Porsche drehte sich und schlug rückwärts in eine Mauer ein, Bellofs Auto krachte ungebremst in die Planken. Der junge Deutsche war auf der Stelle tot. Nach dem Unfall wurde das Rennen abgebrochen und ein Martini-Lancia-LC2 zum Sieger erklärt.

Mugello, Ickx won because his main opposition had to slow down near the end of the race or risk running out of fuel. The second race at Monza was red-flagged after 138 of 173 laps when some old trees in the Lesmo curves fell down and blocked the track. The race however was not restarted and the private Porsche team of Manfred Winkelhock and Marc Surer – which still had a pit stop to make – was declared the winner. Ickx and Mass were fourth, albeit on the same lap as the winners.

There were no problems in England a month later, when Ickx and Mass had a clear win in the 1,000 Kilometres of Silverstone. This event is traditionally the last serious test before going to Le Mans for the 24-hour race. As was to be expected, the French race could only be won with the right fuel consumption. Thus, though Ickx started from the front row alongside the other works Porsche of Bell and Hans-Joachim Stuck, to save fuel he took it easy and after the first hour, he was only lying eighth. He and Mass hit their first problems after two hours when the rear suspension had to be checked. At the three-hour mark, the electronics failed and Ickx had to stop at Tertre Rouge to change the engine's ECU. After that, the team also lost time with a broken transmission cooler and this in its turn eventually led to a complete transmission change during the evening. After six hours, Ickx and Mass lay thirtieth and thus had no chance to win the race but nevertheless they drove hard and worked their way back to finish tenth.

■ *Jochen Mass: "I had several starts with Jacky in sportscars, won many but we never won Le Mans together. Originally I had in my contract not to drive at Le Mans, that is why Jacky often drove there with Derek (Bell). I hated the lack of safety at that track because every year somebody got killed, either a driver or a marshal."*

The ADAC 1,000-kilometre race was to be held at the Hockenheimring for the first time and resulted in a retirement for Ickx and Mass. A broken turbo ended their race just twenty-five laps before the end and the race was won by Bell and Stuck in the other Rothmans Porsche. The same pair also won the Canadian round of the championship at Mosport where Ickx and Mass finished second overall on the same lap as the winners. The race was overshadowed by a fatal accident involving Manfred Winkelhock. This experienced and popular German driver crashed his Porsche, for unknown reasons, into a concrete wall. It took rescue workers twenty-five minutes to get him out of the car after which he was taken to a Toronto hospital by helicopter where he died the following day from major head injuries. It was the first fatal accident in Group C cars that were now in their fourth season.

Three weeks later another fatal crash shocked the motorsport community. At the Spa track, Stefan Bellof died after his car went head on into the wall at Eau Rouge after colliding with Jacky Ickx. After both Porsches had made their last pit stops, they had run side by side for three laps. When Bellof tried to overtake Ickx coming out of La Source and driving down to Eau Rouge, the cars touched and both left the track. Ickx's Porsche spun and hit the wall backwards, while Bellof crashed head on. The young German driver died instantly. After the accident, the race was stopped and a Martini Lancia LC2 was declared the winner.

At the next race, the 1,000 Kilometres at Brands Hatch, the Rothmans Porsches once again finished first and second and again it was Bell and Stuck who came out on top. The ninth round of the

24 Heures du Mans 1985, Porsche 962C

Beim nächsten Rennen, den 1000 Kilometern von Brands Hatch, feierten die Rothmans-Porsche wieder einen Doppelsieg, und wieder hatten Bell/Stuck die Nase vorn. Der neunte WM-Lauf fand Anfang Oktober in Fuji statt und hier bekam es Porsche mit starker Konkurrenz von Toyota und Nissan zu tun. Die Rothmans-Piloten starteten beide aus Reihe eins, steuerten aber schon nach der ersten Runde die Box an. Wegen eines Tropensturms fanden die Fahrer es unverantwortlich und zu gefährlich weiterzufahren. Und mit dieser Meinung waren sie nicht alleine, in den ersten zehn Runden stellten 15 Fahrer ihre Autos an der Box ab. Nach zwei Stunden bzw. 62 Umläufen wurde das Rennen schließlich komplett abgebrochen und der Führende March 85G-Nissan zum Sieger erklärt.

Vor dem Saisonfinale der Langstrecken-WM zog es Ickx erneut in die Wüste. Bei der Pharaonen Rallye in Ägypten pilotierte er zusammen mit Claude Brasseur einen Porsche 959, der während der Rallye komplett ausbrannte.

Das Finale der Langstrecken-WM wurde seinem Prädikat mit nur 16 Autos und weniger als 10.000 Zuschauern nicht gerecht. Ickx und Mass waren dafür wieder obenauf. Sie stellten ihren Porsche auf die Pole und siegten vor dem neuen Jaguar XJR-6 von Jan Lammers, Mike Thackwell und John Nielsen. Nach dem Rennen verkündete Jacky Ickx im Alter von 40 Jahren seinen Rücktritt aus dem Rennsport. In Anbetracht der tragischen Unfälle seiner Kollegen und der kontroversen Regeln zum Spritverbrauch hatte der Belgier genug. Es war ein würdiger Abschied vor einer unwürdigen Kulisse.

◼ *Jochen Mass: „Malaysia war unser letztes gemeinsames Rennen, und wir haben erneut gewonnen. Insgesamt haben Jacky und ich 20 Rennen gewonnen. Das bedeutet, dass wir bei jedem zweiten Start im Porsche gewonnen haben."*

Die vier Jahre im Rothmans Porsche hatten Jacky viele schöne Erlebnisse beschert. Er hatte zwölf Läufe zur FIA Langstrecken-Weltmeisterschaft gewonnen, zehn davon mit Jochen Mass und zwei mit Derek Bell. Ickx wollte sich aber nicht ganz aus dem Motorsport zurückziehen. Er wollte weiterhin an Wüstenrallyes teilnehmen, denn er liebte diese neue Herausforderung und er liebte Afrika.

◼ *Derek Bell: „Jacky war unglaublich talentiert. Er konnte jedes Auto fahren. Im Sportwagen hatten wir den gleichen Fahrstil, und das hat sich bewährt. Viele Leute haben ihn als Sportwagenfahrer in Erinnerung behalten, aber in seiner Blütezeit war er auch ein großartiger Formel-1-Pilot. Für mich war er der Ayrton Senna seiner Zeit."*

Und so ging Jacky Ickx' Rennfahrerkarriere nach 23 spannenden Jahren zu Ende.

championship was held at Fuji in early October and here Porsche could expect strong competition from both Toyota and Nissan. The two Rothmans Porsches started from the front row, but after just one lap they both came into the pits. Because of a tropical rainstorm the drivers found it irresponsible and impossibly dangerous to drive. It was not just the works Porsches who felt that way since fifteen other cars stopped during the first ten laps. Those who continued were red-flagged after two hours and only sixty-two laps at which point a Japanese March-Nissan was declared to be the winner.

Before going to Shah Alam in Malaysia for the final sportscar race of the year, Ickx was back in Egypt to drive a Porsche 959 in the Pharaohs Rally. Unfortunately for him and co-driver, Brasseur, a tire destroyed their Porsche and they retired.

There were only sixteen cars that went to Malaysia for the sportscar race and less than 10,000 people came to see this event, which would be the final race for Jacky Ickx. Together with Mass, he started from pole and won the race ahead of the new V12 Jaguar XJR-6 of Lammers, Mike Thackwell and John Nielsen. After the race, Ickx announced that, at forty years of age, he had had enough of racing. What with the tragic accidents to his colleagues earlier in the year and the effect of the controversial fuel consumption rules, he thought it was time to end his circuit-racing career.

◼ *Jochen Mass: "The Malaysia race was our final one together. And we won again. In total, I won twenty races with Jacky. That amounted to a win in every other start together in a Porsche."*

These four years with Rothmans Porsche provided Ickx with some good memories. He won no less than twelve FIA World Endurance Championship races, most of the time together with Jochen Mass but two in 1982 with Derek Bell. He announced that, in the years to come, he would just do some rallye-raids because he loved the challenge and he enjoyed being in Africa.

◼ *Derek Bell: "Jacky was amazingly talented. He could drive any kind of car. I admired his professionalism. In endurance racing, we had the same driving style and that paid off. People mostly regard him as a sportscar driver, but Jacky in his heyday was also a great Formula One driver, for me he was the Ayrton Senna of his time."*

For Ickx his retirement from racing came after a career that spanned twenty-three years.

Brands Hatch 1000 km 1985, Porsche 962C

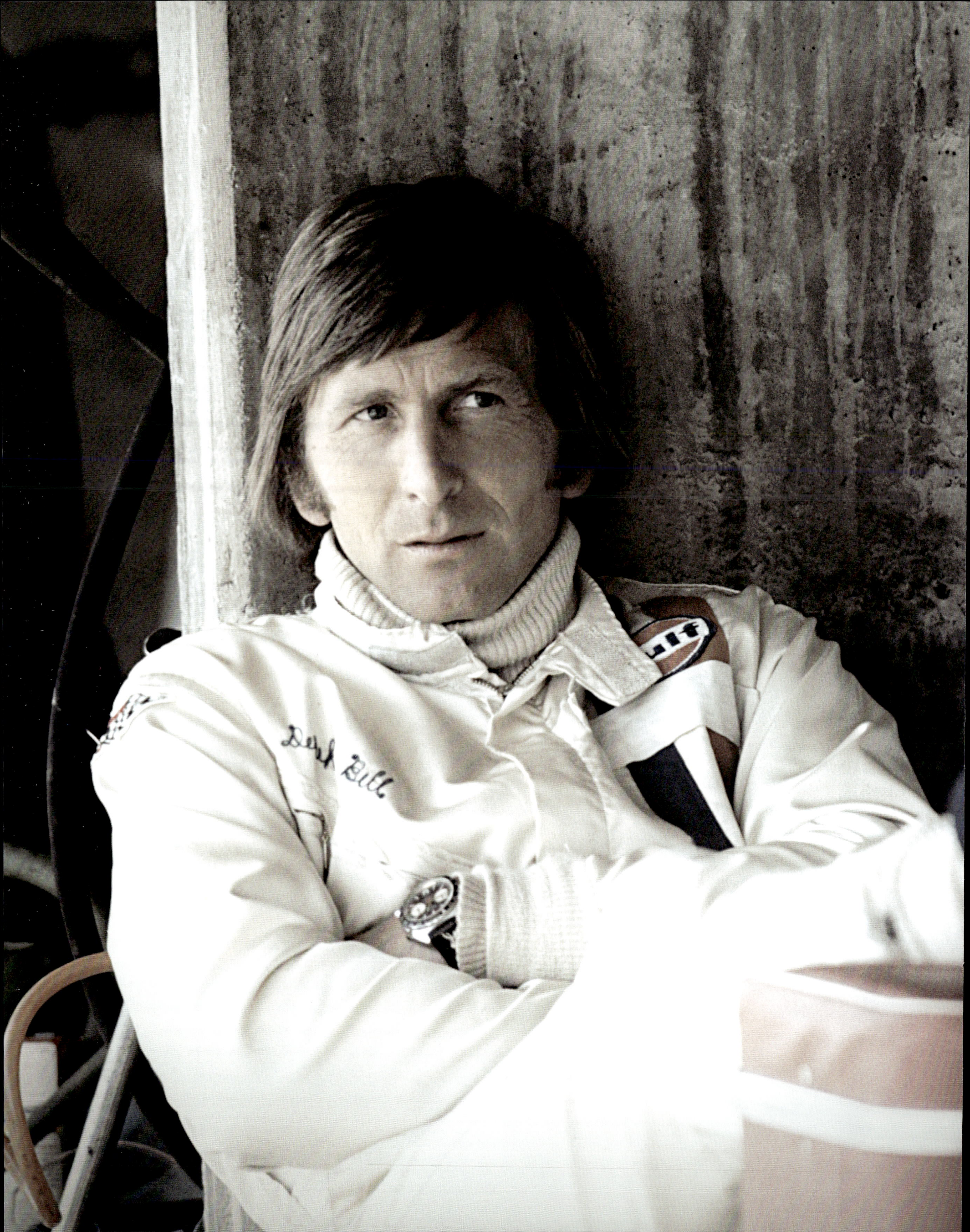
Derek Bell

Derek BELL

Partner von Ickx bei Mirage und Porsche
Partner to Ickx at Mirage and Porsche

„Als Jacky mich fragte, ob ich mit ihm 1975 in Le Mans fahren würde, fühlte ich mich geehrt. Ich fuhr damals für Gulf Racing in der Marken-WM. Eigentlich sollte ich mit Mike Hailwood als Partner starten, der wegen eines Unfalls aber nicht fit war. Dann rief Jacky an und fragte mich. In der Quali erzielten wir die Pole und nach 336 Runden fuhren wir zum Sieg! Für mich war es der erste Le-Mans-Erfolg, für Jacky der zweite. Sechs Jahre später waren wir wieder zusammen in Le Mans, diesmal im Porsche. Das war unser zweiter Sieg – und 1982 haben wir sogar noch einen dritten nachgelegt."

„Wir sind auch auf anderen Strecken zusammen gefahren und hatten immer eine schöne Zeit. Wir waren eines der berühmtesten Fahrerduos der Motorsportgeschichte. Zwischen Jacky und mir stimmte die Chemie. Jacky hat mir – genau wie vorher schon Jo Siffert – beigebracht, wie man ein guter Teamplayer ist."

„Wenn wir mal nicht für ein Team gefahren sind, dann haben wir uns erbitterte Zweikämpfe geliefert, besonders in den früher 70ern. Unsere Duelle waren aber immer fair, wir haben uns gegenseitig respektiert. Jacky ist zwar vier Jahre jünger als ich, trotzdem habe ich ihn immer als einen routinierteren Piloten gesehen – vielleicht, weil er schon mit 21 Jahren in der Formel 1 gefahren ist. Bei Langstreckenrennen muss man zusammenarbeiten und sein Ego zurücknehmen. Man sagt ja immer, dass der Teamkollege dein größter Gegner ist. Wir haben das anders gesehen und es hat funktioniert. Jacky war mir gegenüber immer nett und hat mich respektvoll behandelt. 1975 ließ er mich in Le Mans den Start fahren. Er meinte, er wäre nur der zweite Fahrer, weil ich der Stammpilot bei Gulf war und die ganzen Tests absolviert hatte."

„1981 war Le Mans Jackys einziges Rennen – trotzdem hat er gewonnen. Und das in einem neuen Auto, das ohne Probleme lief. Einfach unglaublich! Das war eine große Leistung."

„Unser letzter Le-Mans-Sieg ist zustande gekommen, weil Jochen Mass nicht gern an der Sarthe fuhr. Also fragte Ickx bei mir an. Es war sein sechster und mein fünfter Sieg. 1983 sind wir mit knappem Rückstand Zweite und 1985 Dritte geworden. Le Mans ist für uns ein Ort mit einer großen Geschichte."

"I was honoured when Jacky asked me to join him for Le Mans in 1975. I was driving for Gulf Racing doing the sportscar series. Actually Mike Hailwood was my partner, but he was not fit after an accident and Jacky just called and asked me to drive. After qualifying we were on pole and after 336 laps, we were the winners. It was the first win at Le Mans for me and the second win for Jacky. Six years later we were back together at Le Mans but this time with Porsche. This was our second win and then we won a third time in 1982 in the fabulous 956."

"But we drove together at other tracks as well and always had a great time. We were known as one of the most famous pairings in motor sport history. Jacky and I achieved that personal chemistry that worked so well in endurance racing. He – and before him, Jo Siffert – taught me how to be a team player."

"Not only did we drive within a team, but when we were in separate cars, we had some fierce battles, especially in the early seventies. But they were always fair battles and we respected each other. Jacky is four years younger than me, but still I considered him as being the more experienced driver probably because he had already driven in F1 when he was twenty-one. In endurance racing, you have to work together and put aside your personal egos. They always say that your team partner is your biggest competitor, but we saw it differently and that worked. And Jacky was always kind and even respectful as when he let me start the race at Le Mans 1975. He told me that I was the team regular who did all the testing and he was just a second driver."

"In 1981, Le Mans was the only race Jacky drove that year and yet he won it. Simply amazing. And he did that in a new car that ran without problems. That is quite an achievement."

"The last time we won Le Mans together in 1982, it was because Jochen Mass did not like driving on that circuit and Ickx asked me to join him. It would be his sixth win and the fifth for me. We came a close second in 1983 and finished third in 1985. Some history there for both of us."

1986 – 2000

Wüstenabenteuer und ein Sieg als Teamchef
Desert adventures and a win as a team boss

Nach dem Sieg beim Finale der Langstrecken-WM 1985 hatte Jacky Ickx zwar den Rücktritt aus dem Rennsport verkündet, seine Fahrerkarriere beendete er aber noch nicht ganz. Auf den Tag genau einen Monat nach seinem letzten Sportwagenrennen nahm er im Porsche 959 an der Rallye Paris–Dakar teil. Gemeinsam mit seinem langjährigen Freund und Beifahrer Claude Brasseur wurde er bei dem dreiwöchigen Wüstenabenteuer Zweiter hinter seinem Teamkollegen René Metge. Die 1985er-Ausgabe ging aber aus einem anderen Grund in die Geschichte ein: Während der Rallye kamen Dakar-Organisator Thierry Sabine und vier andere Personen bei einem Helikopterabsturz ums Leben.

Nach der Wüstenrallye vergingen zwölf Monate, bis Ickx wieder an einer Motorsportveranstaltung teilnahm. Erneut fiel seine Wahl auf „Le Dakar", wo Jacky mit Copilot Christian Tarin einen Lada Niva pilotierte und durch Motorprobleme ausschied. Da die FIA damals einen offiziellen Weltcup für Marathonrallyes gründete, nahm Ickx fortan auch an ähnlichen Rallyes in Afrika teil – erst für Lada, dann für Peugeot und Citroën. Bei der Dakar 1989 holte der Belgier knapp hinter seinem Peugeot-Teamkollegen Ari Vatanen den zweiten Platz. Obwohl Ickx viele Jahre für Werksteams fuhr, holte er nur einen weiteren Sieg: bei der Baja Aragon 1989 in Spanien am Steuer eines Peugeot 405 T16. 1991 ereilte Ickx dann ein persönlicher Schicksalsschlag. Bei der Pharaonen Rallye 1991 brannte sein Citroën nach einem Unfall komplett aus und riss Navigator Christian Tarin in den Tod.

After winning the final race of the 1985 World Endurance Championship, Jacky Ickx announced his retirement from active racing. But he did continue as a driver. Exactly one month after his last sportscar race, he once again participated in the Paris-Dakar Rallye-Raid in a Porsche 959 together with his long-time friend Claude Brasseur. After three weeks driving through western Africa, they finished a commendable second overall behind a similar Porsche 959 driven by René Metge and Dominique Lemoyne. The event was overshadowed by the death of its charismatic organiser, Thierry Sabine, who perished during the event – together with several others – in a helicopter accident.

It was to be another twelve months before Ickx participated again in a motor sports event and again his choice was 'Le Dakar'. This time he competed in a Lada Niva and was partnered by Christian Tarin. They suffered from engine problems and did not finish. As the FIA now sanctioned an official Rallye-Raid Championship, in the years to come, Ickx found himself competing in several such events all over Africa. He drove first with Lada and later with Peugeot and Citroën. In the 1989 Paris-Dakar, he finished a worthy second close behind his Peugeot team-mate, Ari Vatanen. Despite being part of these works teams, he only ever recorded one win, the Baja Aragon in Spain in 1989, where he drove a Peugeot 405 T16. However, during the Pharaohs Rally of 1991, Ickx endured another personal trauma since in the aftermath of a crash, the car burned out and claimed the life of his navigator Tarin.

Paris-Dakar 1986

Paris-Dakar 1989, Peugeot 405 T16, Jacky Ickx & Christian Tarin

Paris-Dakar 1989

■ **Jochen Mass: „Der Unfall bei der Pharaonen Rallye hat Jacky sehr mitgenommen. Seine Hilflosigkeit, als Tarin in den Flammen starb, hat ihn extrem wütend gemacht. Vielleicht war das einer der Gründe, warum Jacky später eine andere Sichtweise auf das Leben erlangt hat. Er wurde philosophisch."**

Die Wüstenrallyes gaben Ickx mehr Befriedigung als Le Mans oder die Formel 1. Sie sind die härtesten und komplexesten Herausforderungen in der Motorsportwelt. Man verbringt Stunde um Stunde bei Vollgas in einer leeren Wüste. Hinzu kommt, dass das Fahren auf Sand nicht so leicht ist, wie man es sich vorstellt. Das Terrain ist unberechenbar, der Fahrer muss jede Sekunde hochkonzentriert sein. Und wenn etwas schief geht, ist die Crew in der leeren Wüste auf sich allein gestellt. Jacky fand die Einsamkeit Afrikas faszinierend, durch sie änderte sich seine Einstellung zum Leben.

Wegen seiner großen Erfahrung bei Langstreckenrennen verpflichtete Mazda den Belgier als Teamchef für die 24 Stunden von Le Mans 1991. Die Marke schickte drei Wankelmotor-Sportwagen an die Sarthe, um die Traditionsveranstaltung als erster japanischer Hersteller zu gewinnen. Unter der Leitung von Ickx sorgte die Mazda-Crew Johnny Herbert, Volker Weidler und Bertrand Gachot für eine Sensation und holte gegen die Favoriten von Peugeot, Mercedes und Jaguar den Gesamtsieg! Die anderen beiden Mazda rundeten den Erfolg mit den Plätzen sechs und acht ab.

1999 machte Ickx sogar einen Familienausflug in die Wüste. Mit seiner Tochter Vanina als Copilotin nahm er in einem Toyota an der UAE Desert Challenge in Dubai teil. In dem Emirat fielen sie aus, zwei Monate später war das Vater-Tochter-Gespann bei der Paris–Dakar aber erfolgreicher und holte Platz 18.

■ **Jochen Mass: "The accident in the Pharaohs Rally was very emotional for Jacky. He was so angry that he was helpless when Tarin died in the fire. Maybe that was one of the reasons that he then acquired a different view on life. He started to become philosophical."**

For Ickx, the Rallye-Raid events gave him more satisfaction than even Le Mans or Formula One. These are the hardest and most complex of motor sport events, hours after hours at full speed alone in the vast deserts. And driving on sand is not as easy as one imagines for it is unpredictable and the driver needs to give his full attention all the time. And, if something goes wrong, the crew are on their own as the desert is empty. And Jacky discovered that the loneliness of Africa was intriguing and it led him a new view of life.

With his vast experience in endurance racing, Ickx was asked to be the team manager for Mazda at the 1991 24 Hours of Le Mans. The Japanese manufacturer sent three prototypes powered by rotary engines to France and hoped to be the first Japanese company to win this prestigious event. Under Ickx's management, the leading Mazda car with Johnny Herbert, Volker Weidler and Bertrand Gachot surprised the favourites – Peugeot, Mercedes-Benz and Jaguar – and won the race with the other two Mazdas finishing sixth and eighth.

In 1999, Ickx competed in the UAE Desert Challenge in Dubai in a private Toyota with his daughter Vanina as navigator. They retired in Dubai but two months later, father and daughter were back together for another Paris-Dakar where they finished eighteenth overall.

Paris-Sirte-Cape Town 1992, Citroën ZX

Rallye des Pharaons 1990, Citroën ZX, Jacky Ickx & Christian Tarin

24 Heures du Mans 1991,
Mazda 787 B, Volker Weidler,
Johnny Herbert & Bertrand Gachot

228

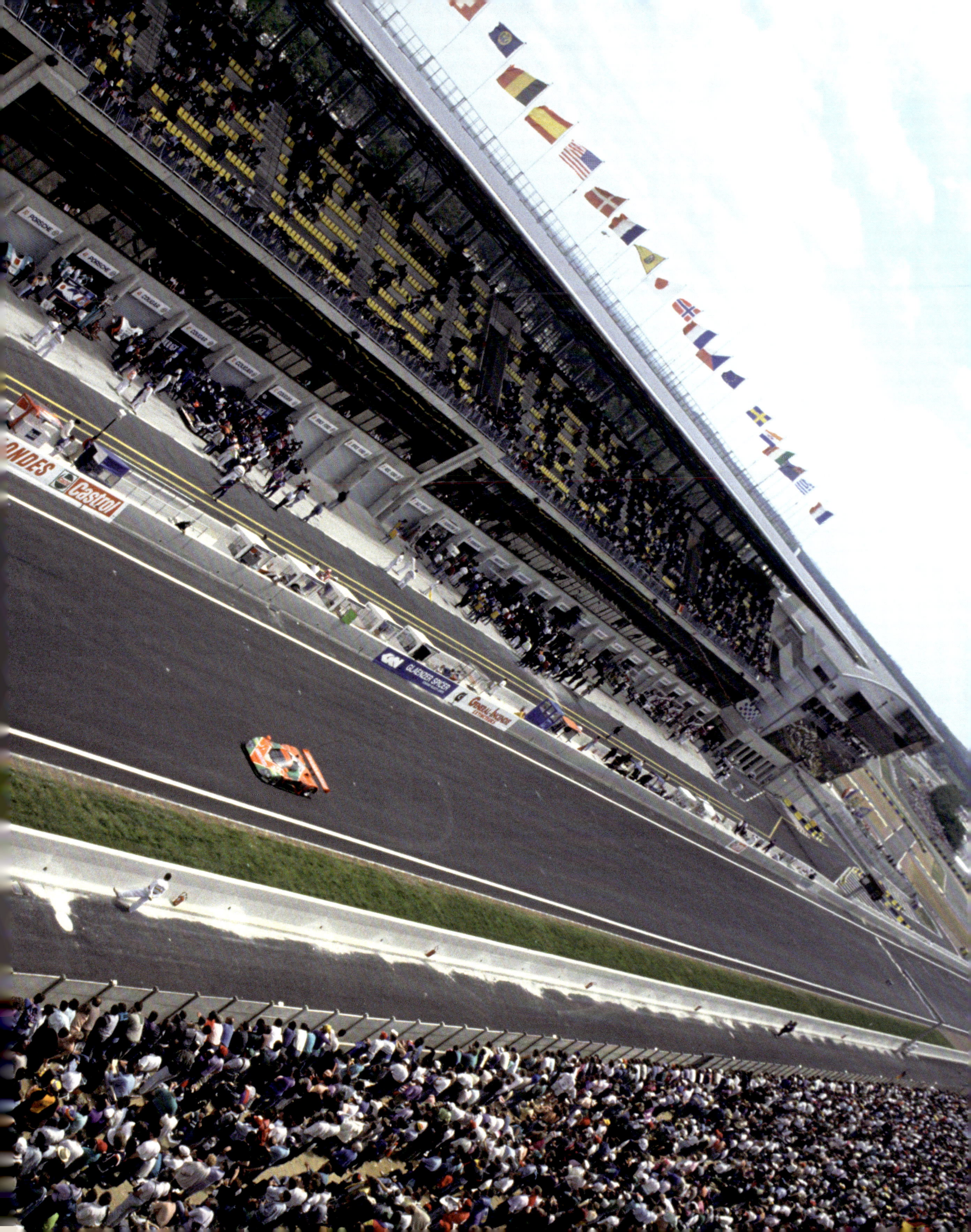
Castrol

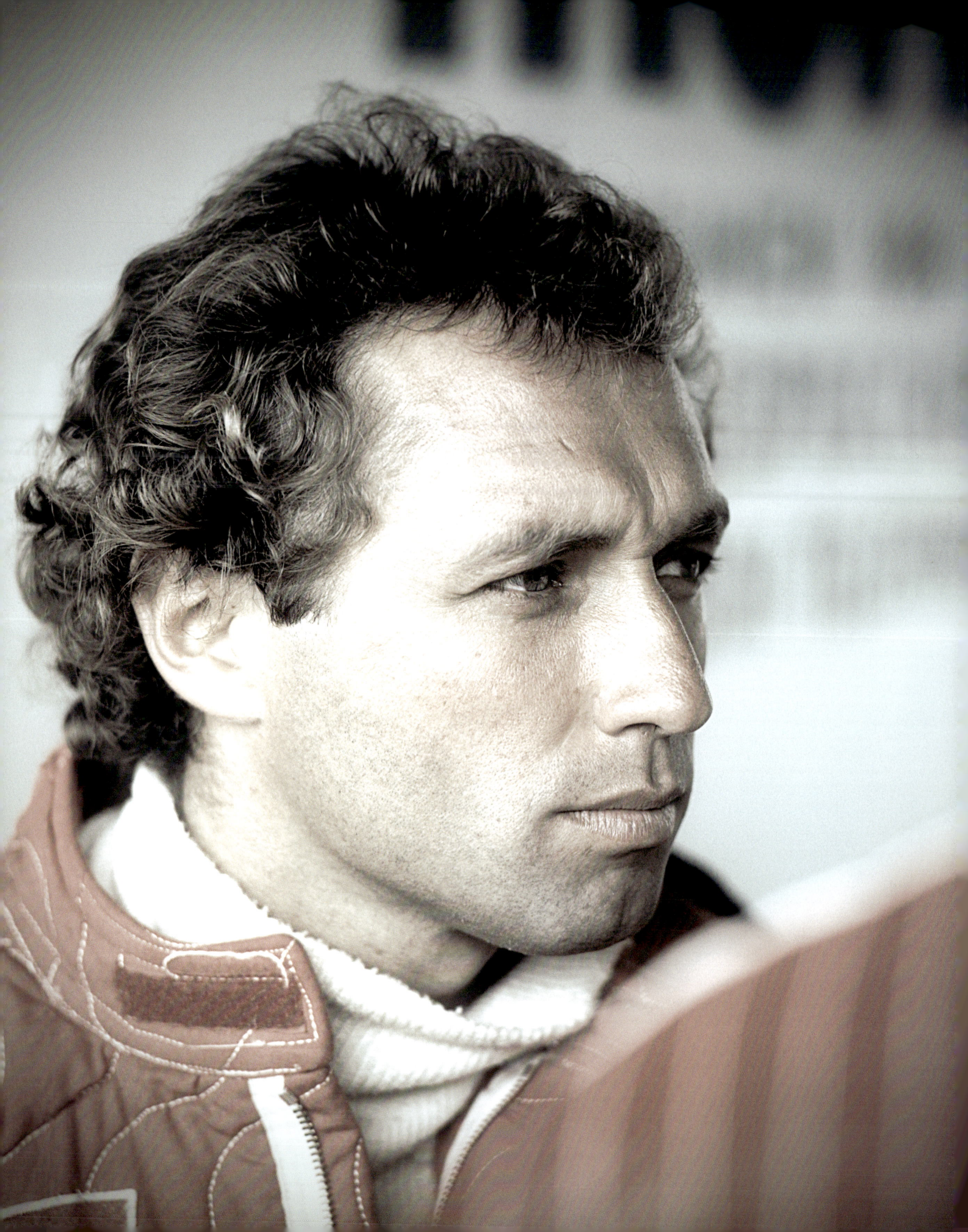

Jochen MASS

Langjähriger Partner von Ickx bei Porsche
Long-time partner of Ickx at Porsche

„Jacky ist ein großartiger Typ. Er war ein toller Rennfahrer und ist ein sehr netter Mensch. Wir sind so viele Rennen zusammen gefahren und sind immer gut miteinander klargekommen. Als wir bei Porsche ein Team gebildet haben, war das in der Endphase seiner Karriere – man könnte es fast seine zweite Karriere nennen. Jacky ist vielleicht egoistisch oder arrogant rübergekommen, aber zu mir war er immer nett. Er hat sich bei Porsche nie als Nummer eins aufgeführt. Wenn man ein Langstreckenrennen gewinnen will, muss man zusammenarbeiten – anders als bei einem Grand Prix. Auf der Langstrecke muss man schnell sein, auf das Auto aufpassen und die richtige Taktik haben. Das hatten wir und das hat zu vielen schönen Siegen geführt."

„Die Dakar hat Jackys Leben verändert. Wenn man durch die einsame afrikanische Wüste fährt, hat man Zeit, über andere Dinge im Leben nachzudenken. Es fördert den inneren Frieden. Die Wüsten sind so weitläufig, dass sie dir eine komplett neue Dimension eröffnen. Ich bin ein begeisterter Segler. Und wenn man alleine auf dem Ozean ist, dann ändert das den eigenen Blickwinkel. Jacky kommt aus einer Familie mit hohen Erwartungen und er war früh erfolgreich. Das sind zwei Zutaten für ein schwieriges Leben. Jacky war sehr intelligent, vielleicht etwas introvertiert – eine Art Einzelgänger. Für die politische Seite des Sports interessierte er sich nicht, er wollte nur Rennen fahren. Dadurch hatten einige Leute den Eindruck, er wäre arrogant. Das war er aber nicht. Er war der netteste Kerl, den man sich vorstellen kann. Das war keine Rolle, die er gespielt hat. Er war wirklich nett. Ich erinnere mich gern an die Zeit, die wir in seinem Haus in Belgien verbracht haben. Er war der perfekte Gastgeber. Er hat immer dafür gesorgt, dass man sich wie zu Hause fühlt. Mit Khadja Nin hat er die perfekte Partnerin gefunden. Sie passt perfekt zu seiner neuen Liebe für Afrika. Es muss großartig sein, in Timbuktu zu leben und die Stille Afrikas zu erleben. Das macht aus dir einen anderen Menschen."

„Jacky hatte aber auch diesen schrecklichen Unfall bei der Pharaonen Rallye, bei dem sein Beifahrer starb. Das war ein schwerer Schlag für ihn. Heute blickt Jacky mit anderen Augen auf seine Karriere zurück. Er ist froh, überlebt zu haben. Und er ist den Menschen, die ihm geholfen haben, und seinen Fans dankbar. Ich denke, dass er zusammen mit Khadja seinen Frieden gefunden hat. Für mich ist es immer wieder schön, mit ihm irgendwo zu sitzen. Wir haben uns so viel zu erzählen – nicht nur über den Rennsport."

"For me, Jacky is a great guy. He was a great racing driver and a very nice person. We drove so many races together and we always got on well. Of course, this was later in his career – his second career, if you can call it that – when we were partners driving Porsches. Perhaps Jacky used to come over as a selfish, maybe arrogant driver, but to me he was always nice. Never acted like the number one within our Porsche team. We did endurance racing where you have to win by working together. It is not like racing for an hour or so in a GP. In endurance racing you must be fast, look after the car and have the right tactics. And that is what we had. It resulted in many nice victories."

"What made him change his way of living was the Dakar event. Doing the Dakar is something completely different. Driving in the lonely African desert gives you time to think about other things in life and promotes inner peace. Those deserts are so vast that they give you a completely different dimension. I do a lot of sailing, and being alone on the ocean also changes one's perspective. Jacky came from a family with high expectations and success for him came early. These were both ingredients for a difficult life. He wanted to race, was very intelligent, maybe a little introvert – a bit of an "Einzelgänger". He had no interest in sport politics and that gave some people the impression that he was arrogant. But he was not. He has always been the nicest guy. It wasn't a role that he played, he really was nice. I remember all the times we spent at his house in Belgium. He was the perfect host. He always tries to make people feel at home. Now with Khadja Nin, he has found the perfect partner. She fits in well with his new love for Africa. Living in Timbuktu must be great, experiencing the silence of the African spaces. That makes you another person."

"And then of course he had that terrible accident in the Pharaohs Rally in which his navigator died. That was a big blow for him. Now, he can look back at his career in a different way. Happy to have survived and thankful to all the people he helped him and also to the fans who followed him. I think he found peace now together with Khadja. But it is always nice to sit with him today. We have so much to talk about, and it is not just about racing."

Bahrain Grand Prix 2008, Jacky & Khadja

Das Leben abseits der Rennstrecke
Personal life away from racing

Die Paris–Dakar 2000 war Jackys letzte Teilnahme im richtigen Wettbewerb. Danach nahm der 55-Jährige nur noch an Demonstrationsfahrten, Gleichmäßigkeits- und Show-Veranstaltungen teil. Als Botschafter von Audi und Chopard war er bei der Mille Miglia, in Goodwood oder bei ähnlichen Events ein häufiger und gern gesehener Gast. Gleichzeitig verbrachte Jacky immer mehr Zeit in seinem geliebten Afrika – weit weg von der Rennszene.

■ *Jacky Ickx: „Der Rennsport liegt hinter mir. Mir fällt es manchmal schwer, an die Vergangenheit zu denken. Ich interessiere mich viel mehr für die Gegenwart. Ich bin heutzutage viel glücklicher, ich bin ein anderer Mensch."*

Die Weite und die Stille der Wüsten Nordafrikas haben ihm die Augen für neue Dinge geöffnet. Dort ist man allein – ein Niemand – und hat Zeit über die Bedeutung des Lebens nachzudenken. Ickx hat 37 Jahre damit verbracht, um die Welt zu rasen. Das hat ihm gewiss viel Spaß gemacht, doch Afrika hat seinem Leben eine neue Bedeutung gegeben.

At 55 years of age, the Paris-Dakar 2000 was the final competitive event for Jacky Ickx. From then on, he would only compete in demonstrations, regularity events and exhibitions. He was to become a familiar face at the Mille Miglia as well as at Goodwood. As an ambassador for Audi and Chopard he was always a popular guest. But Jacky spent more and more time in his beloved Africa, away from the world of racing.

■ *Jacky Ickx: "The racing is behind me. It is sometimes difficult thinking about that past era. I am much more interested in the present. I am happier today, I am another person"*

Ickx's discovery of Africa with its vastness and the silence of the deserts in North Africa opened his eyes to new things. There you are alone – a nobody – and have time to think about the meaning of life. He had spent some thirty-seven years racing around the world and, although he had enjoyed it very much, Africa gave him a new meaning for life.

Zu Beginn seiner Karriere fühlte sich Jacky oft nicht so wohl wie heute. Ickx feierte seine ersten Erfolge als Teenager und musste erst lernen, damit umzugehen. Er hat ein privilegiertes Leben geführt, das auf und abseits der Rennstrecke von Erfolg gesegnet war. Genau wie die Stars von heute wurde er eine berühmte Persönlichkeit, eine Schachfigur für die Medien und Fans. In jungen Jahren war das für Jacky manchmal schwer. Er war ein Rennfahrer, der einfach nur fahren und gewinnen wollte. Selbst wenn die Streckenbedingungen nicht gut waren, ist er trotzdem einfach gefahren. Diese Einstellung zur Sicherheit hat ihm im Fahrerlager viele böse Blicke eingebracht. Aber Jacky wollte seinen eigenen Weg gehen, und das führte manchmal eben zu Konflikten. Im späteren Verlauf seiner F1-Karriere saß Ickx oft in unterlegenen Autos, aber auch da wollte er einfach nur Rennen fahren und zeigen, dass er einer der Schnellsten war. Im Herbst seiner Karriere begann er, über sein Leben als Rennfahrer nachzudenken – und die afrikanische Wüste gab ihm viel Zeit zum Reflektieren. Sein Blick auf den Motorsport vollzog eine 180°-Wende. Er war jetzt nicht mehr der egoistische Rennfahrer, sondern ein dankbarer Ex-Sportler, der den Menschen, die um ihn herum gearbeitet haben, viel zu verdanken hat. Jetzt, im 21. Jahrhundert, gilt Jackys Interesse der Menschheit.

Viele Menschen betrachten Ickx als einen der größten Fahrer in der Geschichte des Motorsports. Er wird als passionierter Sportler gesehen, der immer gewinnen wollte – genau wie Stirling Moss vor ihm und Gilles Villeneuve nach ihm. Die langen Tage in der afrikanischen Wüste haben Ickx' Einstellung zum Rennsport und zum Leben jedoch grundlegend verändert. In seinen 32 Jahren als Rennfahrer ist er möglicherweise mehr Kilometer am Limit gefahren als jeder andere Pilot. Heute ist er dankbar, die gefährlichen 60er- und 70er-Jahre überlebt zu haben. Und rückblickend weiß er auch, dass er seine Erfolge und sein Überleben vielen Leuten zu verdanken hat.

Jackys Kinder sind mittlerweile erwachsen und verfolgen ihre eigene Karriere im Kunst-, Musik- und Motorsportbereich. Jacky selbst ist zum dritten Mal verheiratet, mit der in Burundi geborenen Sängerin Khadja Nin. Er hat die Tür zum Rennsport zugemacht, aber nicht verschlossen. Ab und zu ist er gerne wieder dabei. Gleichzeitig engagiert er sich als Pate der Organisation „FACE for children in need", die Spenden für hilfsbedürftige Kinder sammelt.

Ickx redet heutzutage nicht gerne über sich selbst. Als Rennfahrer muss man egoistisch sein, doch letztlich ist es das Team, das die Autos baut und dem Fahrer die Möglichkeit gibt zu glänzen. Und das möchte Jacky betonen. Heute wünscht er sich, er hätte eine engere Beziehung zu den Menschen gehabt, die ihm in seiner Karriere geholfen haben – den Teambesitzern, Ingenieuren und Mechanikern.

Um sich ihrer Liebe zu Afrika hinzugeben, haben sich Jacky und Khadja ein Haus am Ufer des Niger in Mali gekauft, wo sie einen Großteil ihrer Freizeit verbringen. Gleichzeitig besitzt Jacky noch sein Haus in Brüssel, das einen starken afrikanischen Touch hat. Andenken an Jackys Zeit als Rennfahrer findet man dagegen nur wenige.

◼ *Jacky Ickx: „Rückblickend möchte ich jedem danken, der mir im Laufe meiner Karriere geholfen hat. Den Leuten bei Porsche und Ferrari und natürlich den Vaterfiguren wie Enzo Ferrari, Jack Brabham, John Wyer, Carl Hass und vor allem Ken und Norah Tyrrell. Aber auch den Mechanikern und Fans, die ebenfalls Teil meines Erfolges waren. Es geht nicht nur um mich, sondern auch um alle anderen Menschen. Was ich vermutlich am meisten bereue, ist, dass ich den Leuten um mich herum in meiner Zeit als Rennfahrer nicht genug Dankbarkeit gezeigt habe."*

Sometimes early in his career, Jacky was not as comfortable as he is today. Success came early and as a teenager he had to find a way to live with it. He had a privileged life and was blessed with success, both as a sportsman and in his private life. Having a successful career, he became a popular figure like the stars of today, the pawn of the media and the fans. Sometimes that was hard for the young Belgian. He was a racer whose only goals in life were to race and win. On several occasions, when the track conditions were not good, he just raced and this attitude to safety sometimes got him angry looks from his competitors. Jacky wanted to do it his way and that can sometimes lead to conflict. Later in his career when he got inferior drives in Formula One, he still wanted to be able to race and show that he could be among the fastest. Near the end of his career, he started thinking about his life as a racer and being out in the African deserts gave him plenty of time to reflect. His vision on motor sports made almost a complete U-turn. He was not the selfish driver anymore but a grateful retired sportsman who owed a lot to the people who had worked around him. Now in the twenty-first century, the human race got Jacky's interest.

Many racing people still regard Ickx as one of the greatest drivers in motor sport history. He is considered a passionate driver who wanted to win rather like Stirling Moss before him and Gilles Villeneuve after him. His will to succeed, whatever the circumstances might be, occasionally made him unpopular with his competitors. But now, in hindsight, one might reach a different interpretation. Certainly for Ickx, his long days in the African deserts changed his views on racing and life in general. In a racing career spanning thirty-two years, he probably did more racing miles than any other driver. He is grateful to have survived the dangerous sixties and seventies and looking back on that era, he knows that he has a lot of people to thank for his success and survival.

With his children now grown up, with their own careers in arts, music or racing, Jacky is very happy in his new existence with his third wife, Khadja Nin, the Burundi-born singer. He has almost completely closed the door on racing, but still loves to be around at some events. Jacky is also the godfather of the 'FACE for Children in Need' organisation, helping to raise money for those less fortunate young people.

Today, he does not want to talk about himself a lot anymore, as a racer one is supposed to be selfish but in the end it is the team who build the cars and give a driver the opportunity to shine. And that is what Jacky emphasises now. Now he wishes he had become closer to the people who helped him in his career like the team owners, the engineers and the mechanics.

To indulge his love for Africa, he and Khadja have a house on the banks of the Niger River in Mali where they spend a lot of their free time. But of course, he still has his town house in Brussels but this too now has many African touches with the racing mementoes taking a back seat.

◼ *Jacky Ickx: "Looking back, I want to thank everybody who helped me in my career. The people at Porsche and Ferrari and for sure the father figures like Enzo Ferrari, Jack Brabham, John Wyer, Carl Haas and, above all, Ken and Norah Tyrrell. But also the mechanics and the fans for they too were part of my success. It is not just me – it's about all the other people as well. Maybe my biggest regret is that, when I was racing, I didn't show enough gratitude to those around me."*

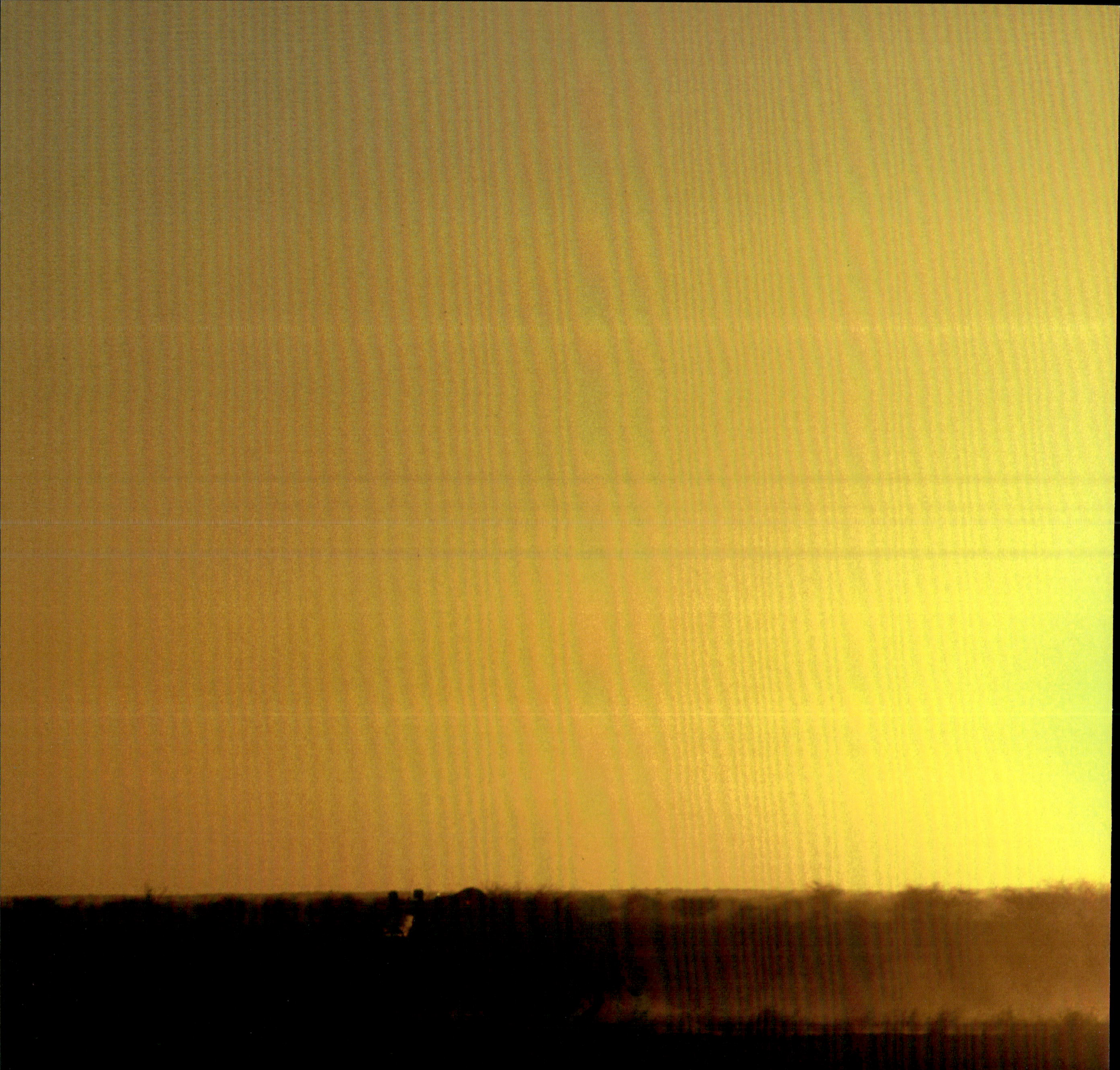

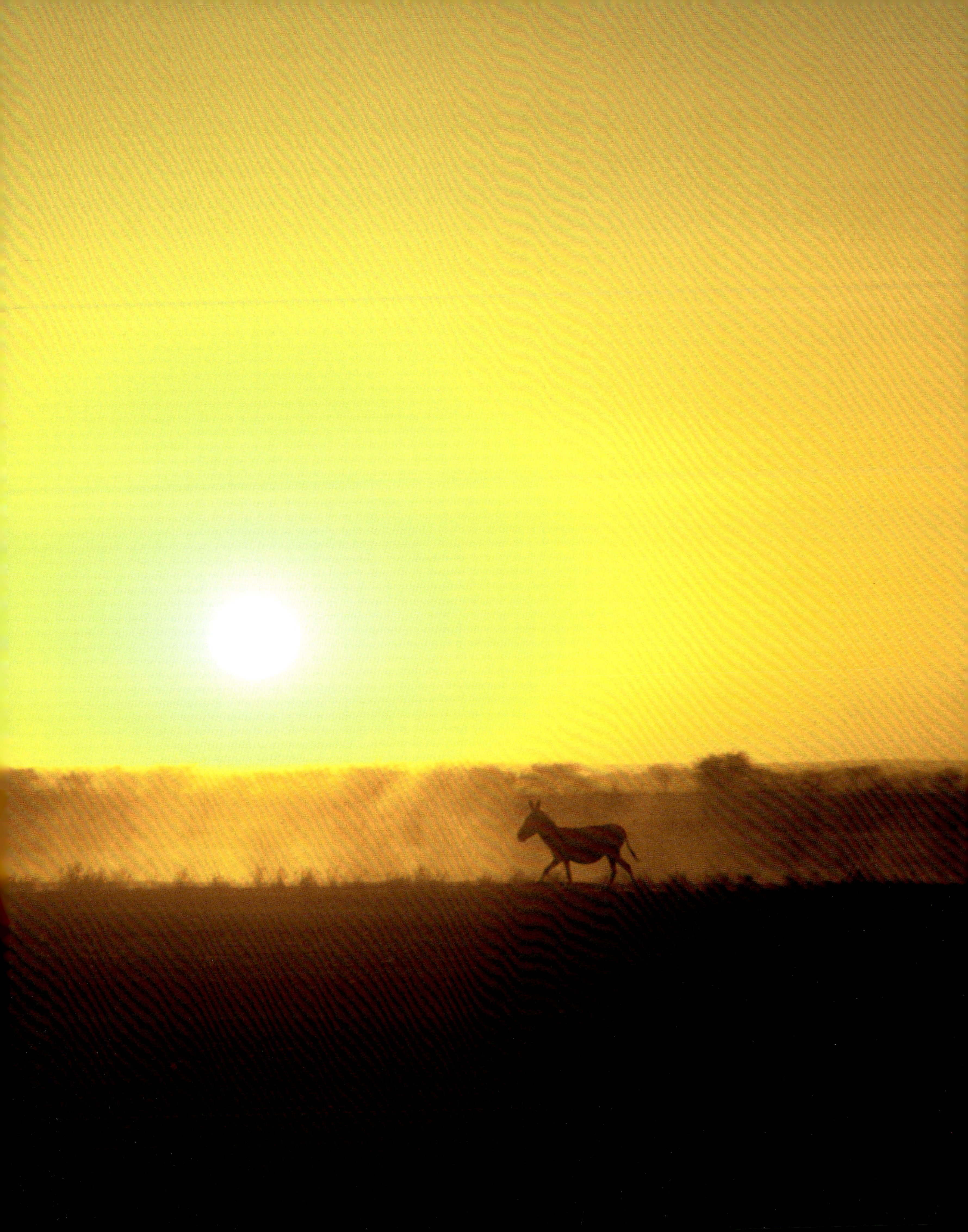

1961 – 2000

Statistik
Statistics

Gran Premio d'Italia 1968

24 Heures du Mans 1969

Datum	Veranstaltung
Date	Event

1961

15.10.	Enghien Trial
12.11.	Nivelles Trial

1962

21.01.	Thuin Trial
08.04.	2 days of Holzkirchen
27.05.	Grand Trophy of Mettet
19.09.	ISDT Garmisch Partenkirchen
21.10.	Marcq-Enghien Trial

1963

	European Championship
17.03.	Belgian Trial Championship
28.04.	Course de Côte de La Roche en Ardennes
11.05.	Scottish Six Days Trial
14.07.	Course de Côte de Gîves
25.08.	Coupe du Benelux (Zolder)
02.09.	Tour de France Automobile
29.09.	Course de Côte de la Citadelle - Namur
29.09.	Course de Côte de la Citadelle - Namur

1964

21.01.	Rixensart Trial
08.03.	Course de Côte de Fléron
15.03.	Driving Course Zolder
22.03.	Course de Côte d'Alle-sur-Semois
28.03.	Coupe de Belgique (Zolder)
05.04.	12 heures de Huy
19.04.	Course de Côte de La Roche en Ardennes
10.05.	Coupe Terlaemen (Zolder)
10.05.	Coupe Terlaemen (Zolder)
17.05.	Coupes de Spa
30.05.	Course de Côte de Ste Cécile - Herbeumont
05.07.	Coupe de Benelux (Zandvoort)
12.07.	Course de Côte de Gîves
12.07.	Course de Côte de Gîves
25.07.	24 Heures de Spa-Francorchamps (Spa-Francorchamps)
09.08.	Course de Côte de Bomerée
09.08.	Course de Côte de Bomerée
23.08.	Course de Côte de Spa-Maquisard
23.08.	European Cup (Zolder)
30.08.	Zandvoort Trophy (Zandvoort)
13.09.	Timmelsjoch Bergrennen
20.09.	Budapest Grand Prix (Budapest)
27.09.	Course de Côte de la Citadelle - Namur
27.09.	Course de Côte de la Citadelle - Namur

Klasse / Class	Fahrzeug / Vehicle	Nr. / No.	Besitzer / Owner	Startpos. / Start pos.	Ergebnis / Results	Beifahrer / Co-driver
Trial	Zündapp					
Trial	Zündapp				1	
Trial	Zündapp	91				
Trial	Zündapp				2	
Trial	Zündapp 50 cc					
Trial	Zündapp	294			2	
Trial	Zündapp	114				
Trial	Zündapp 50cc				1 of class	
Trial	Zündapp				1	
Hill Climb	BMW 700S		Albert Moorkens		DNF-accident	
Trial	Zündapp 98 cc	3				
Hill Climb	BMW 700S	50	Albert Moorkens		1 of class	
Touring Car	BMW 700S		Albert Moorkens		3 of class	
Touring Car	BMW 700S	1	Albert Moorkens		DNF	Harris
Hill Climb	BMW 700S		Albert Moorkens			
Hill Climb	Ford Lotus Cortina	48	Ford Belgium			
Trial	Zündapp	51			1 of class	
Hill Climb	Ford Lotus Cortina		Ford Belgium		1 of class	
Touring Car	Ford Lotus Cortina	55	Ford Belgium		1 of class	
Hill Climb	Ford Lotus Cortina	501	Ford Belgium		1 of class	
Touring Car	Ford Lotus Cortina	34	Ford Belgium		2 of class	
Rally	Hillman Imp	45			1 of class / 2nd overall	
Hill Climb	Ford Lotus Cortina	308	Ford Belgium		DNF	
Touring Car	Ford Lotus Cortina		Ford Belgium		DNF	
Touring Car	BMW 700S	30	Albert Moorkens	2	DNF-accident	
Touring Car	Ford Lotus Cortina		Ford Belgium		DNF-accident	
Hill Climb	Ford Lotus Cortina		Ford Belgium		3 of class	
Touring Car	BMW 700S		Albert Moorkens		1 of class	
Hill Climb	BMW 700S		Albert Moorkens		1 of class	
Hill Climb	Ford Lotus Cortina		Ford Belgium		4 of class / 14th overall	
Touring Car	Ford Lotus Cortina	304	Ford Belgium			Pilette
Hill Climb	BMW 700S	5	Albert Moorkens		1 of class	
Hill Climb	Ford Lotus Cortina	50	Ford Belgium		1 of class	
Hill Climb	Ford Lotus Cortina		Ford Belgium			
Touring Car	BMW 700S	101	Albert Moorkens			
Touring Car	Ford Lotus Cortina	122	Alan Mann Racing		4	
Hill Climb	Ford Lotus Cortina	37	Alan Mann Racing		2 of class	
Touring Car	Ford Lotus Cortina	23	Alan Mann Racing		DNF-3 of class	
Hill Climb	BMW 700S		Albert Moorkens		1 of class	
Hill Climb	Ford Lotus Cortina	69	Ford Belgium		1 of class	

ADAC-1000-km-Rennen 1968

Großer Preis von Deutschland 1966

ADAC-1000-km-Rennen 1969

| Datum | Veranstaltung |
| Date | Event |

1965

	Belgian Trial Championship
07.03.	Course de Côte de Fléron
14.03.	Course de Côte d'Alle-sur-Semois
21.03.	Coupe de Belgique
21.03.	Coupe de Belgique
28.03.	Course de Côte de Kautenbach
11.04.	Course de Côte de La Roche en Ardennes
30.04.	Tulpenrallye
16.05.	Coupes de Spa
30.05.	Course de Côte de Ste Cécile - Herbeumont
13.06.	ADAC-1000-km-Rennen (Nürburgring)
26.06.	Coupe Terlaemen (Zolder)
26.06.	Coupe Terlaemen (Zolder)
04.07.	Coupe de Benelux (Zandvoort)
04.07.	Coupe de Benelux (Zandvoort)
25.07.	24 Heures de Spa-Francorchamps (Spa-Francorchamps)
22.08.	Course de Côte de Spa-Maquisard
26.08.	Trans-Am Marlboro (Maryland)
28.08.	Marathon de la Route (Nürburgring)
29.08.	Zandvoort Trophy (Zandvoort)
12.09.	Limborg Trophy
19.09.	Course de Côte de Houyet
03.10.	Course de Côte de la Citadelle - Namur

1966

	Course de Côte des Tros-Marêts
	Marche Trial
	St Martin Aywaille Trial
06.02.	24 Hours of Daytona (Daytona Beach)
13.03.	Course de Côte de Fléron
20.03.	Course de Côte de La Roche en Ardennes
27.03.	Grand National (Zolder)
02.04.	XXI B.A.R.C. "200" (Oulton Park)
11.04.	II Sunday Mirror Trophy (Goodwood)
17.04.	XXVI Grand Prix Automobile de Pau (Pau)
24.04.	Coupe de Belgique
08.05.	III Grote Prijs van Limborg (Zolder)
08.05.	Grote Prijs van Limborg (Zolder)
14.05.	XVIII BRDC International Trophy
15.05.	Course de Côte d'Alle-sur-Semois
21.05.	Grand Prix de Monaco (Monaco)
22.05.	Coupes de Spa
29.05.	Grand Prix des Frontières (Chimay)
30.05.	London Trophy (Crystal Palace)
12.06.	Trans-Am Mid-America 300 (Mid-America)
19.06.	24 Heures du Mans (Le Mans)
03.07.	XXXII Grand Prix de Reims (Reims)
03.07.	Großer Preis der Tourenwagen (Nürburgring)
09.07.	VII Aston Martin Owners Club Trophy (Silverstone)
10.07.	XIV Grand Prix de Rouen-les-Essarts (Rouen-les-Essarts)
16.07.	Peter England Trophy (Brands Hatch)
16.07.	British Eagle Trophy (Brands Hatch)
23.07.	24 Heures de Spa-Francorchamps (Spa-Francorchamps)
07.08.	Großer Preis von Deutschland (Nürburgring)
14.08.	Trans-Am Marlboro 12 hours (Maryland)
20.08.	Le Marathon de la Route (Nürburgring)
21.08.	Course de Côte de Spa-Maquisard
29.08.	Guards' Trophy (Brands Hatch)
04.09.	Zandvoort Trophyée (Zandvoort)
04.09.	Zandvoort Trophyée (Zandvoort)
11.09.	Coupes de l'Avenir (Zolder)
11.09.	Coupes de l'Avenir (Zolder)
18.09.	Trophée Craven A – Le Mans
25.09.	XXV Grand Prix d'Albi (Albi)

Klasse / Class	Fahrzeug / Vehicle	Nr. / No.	Besitzer / Owner	Startpos. / Start pos.	Ergebnis / Results	Beifahrer / Co-driver
Trial	Zündapp					
Hill Climb	Ford Lotus Cortina	71		-		
Hill Climb	Ford Lotus Cortina			-	1 of class	
Touring Car	Ford Lotus Cortina	69			1	
Touring Car	Ford Mustang	43			1	
Hill Climb	Ford Lotus Cortina	39		-	1 of class	
Hill Climb	Ford Lotus Cortina			-	1 of class	
Rally	Ford Lotus Cortina	116		-	11	Staepelaere
Touring Car	Ford Mustang	1		1	14	
Hill Climb	Ford Lotus Cortina			-	1 of class	
Touring Car	Ford Lotus Cortina		Alan Mann Racing		NC	Baillie
Touring Car	Ford Mustang	8	Alan Mann Racing		1 Div 3	
Touring Car	Ford Lotus Cortina	20	Ford Belgium		4 Div 2	
Touring Car	Ford Mustang				1	
Touring Car	Ford Lotus Cortina				1	
Touring Car	BMW 1800 TISA			2	DNF-head gasket	Glemser
Hill Climb	Ford Lotus Cortina			-	1 of class	
Touring Car	Ford Lotus Cortina	22	Alan Mann Racing	2	9	Taylor
Touring Car	Ford Mustang	31			2	Staepelaere
Touring Car	Ford Lotus Cortina	107	Ford Belgium		DNF-suspension	
Touring Car	Ford Mustang	1			1	
Hill Climb	Ford Lotus Cortina			-	1 of class	
Hill Climb	Ford Lotus Cortina	59		-	1 of class	

Klasse / Class	Fahrzeug / Vehicle	Nr. / No.	Besitzer / Owner	Startpos. / Start pos.	Ergebnis / Results	Beifahrer / Co-driver
Hill Climb	Ford Lotus Cortina	61		-	1	
Trial	Zündapp	58				
Trial	Zündapp	37				
Sports Cars	Ferrari 250LM	26	Jacques Swaters	20	DNF-transmission	Dernier-Blaton
Hill Climb	Ford Lotus Cortina			-		
Hill Climb	Ford Lotus Cortina			-	2	
Touring Car	Ford Mustang	64			1	
Formula 2	Matra MS5 - BRM	8	Tyrrell Racing Organisation		Cancelled (snow on track)	
Formula 2	Matra MS5 - BRM	8	Tyrrell Racing Organisation		6	Shared his car with J. Stewart
Formula 2	Matra MS5 - BRM	24	Tyrrell Racing Organisation	17	4	Shared his car with J. Stewart
Touring Car	Ford Mustang				1	
Formula 2	Matra MS5 - SCA	20	Tyrrell Racing Organisation		DNF-engine	
Touring Car	Ford Lotus Cortina	44			2	
Touring Car	Ford Lotus Cortina	42			4	
Hill Climb	Ford Lotus Cortina	70		-	1 Gr 1&2	
Formula 3	Matra MS5 - Ford	67	Tyrrell Racing Organisation		Not qualified - accident	
Touring Car	Ford Mustang	1			1	
Touring Car	Ford Lotus Cortina	15			DNF	
Touring Car	Ford Lotus Cortina	73		4	3	
Touring Car	Ford Lotus Cortina				3	Hahne
Sports Cars	Ford GT40	60	Essex Wire	14	DNF-engine	Neerpasch
Formula 2	Matra MS5 - BRM	26	Tyrrell Racing Organisation	13	DNF	
Touring Car	Ford Lotus Cortina		Alan Mann Racing		DNF-bearing	Hawkins
Formula 3	Matra MS5 - Ford	38	Tyrrell Racing Organisation		3	
Formula 2	Matra MS5 - BRM	14	Tyrrell Racing Organisation		DNF	
Touring Car	Ford Lotus Cortina	86		4	5	
Can-Am	McLaren Elva	48	Alan Brown	3	5	
Touring Car	BMW 2000 TI	17		1	1	Hahne
Formula 2	Matra MS5 - SCA	27	Tyrrell Racing Organisation	1	DNF-accident	
Touring Car	Ford Lotus Cortina		Alan Mann Racing		DNF-engine	Hahne
Touring Car	Ford Lotus Cortina	31			1	Staepelaere
Hill Climb	Ford Lotus Cortina			-	1	
Formula 3	Matra MS5 - SCA	79	Tyrrell Racing Organisation	13	13	
Formula 3	Matra MS5 - SCA	6	Tyrrell Racing Organisation	9	2	
Touring Car	Ford Lotus Cortina	51			5 Div 2	
Touring Car	Ford Lotus Cortina	74			1	
Formula 3	Brabham BT18 - Ford	30	Tyrrell Racing Organisation	4	2	
Formula 2	Matra MS5 - BRM	16	Tyrrell Racing Organisation		DNF-electrical	
Formula 2	Matra MS5 - BRM	24	Tyrrell Racing Organisation		4	

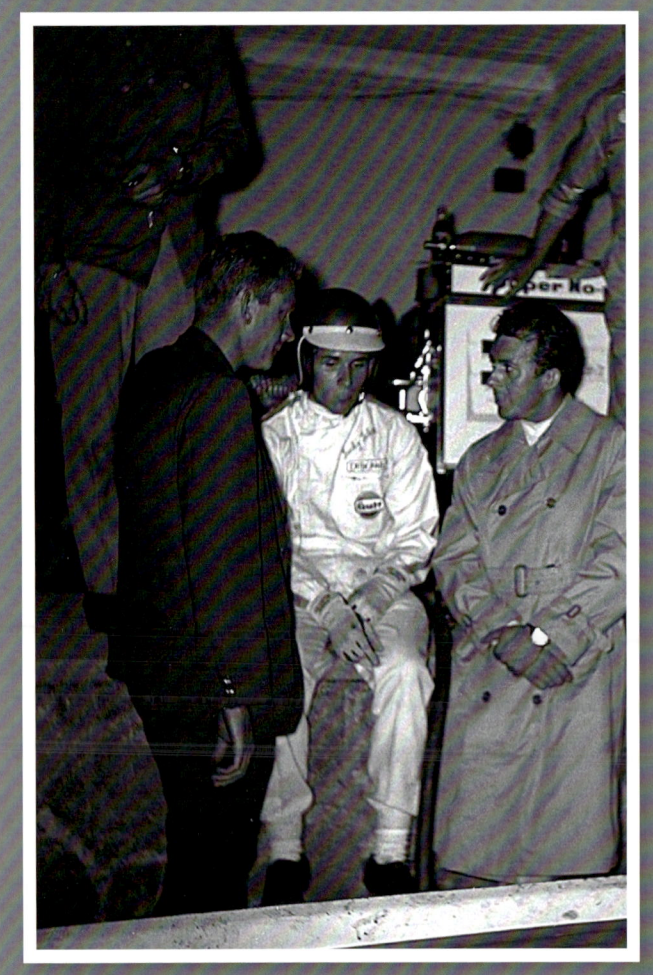

24 Heures de Spa-Francorchamps 1967

Flugplatzrennen Tulln-Langenlebarn 1967

| Datum | Veranstaltung |
| Date | Event |

1966

02.10.	European Formula 3 International Challenge (Brands Hatch)
16.10.	Course de Côte des Fagnes
30.10.	I Motor Show "200" (Brands Hatch)
05.11.	9 Hours of Kyalami (Kyalami)
09.11.	Course de Côte de la Citadelle - Namur

1967

05.02.	24 Hours of Daytona (Daytona Beach)
12.03.	Race of Champions (Brands Hatch)
24.03.	I Guards "100" (Snetterton)
27.03.	XXII B.A.R.C. "200" (Silverstone)
27.03.	XXII B.A.R.C. "200" (Silverstone)
04.04.	XXVII Grand Prix Automobile de Pau (Pau)
09.04.	II Gran Premio de Barcelona (Montjuïc)
23.04.	Eifelrennen (Nürburgring)
25.04.	1000 km di Monza (Monza)
01.05.	1000 km de Spa-Francorchamps (Spa-Francorchamps)
14.05.	Guards' International Trophy (Mallory Park)
21.05.	Grote Prijs van Limborg (Zolder)
21.05.	Grote Prijs van Limborg (Zolder)
28.05.	ADAC-1000-km-Rennen (Nürburgring)
29.05.	London Trophy (Crystal Palace)
11.06.	24 Heures du Mans (Le Mans)
25.06.	Grand Prix de Reims (Reims)
09.07.	Deutschland Trophäe (Hockenheim)
16.07.	Flugplatzrennen Tulln-Langenlebarn (Tulln-Langenlebarn)
22.07.	24 Heures de Spa-Francorchamps (Spa-Francorchamps)
30.07.	Grote Prijs van Zandvoort (Zandvoort)
06.08.	Großer Preis von Deutschland (Nürburgring)
13.08.	Sveriges Grand Prix (Karlskoga)
13.08.	Sveriges Grand Prix (Karlskoga)
20.08.	Gran Premio del Mediterraneo (Enna-Pergusa)
26.08.	Le Marathon de la Route (Nürburgring)
28.08.	Guards' Trophy (Brands Hatch)
28.08.	Guards' Trophy (Brands Hatch)
10.09.	Gran Premio d'Italia (Monza)
16.09.	Gold Cup (Oulton Park)
16.09.	Gold Cup (Oulton Park)
24.09.	Grand Prix d'Albi (Albi)
01.10.	United States Grand Prix (Watkins Glen)
08.10.	Gran Premio di Roma (Vallelunga)
15.10.	1000 km de Paris (Montlhéry)
04.11.	9 Hours of Kyalami (Kyalami)
12.11.	Gran Premio de España (Jarama)

1968

01.01.	South African Grand Prix (Kyalami)
04.02.	24 Hours of Daytona (Daytona Beach)
17.03.	Race of Champions (Brands Hatch)
23.03.	Sebring 12-Hour Endurance Race (Sebring)
31.03.	Gran Premio de Barcelona (Montjuïc)
07.04.	BOAC 500m (Brands Hatch)
21.04.	Internationales ADAC-Eifelrennen (Nürburgring)
24.04.	Daily Express International Trophy (Silverstone)
25.04.	1000 km di Monza (Monza)
05.05.	Grote Prijs van Limborg (Zolder)
12.05.	Gran Premio de España (Jarama)
19.05.	ADAC-1000-km-Rennen (Nürburgring)
26.05.	1000 km de Spa-Francorchamps (Spa-Francorchamps)
26.05.	Coupes de Spa
03.06.	London Trophy (Crystal Palace)

Klasse / Class	Fahrzeug / Vehicle	Nr. / No.	Besitzer / Owner	Startpos. / Start pos.	Ergebnis / Results	Beifahrer / Co-driver
Formula 3	Matra F3	1	RAC de Belgique	3	7	
Hill Climb	Ford Lotus Cortina			-	1 of class	
Formula 2	Matra MS5 - SCA	15	Tyrrell Racing Organisation	9	4	
Sports Cars	Ferrari 275 LM	5	Jacques Swaters		DNF-head gasket	Dernier
Hill Climb	Ford Lotus Cortina			-		

Klasse / Class	Fahrzeug / Vehicle	Nr. / No.	Besitzer / Owner	Startpos. / Start pos.	Ergebnis / Results	Beifahrer / Co-driver
Sports Cars	Ford GT40	11	Grady Davis	13	6	Thompson
Formula 2	Matra MS5	21	Matra Sports	12	DNF-fuel pump	
Formula 2	Matra MS5 - FVA	24	Tyrrell Racing Organisation		DNF-ignition	
Formula 2	Matra MS5 - FVA	17	Tyrrell Racing Organisation	10	7	
Touring Car	Ford Cortina MK2	17		10		
Formula 2	Matra MS5 - FVA	22	Tyrrell Racing Organisation	10	5	
Formula 2	Matra MS5 - FVA	7	Tyrrell Racing Organisation	8	DNF-engine	
Formula 2	Matra MS5 - FVA	16	Tyrrell Racing Organisation	5	3	
Sports Cars	Mirage M1 - Ford	6	JWA Automotive	5	DNF-ignition	Rees
Sports Cars	Mirage M1 - Ford	6	JWA Automotive	2	1	Thompson
Formula 2	Matra MS5 - FVA	14	Tyrrell Racing Organisation	2	4	
Formula 2	Matra MS5 - FVA	5	Tyrrell Racing Organisation	7	DNF-engine	
Touring Car	Ford Lotus Cortina		Ford Belgium		4 Div 2	
Sports Cars	Mirage M1 - Ford	6	JWA Automotive	9	DNF-punctures	Attwood
Formula 2	Matra MS5 - FVA	31	Tyrrell Racing Organisation	8	1	
Sports Cars	Mirage M1 - Ford	15	JWA Automotive	15	DNF-head gasket	Muir-Piper
Formula 2	Matra MS5 - FVA	26	Tyrrell Racing Organisation	7	6	
Formula 2	Matra MS5 - FVA	10	Tyrrell Racing Organisation		10	
Formula 2	Matra MS7 - FVA	16	Tyrrell Racing Organisation	5	5	
Touring Car	Ford Mustang	1	Alan Mann Racing	1	DNF-rear axle	Hahne
Formula 2	Matra MS5 - FVA	3	Tyrrell Racing Organisation	1	1	
Formula 2	Matra MS5 - FVA	29	Tyrrell Racing Organisation	1	4 (DNF-accident)	
Sports Cars	Mirage M1 - Ford	1	JWA Automotive		1	
Formula 2	Matra MS5 - FVA	9	Tyrrell Racing Organisation	5	6	
Formula 2	Matra MS5 - FVA	14	Tyrrell Racing Organisation	2	3	
Touring Car	Ford Mustang				DNF-transmission	Staepelaere-Gautot
Formula 2	Matra MS5 - FVA	14	Tyrrell Racing Organisation	9	5	
Touring Car	Ford Lotus Cortina MK2				2	
Formula 1	Cooper T81B - Maserati	32	Cooper Car Company	15	6	
Touring Car	Ford Lotus Cortina MK2				DNF-accident	
Formula 2	Matra MS5 - FVA	10	Tyrrell Racing Organisation	5	DNF-accident	
Formula 2	Matra MS5 - FVA	32	Tyrrell Racing Organisation	9	4	
Formula 1	Cooper T86 - Maserati	21	Cooper Car Company	16	DNF-piston/overheat	
Formula 2	Matra MS7 - FVA	34	Tyrrell Racing Organisation	1	1	
Sports Cars	Mirage M1 - Ford	3	JWA Automotive	1	1	Hawkins
Sports Cars	Mirage M1 - Ford	4	JWA Automotive	3	1	Redman
Formula 1 NC	Matra MS5 - FVA	4	Tyrrell Racing Organisation	8	6	

Klasse / Class	Fahrzeug / Vehicle	Nr. / No.	Besitzer / Owner	Startpos. / Start pos.	Ergebnis / Results	Beifahrer / Co-driver
Formula 1	Ferrari 312	9	Ferrari Automobili	11	DNF-oil leak	
Sports Cars	Ford GT40	8	JWA Automotive	1	DNF-gearbox	Redman
Formula 1 NC	Ferrari 312	9	Scuderia Ferrari SpA SEFAC	8	8	
Sports Cars	Ford GT40	28	JWA Automotive	2	DNF-clutch	Redman
Formula 2	Ferrari Dino 166 V6	24	Ferrari Automobili	5	DNF-accident	
Sports Cars	Ford GT40	4	JWA Automotive	5	1	Redman
Formula 2	Ferrari Dino 166 V6	3	Scuderia Ferrari SpA SEFAC	1	DNF-radiator	
Formula 1 NC	Ferrari 312	6	Scuderia Ferrari SpA SEFAC	7	4	
Sports Cars	Ford GT40	39	JWA Automotive	1	DNF-broken exhaust	Redman
Formula 2	Ferrari Dino 166 V6	4	Scuderia Ferrari SpA SEFAC	8	4	
Formula 1	Ferrari 312	21	Scuderia Ferrari SpA SEFAC	8	DNF-ignition	
Sports Cars	Ford GT40	65	JWA Automotive	2	3	Hawkins
Sports Cars	Ford GT40	33	JWA Automotive	2	1	Redman
Touring Car	Ford Mustang	3			1	
Formula 2	Ferrari Dino 166 V6	25	Scuderia Ferrari SpA SEFAC	5	DNF-accident	

Grand Prix de Monaco 1969

ADAC-1000-km-Rennen 1969

Datum / Date	Veranstaltung / Event

1968

09.06.	Grand Prix de Belgique (Spa-Francorchamps)
16.06.	Rhein-Pokalrennen (Hockenheim)
23.06.	Grote Prijs van Nederland (Zandvoort)
07.07.	Grand Prix de France (Rouen-Les-Essarts)
14.07.	6 Hours of Watkins Glen (Watkins Glen)
20.07.	British Grand Prix (Brands Hatch)
04.08.	Großer Preis von Deutschland (Nürburgring)
17.08.	Gold Cup (Oulton Park)
25.08.	Gran Premio del Mediterraneo (Enna-Pergusa)
08.09.	Gran Premio d'Italia (Monza)
22.09.	Canadian Grand Prix (Mont-Tremblant)
03.11.	Gran Premio de Mexico (Mexico City)
09.11.	9 Hours of Kyalami (Kyalami)

1969

02.02.	24 Hours of Daytona (Daytona Beach)
23.02.	Daytona 500 (Daytona Beach)
01.03.	South African Grand Prix (Kyalami)
16.03.	Race of Champions (Brands Hatch)
22.03.	Sebring 12-Hour Endurance Race (Sebring)
30.03.	BRDC International Trophy (Silverstone)
13.04.	BOAC 500m (Brands Hatch)
20.04.	Coupe de Belgique (Zolder)
04.05.	Gran Premio de España (Montjuïc)
10.05.	Coupes de Spa
11.05.	1000 km de Spa-Francorchamps (Spa-Francorchamps)
18.05.	Grand Prix de Monaco (Monaco)
01.06.	ADAC-1000-km-Rennen (Nürburgring)
08.06.	Grote Prijs van Limborg (Zolder)
15.06.	24 Heures du Mans (Le Mans)
21.06.	Grote Prijs van Nederland (Zandvoort)
29.06.	Grand Prix de Reims (Reims)
06.07.	Grand Prix de France (Charade)
12.07.	6 Hours of Watkins Glen (Watkins Glen)
19.07.	British Grand Prix (Silverstone)
03.08.	Großer Preis von Deutschland (Nürburgring)
10.08.	1000 km Österreichring (Zeltweg)
16.08.	Gold Cup (Oulton Park)
24.08.	Gran Premio del Mediterraneo (Enna-Pergusa)
07.09.	Gran Premio d'Italia (Monza)
14.09.	500 km di Imola (Imola)
20.09.	Canadian Grand Prix (Mosport Park)
05.10.	United States Grand Prix (Watkins Glen)
19.10.	Gran Premio de Mexico (Mexico City)

1970

01.02.	24 Hours of Daytona (Daytona Beach)
01.02.	24 Hours of Daytona (Daytona Beach)
07.03.	South African GP (Kyalami)
21.03.	Sebring 12-Hour Endurance Race (Sebring)
30.03.	BARC Thruxton (Thruxton)
12.04.	BOAC 1000 km (Brands Hatch)
19.04.	Gran Premio de España (Jarama)
26.04.	Gran Premio de Barcelona (Montjuïc)
10.05.	Grand Prix de Monaco (Monaco)
17.05.	1000 km de Spa-Francorchamps (Spa-Francorchamps)
17.05.	Coupes de Spa
24.05.	Grote Prijs van Limborg (Zolder)
31.05.	ADAC-1000-km-Rennen (Nürburgring)
07.06.	Grand Prix de Belgique (Zolder)

Klasse / Class	Fahrzeug / Vehicle	Nr. / No.	Besitzer / Owner	Startpos. / Start pos.	Ergebnis / Results	Beifahrer / Co-driver
Formula 1	Ferrari 312	23	Scuderia Ferrari SpA SEFAC	3	3	
Formula 2	Ferrari Dino 166 V6	6	Scuderia Ferrari SpA SEFAC	4	5	
Formula 1	Ferrari 312	10	Scuderia Ferrari SpA SEFAC	6	4	
Formula 1	Ferrari 312	26	Scuderia Ferrari SpA SEFAC	3	1	
Sports Cars	Ford GT40	5	JWA Automotive	2	1	Bianchi
Formula 1	Ferrari 312	6	Scuderia Ferrari SpA SEFAC	12	3	
Formula 1	Ferrari 312	9	Scuderia Ferrari SpA SEFAC	1	4	
Formula 1 NC	Ferrari 312	9	Scuderia Ferrari SpA SEFAC	5	DNF-ignition	
Formula 2	Ferrari Dino 166 V6	18	Scuderia Ferrari SpA SEFAC	5	6	
Formula 1	Ferrari 312	8	Scuderia Ferrari SpA SEFAC	4	3	
Formula 1	Ferrari 312	10	Scuderia Ferrari SpA SEFAC	21	Accident in practice	
Formula 1	Ferrari 312	7	Scuderia Ferrari SpA SEFAC	15	DNF-ignition	
Sports Cars	Mirage M1 - Ford	1		3	1	Hobbs

Klasse / Class	Fahrzeug / Vehicle	Nr. / No.	Besitzer / Owner	Startpos. / Start pos.	Ergebnis / Results	Beifahrer / Co-driver
Sports Cars	Ford GT40	1	JWA Automotive	8	26 (DNF-accident)	Oliver
NASCAR	Mercury Cyclone	97	Holman & Moody		Not qualified - accident	
Formula 1	Brabham BT26 - Ford	15	Brabham Racing Organisation	13	DNF ignition	
Formula 1 NC	Brabham BT26 - Ford	6	Brabham Racing Organisation	10	DNF-fuel metering unit	
Sports Cars	Ford GT40	22	JWA Automotive	12	1	Oliver
Formula 1 NC	Brabham BT26 - Ford	9	Brabham Racing Organisation	4	4	
Sports Cars	Mirage M2/300 - BRM	51	JWA Automotive	11	DNF-drive shaft	Oliver
Touring Car	Ford Escort TC	94		3	DNF-gearbox	
Formula 1	Brabham BT26 - Ford	4	Motor Racing Developments Ltd	7	6 (DNF-suspension)	
Touring Car	Ford Falcon	1	Alan Mann Racing	1	1	
Sports Cars	Mirage M2/300 - BRM	1	JWA Automotive	2	DNF-fuel pump	Oliver
Formula 1	Brabham BT26 - Ford	6	Motor Racing Developments Ltd	7	DNF-suspension	
Sports Cars	Mirage M2/300 - Ford	8	JWA Automotive	8	DNF-suspension	Oliver
Formula 2	Brabham BT23C - FVA	9	Frank Williams Racing Cars	4	2	
Sports Cars	Ford GT40	6	JWA Automotive	13	1	Oliver
Formula 1	Brabham BT26 - Ford	12	Motor Racing Developments Ltd	5	5	
Formula 2	Brabham BT23C - FVA	30	Alistair Walker Racing	1	DNF-engine	
Formula 1	Brabham BT26 - Ford	11	Motor Racing Developments Ltd	4	3	
Sports Cars	Mirage M2/300 - Ford	5	JWA Automotive	5	DNF-camshaft	Oliver
Formula 1	Brabham BT26 - Ford	7	Motor Racing Developments Ltd	4	2	
Formula 1	Brabham BT26 - Ford	6	Motor Racing Developments Ltd	1	1	
Sports Cars	Mirage M2/300 - Ford	9	JWA Automotive	1	DNF-steering	Oliver
Formula 1 NC	Brabham BT26 - Ford	6	Motor Racing Developments Ltd	2	1	
Formula 2	De Tomaso 103 - FVA	12	Alessandro de Tomaso	5	DNF-engine	
Formula 1	Brabham BT26 - Ford	26	Motor Racing Developments Ltd	15	10 (DNF-fuel supply)	
Sports Cars	Mirage M3	4	JWA Automotive	3	1	
Formula 1	Brabham BT26 - Ford	11	Motor Racing Developments Ltd	1	1	
Formula 1	Brabham BT26 - Ford	7	Motor Racing Developments Ltd	8	DNF-engine	
Formula 1	Brabham BT26 - Ford	7	Motor Racing Developments Ltd	2	2	

Klasse / Class	Fahrzeug / Vehicle	Nr. / No.	Besitzer / Owner	Startpos. / Start pos.	Ergebnis / Results	Beifahrer / Co-driver
Sports Cars	Ferrari 512S	27	Ferrari	5	DNF-accident damage	Schetty
Sports Cars	Ferrari 512S	28	Ferrari	1	3	Andretti-Merzario
Formula 1	Ferrari 312B	17	Scuderia Ferrari SpA SEFAC	5	DNF-engine	
Sports Cars	Ferrari 512S	20	Ferrari	4	DNF-valve	Schetty
Formula 2	BMW 270	30	BMW	2	6	
Sports Cars	Ferrari 512S	1	Ferrari	2	8	Oliver
Formula 1	Ferrari 312B	2	Scuderia Ferrari SpA SEFAC	7	DNF-accident	
Formula 2	BMW 270	1	BMW		DNF-accident	
Formula 1	Ferrari 312B	26	Scuderia Ferrari SpA SEFAC	5	DNF-drive shaft	
Sports Cars	Ferrari 512S	20	Ferrari	3	2	Surtees
Touring Car	Ford Mustang	1		3	DNF	
Formula 2	BMW 270	4	BMW	3	DNF-engine	
Sports Cars	Ferrari 512S	56	Ferrari	4	Accident in practice	Schetty
Formula 1	Ferrari 312B	27	Scuderia Ferrari SpA SEFAC	4	8	

Grand Prix de Monaco 1971

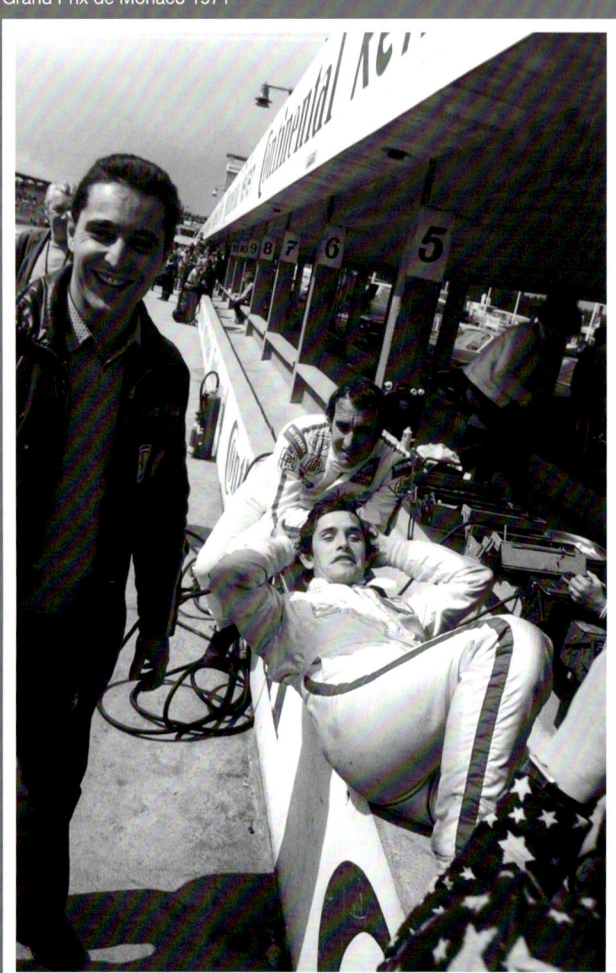

Rindt Memorial 1971

| Datum | Veranstaltung |
| Date | Event |

1970

13.06.	24 Heures du Mans (Le Mans)
21.06.	Grote Prijs van Nederland (Zandvoort)
28.06.	Gran Prix de Rouen (Rouen-les-Essarts)
05.07.	Grand Prix de France (Charade)
11.07.	6 Hours of Watkins Glen (Watkins Glen)
12.07.	Watkins Glen
19.07.	British Grand Prix (Brands Hatch)
26.07.	Trophée de France Formule 2 (Le Castellet)
02.08.	Großer Preis von Deutschland (Hockenheim)
16.08.	Großer Preis von Österreich (Zeltweg)
23.08.	Gran Premio del Mediterraneo (Enna-Pergusa)
30.08.	Festspielpreis der Stadt Salzburg (Salzburgring)
06.09.	Gran Premio d'Italia (Monza)
13.09.	Flugplatzrennen Tulln-Langenlebarn (Tulln-Langenlebarn)
20.09.	Canadian Grand Prix (Mont-Tremblant)
27.09.	Gran Premio di Imola (Imola)
04.10.	United States Grand Prix (Watkins Glen)
11.10.	1000 km Österreichring (Zeltweg)
25.10.	Gran Premio de Mexico (Mexico City)
07.11.	9 Hours of Kyalami (Kyalami)

1971

06.03.	South African Grand Prix (Kyalami)
20.03.	Sebring 12-Hour Endurance Race (Sebring)
28.03.	Questor Grand Prix (Ontario)
04.04.	BOAC 1000 km (Brands Hatch)
18.04.	Gran Premio de España (Montjuïc)
25.04.	1000 km di Monza (Monza)
09.05.	1000 km de Spa-Francorchamps (Spa-Francorchamps)
23.05.	Grand Prix de Monaco (Monaco)
30.05.	ADAC-1000-km-Rennen (Nürburgring)
13.06.	Rindt Memorial (Hockenheim)
20.06.	Grote Prijs van Nederland (Zandvoort)
27.06.	1000 km Österreichring (Zeltweg)
04.07.	Grand Prix de France (Paul Ricard)
17.07.	RAC British Grand Prix (Silverstone)
24.07.	Watkins Glen 6 Hours (Watkins Glen)
01.08.	Großer Preis von Deutschland (Nürburgring)
15.08.	Großer Preis von Österreich (Zeltweg)
05.09.	Gran Premio d'Italia (Monza)
12.09.	6 heures du Castellet (Paul Ricard)
19.09.	Canadian Grand Prix (Mosport Park)
03.10.	United States Grand Prix (Watkins Glen)
06.11.	9 Hours of Kyalami (Kyalami)

1972

09.01.	1000 km Buenos Aires (Buenos Aires)
23.01.	Gran Premio de la Republica Argentina (Buenos Aires)
06.02.	6 Hours of Daytona (Daytona Beach)
04.03.	South African Grand Prix (Kyalami)
25.03.	Sebring 12-Hour Endurance Race (Sebring)
16.04.	BOAC 1000 km (Brands Hatch)
25.04.	1000 km de Monza (Monza)
01.05.	Gran Premio de España (Jarama)
07.05.	1000 km de Spa-Francorchamps (Spa-Francorchamps)
07.05.	Coupes de Spa
14.05.	Grand Prix de Monaco (Monaco)
28.05.	1000 km Nürburgring (Nürburgring)
04.06.	Grand Prix de Belgique (Nivelles)
25.06.	1000 km Österreichring (Zeltweg)
02.07.	Grand Prix de France (Charade)

Klasse / Class	Fahrzeug / Vehicle	Nr. / No.	Besitzer / Owner	Startpos. / Start pos.	Ergebnis / Results	Beifahrer / Co-driver
Sports Cars	Ferrari 512S	5	Ferrari	6	DNF-accident	Schetty-Giunti-Vaccarella
Formula 1	Ferrari 312B	25	Scuderia Ferrari SpA SEFAC	3	3	
Formula 2	BMW 270	5	BMW	16	4	
Formula 1	Ferrari 312B	10	Scuderia Ferrari SpA SEFAC	1	DNF-engine	
Sports Cars	Ferrari 512S	91	Ferrari	4	5	Schetty
Can-Am	Ferrari 512S	91		8	DNF	
Formula 1	Ferrari 312B	3	Scuderia Ferrari SpA SEFAC	3	DNF-transmission	
Formula 2	BMW 270	17	BMW	1	DNF-oil pressure	
Formula 1	Ferrari 312B	10	Scuderia Ferrari SpA SEFAC	1	2	
Formula 1	Ferrari 312B	12	Scuderia Ferrari SpA SEFAC	3	1	
Formula 2	BMW 270	6	BMW	1	3	
Formula 2	BMW 270	19	BMW		1	
Formula 1	Ferrari 312B	2	Scuderia Ferrari SpA SEFAC	1	DNF-clutch	
Formula 2	BMW 270	9	BMW	7	1	
Formula 1	Ferrari 312B	18	Scuderia Ferrari SpA SEFAC	2	1	
Formula 2	BMW 270	6	BMW	12	DNF-alternator	
Formula 1	Ferrari 312B	3	Scuderia Ferrari SpA SEFAC	1	4	
Sports Cars	Ferrari 512M	31	Ferrari	2	DNF-electrics	Giunti-Schetty
Formula 1	Ferrari 312B	3	Scuderia Ferrari SpA SEFAC	3	1	
Sports Cars	Ferrari 512M	4	Ferrari	2	1	Giunti

Klasse / Class	Fahrzeug / Vehicle	Nr. / No.	Besitzer / Owner	Startpos. / Start pos.	Ergebnis / Results	Beifahrer / Co-driver
Formula 1	Ferrari 312B	4	Scuderia Ferrari SpA SEFAC	8	8	
Sports Cars	Ferrari 312PB	25	Ferrari	2	DNF-gearbox	Andretti
Formula 1 NC	Ferrari 312B	4	Scuderia Ferrari SpA SEFAC	3	11	
Sports Cars	Ferrari 312PB	51	Ferrari	1	2	Regazzoni
Formula 1	Ferrari 312B	4	Scuderia Ferrari SpA SEFAC	1	2	
Sports Cars	Ferrari 312PB	15	Ferrari	2	DNF-accident	Regazzoni
Sports Cars	Ferrari 312PB	1	Ferrari	5	8 (DNF-accident)	Regazzoni
Formula 1	Ferrari 312B2	4	Scuderia Ferrari SpA SEFAC	2	3	
Sports Cars	Ferrari 312PB	15	Ferrari	1	DNF-overheat	Regazzoni
Formula 1 NC	Ferrari 312B	4	Scuderia Ferrari SpA SEFAC	2	1	
Formula 1	Ferrari 312B2	2	Scuderia Ferrari SpA SEFAC	1	1	
Sports Cars	Ferrari 312PB	7	Ferrari	2	DNF-accident	Regazzoni
Formula 1	Ferrari 312B2	4	Scuderia Ferrari SpA SEFAC	3	DNF-engine	
Formula 1	Ferrari 312B2	4	Scuderia Ferrari SpA SEFAC	6	DNF-engine	
Sports Cars	Ferrari 312PB	40	Ferrari	3	DNF-start motor	Andretti
Formula 1	Ferrari 312B2	4	Scuderia Ferrari SpA SEFAC	2	DNF-accident	
Formula 1	Ferrari 312B2	4	Scuderia Ferrari SpA SEFAC	6	DNF-engine	
Formula 1	Ferrari 312B	3	Scuderia Ferrari SpA SEFAC	2	DNF-transmission	
Touring Car	BMW 2800 CS	14	BMW		DNF-brakes	Stuck
Formula 1	Ferrari 312B2	4	Scuderia Ferrari SpA SEFAC	12	8	
Formula 1	Ferrari 312B	32	Scuderia Ferrari SpA SEFAC	7	19 (DNF-alternator)	
Sports Cars	Ferrari 312PB	5	Ferrari	2	2	Andretti

Klasse / Class	Fahrzeug / Vehicle	Nr. / No.	Besitzer / Owner	Startpos. / Start pos.	Ergebnis / Results	Beifahrer / Co-driver
Sports Cars	Ferrari 312PB	28	Ferrari	3	10	Andretti
Formula 1	Ferrari 312B2	8	Scuderia Ferrari SpA SEFAC	8	3	
Sports Cars	Ferrari 312PB	2	Ferrari	1	1	Andretti
Formula 1	Ferrari 312B2	5	Scuderia Ferrari SpA SEFAC	7	8	
Sports Cars	Ferrari 312PB	2	Ferrari	1	1	Andretti
Sports Cars	Ferrari 312PB	11	Ferrari	2	1	Andretti
Sports Cars	Ferrari 312PB	1	Ferrari	2	1	Regazzoni
Formula 1	Ferrari 312B2	4	Scuderia Ferrari SpA SEFAC	1	2	
Sports Cars	Ferrari 312PB	1	Ferrari	1	2	Regazzoni
Touring Car	BMW 2800 CS	4	Team Schnitzer	1	1	
Formula 1	Ferrari 312B2	6	Scuderia Ferrari SpA SEFAC	2	2	
Sports Cars	Ferrari 312PB	1	Ferrari	8	DNF-accident	Regazzoni
Formula 1	Ferrari 312B2	29	Scuderia Ferrari SpA SEFAC	4	DNF-injection	
Sports Cars	Ferrari 312PB	1	Ferrari	3	1	Redman
Formula 1	Ferrari 312B2	3	Scuderia Ferrari SpA SEFAC	4	11	

1000 km Nürburgring 1974

Grand Prix de Monaco 1975

Datum / Date	Veranstaltung / Event
1972	
15.07.	RAC British Grand Prix (Brands Hatch)
22.07.	Watkins Glen 6 Hours (Watkins Glen)
30.07.	Großer Preis von Deutschland (Nürburgring)
13.08.	Großer Preis von Österreich (Zeltweg)
10.09.	Gran Premio d'Italia (Monza)
17.09.	500 km di Imola (Imola)
24.09.	Canadian Grand Prix (Mosport Park)
08.10.	United States Grand Prix (Watkins Glen)
04.11.	9 Hours of Kyalami (Kyalami)

1973	
28.01.	Gran Premio de la Republica Argentina (Buenos Aires)
11.02.	Grande Prêmio do Brasil (Interlagos)
03.03.	South African Grand Prix (Kyalami)
25.03.	6 Heures de Vallelunga (Vallelunga)
15.04.	1000 km de Dijon (Dijon-Prenois)
25.04.	1000 km de Monza (Monza)
29.04.	Gran Premio de España (Jarama)
06.05.	1000 km de Spa-Francorchamps (Spa-Francorchamps)
13.05.	Targa Florio
20.05.	Grand Prix de Belgique (Zolder)
27.05.	1000 km Nürburgring (Nürburgring)
03.06.	Grand Prix de Monaco (Monaco)
10.06.	24 heures du Mans (Le Mans)
17.06.	Großer Preis von Schweden (Anderstorp)
24.06.	1000 km Österreichring (Zeltweg)
01.07.	Grand Prix de France (Paul Ricard)
14.07.	British Grand Prix (Silverstone)
21.07.	Watkins Glen 6 Hours (Watkins Glen)
05.08.	Großer Preis von Deutschland (Nürburgring)
02.09.	6 heures du Castellet (Paul Ricard)
09.09.	Gran Premio d'Italia (Monza)
07.10.	United States Grand Prix (Watkins Glen)
13.10.	24 heures à Nivelles
03.11.	9 Hours of Kyalami (Kyalami)

1974	
13.01.	Gran Premio de la Republica Argentina (Buenos Aires)
27.01.	Grande Prêmio do Brasil (Interlagos)
17.03.	Race of Champions (Brands Hatch)
30.03.	South African Grand Prix (Kyalami)
21.04.	Austria-Trophäe (Salzburgring)
25.04.	1000 km de Monza (Monza)
28.04.	Gran Premio de España (Jarama)
05.05.	1000 km de Spa-Francorchamps (Spa-Francorchamps)
12.05.	Grand Prix de Belgique (Zolder)
19.05.	1000 km Nürburgring (Nürburgring)
26.05.	Grand Prix de Monaco (Monaco)
02.06.	1000 km di Imola (Imola)
09.06.	Sveriges Grand Prix (Anderstorp)
23.06.	Grote Prijs van Nederland (Zandvoort)
30.06.	1000 km Österreichring (Zeltweg)
07.07.	Grand Prix de France (Paul Ricard)
14.07.	Großer Preis der Tourenwagen (Nürburgring)
20.07.	British Grand Prix (Brands Hatch)
04.08.	Großer Preis von Deutschland (Nürburgring)
15.08.	1000 km du Castellet (Paul Ricard)
18.08.	Großer Preis von Österreich (Zeltweg)
08.09.	Gran Premio d'Italia (Monza)
22.09.	Canadian Grand Prix (Mosport Park)
06.10.	United States Grand Prix (Watkins Glen)

Klasse / Class	Fahrzeug / Vehicle	Nr. / No.	Besitzer / Owner	Startpos. / Start pos.	Ergebnis / Results	Beifahrer / Co-driver
Formula 1	Ferrari 312B2	5	Scuderia Ferrari SpA SEFAC	1	DNF-oil pressure	
Sports Cars	Ferrari 312PB	85	Ferrari	2	1	Andretti
Formula 1	Ferrari 312B2	4	Scuderia Ferrari SpA SEFAC	1	1	
Formula 1	Ferrari 312B2	18	Scuderia Ferrari SpA SEFAC	9	DNF-fuel system	
Formula 1	Ferrari 312B2	4	Scuderia Ferrari SpA SEFAC	1	DNF-electrics	
Sports Cars	Ferrari 312PB	2	Ferrari	1	2	
Formula 1	Ferrari 312B2	10	Scuderia Ferrari SpA SEFAC	8	12	
Formula 1	Ferrari 312B2	7	Scuderia Ferrari SpA SEFAC	12	5	
Sports Cars	Ferrari 312PB	1	Ferrari	2	DNF-engine	Redman

Klasse / Class	Fahrzeug / Vehicle	Nr. / No.	Besitzer / Owner	Startpos. / Start pos.	Ergebnis / Results	Beifahrer / Co-driver
Formula 1	Ferrari 312B2	18	Scuderia Ferrari SpA SEFAC	3	4	
Formula 1	Ferrari 312B2	9	Scuderia Ferrari SpA SEFAC	3	5	
Formula 1	Ferrari 312B2	8	Scuderia Ferrari SpA SEFAC	11	DNF-accident	
Sports Cars	Ferrari 312PB	1	Ferrari	2	3	Redman
Sports Cars	Ferrari 312PB	3	Ferrari	5	2	Redman
Sports Cars	Ferrari 312PB	1	Ferrari	2	1	Redman
Formula 1	Ferrari 312B3	7	Scuderia Ferrari SpA SEFAC	6	12	
Sports Cars	Ferrari 312PB	1	Ferrari	1	DNF-gearbox	Redman
Sports Cars	Ferrari 312PB	5	Ferrari	4	DNF-accident	Redman
Formula 1	Ferrari 312B3	3	Scuderia Ferrari SpA SEFAC	3	DNF-oil pump	
Sports Cars	Ferrari 312PB	1	Ferrari	2	1	Redman
Formula 1	Ferrari 312B3	3	Scuderia Ferrari SpA SEFAC	7	DNF-transmission	
Sports Cars	Ferrari 312PB	15	Ferrari	2	DNF-engine	Redman
Formula 1	Ferrari 312B3	3	Scuderia Ferrari SpA SEFAC	8	6	
Sports Cars	Ferrari 312PB	1	Ferrari	3	3	Redman
Formula 1	Ferrari 312B3	3	Scuderia Ferrari SpA SEFAC	12	5	
Formula 1	Ferrari 312B3	3	Scuderia Ferrari SpA SEFAC	19	8	
Sports Cars	Ferrari 312PB	10	Ferrari	5	2	Redman
Formula 1	McLaren M23 - Ford	30	Yardley Team McLaren	4	3	
Touring Car	BMW 3.0 CSL	2	BMW	5	2	Hunt
Formula 1	Ferrari 312B3	3	Scuderia Ferrari SpA SEFAC	14	8	
Formula 1	Iso Marlboro IR01 - Ford	26	Frank Williams Racing Cars	23	7	
Touring Car	BMW Alpina 3.0 CSL	1		2	20 (DNF-engine)	Muir
Touring Car	BMW 3.5 CSL	4	BMW	10	7	Stuck

Klasse / Class	Fahrzeug / Vehicle	Nr. / No.	Besitzer / Owner	Startpos. / Start pos.	Ergebnis / Results	Beifahrer / Co-driver
Formula 1	Lotus 72E - Ford	2	John Player Team Lotus	7	DNF-clutch	
Formula 1	Lotus 72E - Ford	2	John Player Team Lotus	5	3	
Formula 1 NC	Lotus 72E - Ford	2	John Player Team Lotus	11	1	
Formula 1	Lotus 76/2 - Ford	2	John Player Team Lotus	10	DNF-brakes	
Touring Car	BMW 3.0 CSL	1		1	1	Stuck
Sports Cars	Alfa Romeo 33TT12	4	Autodelta	5	2	Stommelen
Formula 1	Lotus 76/2 - Ford	2	John Player Team Lotus	5	DNF-brakes	
Sports Cars	Matra-Simca MS670C	4	Matra-Simca	2	1	Jarier
Formula 1	Lotus 76/2 - Ford	2	John Player Team Lotus	16	DNF-overheat	
Sports Cars	BMW 3.0 CSL	71		17	DNF-gearbox	Stuck
Formula 1	Lotus 72E - Ford	2	John Player Team Lotus	19	DNF-oil pipe	
Sports Cars	Alfa Romeo 33TT12	3	Autodelta	3	DNF-accident	Merzario
Formula 1	Lotus 72E - Ford	2	John Player Team Lotus	7	DNF-engine	
Formula 1	Lotus 72E - Ford	2	John Player Team Lotus	18	11	
Sports Cars	Alfa Romeo 33TT12	1	Autodelta	4	5 (DNF-valves)	Merzario-Brambilla
Formula 1	Lotus 72E - Ford	2	John Player Team Lotus	13	5	
Touring Car	BMW 3.0 CSL	2			DNF-gearbox	Bell
Formula 1	Lotus 72E - Ford	2	John Player Team Lotus	12	3	
Formula 1	Lotus 72E - Ford	2	John Player Team Lotus	9	5	
Sports Cars	Gulf Mirage GR7 - Ford	7	JWA Automotive	3	3	Bell
Formula 1	Lotus 76/2 - Ford	2	John Player Team Lotus	22	DNF-accident	
Formula 1	Lotus 76/2 - Ford	2	John Player Team Lotus	16	DNF-fuel injection	
Formula 1	Lotus 72E - Ford	2	John Player Team Lotus	21	13	
Formula 1	Lotus 72E - Ford	2	John Player Team Lotus	16	DNF-accident	

500 km di Imola 1976

1000 km Nürburgring 1978

| Datum | Veranstaltung |
| Date | Event |

1975

12.01.	Gran Premio de la Republica Argentina (Buenos Aires)
26.01.	Grande Prêmio do Brasil (Interlagos)
01.03.	South African Grand Prix (Kyalami)
16.03.	Race of Champions (Brands Hatch)
23.03.	1000 km di Mugello (Mugello)
27.04.	Gran Premio de España (Montjuïc)
04.05.	1000 km de Spa-Francorchamps (Spa-Francorchamps)
11.05.	Grand Prix de Monaco (Monaco)
25.05.	Grand Prix de Belgique (Zolder)
08.06.	Sveriges Grand Prix (Anderstorp)
15.06.	24 Heures du Mans (Le Mans)
22.06.	Grote Prijs van Nederland (Zandvoort)
06.07.	Grand Prix de France (Paul Ricard)

1976

25.01.	Grande Prêmio do Brasil (Interlagos)
06.03.	South African Grand Prix (Kyalami)
14.03.	Race of Champions (Brands Hatch)
21.03.	1000 km di Mugello (Mugello)
28.03.	United States Grand Prix West (Long Beach)
04.04.	6 Ore di Vallelunga (Vallelunga)
11.04.	BRDC International Trophy (Silverstone)
25.04.	4 ore di Monza (Monza)
02.05.	Gran Premio de España (Jarama)
09.05.	Silverstone 6 Hours (Silverstone)
16.05.	Grand Prix de Belgique (Zolder)
23.05.	500 km di Imola (Imola)
30.05.	Grand Prix de Monaco (Monaco)
13.06.	24 Heures du Mans (Le Mans)
27.06.	Martha 1000 - Österreichring 6 hours (Zeltweg)
04.07.	Grand Prix de France (Paul Ricard)
10.07.	Watkins Glen 6 Hours (Watkins Glen)
18.07.	British Grand Prix (Brands Hatch)
22.08.	Mosport 200 Miles (Mosport)
29.08.	Grote Prijs van Nederland (Zandvoort)
04.09.	6 heures de Dijon (Dijon-Prenois)
05.09.	500 km de Dijon (Dijon-Prenois)
12.09.	Gran Premio d'Italia (Monza)
03.10.	Canadian Grand Prix (Mosport)
10.10.	United States Grand Prix (Watkins Glen)

1977

06.02.	Daytona 24 Hours (Daytona Beach)
15.05.	Silverstone 6 Hours (Silverstone)
22.05.	Grand Prix de Monaco (Monaco)
29.05.	Nürburgring 1000 km (Nürburgring)
12.06.	24 Heures du Mans (Le Mans)
12.06.	24 Heures du Mans (Le Mans)
03.07.	DRM Norisring
03.07.	200 Meilen von Nürnberg (Norisring)
09.07.	Watkins Glen 6 Hours (Watkins Glen)
30.07.	DRM Hockenheim
20.08.	Mosport 6 Hours (Mosport)
28.08.	Mid-Ohio 3 hours (Mid-Ohio)
17.09.	Michigan International Speedway, Race One
25.09.	Brands Hatch 6 Hours (Brands Hatch)
09.10.	Preis von Hessen-Hockenheim 2x3 Hours (Hockenheim)
15.10.	Riverside International Raceway, Race Two
16.10.	Riverside International Raceway, Race Three
01.11.	Bathurst 1000 (Mount Panorama)

Klasse Class	Fahrzeug Vehicle	Nr. No.	Besitzer Owner	Startpos. Start pos.	Ergebnis Results	Beifahrer Co-driver
Formula 1	Lotus 72E - Ford	6	John Player Team Lotus	18	8	
Formula 1	Lotus 72E - Ford	6	John Player Team Lotus	12	9	
Formula 1	Lotus 72E - Ford	6	John Player Team Lotus	21	12	
Formula 1 NC	Lotus 72E - Ford	6	John Player Team Lotus	4	4	
Sports Cars	Alfa Romeo 33TT12	1	Willy Kauhsen	1	2	Merzario
Formula 1	Lotus 72E - Ford	6	John Player Team Lotus	16	2	
Sports Cars	Alfa Romeo 33TT12	1	Willy Kauhsen	2	2	Merzario
Formula 1	Lotus 72E - Ford	6	John Player Team Lotus	14	8	
Formula 1	Lotus 72E - Ford	6	John Player Team Lotus	16	DNF-stub axle	
Formula 1	Lotus 72E - Ford	6	John Player Team Lotus	18	15	
Sports Cars	Gulf Mirage GR8 - Ford	11	JWA Automotive	1	1	Bell
Formula 1	Lotus 72E - Ford	6	John Player Team Lotus	21	DNF-engine	
Formula 1	Lotus 72E - Ford	6	John Player Team Lotus	19	DNF-brakes	

Klasse Class	Fahrzeug Vehicle	Nr. No.	Besitzer Owner	Startpos. Start pos.	Ergebnis Results	Beifahrer Co-driver
Formula 1	Wolf-Williams FW05 - Ford	20	Frank Williams Racing Cars	19	8	
Formula 1	Wolf-Williams FW05 - Ford	20	Frank Williams Racing Cars	19	16	
Formula 1 NC	Wolf-Williams FW05 - Ford	20	Frank Williams Racing Cars	4	3	
Sports Cars	Porsche 936	4	Porsche	1	1	Mass
Formula 1	Wolf-Williams FW05 - Ford	20	Frank Williams Racing Cars	-	Not Qualified	
Sports Cars	Porsche 935	1	Porsche	1	1	Mass
Formula 1 NC	Wolf-Williams FW05 - Ford	20	Frank Williams Racing Cars	15	DNF-gear lever	
Sports Cars	Porsche 936	3	Porsche	1	1	Mass
Formula 1	Wolf-Williams FW05 - Ford	20	Frank Williams Racing Cars	21	7	
Sports Cars	Porsche 935	9	Porsche	1	10	Mass
Formula 1	Wolf-Williams FW05 - Ford	20	Frank Williams Racing Cars	-	Not Qualified	
Sports Cars	Porsche 936	7	Porsche	3	1	Mass
Formula 1	Wolf-Williams FW05 - Ford	20	Frank Williams Racing Cars	-	Not Qualified	
Sports Cars	Porsche 936	20	Porsche	2	1	van Lennep
Sports Cars	Porsche 935	1	Porsche	1	DNF-engine	Schurti
Formula 1	Wolf-Williams FW05 - Ford	20	Frank Williams Racing Cars	19	10	
Sports Cars	Porsche 935	2	Porsche	1	3	Mass
Formula 1	Wolf-Williams FW05 - Ford	20	Frank Williams Racing Cars	-	Not Qualified	
Sports Cars	Porsche 936	20	Porsche	3	3	
Formula 1	Ensign N176 - Ford	22	Team Tissot Ensign	11	DNF-electrics	
Sports Cars	Porsche 935	1	Porsche	1	1	Mass
Sports Cars	Porsche 936	6	Porsche	2	1	Mass
Formula 1	Ensign N176 - Ford	22	Team Ensign	10	10	
Formula 1	Ensign N176 - Ford	22	Team Ensign	16	13	
Formula 1	Ensign N176 - Ford	22	Team Ensign	19	DNF-accident	

Klasse Class	Fahrzeug Vehicle	Nr. No.	Besitzer Owner	Startpos. Start pos.	Ergebnis Results	Beifahrer Co-driver
Sports Cars	Porsche 935	1	Porsche	1	DNF-puncture	Mass
Sports Cars	Porsche 935-77	1	Porsche	1	1	Mass
Formula 1	Ensign N177 - Ford	22	Team Tissot Ensign with Castrol	17	10	
Sports Cars	Porsche 935-77	1	Porsche	1	DNF-injection	Mass
Sports Cars	Porsche 936-77	4	Porsche	7	1	Barth-Haywood
Sports Cars	Porsche 936-77	3	Porsche	3	DNF-engine	Pescarolo
Sports Cars	Porsche 935-1.4	40			DNF-electrical	
Sports Cars	Porsche 935-77	40			7	
Sports Cars	Porsche 935-77	1	Porsche	1	1	Mass
Sports Cars	Porsche 935-2	40		1	1 Div 2	
Sports Cars	Porsche 935-77	1	Porsche	1	DNF-head gasket	Schurti
Sports Cars	Porsche 935-77	15		11	2	McKitterick
IROC	Chevrolet Camaro			11	12 (DNF-accident)	
Sports Cars	Porsche 935-77	1	Porsche	1	1	Mass
Sports Cars	Porsche 935-77	1	Porsche	2	DNF-head gasket	Schurti
IROC	Chevrolet Camaro			10	8	
IROC	Chevrolet Camaro			5	7	
Touring Car	Ford Falcon Cobra	1		3	1	Moffat

British Grand Prix 1979

24 Heures du Mans 1982

| Datum | Veranstaltung |
Date	Event
1978	
17.02.	Daytona International Speedway, Race Four
19.03.	BRDC International Trophy (Silverstone)
07.05.	Grand Prix de Monaco (Monaco)
14.05.	Silverstone 6 Hours (Silverstone)
21.05.	Grand Prix de Belgique (Zolder)
28.05.	1000 km Nürburgring (Nürburgring)
04.06.	Gran Premio de España (Jarama)
11.06.	24 Heures du Mans (Le Mans)
11.06.	24 Heures du Mans (Le Mans)
17.06.	Sveriges Grand Prix (Anderstorp)
08.07.	Watkins Glen 6 Hours (Watkins Glen)
15.07.	24 Hours of Spa-Francorchamps (Spa-Francorchamps)
03.09.	6 Ore Vallelunga (Vallelunga)
17.09.	200 Meilen von Nürnberg (Norisring)
15.10.	Bathurst 1000 (Mount Panorama)
19.11.	Race of Giants (Macao)
1979	
04.02.	Daytona 24 Hours (Daytona Beach)
18.03.	6 Ore di Mugello (Mugello)
22.04.	6 heures de Dijon (Dijon-Prenois)
06.05.	Road Atlanta
20.05.	Charlotte
03.06.	Mosport
10.06.	24 Heures du Mans (Le Mans)
01.07.	Grand Prix de France (Dijon-Prenois)
08.07.	Watkins Glen
14.07.	British Grand Prix (Silverstone)
22.07.	Elkhart Lake
29.07.	Großer Preis von Deutschland (Hockenheim)
12.08.	Großer Preis von Österreich (Österreichring)
19.08.	Brainerd
26.08.	Grote Prijs van Nederland (Zandvoort)
02.09.	Trois-Rivières
09.09.	Gran Premio d'Italia (Monza)
30.09.	Canadian Grand Prix (Montreal)
07.10.	United States Grand Prix (Watkins Glen)
14.10.	Laguna Seca
28.10.	Riverside
1980	
15.06.	24 Heures du Mans (Le Mans)
21.06.	Croisière Verte
1981	
20.01.	Paris-Dakar
14.06.	24 Heures du Mans (Le Mans)
1982	
20.01.	Paris-Dakar
07.02.	Boucles de Spa
16.05.	Silverstone 6 Hours (Silverstone)
20.06.	24 Heures du Mans (Le Mans)
05.09.	1000 km de Spa (Spa-Francorchamps)

| Klasse | Fahrzeug | Nr. | Besitzer | Startpos. | Ergebnis | Beifahrer |
Class	Vehicle	No.	Owner	Start pos.	Results	Co-driver
IROC	Chevrolet Camaro			9	6	
Formula 1 NC	Ensign N177 - Ford	22	Team Tissot Ensign	13	DNF-spun	
Formula 1	Ensign N177 - Ford	22	Team Tissot Ensign	16	DNF-brakes	
Sports Cars	Porsche 935-78	1	Porsche	1	1	Mass
Formula 1	Ensign N177 - Ford	22	Team Tissot Ensign	22	12	
Sports Cars	Porsche 935-77A	8	Max Moritz	3	2	Schurti
Formula 1	Ensign N177 - Ford	22	Team Tissot Ensign	21	DNF-engine	
Sports Cars	Porsche 936-78	5	Porsche	1	DNF-accident	Pescarolo-Mass
Sports Cars	Porsche 936-78	6	Porsche	4	2	Wollek-Barth
Formula 1	Ensign N177 - Ford	22	Team Tissot Ensign		Not Qualified	
Sports Cars	Porsche 935-77A	1	Vasek Polak	16	26 (DNF-engine)	Follmer
Touring Car	VW Scirocco	74			DNF	Redman
Sports Cars	Porsche 935-78	1	Porsche	1	DNF-injection	Schurti
Sports Cars	Porsche 935-78	40		4	DNF-engine	
Touring Car	Ford Falcon Cobra	1		4	DNF-engine	Moffat
Touring Car	Ford Escort	4			1	

Sports Cars	Porsche 935-77A	1	Georg Loos	3	32 (DNF-valves)	Wollek-Gregg
Sports Cars	Porsche 935-77A	11	Georg Loos	4	2	Wollek-Schurti
Sports Cars	Porsche 935-77A	1	Georg Loos	4	2	Wollek-Schurti
Can-Am	Lola T333CS - Chevrolet	1		1	2	
Can-Am	Lola T333CS - Chevrolet	1		2	1	
Can-Am	Lola T333CS - Chevrolet	1		4	1	
Sports Cars	Porsche 936-78	12	Porsche	2	Disq-External help	Redman
Formula 1	Ligier JS11 - Ford	25	Equipe Ligier	14	DNF-engine	
Can-Am	Lola T333CS - Chevrolet	1		4	8	
Formula 1	Ligier JS11 - Ford	25	Equipe Ligier	17	6	
Can-Am	Lola T333CS - Chevrolet	1		3	1	
Formula 1	Ligier JS11 - Ford	25	Equipe Ligier	14	DNF-tyre	
Formula 1	Ligier JS11 - Ford	25	Equipe Ligier	21	DNF-engine	
Can-Am	Lola T333CS - Chevrolet	1		3	1	
Formula 1	Ligier JS11 - Ford	25	Equipe Ligier	20	5	
Can-Am	Lola T333CS - Chevrolet	1		3	13 (DNF-accident)	
Formula 1	Ligier JS11 - Ford	25	Equipe Ligier	11	DNF-engine	
Formula 1	Ligier JS11 - Ford	25	Equipe Ligier	16	DNF-gearbox	
Formula 1	Ligier JS11 - Ford	25	Equipe Ligier	24	DNF-accident	
Can-Am	Lola T333CS - Chevrolet	1		6	8	
Can-Am	Lola T333CS - Chevrolet	1		3	1	

| Sports Cars | Porsche 908-80 | 9 | Martini Racing | 4 | 2 | Joest |
| Rally Raid | Zündapp 125 cc | 40 | | | 1 category | |

| Rally Raid | Citroën CX 2400 GTI | 125 | | | DNF-accident | Brasseur |
| Sports Cars | Porsche 936-81 | 11 | Porsche | 1 | 1 | Bell |

Rally Raid	Mercedes 280GE	154			5	Brasseur
Rally	Porsche 944	4			DNF-steering	Goossens
Sports Cars	Porsche 956	1	Porsche	1	2	Bell
Sports Cars	Porsche 956	1	Porsche	1	1	Bell
Sports Cars	Porsche 956	1	Porsche	1	1	Mass

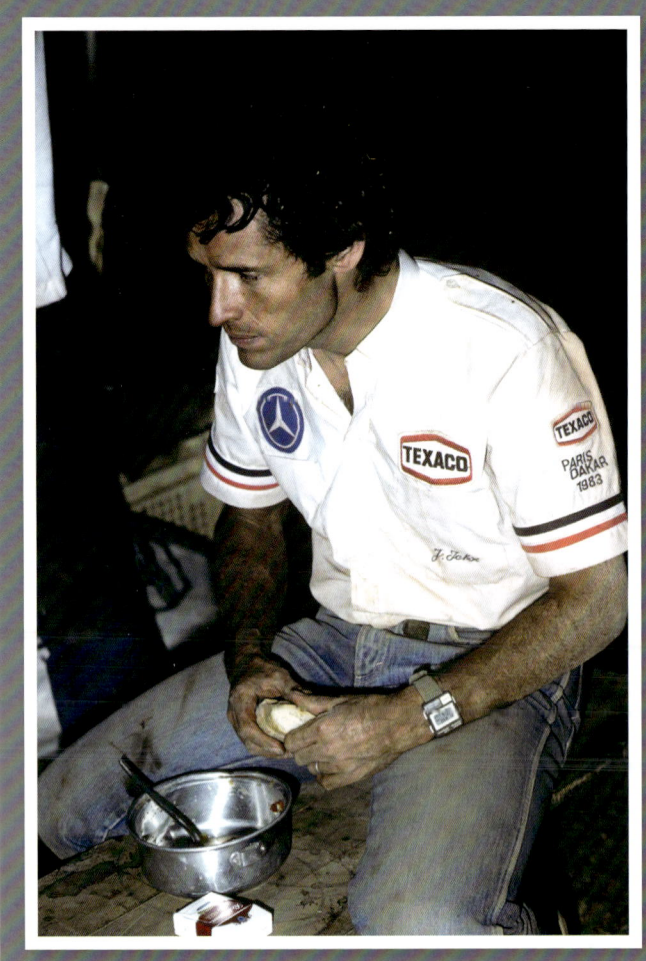

Paris-Dakar 1983

1000 km de Spa-Francorchamps 1984

| Datum | Veranstaltung |
Date	Event
1982	
03.10.	Fuji 1000 km (Fuji)
17.10.	Brands Hatch 1000 km (Brands Hatch)
06.11.	9 Hours of Kyalami (Kyalami)
1983	
20.01.	Paris-Dakar
10.04.	1000 km di Monza (Monza)
08.05.	Silverstone 1000 km (Silverstone)
29.05.	ADAC 1000 km (Nürburgring)
19.06.	24 Heures du Mans (Le Mans)
04.09.	1000 km de Spa-Francorchamps (Spa-Francorchamps)
18.09.	Brands Hatch 1000 km (Brands Hatch)
02.10.	Fuji 1000 km (Fuji)
15.10.	Rallye des Pharaons
10.12.	1000 km of Kyalami (Kyalami)
1984	
20.01.	Paris-Dakar
23.04.	1000 km di Monza (Monza)
13.05.	Silverstone 1000 km (Silverstone)
16.06.	Michigan International Speedway, Race One
07.07.	Burke Lakefront Airport, Race Two
15.07.	ADAC 1000 km (Nürburgring)
15.07.	ADAC 1000 km (Nürburgring)
28.07.	Talladega Superspeedway, Race Three
05.08.	Mosport 1000 km (Mosport)
11.08.	Michigan International Speedway, Race Four
02.09.	1000 km de Spa-Francorchamps (Spa-Francorchamps)
16.09.	1000 km di Imola (Imola)
30.09.	Fuji 1000 km (Fuji)
02.12.	1000 km of Sandown Park (Sandown Park)
1985	
22.01.	Paris-Dakar
14.04.	1000 km di Mugello (Mugello)
28.04.	1000 km di Monza (Monza)
12.05.	Silverstone 1000 km (Silverstone)
16.06.	24 Heures du Mans (Le Mans)
14.07.	1000-km-Rennen (Hockenheim)
11.08.	Mosport 1000 km (Mosport)
01.09.	1000 km de Spa-Francorchamps (Spa-Francorchamps)
22.09.	Brands Hatch 1000 km (Brands Hatch)
06.10.	Fuji 1000 km (Fuji)
19.10.	Rallye des Pharaons
01.12.	800 km of Selangor (Shah Alam)
1986	
23.01.	Paris-Dakar
1987	
22.01.	Paris-Dakar

Klasse / Class	Fahrzeug / Vehicle	Nr. / No.	Besitzer / Owner	Startpos. / Start pos.	Ergebnis / Results	Beifahrer / Co-driver
Sports Cars	Porsche 956	1	Porsche	2	1	Mass
Sports Cars	Porsche 956	11	Porsche	1	1	Bell
Sports Cars	Porsche 956	3		1	1	Mass
Rally Raid	Mercedes 280GE	142			1	Brasseur
Sports Cars	Porsche 956-83	1	Porsche	3	2	Mass
Sports Cars	Porsche 956-83	1	Porsche	3	DNF-accident	Mass
Sports Cars	Porsche 956-83	1	Porsche	2	1	Mass
Sports Cars	Porsche 956-83	1	Porsche	1	2	Bell
Sports Cars	Porsche 956-83	1	Porsche	1	1	Mass
Sports Cars	Porsche 956-83	1	Porsche	1	2	Mass
Sports Cars	Porsche 956-83	1	Porsche	2	2	Mass
Rally Raid	Mercedes 280GE	1			1	Da Silva
Sports Cars	Porsche 956	1	Porsche	2	3	Mass
Rally Raid	Porsche 911	175			6	Brasseur
Sports Cars	Porsche 956-83	1	Porsche	8	2	Mass
Sports Cars	Porsche 956-83	1	Porsche	2	1	Mass
IROC	Chevrolet Camaro Z28			3	9	
IROC	Chevrolet Camaro Z28			4	12	
Sports Cars	Porsche 956-83	1	Porsche	4	7	Mass
Sports Cars	Porsche 956	3	Porsche	-	Practice	Mass
IROC	Chevrolet Camaro Z28			2	10	
Sports Cars	Porsche 956-83	1	Porsche	2	1	Mass
IROC	Chevrolet Camaro Z28			12	12	
Sports Cars	Porsche 956-83	1	Porsche	2	2	Mass
Sports Cars	Porsche 956	1	Porsche	24	DNF-clutch	Watson
Sports Cars	Porsche 956-83	1	Porsche	2	2	Watson
Sports Cars	Porsche 956-83	1	Porsche	2	2	Mass
Rally Raid	Porsche 959	185		-	DNF-suspension	Brasseur
Sports Cars	Porsche 962C	1	Porsche	4	1	Mass
Sports Cars	Porsche 962C	1	Porsche	4	4	Mass
Sports Cars	Porsche 962C	1	Porsche	7	1	Mass
Sports Cars	Porsche 962C	1	Porsche	2	10	Mass
Sports Cars	Porsche 962C	1	Porsche	1	DNF-turbo	Mass
Sports Cars	Porsche 962C	1	Porsche	2	2	Mass
Sports Cars	Porsche 962C	1	Porsche	6	DNF-accident	Mass
Sports Cars	Porsche 962C	1	Porsche	4	2	Mass
Sports Cars	Porsche 962C	1	Porsche	2	AB	Mass
Rally Raid	Porsche 959	1		-	DNF-fire	Brasseur
Sports Cars	Porsche 962C	1	Porsche	1	1	Mass
Rally Raid	Porsche 959	185		-	2	Brasseur
Rally Raid	Lada Niva	185		-	DNF-piston	Tarin

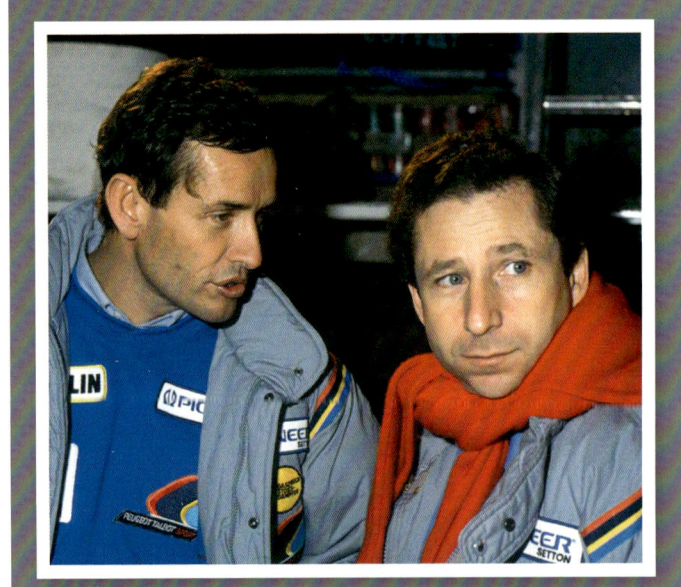

Paris-Dakar 1989

Paris-Dakar 1991

Paris-Dakar 1991

Datum	Veranstaltung
Date	Event

1988

22.01.	Paris-Dakar
15.05.	Atlas Rally
27.10.	Rallye des Pharaons

1989

13.01.	Paris-Dakar
09.05.	Rallye des Pharaons
23.07.	Baja Aragon

1990

16.01.	Paris-Dakar
	Rallye de Tunisie
21.07.	Baja Aragon
15.10.	Rallye des Pharaons

1991

16.01.	Paris-Tripoli-Dakar
20.06.	Baja Aragon
16.10.	Rallye des Pharaons

1992

| 16.01. | Paris-Sirte-Cape Town |

1995

| 15.01. | Granada-Dakar |

1998

| 04.07. | 24 Heures de Spa-Francorchamps (Spa-Francorchamps) |

1999

| 06.11. | UAE Desert Challenge |

2000

| 23.01. | Paris-Dakar |

Legends / Legende:
English abbreviations:
AB = Race aborted; Div = Division; DNF = Did not finish; Formula 1 NC = Formula 1 non-championship race; Gr = Group; IROC = International Race of Champions
Deutsche Übersetzung:
Klasse: Formula 1 = Formel 1; Formula 1 NC = Formel-1-Rennen ohne WM-Status; Formula 2 = Formel 2; Formula 3 = Formel 3; Hill Climb = Bergrennen; IROC = International Race of Champions; Rally = Rallye; Rally Raid = Marathonrallye; Sports Car = Sportwagen; Touring Car = Tourenwagen; Trial = Trial

Klasse / Class	Fahrzeug / Vehicle	Nr. / No.	Besitzer / Owner	Startpos. / Start pos.	Ergebnis / Results	Beifahrer / Co-driver
Rally Raid	Lada Niva	218		-	38	Tarin
Rally Raid	Lada Niva	211		-	10	Tarin
Rally Raid	Lada Niva	205		-	3	Poch
Rally Raid	Peugeot 405 T16	206	Peugeot Sport	-	2	Tarin
Rally Raid	Peugeot 405 T16	202	Peugeot Sport	-	2	Tarin
Rally Raid	Peugeot 405 T16	124	Peugeot Sport	-	1	Tarin
Rally Raid	Lada Samara	213		-	7	Tarin
Rally Raid	Lada Samara	203		-	3	Tarin
Rally Raid	Citroën ZX		Citroën Sport	-	2	Tarin
Rally Raid	Citroën ZX		Citroën Sport	-	5	Tarin
Rally Raid	Citroën ZX	203	Citroën Sport	-	DNF-fire	Tarin
Rally Raid	Citroën ZX		Citroën Sport	-	DNF-accident	Tarin
Rally Raid	Citroën ZX	203	Citroën Sport	-	DNF-fire	Tarin
Rally Raid	Citroën ZX	205	Citroën Sport	-	6	Lemoyne
Rally Raid	Toyota Land Cruiser HDJ80	220		-	18/1st cat	
Touring Car	Renault Megane	1	Renault Sport Belgium	11	DNF-accident	Vanina Ickx
Rally Raid	Toyota Land Cruiser	209		-	DNF	Vanina Ickx
Rally Raid	Toyota Land Cruiser	274	VJX	-	18	Vanina Ickx

Deutsche Übersetzung:

<u>Ergebnis:</u> 1 of class = 1. in der Klasse; 1 overall = 1. in der Gesamtwertung; AB = Rennen abgebrochen; accident = Unfall; accident in practice = Trainingsunfall; accident damage = Unfallschäden; alternator = Lichtmaschine; bearing = Lager; brakes = Bremsen; broken exhaust = Auspuff gebrochen; camshaft = Nockenwelle; cancelled (snow on track) = Abgesagt (wg. Schneefalls); category = Kategorie; clutch = Kupplung; disq (external help) = Disqualifiziert (wg. fremder Hilfe); Div = Division; DNF = Ausgefallen; drive shaft = Antriebswelle; electrical = Elektrik; engine = Motor; fire = Feuer; fuel injection = Kraftstoffeinspritzung; fuel metering unit = Kraftstoffdosierungssystem; fuel pump = Kraftstoffpumpe; fuel supply = Kraftstoffzufuhr; fuel system = Kraftstoffsystem; gear lever = Schalthebel; gearbox = Getriebe; Gr = Gruppe; head gasket = Zylinderkopfdichtung; ignition = Zündung; injection = Einspritzung; not qualified = nicht qualifiziert; oil leak = Ölleck; oil pressure = Öldruck; oil pump = Ölpumpe; overheat = Überhitzung; piston = Kolben; practice = Training; puncture = Reifenschaden; radiator = Kühler; rear axle = Hinterachse; spun = Dreher; starter motor = Anlasser; steering = Lenkung; stub axle = Achsschenkel; suspension = Aufhängung; transmission = Kraftübertragung; turbo = Turbolader; tyre = Reifen; valve(s) = Ventil(e)

<u>Beifahrer:</u> Shared his car with Jackie Stewart = Er hat sich das Auto mit Jackie Stewart geteilt

McKLEIN PUBLISHING

Targa Florio
1955–1973

Die Targa Florio war früher eines der größten Autorennen der Welt. Dieses Buch vermittelt den Mythos des Rennens über die schmalen Bergstraßen Siziliens von A bis Z mit faszinierenden, großformatigen Bildern.

This book looks back on the history of the legendary race on the narrow mountain roads of Sicily from A to Z, with many fascinating large-format photographs.

By Ed Heuvink
Size: 29 x 29 cm, 400 pages
Hardcover, in a slipcase
Texts in English, German & Italian
ISBN: 978-3-927458-66-6
Price: 99.90 euros*

Jim Clark
Rennfahrerlegende
Racing Hero

Dieses Werk von Graham Gauld, einem von Clarks engen Wegbegleitern, fasst das Leben des Formel-1-Weltmeisters von A bis Z zusammen und zeigt den bescheidenen Schotten so persönlich wie nie zuvor.

This book written by Graham Gauld – one of Clark's close companions – reviews the life and career of the Formula One World Champion from A to Z and portrays the Scotsman more intimately than ever before.

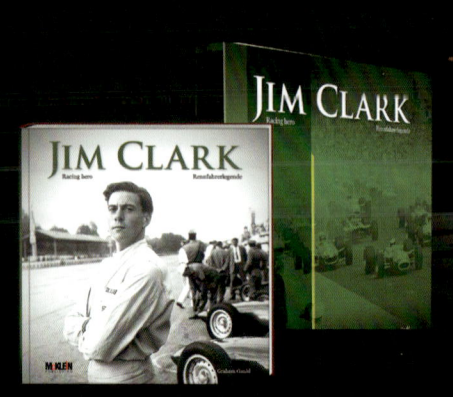

By Graham Gauld
Size: 29 x 29 cm, 400 pages
Hardcover, in a slipcase
Texts in English & German
ISBN: 978-3-927458-75-8
Price: 99.90 euros*

1965–1969
DETAILS
Legendäre Sportwagen ganz nah
Legendary sports cars up close

Exotische Materialien, hauchdünne Karossen und überdimensionierte Motoren: Dieses Buch porträtiert die Rennsportwagen und Prototypen von 1965 bis 1969 mit unveröffentlichten Fotos und unterhaltsamen Storys.

Exotic materials, wafer-thin bodies, over-powered engines: This 400-page book gives an inside view of the sports and prototype racing machines used from 1965 to 1969 with many photos and entertaining stories.

By Wilfried Müller
Size: 29 x 29 cm, 400 pages
Hardcover, in a slipcase
Texts in English & German
ISBN: 978-3-927458-76-5
Price: 99.90 euros*

Auch von McKlein Publishing
Also available

Group 2
The genesis of world rallying
English & German texts in separate books
Deutsche ISBN: 978-3-927458-72-7
English ISBN: 978-3-927458-73-4
Price: 49.90 euros*

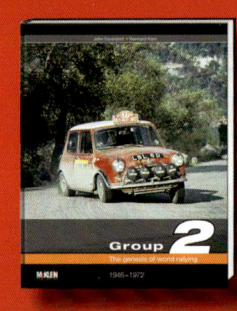

Group 4
From Stratos to Quattro
English & German texts in separate books
Deutsche ISBN: 978-3-927458-53-6
English ISBN: 978-3-927458-54-3
Price: 49.90 euros*

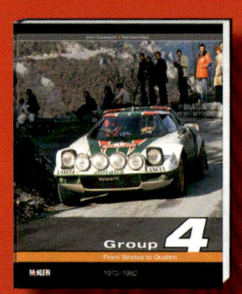

Group B
The rise and fall of rallying's wildest cars
English & German texts in separate books
Deutsche ISBN: 978-3-927458-55-0
English ISBN: 978-3-927458-56-7
Price: 49.90 euros*

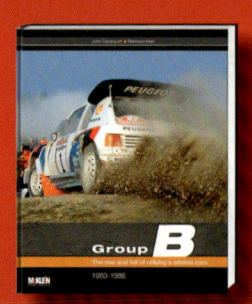

Rally and Racing WebShop - Hauptstraße 172 - 51143 Köln - Germany - Tel: 0049-2203-9242570 - www.racingwebshop.com

RacingWebShop.com